Second Edition

ENTERPRISE SYSTEMS FOR MANAGEMENT

Luvai F. Motiwalla

University of Massachusetts Lowell

and

Jeff Thompson

Oracle Consulting

PEARSON

Boston   Columbus   Indianapolis   New York   San Francisco   Upper Saddle River
Amsterdam   Cape Town   Dubai   London   Madrid   Milan   Munich   Paris   Montreal   Toronto
Delhi   Mexico City   Sao Paulo   Sydney   Hong Kong   Seoul   Singapore   Taipei   Tokyo

Editorial Director: Sally Yagan
Editor in Chief: Eric Svendsen
Executive Editor: Bob Horan
Director of Editorial Services: Ashley Santora
Editorial Project Manager: Kelly Loftus
Director of Marketing: Patrice Lumumba Jones
Senior Marketing Manager: Anne Fahlgren
Senior Managing Editor: Judy Leale
Production Project Manager: Clara Bartunek
Creative Art Director: Jayne Conte
Cover Designer: Suzanne Behnke
Cover Art: Fotolia
Lead Media Project Manager: Lisa Rinaldi
Full-Service Project Management: Abinaya Rajendran / Integra Software Services Pvt. Ltd.
Printer/Binder: STP / RRD / Harrisonburg
Cover Printer: STP / RRD / Harrisonburg
Text Font: 10/12, Times

Credits and acknowledgments borrowed from other sources and reproduced, with permission, in this textbook appear on appropriate page within text.

Library of Congress Cataloging-in-Publication Data
Motiwalla, Luvai F.
  Enterprise systems for management / Luvai F. Motiwalla, Jeff Thompson.—2nd ed.
    p. cm.
  Includes bibliographical references and index.
  ISBN-13: 978-0-13-214576-3 (alk. paper)
  ISBN-10: 0-13-214576-6 (alk. paper)
  1. Management information systems.   I. Thompson, Jeffrey,   II. Title.
  HD30.213.M68 2012
  658.4'038011—dc22

                                        2011007275

11

ISBN 10:   0-13-214576-6
ISBN 13: 978-0-13-214576-3

This book is first and foremost dedicated to the many students whom I have taught and learned from over the years including the design and implementation of ERP systems in the real-world organizations. They have helped me understand and appreciate the often-complex concepts and render them in terms that are familiar and related to their everyday lives. The book is also dedicated to the many friends and colleagues with whom I have interacted over the past 20 years. In addition, I dedicate this book to my wife, Rashida, our caring parents, and our kids, Taher and Naqiya, who encouraged and supported me while writing this book. Finally, I dedicate this book to the memory of my father, Fazle, who passed away in 2007!

Luvai Motiwalla

I would like to dedicate this book to my wife, Deb, and our two children, Trevor and Taylor. They are my inspiration and motivation. They keep me balanced and centered on what is important in life.

Jeff Thompson

BRIEF CONTENTS

CONTENTS

PREFACE

Enterprise systems include enterprise resource planning (ERP), supply chain management (SCM), customer resource management (CRM), and other enterprise-level systems that are critical to all dynamic, globally aware companies. ERP systems are important factors in the success of corporations today. With a diversified global market, technology is utilized to overcome distance, language, and culture. Today's information systems have permeated well beyond the traditional functional applications, and even the more technologically current client–server applications, to mission-focused enterprise systems.

This second edition of the book describes the components of an ERP system and provides an introduction to the process of implementing a successful system in today's organizations. Because ERP systems are complex, they often require a large investment of money and time. An ERP implementation impacts a large number of people, both inside and outside the organization. It also requires both carefully crafted business needs and a comprehensive change management strategy. Enterprise systems extend from the back-end supply chain operations to front-end customer-facing services that extend beyond the boundaries of the enterprise. As such, the implementation process is increasingly expensive, intense, and prone to failure than were traditional information system implementations.

Organizations considering an investment in enterprise systems should be educated on enterprise systems components and architecture, as well as both their short- and long-term impacts on the organizational business processes. Management needs to be prepared to address the technology issues of enterprise systems and, more importantly, the business processes, corporate policies, change management, and people expectations. The goal of this book is to educate students on these issues and on the value that enterprise systems add to today's companies. Students will learn how enterprise systems can remove structural and functional barriers to make organizations more cross-functional and productive. Students will also learn about the enterprise system's technology and implementation life cycle and develop an understanding of the impact on processes and people in an organization. This book places major importance on the strategic role of ERP systems in providing a platform for improved business operations and productivity.

In addition, the book emphasizes both business and managerial aspects of enterprise systems from planning to postimplementation. This edition specifically

- provides several examples of real-world company issues that occurred while implementing enterprise systems;
- provides a step-by-step learning process for students, using organized materials, and learning about enterprise system implementations;
- focuses on a pedagogy that lays out concise learning goals and reinforces the concepts learned using cases, discussion questions, and exercises; and
- highlights issues within the implementation process that have implications for management.

The widespread implementation of enterprise systems in large to small organizations has created a tremendous demand for employees with a strong knowledge foundation in both the technical and organizational aspects of enterprise system and the implementation process. This book can be used for an enterprise systems course in both graduate (MBA program) and undergraduate courses (MIS program) at a business college. It is written to provide students with a comprehensive source for foundational concepts in ERP, SCM, and CRM systems. The goal of this book is to assist students in becoming knowledgeable participants in the enterprise system implementation process and have the confidence to ask complex questions. Students taking this course ideally should have taken the introduction to management information systems (MIS) course, which would provide them with a basic understanding of information technology (IT) components, the evolution of MIS in organizations, and a systems development life cycle.

In addition to students, this book would be helpful for professionals, top management, and such other participants as subject matter experts (SMEs), who are involved in an enterprise systems implementation project. Professionals will find this book to be a good reference resource for terminology and a knowledge base for launching enterprise systems. Top management will gain a perspective on strategies for implementing enterprise systems and resource requirements and providing an understanding on the need for organizational commitment for the enterprise systems project. They will be able to make better decisions and interact better with the implementation team.

WHAT'S NEW IN THIS EDITION

This edition has made some significant changes in the content to make the material more current for today's enterprise systems environment. Following are some of the key changes:

- Chapter 1 has been revised and edited with more focus on the evolution of the enterprise system rather than on information system; the focus of this chapter is now entirely on ERP components, architecture, and life cycle.
- Similarly, several changes have been made to other chapters, for example, business process management and reengineering in Chapter 9, new architectures such as cloud computing and mobile computing in Chapter 3, and new ERP implementation methodologies, such as agile methodology, in Chapter 4.
- Several case studies were modified and updated with current material to reflect changes that may have happened to the companies discussed in the case.
- Complete new sections have been added on business process management, project management, ERP virtualization, ERP training, green computing and its impact on enterprise systems, and RFID.
- Materials have been reorganized to improve the flow of the book and assist in the teaching of the course. For example, change management topic has been consolidated in one chapter instead of spreading it around in the book, outdated diagrams and figures have been removed, and some of the detail lists, like roles and responsibilities of ERP teams, have been moved to the appendix area.

BOOK FEATURES

In reviewing the academic and trade books on teaching an enterprise system course, it was difficult to find a comprehensive textbook for ERP implementations. Another problem with textbooks in MIS today is that the information is often outdated prior to its usage in the classroom. With this in mind, we have taken the approach of summarizing the *timeless* concepts of implementing enterprise systems in organizations. Although the textbook is complete in and of itself, currency of topics is maintained by supplementing the text with Web materials and links on the book materials. Adopting professors will benefit from the instructor's manual, which provides such materials as a course syllabus template, chapter overviews, answers to discussion questions and case study analysis, and PowerPoint slide presentations.

The second edition still maintains the same learning pedagogy as the first edition. Each chapter begins with learning objectives and an opening real-world case to lead students through the major concepts of the chapter and ends with managerial implications and a closing case study to show the application of these concepts. All chapters have such visual supplements as diagrams, figures, or tables to reinforce the concepts and end-of-chapter review and discussion questions and exercises.

CHAPTER ORGANIZATION

This book is organized to teach the underlying technology of implementing such enterprise systems as ERP, CRM, and SCM, as well as to discuss their implications to organizations. The main focus is on the ERP implementation process, which is covered from the development life cycle and implementation strategy to postimplementation stabilization and production support, as shown in four-area ERP implementation framework (i.e., technology, life cycle, people and organizations, and application extensions) to simplify the understanding of introducing ERP in organizations. Readers are exposed at each stage to technical as well as managerial issues and solutions adopted by real-world organizations to solve these problems.

The chapters are arranged to give readers a quick understanding of an ERP system prior to addressing the ERP implementation process and organizational issues as shown in Figure 1. Readers are given increasingly complex concepts, which build upon previous discussions. The different phases of an implementation process are discussed with cases and examples. They are examined from various perspectives to create an understanding of the reasons ERP systems require organizational changes in order to be effective.

In addition to the introduction to enterprise systems in Chapter 1, the book is broken down into four sections to assist instructors in focusing on specific aspects for their course:

Section I: ERP Systems (Chapters 2 and 3) provides the technical foundation on ERP systems and provides motivation to learn about enterprise systems implementation process. It also introduces the concept of systems integration and the role of ERP in systems integration and discusses the ERP system components and architecture.

Section II: ERP Implementation (Chapters 4–7) helps readers in understanding the ERP development life cycle, the process of selecting ERP software and vendor, how to manage an ERP implementation project, and the concept of metrics and evaluation of ERP implementation in organization.

Section III: People and Organization (Chapters 8–10) highlights the issues dealing with people and organization change, business process reengineering, change management, operational and postimplementation activities, and the role of ethics and globalization in ERP implementation.

Section IV: ERP Extensions (Chapters 11 and 12) deals with two other enterprise-level applications, namely, supply chain management and customer resource management, which are often integrated with ERP systems.

We realize that instructors today require flexibility in teaching this course with a blend of coverage on technological and organizational issues. This book provides this flexibility by allowing instructors to mix and match various chapters without losing continuity. Instructors who wish to focus on the ERP implementation process without covering the technology could

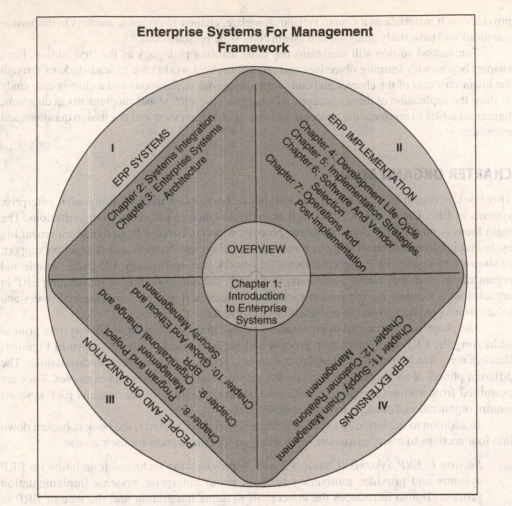

Enterprise Systems For Management Framework

I — ERP SYSTEMS
Chapter 2: Systems Integration
Chapter 3: Enterprise Systems Architecture

II — ERP IMPLEMENTATION
Chapter 4: Development Life Cycle
Chapter 5: Implementation Strategies
Chapter 6: Software And Vendor Selection And
Chapter 7: Operations And Post-implementation

OVERVIEW
Chapter 1: Introduction to Enterprise Systems

III — PEOPLE AND ORGANIZATION
Chapter 8: Program and Project Management
Chapter 9: Organizational Change and BPR
Chapter 10: Global And Ethical and Security Management

IV — ERP EXTENSIONS
Chapter 11: Supply Chain Management
Chapter 12: Customer Relations Management

FIGURE 1 Book Framework

cover Chapters 1 and 4–10, while instructors wishing to focus on the technology could cover Chapters 1–7, 11, and 12. An undergraduate course similarly could skip Chapters 11 and 12 and all the closing case studies, whereas a graduate course could skip Chapters 2 and 3.

FACULTY RESOURCES

Instructor's Resource Center

The following supplements are available to adopting instructors:

> *Instructor's Manual*—contains a chapter summary and answers to all discussion questions for each chapter of the text.

> *PowerPoint Presentations*—feature lecture notes that highlight key text terms and concepts. Professors can customize the presentation by adding their own slides or by editing the existing ones.

Test Bank Item File—an extensive set of multiple choice, true or false, and essay questions for each chapter of the text. Questions are ranked according to difficulty level and referenced with page numbers from the text. The test item file is available in Microsoft Word format and as the computerized Prentice-Hall TestGen software.

TestGen—Pearson Education's test-generating software is available from www.pearson highered.com/irc. The software is PC/MAC compatible and is preloaded with all of the test item file questions. You can manually or randomly view test questions and drag and drop to create a test. You can add or modify test bank questions as needed. Our TestGens are converted for use in BlackBoard and WebCT. These conversions can be found on the Instructor's Resource Center. Conversions to Moodle, D2L, or Angel can be requested through your local Pearson Sales Representative.

Image Library—a collection of the text art organized by chapter. This collection includes all of the figures, tables, and screenshots from the book. These images can be used to enhance class lectures and PowerPoint slides.

ACKNOWLEDGMENTS

Many people have provided helpful contributions to make this book possible. First, I would like to thank my coauthor, Jeff Thompson, for taking time out of his busy schedule as IT consultant with Oracle Corp and agreeing to participate in updating the contents for the second edition. This book would not have the practical or hands-on knowledge of ERP implementation without his contributions. I would also like to thank all the MBA students who took my elective course in enterprise management in the last three years—they have provided valuable comments and feedback on the early versions of the book's materials as well as some of its case materials. Finally, thanks to my parents, wife, son, and daughter, who encouraged me to work on this book project and have been patient with me during my frustrations with it.

Luvai Motiwalla,
Professor of MIS

First and foremost, my thanks to Luvai for working together on writing this book. This book was his brainchild, and I was honored that he and I had a chance to take the idea and make it a reality. I believe this text is a unique combination of theory and practical experience that will help students fully understand the complexities of ERP implementations.

I would also like to thank all those that I ever had a chance to work with on project teams for all their support and dedication. With each implementation, we shared and learned and understood that projects are successful due largely to teamwork. I owe a special debt of gratitude to Russell Utterberg (deceased), who mentored me in my early years of learning project management.

Jeff Thompson

We are very thankful to Bob Horan (executive editor), Kelly Loftus (editorial project manager), and the entire production staff of Pearson Prentice Hall publishers for helping us make this book a professional publication. We have had a wonderful experience working with everyone at Pearson Prentice Hall. Everyone at PH approached this book with commitment and enthusiasm. They have made us feel like partners on this book project. We appreciate the commitment they displayed and would like to thank them for the experience. In addition, we would like to thank the following external reviewers for their valuable comments and feedback to make this book successful in the classroom environment.

- Yvonne Lederer Antonucci, Widener University
- Omar Chaudhry, Golden Gate University
- Nikunj Dalal, Oklahoma State University
- Stephen De Lurgio, University of Missouri
- Mary Goodrich, University of Texas at Dallas
- Severin Grabski, Michigan State University
- Yair Levy, Nova Southern University

- Alan R. Peslak, Pennsylvania State University
- Jeffrey Schaller, Eastern Connecticut State University
- Shu Schiller, Wright State University
- Lou Thompson, University of Texas at Dallas
- F.C. Weston, Jr., Colorado State University

ABOUT THE AUTHORS

Luvai Motiwalla, Ph.D.   Luvai F. Motiwalla is professor of MIS at the College of Management at the University of Massachusetts Lowell (UML). He has a Ph.D. from the University of Arizona (1989). Before joining UML, he worked at University of Hartford, Connecticut, and his current research and teaching mainly focuses on the areas of e-business and enterprise systems. He has developed and taught the first e-Business and enterprise systems courses offered by his department. Professor Motiwalla has published several articles in highly recognized journals such as *Journal of MIS, Communications of ACM, Journal of Electronic Commerce, Information & Management, Computers & Education,* and others. In addition, he has presented his research in several regional, national, and international academic conferences and served as a reviewer for many MIS journals and conferences. His professional experience includes work on research grants funded by U.S. Department of Education, NSF, Davis Foundation, Connecticut, Department of Health Services, IBM, NCR, and U.S. Army and consulted with several regional and national corporations.

Jeff Thompson   Thompson has over 30 years' experience in information technology including 20 years' experience in a management role in higher education. During the last 12 years Mr. Thompson was a chief information officer. He has an extensive background in information technology and communications and change management and has been successful at directing and managing a variety of system implementations including large ERP systems, network infrastructure, high-performance computing, academic technology, and online Web-based learning. For the last seven years, Mr. Thompson served as the vice chancellor of Information Technology and Institutional Research at the University of Massachusetts Lowell. During his tenure there, he was in charge of campus legacy administrative systems and successfully replaced it with the PeopleSoft ERP, in a multi-institution single database implementation. He is now a senior program director for Oracle, North America Consulting, working with Oracle clients implementing ERP systems as the implementation partner.

1

Introduction to Enterprise Systems for Management

LEARNING OBJECTIVES

After reading this chapter, you should be able to:

- Understand the information systems evolution and its historical role in organizations leading to systems integration and eventually Enterprise Resource Planning (ERP).

- Learn about ERP systems and their evolution, components, and architecture. Understand the benefits and drawbacks of implementing ERP systems and how they can help an organization improve its efficiency and worker productivity.

- Have an overview of the implementation process (e.g., the ERP life cycle, business process reengineering, project management, and change management). Understand the role of staff, vendors, consultants, and the organization in making the ERP implementation process successful.

- Comprehend the ethical, global, and security challenges while implementing an ERP system as well as get an overview of ERP vendors and industry trends.

CASE 1.1
Opening Case
Hershey's Enterprise 21 Project

Source: Based on article David F. Carr, "Hershey's Sweet Victory," December 16, 2002, issue of *Baseline Magazine*.

Hershey Foods, Inc., completed an upgrade to their SAP/R3 enterprise software installation on schedule in September 2002, and they did it below their projected budget. This was considered a big achievement for a company that had experienced $150 million in lost sales due to problems associated with its new ERP system just a few years earlier in 1999. Hershey's CIO, George Davis, wondered why things went so smoothly with the upgrade compared with the original installation. Was it a technology problem? Or was it a people and organization change problem?

Hershey began its ERP journey with the Enterprise 21 Project late in 1996 when management approved the project in an effort to fix the Y2K problem and, at the same time, upgrade Hershey's IT environment to a twenty-first century system. This system was supposed to be an integrated system that used the client–server architecture and an SAP/R3 application suite. This was a complete overhaul of existing legacy enterprise system involving replacements of current Information Systems (IS) with packaged software solutions with the following goals:

- Establish a single company-wide supply chain strategy across all divisions.
- Streamline entire business process by reengineering all the functional areas throughout the company.
- Use new supply chain efficiencies to help increase gross margin.
- Maintain sales growth of at least 3–4 percent per year.
- Save $75–80 million by the end of 2002 through corporate restructuring and the closing of older distribution sites.
- Replace existing legacy software due to Y2K date-related problems.
- Replace legacy mainframe IS with an enterprise client–server architecture.

The initial plan of implementation was for four years with a budget of $112 million. Although Hershey's management vision was excellent, they lacked the necessary people at the top management level to make proper decisions on the implementation plan. Hershey did not have any high-ranking IT executive before hiring George Davis sometime in early 2000. They had lower-level managers making decisions that were aligned to their functional areas of business with no one at the top integrating these decisions to create a system that would work for the whole business. They had lots of committees with little or no oversight. As a result, Hershey's confectionary manufacturing and distribution operations' entire supply chain system ground to a halt in 1999, making it impossible to fulfil $100 million worth of orders.

The initial implementation was riddled with several problems from the beginning. First, Hershey tried to implement too many changes too fast. The Enterprise 21 project went for a complete discarding of the older mainframe legacy system used at Hershey and replacing it with the following three new software applications at the same time:

- SAP/R3 enterprise application suite
- Manugistics (demand planning and transportation) Systems
- Siebel Systems (CRM and sales tools)

The complexity of integrating SAP with Manugistics software and Seibel software was so overwhelming even with the help of an experienced consulting firm that this integration was dropped. In addition, due to project delays and Y2K, the Hershey's IT department decided to go with a direct cut over strategy (Big-Bang implementation) instead of a phased-in approach during their peak sales season right before Halloween.

Data entry in the new ERP system was another problem. SAP is very rigid software in terms of how, when, and where the data must be entered into the system for inventory tracking and management. Hershey's employees were not trained for this rigid data entry because their legacy system was flexible in terms of how the data were stored. This created a major crisis when the new system was used during the Halloween season. Customer orders were missed despite sufficient inventory on hand. System workarounds caused many headaches for workers. Extra capacity in warehouse space was not recorded into the SAP system, which caused communication failure between logistics and IT.

Finally, a lack of top management support and involvement also played a role in the Enterprise 21 project. In addition to lacking a CIO at the top decision-making level, Hershey's management took a hands-off approach by not getting involved in the decision-making process. For example, some managers recommended supplementing the major consultants for this project, IBM Global Services, with another consulting firm that had more experience with SAP–Manugistics. Top management stayed away from making any decision in this area. In general, Hershey's management did not understand the amount of effort necessary for both the technical and organizational change issues for this project.

What do you think about Hershey's ERP strategy? What lessons can be learned from the Hershey experience?

PREVIEW

Hershey's strategy shows the complexity of implementing ERP systems in organizations. In the early days of ERP implementation, management generally did not understand the magnitude of the issues an organization has to consider before, during, and after implementing ERP systems. Although they are packaged software, ERP systems are very different from such conventional packaged software as Microsoft Office and others. An ERP implementation goes beyond the technical issues of infrastructure and incompatibility of systems to management and people issues of process change and change management that will be discussed throughout this book. Any manager thinking about implementing or planning to implement ERP can take away two valuable lessons from the Hershey case: (1) test the business processes and systems using a methodology designed to simulate realistic operating scenarios and (2) pay close attention to ERP scheduling.

This initial failure in 1999 opened the eyes of Hershey's management to the problems and issues with implementing ERP software. Management stayed involved with the project from beginning to end during the 2002 upgrade phase and hired a CIO to oversee the project. The following are some key lessons learned from Hershey's ERP implementation:

- Go slowly and stick to the initial implementation plan
- Using a phased strategy can be a slow but safe choice.
- Spend appropriate time and resources to test the new system thoroughly.
- Keep things simple by limiting the number of software applications.
- Functional groups must communicate their specific data requirements to the implementation team. Spend extra time to ensure that all of the data requirements from all groups are mapped correctly before proceeding with the implementation.
- Definitions of basic business processes that should be addressed by insiders are often left for outsiders (e.g., consultants).
- Oversight matters, especially with a project of this magnitude.
- A steering committee must include such top management as the CEO and CIO.

Hershey's successful upgrade of SAP/R3, after the initial disaster, clearly shows that the company learned from its mistakes and has moved forward. Hershey has also met its business and IT goals since the full ERP implementation took place. Other companies can use the Hershey case to their advantage as they embark on their own ERP journeys. There are no shortcuts when it comes to implementing an enterprise system similar in scope to Hershey's. The most important lesson that Hershey learned might have been to proceed with the project slowly so nothing is left out during implementation.

ENTERPRISE SYSTEMS IN ORGANIZATIONS

Before delving into the details of ERP systems, we will quickly review the evolution of enterprise systems in organizations.

Business organizations have become very complex. This is due to an increased layer of management hierarchy and an increased level of coordination across departments. Each staff role and management layer has different information needs and requirements. As such, no single information system can support all the business needs. Figure 1-1 shows the typical levels of management and corresponding information needs. Management is generally categorized into three levels: strategic, middle or mid-management, and operational. At the strategic level, functions are highly unstructured and resources are undefined, whereas functions are highly structured and resources are predefined at the operational level. The mid-management level is somewhere in between depending on the hierarchy and organizational size.

The pyramid shape in Figure 1-1 illustrates the information needs at each level of management. The quantitative requirements are much less at the strategic level than they are at the operational level; however, the quality of information needed at the top requires sophisticated processing and presentation. The pyramid should assess and display the performance of the entire organization. For example, the CEO of a company may need a report that quickly states how a particular product is performing in the market vis-à-vis other company products over a period of time and in different geographical regions. Such a report is not useful to an operations manager, who is more interested in the detailed sales report of all products he or she is responsible for in the last month. The pyramid therefore suggests that managers at the higher level require a smaller quantity of information, but that it is a very high quality of information. On the other hand, the operational-level manager requires more detailed information and does not require a high level of analysis or aggregation as do their strategic counterparts. Today's enterprise systems are designed to serve these varied organizational requirements.

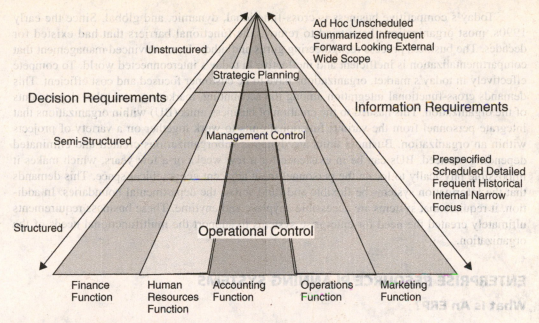

FIGURE 1-1 Management Pyramid with Information Requirements

Enterprise systems, therefore, are a crucial component of any successful organization today. They are an integral part of the organization and provide computer automation support for most business functions such as accounting, finance, marketing, customer service, human resource management, operations, and more. In general, they play a critical role in both the primary and secondary activities of the organization's value chain.[1]

Information Silos and Systems Integration

As organizations become larger and more complex, they tend to break functions into smaller units by assigning a group of staff to specialize in these activities. This allows the organization to manage complexity as well as some of the staff to specialize in those activities to enhance productivity and efficiency. The role of information systems has been and always will be one of supporting business activities and enhancing the workers' efficiency. Over time, however, as business changes and expands, systems need to change to keep pace. The result is sometimes a wide variety of information systems and computer architecture configurations, which creates a hodgepodge of independent nonintegrated systems. These systems ultimately create bottlenecks and interfere with productivity.

In today's globally competitive environment, an organization will find it very difficult to operate and survive with silo information systems. Organizations need to be agile and flexible, and will require the same from their information systems. These systems need to have integrated data, applications, and resources from across the organization. Integrated information systems are needed today to focus on customers, to process efficiency, and to help build teams that bring employees together that cross functional areas.

---

[1] Porter, M., and Millar, V. (July–August 1985). How Information Gives You Competitive Advantage. *Harvard Business Review*.

Today's competitive business is cross-functional, dynamic, and global. Since the early 1990s, most organizations have tried to remove the functional barriers that had existed for decades. The business process reengineering gurus and others have convinced management that compartmentalization is inefficient and ineffective in today's interconnected world. To compete effectively in today's market, organizations have to be customer focused and cost efficient. This demands cross-functional integration among the accounting, marketing, and other departments of the organization. This has led to the creation of business units (BU) within organizations that integrate personnel from the various functional units to work together on a variety of projects within an organization. Business units are dynamic suborganizations created and eliminated depending on need. BUs can be in existence for a few weeks or a few years, which makes it impossible physically to locate the personnel in an adjacent geographical space. This demands that the information systems be flexible and fluid across the departmental boundaries. In addition, it requires that systems are accessible anyplace and anytime. These business requirements ultimately created the need for enterprise systems to support the multifunctional needs of the organization.

ENTERPRISE RESOURCE PLANNING SYSTEMS

What Is An ERP?

Enterprise resource planning (ERP) systems are the specific kind of enterprise systems to integrate data across and be comprehensive in supporting all the major functions of the organization. In this book, enterprise systems are referred to as ERP systems mainly because the term ERP is more popular and commonly understood in the IT industry. ERPs, shown in Figure 1-2, are basically integrated information systems that support such enterprise functions as accounting, financial, marketing, and production requirements of organizations. This allows for real-time data flows between the functional applications.

ERP systems are comprehensive software applications that support critical organizational functions. As shown in Figure 1-2, they integrate both the various functional aspects of the organization and the systems within the organization with those of its partners and suppliers. Furthermore, these systems are "Web enabled," meaning that they work using Web clients, making them accessible to all of the organization's employees, clients, partners, and vendors from anytime and anyplace, thereby promoting the BUs' effectiveness.

ERP system's goal is to make information flow be both dynamic and immediate, therefore increasing the usefulness and value of the information. In addition, an ERP system acts as a central repository eliminating data redundancy and adding flexibility. A few of the reasons companies choose to implement ERP systems is the need to "increase supply chain efficiency, increase customer access to products and services, reduce operating costs, respond more rapidly to a changing marketplace, and extract business intelligence from the data."[2]

Another goal of ERP system is to integrate departments and functions across an organization onto a single infrastructure that serves the needs of each department. This is a difficult, if not an impossible, task considering that employees in the procurement department will have very different needs than will employees in the accounting department. Each department historically has its own computer system optimized for the particular ways that the department does its work.

---

[2] Robinson, S. (December 10, 2004). A Developer's Overview of ERP. www.developer.com/design/print.php/3446551 (accessed February 15, 2006).

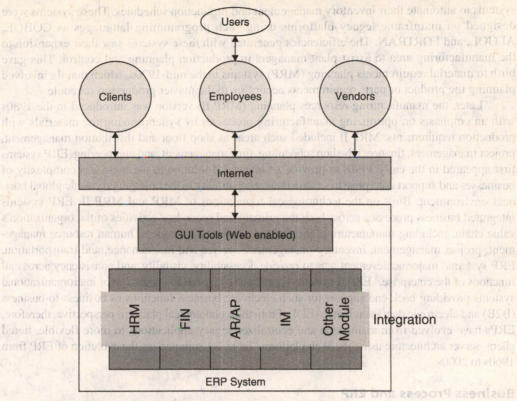

FIGURE 1-2   Integrated Systems—ERP

An ERP system, however, combines them all together into a single, integrated software environment that works on a single database, thereby allowing various departments to share information and communicate with each other more easily. To achieve this high level of integration, however, departments may sometimes give up some functionality for the overall benefit of being integrated. The central idea behind data integration is that clean data can be entered once into the system and then reused across all applications.

In summary, ERP systems are the mission-critical information systems in today's business organization. They replace an assortment of systems that typically existed in those organizations (e.g., accounting, finance, HR, transaction processing systems, materials planning systems, and management information systems). In addition, they solve the critical problem of integrating information from various sources inside and outside the organization's environment and make it available, in real time, to all employees and partners of the organization. We will discuss further ERP systems and their implications to organizations both before and after their implementation later in this book.

Evolution of ERP

During the 1960s and 1970s, most organizations designed silo systems for their departments. As the production department grew bigger, with more complex inventory management and production scheduling, they designed, developed, and implemented centralized production systems to automate their inventory management and production schedules. These systems were designed on mainframe legacy platforms using such programming languages as COBOL, ALGOL, and FORTRAN. The efficiencies generated with these systems saw their expansion to the manufacturing area to assist plant managers in production planning and control. This gave birth to material requirements planning (MRP) systems in the mid-1970s, which mainly involved planning the product or parts requirements according to the master production schedule.

Later, the manufacturing resources planning (MRP II) version was introduced in the 1980s with an emphasis on optimizing manufacturing processes by synchronizing the materials with production requirements. MRP II included such areas as shop floor and distribution management, project management, finance, job-shop scheduling, time management, and engineering. ERP systems first appeared in the early 1990s to provide an integrated solution to the increased complexity of businesses and support enterprise to sustain their compatibility in the emerging dynamic global business environment. Built on the technological foundations of MRP and MRP II, ERP systems integrated business processes across both the primary and secondary activities of the organization's value chain, including manufacturing, distribution, accounting, finances, human resource management, project management, inventory management, service and maintenance, and transportation. ERP systems' major achievement was to provide accessibility, visibility, and consistency across all functions of the enterprise.[3] ERP II systems today have expanded to integration of interorganizational systems providing back-end support for such electronic business functions as business-to-business (B2B) and electronic data interchange (EDI). From the technological platform perspective, therefore, ERPs have evolved from mainframe and centralized legacy applications to more flexible, tiered client–server architecture using the Web platform. Table 1-1 summarizes the evolution of ERP from 1960s to 2000s.

Business Process and ERP

A crucial role of ERP in business, beside integration of functional applications and organization information, is to better position the organization to change its business processes. As defined, a business process is a series of tasks or activities grouped to achieve a business function or goal. For example, order processing may include such tasks as taking an order, checking inventory, and preparing invoices. Most organizations have a set of policies and procedures to guide their business process. The ERP software has hundreds of business processes built into the logic of the system. These processes may or may not agree with the organization's current business processes. An organization has two choices when implementing ERP: change business processes to match the software's functionality or modify the ERP software. The consequences of selecting either option have a long-term impact on the organization in terms of its bottom line and the performance of its employees, customers, and other stakeholders.

Vendors assert that they have embedded the "best practices or leading practices" of a business process in their software. It is therefore possible for organizations to maximize their benefits by taking advantage of these best practices. This occurs only when organizations do not make major modifications to their ERP software during implementation. In reality, there are other negative consequences for an organization when modifying the ERP system to match existing processes. For example, any future upgrades to the system once it has been modified become cumbersome and expensive due to the fact that the modified system logic needs to be

---

[3] Somers, T. M., Nelson, K., and Karimi, J. (2003). Confirmatory Factor Analysis of the End-User Computing Satisfaction Instrument: Replication within an ERP Domain. *Decision Sciences, 34* (3), 595–621.

TABLE 1-1   Evolution of Enterprise Systems

Timeline	System	Platform	Description
1960s	Inventory management and control	Mainframe legacy using third-generation software (e.g., Cobol, Fortran)	With a focus on efficiency, these systems were designed to manage and track inventory of raw materials and guide plant supervisors on purchase orders, alerts, and targets, providing replenishment techniques and options, inventory reconciliation, and inventory reports.
1970s	Material requirements planning (MRP)	Mainframe legacy using third-generation software (e.g., Cobol, Fortran)	With a focus on sales and marketing, these systems were designed for job shop scheduling processes. MRP generates schedules for production planning, operations control, and inventory management.
1980s	Manufacturing requirements planning (MRP II)	Mainframe legacy using fourth-generation database software and manufacturing applications	With a focus on manufacturing strategy and quality control, these systems were designed for helping production managers in designing production supply chain processes—from product planning, parts purchasing, inventory control, and overhead cost management to product distribution.
1990s	Enterprise resource planning (ERP)	Mainframe or client–server using fourth-generation database software and package software application to support most organizational functions	With a focus on application integration and customer service, these systems were designed for improving the performance of the internal business processes across the complete value chain of the organization. They integrate both primary business activities like product planning, purchasing, logistics control, distribution, fulfillment, and sales; additionally, they integrate secondary or support activities like marketing, finance, accounting, and human resources.
2000s	Extended ERP or ERP II	Client–server using Web platform, open source and integrated with fifth-generation applications like SCM, CRM, SFA. Also available on Software as a Service (SaaS) environments	With a focus on agility and customer-centric global environment, these systems extended the first-generation ERP into interorganizational systems ready for e-Business operations. They provide anywhere anytime access to resources of the organization and their partners; additionally, they integrate with newer external business modules such as supply chain management, customer relationship management, sales force automation (SFA), advanced planning and scheduling (APS), etc.

updated separately on every new version of the software. Thus, every time an organization has to upgrade the ERP system, the IT staff will have to upgrade the application and upgrade the modifications. Modifications will have to be reengineered into the system when they are incompatible with the new version.

On the other hand, if the organization decides to implement the ERP system "as-is" (aka. *vanilla implementation*), disruptions will occur with the functioning of the organization. Employees, business partners, and clients will have to be retrained in the new business processes (in addition to the ERP system). This does generate resistance from the users, adding to the training expense for the implementation. Thus, management must pay very close attention to the organizational consequences of modifying or not modifying the ERP software to match their organizations' business process. This is not an easy decision. A wrong decision can bring down the entire organization, whereas a right decision can reap enormous benefits. We will later discuss several ERP implementation examples (e.g., Hershey Foods, Microsoft, and Cisco Systems) that will highlight the consequences of early management decisions on their organization. A good understanding of ERP technology and its implementation process can significantly improve efficiency and effectiveness of the organization's business processes.

ERP System Components

As shown in Figure 1-3, an ERP system, like its information system counterpart, has similar components such as hardware, software, database, information, process, and people. These components work together to achieve an organization's goal of enhanced efficiency and effectiveness in their business processes.

An ERP system depends on hardware (i.e., servers and peripherals), software (i.e., operating systems and database), information (i.e., organizational data from internal and external resources), process (i.e., business processes, procedures, and policies), and people (i.e., end users and IT staff) to perform the input, process, and output phases of a system. The basic goal of ERP, like any other information system, is to serve the organization by converting data into useful information for all the organizational stakeholders.

The key components for an ERP implementation are hardware, software, database, processes, and people. These components must work together seamlessly for the implementation to be successful. The implementation team must carefully evaluate each component in relation to the others while developing an implementation plan. Hardware, software, and data play a significant role in an ERP system implementation. Failures are often caused by a lack of

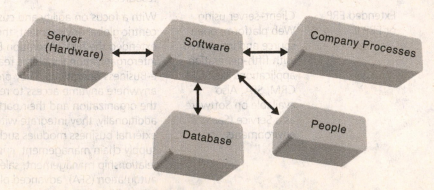

FIGURE 1-3   ERP Components

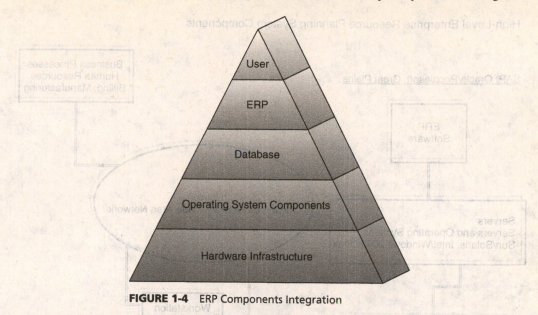

FIGURE 1-4   ERP Components Integration

attention to the business processes and people components. Both people involvement and process integration will need to be addressed from the very early stages in the implementation plan. Staff must be allowed to play a key role in the project from the beginning. As shown in Figure 1-4, each component must be layered appropriately and each layer must support the efficiency of the other layers. The layered approach also provides the ability to change layers without significantly affecting the other layers. This can help organizations lower the long-term maintenance of the ERP application because changes in one layer do not necessarily require changes in other layers.

ERP Architecture

The architecture of the ERP implementation influences the cost, maintenance, and the use of the system. A flexible architecture is best because it allows for scalability as the needs of the organization change and grow. A system's architecture is a blueprint of the actual ERP system and transforms the high-level ERP implementation strategy into an information flow with interrelationships in the organization. The ERP architecture helps the implementation team build the ERP system for an organization. The role of system architecture is similar to the architecture of a home, which takes the vision of the homeowners with the system components similar to the wiring, plumbing, and furnishings of a home.

The process of designing ERP system architecture is slightly different from other IT architectures. Whereas other IT architectures are driven by organizational strategy and business processes, if purchased, ERP architecture is often driven by the ERP vendor. This is often referred to as *package-driven* architecture. The reason for this reversal is that most ERP vendors claim to have the best practices of their industry's business processes captured in their system logic. This argument has proven very powerful in convincing organizations to spend millions of dollars for the ERP package. In order to leverage this investment and maximize the return on investment, an ERP implementation is driven by the requirements contained in the package.

High-Level Enterprise Resource Planning System Components

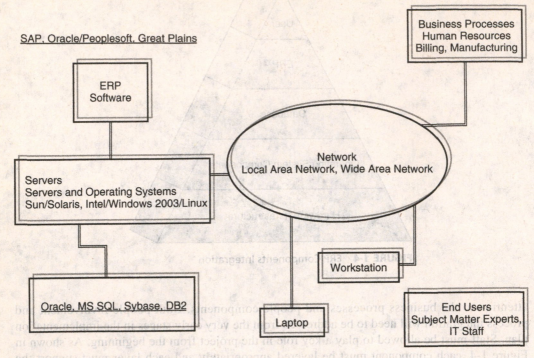

FIGURE 1-5   Example of Architecture of ERP at Large University

The architecture must therefore be conceived after the selection of ERP software, whereas the architecture is conceived well before buying or developing software in other IT implementations.

An ERP package can have a very different implementation outcome from one organization to another. In the architecture of a large university, an ERP system can be very complex and must be designed and tested thoroughly before implementing it in the organization (Figure 1-5). The architecture sets the stage for modifications or customizations to support an organization's policies and procedures, data conversion, system maintenance, upgrades, backups, security, access, and controls. Many organizations often make the mistake of ignoring the system architecture stage and jumping directly into ERP implementation because they have planned a "vanilla" or "as-is" implementation. This can be disastrous because the organization will not be prepared for long-term maintenance and upkeep of the system.

The two types of architectures for an ERP system are logical (see Figure 1-6) and physical or tiered (see Figure 1-7). The logical architecture, shown in Figure 1-6, focuses on supporting the requirements of the end users, whereas the physical architecture focuses on the efficiency (cost, response time, etc.) of the system. The logical architecture provides the database schemas of entities and relationships at the lowest tier, followed by the core business processes and business logic handled by the system at the second tier. The third tier provides details on the applications that support the various business functions built in to the ERP system. The end users do not ever see the first and second tiers because they interact primarily with the client–user interface application tier that provides them access to the functional applications.

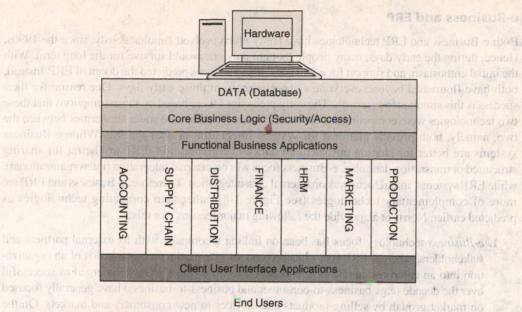

FIGURE 1-6 Logical Architecture of an ERP System

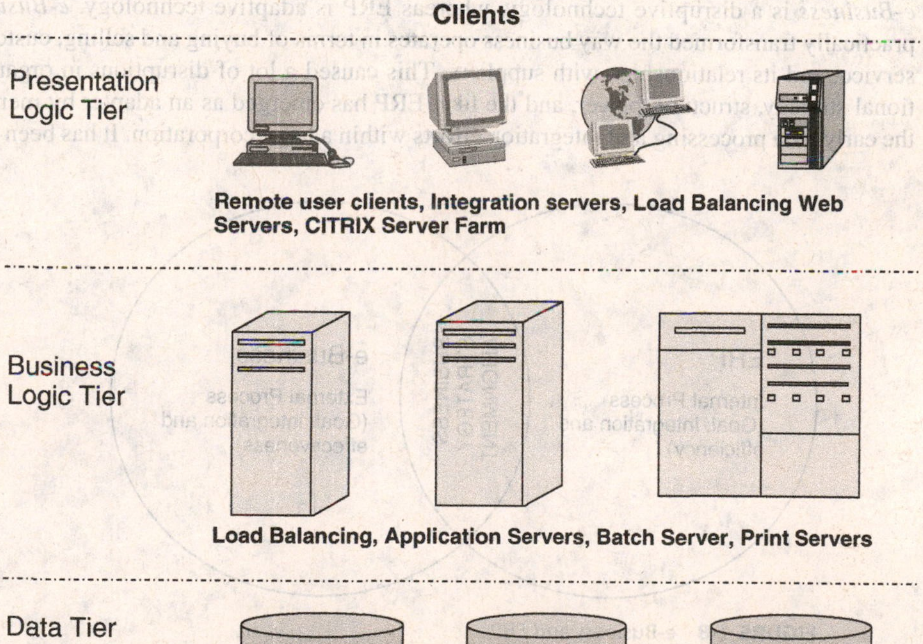

FIGURE 1-7 Tiered Architecture Example of ERP System

e-Business and ERP

Both e-Business and ERP technologies have pretty much evolved simultaneously, since the 1990s. Hence, during the early days, many people thought only one would survive for the long term. With the initial enthusiasm and support for e-Business, many analysts predicted the doom of ERP. Instead, both have flourished beyond everyone's expectation from those early days. One reason for their success is this simultaneous growth. The early predictions were based on the assumptions that these two technologies were competing for the same market. Yes there are some similarities between the two, namely, both provide platform for systems integration or data sharing. While e-Business systems are better for sharing unstructured data and collaboration, ERP are better for sharing structured or transaction data; also, e-Business focus was on external integration (interorganizational), while ERP systems' initial focus was on internal data integration. Therefore, e-Business and ERP are more of complementary technologies (see Figure 1-8) rather than competing technologies as predicted earlier. Norris et al. provide the following major reasons[4] for this.

1. *e-Business* technology focus has been on linking a company with its external partners and stakeholders, whereas ERP focus has been on integrating the functional silos of an organization into an enterprise application. *e-Business* technologies that have emerged as successful over the decade (e.g., business-to-consumer and business-to-business) have generally focused on market growth by selling products and services to new consumers and markets. On the other hand, ERP technology has been successful in integrating business processes across the functional spectrum of the organization and in providing a central repository of all corporate data, information, and knowledge, thereby increasing organizational efficiency and worker productivity.

2. *e-Business* is a disruptive technology, whereas ERP is adaptive technology. *e-Business* practically transformed the way business operates in terms of buying and selling, customer service, and its relationships with suppliers. This caused a lot of disruptions in organizational strategy, structure, power, and the like. ERP has emerged as an adapter by merging the early data processing and integration efforts within a large corporation. It has been very

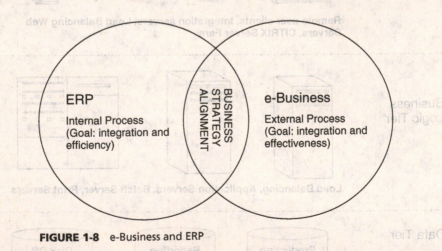

ERP

Internal Process
(Goal: integration and
efficiency)

BUSINESS
STRATEGY
ALIGNMENT

e-Business

External Process
(Goal: integration and
effectiveness)

FIGURE 1-8   e-Business and ERP

---

[4] Norris, G., Hurley, J. R., Hartley, K. M., Dunleavy, J. R., and Balls, J. D. (2000). *E-Business and ERP Transforming the Enterprise.* New York, NY: PriceWaterhouseCoopers and Wiley Publishers.

successful in aligning and integrating accounting, finance, human resource, and manufacturing technologies by aligning business processes with information processing logic and in transforming these organizations from pure hierarchical structures to matrix and other hybrid or flexible organizational structures. Thus, even though *e-Business* caused a lot of disruptions in business, ERP helped these businesses survive by allowing them to adapt quickly to these disruptions.

3. Finally, the early focus of e-Business was on communication (e-mail), collaboration (calendaring, scheduling, group support), marketing and promotion (Web sites), and electronic commerce. These can all be considered front-office functions that involve user and/or customer interactions. In contrast, the focus of ERP systems was mainly on data sharing, systems integration, business process change, and improving decision making through the access of data from a single source. These functions can all be considered back-office functions helping the operational efficiencies of employees, vendors, and suppliers. For example, e-commerce, which facilitates selling of products online, requires tremendous back-end support, namely, fulfillment of the online order. This task can be efficient if an organization has an ERP system in place.

The above reasons show why these two technologies have successfully cohabitated in organizations for the last decade, thereby refuting the earlier claims that one will replace the other. Even in intranet applications, the functionality is one of ERP applications only, and it is delivered via Internet-based protocols. Today, both technologies are evolving toward a single model in which ERP vendors provide e-commerce and e-Business modules as part of the system. In future, e-business Web site implementation will become a part of ERP implementation.

Benefits and Limitations of ERP

ERP systems require a substantial investment from an organization in terms of cost, time, and people. These investments can run into millions of dollars over several years and involve hundreds of people from the organization. No organization will be willing to invest a huge amount of resources unless the benefits outweigh the costs. The benefits and limitations of ERP can be looked at from a systems and business viewpoint; similarly, like other IT projects, the returns can be tangible and intangible, as well as short term and long term. The management within an organization that implements an ERP system has to account for the benefits and limitations of this system from all viewpoints and focus on the big picture to justify the huge investments in this system to the stakeholders. A strong commitment from management is critical for the success of ERP systems. This commitment will not be internalized unless a thorough analysis of benefits and limitations is communicated.

The system benefits and limitations of ERP systems are as follows:

- Integration of data and applications across functional areas of the organization (i.e., data can be entered once and used by all applications in the organization, improving accuracy and quality of the data).
- Maintenance and support of the system improves as the IT staff is centralized and is trained to support the needs of users across the organization.
- Consistency of the user interface across various applications means less employee training, better productivity, and cross-functional job movements.
- Security of data and applications is enhanced due to better controls and centralization of hardware, software, and network facilities.

- Complexity of installing, configuring, and maintaining the system increases, thereby requiring specialized IT staff, hardware, network, and software resources.
- Consolidation of IT hardware, software, and people resources can be cumbersome and difficult to attain.
- Data conversion and transformation from an old system to a new system can be an extremely tedious and complex process.
- Retraining of IT staff and personnel to the new ERP system can produce resistance and reduce productivity over a period of time.

The business benefits and limitations of ERP systems are as follows:

- Increasing agility of the organization in terms of responding to changes in the environment for growth and maintaining the market share in the industry.
- Sharing of information across the functional departments means employees can collaborate easily with each other and work in teams.
- Linking and exchanging information in real time with its supply chain partners can improve efficiency and lower costs of products and services.
- Quality of customer service is better and quicker as information flows both up and down the organization hierarchy and across all business units.
- Efficiency of business processes are enhanced due to business process reengineering of organization functions.
- Retraining of all employees with the new system can be costly and time consuming.
- Change of business roles and department boundaries can create upheaval and resistance to the new system.
- Reduction in cycle time in the supply chain from procurement of raw materials to production, distribution, warehousing, and collection (see example in Box 1-1).

BOX 1-1   Microsoft's ERP Implementation

Microsoft's rapid growth in the 1990s created major support problems for the IT staff, which felt it had lost control over the systems they administered. The problems arose due to the number of redundant applications that had been developed to support the company's operation. At one point as many as 90 percent of the 20,000 batch programs that were retrieving and passing data between applications were redundant. The move to a single architecture with SAP improved integration between Microsoft's business units and its suppliers and customers. Microsoft spent 10 months and $25 million replacing 33 existing systems in 26 sites with SAP. Microsoft claims to have saved $18 million annually as a result, and Bill Gates (founder of Microsoft) reportedly has expressed great satisfaction with the SAP software.[5,6] The key production benefits of ERP systems were as follows:

- Reduction of planning cycle (95 percent)
- Reduction of delivery times (10–40 percent)
- Reduction of production times (10–50 percent)
- Lower stock levels (10–25 percent)
- Reduction of late deliveries (25–50 percent)
- Increase in productivity (2–5 percent)

---

[5] Kalakota, R., and Robinson, M. (1999). *E-Business—Roadmap to Success.* Reading, MA: Addison-Wesley.
[6] White, B., Clark, D., and Ascarely, S. (March 14, 1997). Program of Pain. *Wall Street Journal,* 6.

ERP IMPLEMENTATION

ERP systems are continuously changing and evolving to provide the organization with a new way of looking at business processes and decision making. Organizations are also continuously changing to match their environments. Both need the flexibility to adapt with each other in order to be successful. System implementations are generally very complex, time consuming, and resource intensive. Because of its size and impact on the organization, an ERP system only increases this complexity; therefore, before implementing ERP, an organization has to plan and understand the life cycle of these systems. This section will provide a quick overview of the ERP implementation process, which begins with business process management (BPM). BPM lays the foundation for the remaining chapters; the ERP implementation concepts introduced in this section will be discussed in more detail later.

Business Process Management

Business process management is the understanding, visibility, and control of business processes. A business process represents a discrete series of activities or tasks that can span people, applications, business activities, and organizations. BPM is similar to other process improvement disciplines, such as Lean Six Sigma, which are used by companies like General Electric to improve organizations' performance and employee productivity. BPM has a prescribed process or methodology that should be followed to help an organization document their business processes and understand where they are being used throughout their business. The initial stage of BPM is to create an "as-is" process map that defines the current process. The as-is process is then used as a baseline for determining where the process may be improved. However, simply documenting the current process does not give the business managers control over the process.

The real value of BPM comes from gaining visibility and control of the business process. BPM can activate the process, orchestrate the people, data, and systems that are involved in the process, give the business managers a detailed view into how the process is operating and where the bottlenecks are occurring, and highlight possible process optimization. Process operational metrics are automatically collected by the BPM software. Armed with data on how the current process is operating, business process managers can use various process improvement techniques to optimize the process. The impact of an improved business process can be realized in many ways, including improved customer satisfaction, reductions in cost, and increased productivity by allocating resources to more value-added activities. One way of achieving these improvements is through implementing ERP system, which has embedded business process designed to improve employee and organization's performance. Taking a life cycle approach will help organizations achieve their process improvement goals with ERP. BPM would be part of this ERP life cycle.

ERP Life Cycle

Understanding an ERP system life cycle and its effects on today's organizations is fundamental to fulfilling the long-term investment in an ERP system. As shown in Figure 1-9, ERP implementation is not a onetime implementation. It requires a continuous cycle of product release and support.

The key to a successful implementation, therefore, is to use a proven methodology, to take it one step at a time, and to begin with an understanding of the ERP life cycle. When a system implementation does not have a well-defined methodology, deadlines will likely be missed, budgets will be overspent, and functionality will not meet the client's needs and requirements.

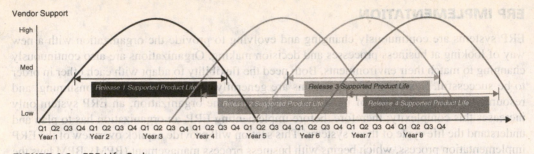

FIGURE 1-9   ERP Life Cycle

ERP system implementations are very risky, and using a well-defined project plan with a proven methodology will assist in managing those risks.

There must be a strong well-communicated need to make the change from the existing information systems/applications to an ERP system before starting any ERP development or implementation. There should also be clear and well-defined business objectives written and communicated to the organization. The project methodology needs to be documented, reviewed, and fully understood by everyone involved in the project once objectives are outlined.

There are many methodologies documented and used in system implementations. Figure 1-10 shows a sample ERP implementation methodology in which there are five phases of the life cycle from requirement gathering analysis to stabilization and production support, which are applied to the three levels of ERP implementation: functional, technical, and organizational. When selecting a methodology, make sure it is robust and addresses issues at all components and levels of the enterprise system. If an external implementation partner or consultant is involved, be sure to review their methodology and determine whether it is appropriate for your organization. Implementation partners may have good expertise in the functional areas, but their most important criteria are a knowledge base of how to design and implement systems successfully.

ERP Implementation Strategies

Implementing an ERP system is problematic without first considering current business processes and changes to those processes based on the functionality of the new system. If business processes are not analyzed and compared with what the new system can do, it is very

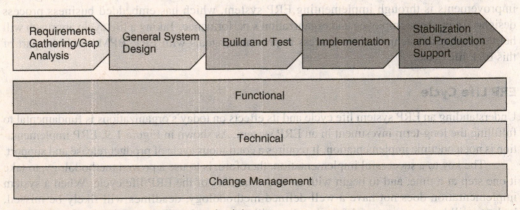

FIGURE 1-10   ERP Implementation Methodology

likely the implementation will require significant system modifications after implementation. In developing the business case for an ERP implementation one must make a decision on the number of modifications to be made to address business requirements. An implementation with considerable modifications to the ERP software package, sometimes referred to as "chocolate" implementation, can increase the chances of success with the users because the package has been customized based on user requirements; however, modifications increase the investment in the system and introduce higher implementation risk.

In a purchased system like ERP, modifying the system means that every modification will have to be addressed each time the system is upgraded. It is like paying for the modification over and over again. Most purchased ERP systems today are minimally modified (or as-is) to protect the investment in the system. This is sometimes called a "vanilla" implementation. Every ERP vendor upgrades their system on a regular basis, adding functionality, fixing problems, and generally keeping the product current with the ever-changing technology innovations to remain competitive. Product life cycles are shown in Figure 1-11.

Software and Vendor Selection

The number of organizations using the Internet has increased dramatically since the early 1990s. The Internet and Web browsers have created an environment that allows for information systems to move out of the back room and onto desktops everywhere. Information systems have grown in functionality and availability. They have also become increasingly complex and difficult to develop. From the 1960s through the early 1990s many organizations were very capable of developing an information system application in-house. The development time was not lengthy, and the systems developed were certainly not as complex. It is very different today. Most organizations lack the skill-set and desire to spend the time and money developing an ERP system "in-house." For many of the reasons identified earlier many more organizations today have chosen to purchase ERPs on the market.

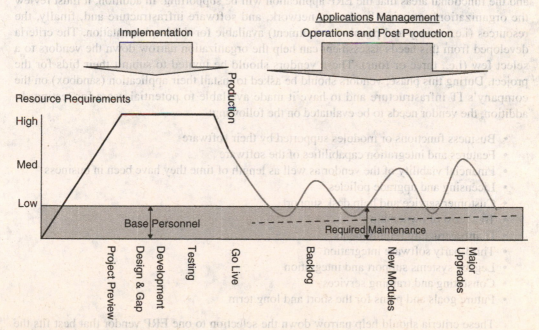

FIGURE 1-11 Product Life Cycle

It is best for an organization that does not have the experience in developing ERP systems to purchase one; however, it does bring forward several issues that should be addressed. Even though it may seem that the vendor selection is the most important issue, the key is the organizational culture. Is the organization ready for change? Organizations need more preparation for change with a purchased system. Setting expectations, developing organizational buy-in, and communicating the need for the change are essential. The "old" days of changing a system within a "silo'd" department are gone. Changing or modifying a system needs to be addressed in the context of the whole organization. In addition, most organizations that move from an in-house developed system to a purchased one find they have to address the notion of system "personality" (i.e., owning the system, its functionality, and how it works). In-house–developed systems fit an organization and its business processes very closely. With purchased systems, each is developed with its own "personality" and requires adjusting to it. To utilize a purchased ERP system fully requires time to continually learn how the system can work best within the organization.

ERP systems consist of computer applications that support and connect all aspects of an organization's business processes and offer a link to customers and suppliers. The data flow freely and are integrated in "real time." When an organization realizes that its legacy system is keeping it from properly and efficiently servicing customers and that their operations are in need of process improvements, they realize they should consider investing in an ERP system. The selection of a vendor-developed ERP system is a challenging job because the organization has to find both a system that is most appropriate for its operational needs and a vendor to become a "partner" for quite some time.

Before selecting a vendor, the organization must carefully evaluate its current and future needs in enterprise management systems. This needs assessment can begin very simply by looking at the size of the organization in terms of the number of employees that will be accessing the ERP applications. The assessment must look at the industry that the organization belongs to and the functional areas that the ERP application will be supporting. In addition, it must review the organization's existing hardware, network, and software infrastructure and, finally, the resources (i.e., money and people commitment) available for the implementation. The criteria developed from this needs assessment can help the organization narrow down the vendors to a select few (i.e., three or four). These vendors should be invited to submit their bids for the project. During this phase, vendors should be asked to install their application (sandbox) on the company's IT infrastructure and to have it made available to potential users for testing. In addition, the vendor needs to be evaluated on the following:

- Business functions or modules supported by their software
- Features and integration capabilities of the software
- Financial viability of the vendor as well as length of time they have been in business
- Licensing and upgrade policies
- Customer service and help desk support
- Total cost of ownership
- IT infrastructure requirements
- Third-party software integration
- Legacy systems support and integration
- Consulting and training services
- Future goals and plans for the short and long term

These criteria should help narrow down the selection to one ERP vendor that best fits the organization. The purchasing and contract discussions should then start with that vendor.

Operations and Post-Implementation

Going live ("Go-live") is one of the most critical points in a project's success. A lot of time and resources have been spent to get to this point. In assessing an ERP project's readiness for Go-live, it is vital to focus the efforts of the teams to ensure that task and activities are completed before going live. This allows project management to address any outstanding issues that may jeopardize the Go-live date. This involves a readiness process that needs to include as many team members and appropriate users and managers as possible because it helps the overall organization understand that the implementation is near and that changes will be taking place. During a project it seems like the system will never be implemented. An effective readiness process lets the teams and organization know that going live is close.

Many ERP implementations have turned into disastrous endeavors during or after the Go-live stage. For instance, FoxMeyer Drug actually collapsed during the stabilization stage, following SAP implementation, in late 1990s, and filed a $500 million lawsuit against SAP/R3. Much of the success of the implementation, therefore, is in the stabilization and postproduction support processes. Stabilization is the time from Go-live to about 90 days after, or until the number of issues and problems has been reduced. An effective response to stabilization issues will determine how well the system is accepted by the end users and management. Five areas of stabilization are important:

1. Training for end users
2. Reactive support (i.e., help desk for troubleshooting)
3. Auditing support to make sure data quality is not compromised by new system
4. Data fix to resolve data migration and errors that are revealed by audits
5. New features and functionalities to support the evolving needs of the organization

Daily and continual monitoring of the implementation issues will provide an appropriate time to move to the postproduction support phase. This phase also addresses the backlog of development issues, evaluates new business processes, and provides more updated training, all of which are a part of the continued implementation.

PEOPLE AND ORGANIZATION

Project Management

For an ERP system to be implemented successfully, project management must provide strong leadership, a clear and understood implementation plan, and close monitoring of the budget. Project management is the glue that holds the project together. Project management must also follow a process that leads to sound decision making and creates a high level of trust and accountability with all involved in the implementation.

Figure 1-12 depicts the fundamental balance of project management. Any change to one side of the triangle will require a change to one or more sides.

The role of the project manager is one of the most exciting yet risky jobs in an implementation. A successful project manager must be process driven and understand the value of an implementation methodology. The project manager role is the single most important role in an ERP system implementation. To be successful one must be prepared to work long hours in a highly charged environment.

A key component to project management is to understand and communicate the ERP system application management life cycle. The system, whether purchased or "homegrown," has the cycle

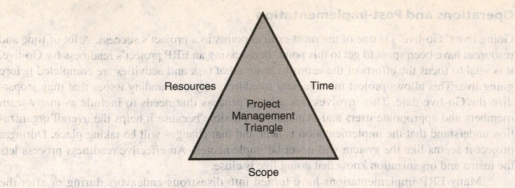

FIGURE 1-12 Project Management

shown (see Figure 1-13). One of the foundations in an implementation is communication of the different project life cycle phases to senior management and staff. All decisions made during an implementation phase will have an effect (i.e., cost and staffing) on the application management phase. The product life cycle application management phase is by far the more costly phase.

Role of Consultants

Many organizations are quite sophisticated at implementing systems, whereas others only do it once or twice every 10–15 years. As stated previously, ERP systems implementations are high risk. It is critical to assess and understand the organization's capacity for implementing such a complex system. The costs of failure are great, and the number of failures is much too high. The development of a credible implementation plan, budget estimates, and deadlines is critical to a project's success.

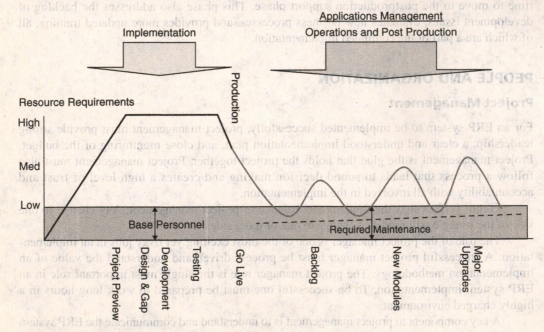

FIGURE 1-13 Project Life Cycle

Before trying to implement a major ERP system, organizations must assess their ability to be successful. There is a model that exists to help organizations understand and assess that ability: the Capability Maturity Model. This model has five levels of organizational capability, with level one being the least capable and level five the most capable. If an organization's assessment criterion is on the lower end of the model, the organization should look seriously at hiring a consulting company as an implementation partner to assist and possibly lead the organization through the implementation.

As stated, it is often the case for organizations without much ERP implementation experience to use implementation partners. The use of consultants may appear to increase the project cost, but in most cases it does not. In the case where an organization does have the experience, the need for consulting should only be considered to address gaps in skills.

Change Management

For major system implementations, the change management role is essential because it prepares an organization for changes to how its business is done. In implementing any new system, communicating, preparing, and setting expectations are just as important as training and supporting the implementation. Effective communication of expectations will reduce risk and better insure that the system is accepted once it is implemented. Change management was historically always thought of as important, but it was rarely funded or staffed appropriately. Today that is changing, and there is an increased awareness that the success of a project is the result of a well planned and thorough change management process. Research has shown that many projects fail due to lack of communication between technical staff and customers, and this one factor is often cited as a component overlooked in implementations. It is essential to develop, understand, and communicate the return on investment, business processes, and the need for change. It is rare that an ERP system implementation failure is based on hardware or software not working appropriately.

Business Process Reengineering

While the phrase *business process reengineering* is overused, it is often the case that current business processes will need to be changed to use the functionality of an ERP system fully. It is best to make it clear to clients and users that processes will need to be changed, adjusted, or adapted as the ERP system is implemented. A business process is a group of activities or tasks that are coordinated for achieving a business goal. A business process can be ordering supplies or designing a new product for the market. Most organizations have defined policies or procedures for a business process. For example, in order to buy office supplies the administrative assistant has to collect order requests from the department members, consolidate them into one order, find prices from the vendor manuals, fill out purchase order forms, get manager's approval, and so on. The business process task for ordering supplies may not work in the same way after the ERP system is installed. The way decisions on ordering supplies are made may also change after the installation of the system; therefore, an organization has to prepare its employees, IT staff, suppliers, managers, and other affected parties for the arrival of the new system.

Global, Ethical, and Security Management

Between the years 1997 and 2007, the IT industry has experienced massive globalization of its services. Outsourcing and offshoring have become common themes across all industries when it comes to IT development, maintenance, and support. Whereas large companies have been outsourcing for a number of years, small and medium-size companies have only recently come to rely on outsourcing partners for a majority of their IT support. Globalization has impacted ERP systems in many ways. First, a majority of ERP vendors are global. SAP, Oracle, Microsoft, and others have support offices and development teams spread around the globe. Second, large ERP implementation consultants have global offices and staffs to help clients in ERP implementation projects all over the world; several consultants are emerging from countries like India. Finally, software leasing or Software as a Service (SaaS) is an emerging model for outsourcing for many companies that do not want to invest large amounts of money on in-house ERP implementations.

Ethics and security are other areas that have attracted a lot of attention. There has been a wide-spread increase in corporate white-collar crimes such as unscrupulous accounting and marketing practices, privacy violations, unauthorized data sharing, spam mail, viruses, snooping, phishing, and identity theft. All these unethical practices have indirectly impacted ERP systems due to their centrality in organization and direct integration with the database. Compliance management due to such regulations as the Sarbanes–Oxley (SOX) Act and the Health Insurance Portability and Accountability Act (HIPAA) are fast-growing software support areas, and several ERP vendors have started providing software modules or tools to support compliance management.

Along with additional modules, organizations are implementing security services to manage access and control in ERP systems, and they are developing awareness programs across their organizations to help staff and management understand the seriousness of security breaches within an ERP; however, security unfortunately remains an afterthought. The seamless integration of ERP software only increases the risk of both hackers who break through perimeter security and insiders who abuse system privileges to misappropriate assets through acts of fraud. The ERP world requires a new way of thinking about security, namely, about business transactions that inflict financial losses from systems-based fraud, abuse, and errors, and not just the bits and bytes of network traffic.

ERP VENDORS

The ERP software market has experienced tremendous growth in the last decade, even after analysts had predicted its early demise in 1990s. The Global Industry Analysts, Inc.,[7] analyzed ERP software market worldwide (North America, Europe, Latin America, Asia, and rest of world) by revenue and application type. They predict that world market for ERP software will reach $67.8 billion by the year 2015, dominated by North America and Europe, from the $36 billion in 2008. Tight budget amid the global economic crisis forces the enterprises to remain more accountable toward spending on business process and applications. The focus has now shifted toward reducing the operating costs, implementation time, and the cost of maintenance of the ERP system. In turn, the vendors too are concentrating on the smaller projects that result in quick returns, rather than on longer ones with higher implementation periods and delayed payments. In turn, the enterprises are now opting for single application systems over multiple systems, in order to save on costs and bring in more functional efficiencies.

Key players dominating the global ERP software market include ABAS Software AG, CDC Software Inc., Consona Corporation, Epicor Software Corporation, Industrial and Financial Systems AB, Microsoft, NetSuite Inc., Oracle Corporation, Plex Systems, Inc., QAD Inc., Ramco Systems, The Sage Group plc, SAP AG, Unit 4 Agresso NV, and Visma AS, among others. This vast market can be grouped into three tiers as shown in Table 1-2 below. Tier I

---

[7] Global Industry Analysts. (April 2010). ERP Software: A Global Strategic Business Report. www.StrategyR.com, 562.

TABLE 1-2   ERP Market Tiers

Tier I, Tier II, and Tier III ERP Software Vendors

Sample Vendors

Tier I	Tier II	Tier IIII
SAP	Epicor	ABAS
Oracle	Sage	Activant Solutions Inc.
Oracle—e-Business Suite	Infor	Bowen and Groves
Oracle—JD Edwards	IFS	Compiere
Oracle—Peoplesoft	QAD	Exact
Microsoft Dynamics	Lawson	NetSuite
	CDC Software	Visibility
		CGS
		Hansa World
		Consona
		Syspro

includes large vendors like SAP, Oracle, and Microsoft, who provide support for large companies; Tier II includes vendors supporting the midsize companies; and Tier III vendors support small companies. Recently, the midsize and small company markets have shown tremendous growth. Small companies, which usually have less than 30 users and less demanding needs, prefer using Tier III software. Midsize companies (with less than 100 users) that have outgrown Tier III packages often become Tier II clients. They usually have just a few localized sites and prefer short-term investments. Tier I software is targeted for a large enterprise company.

Here is the market share vendor between Tier II and top three Tier I vendors.

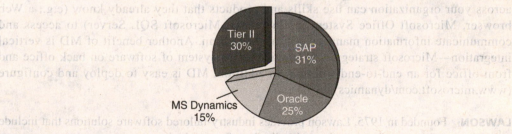

Key Vendors

The competition among ERP vendors has become fierce, and mergers and acquisitions have become the latest trend. The key ERP vendors (i.e., SAP, Oracle, Microsoft, and Infor) are likely to hold on to their 46 percent of the ERP applications market. Many organizations who are shopping for a system will opt for a vendor who is a leader in the industry, whereas others take the time to examine products from many vendors before making a decision. The ERP industry is continually changing and evolving as more and more businesses have started using packaged solutions to support their enterprise functions. The following is a brief description of the current major ERP vendors.

SAP

Founded in 1972, SAP is the recognized leader among ERP vendors, claiming the largest current market share. Its solutions are for all types of industries and for every major market. SAP is headquartered in Walldorf, Germany, with 12 million users, 88,700 installations, and more than 1500 partners. It employs more than 32,000 people in more than 50 countries. Its products include mySAP Business Suite, SAP NetWeaver, and solutions for small and midsize companies (e.g., SAP Business One and SAP All-in-One) (www.sap.com).

ORACLE   Oracle technology can be found in nearly every industry around the world and in the offices of 98 of the Fortune 100 companies. Oracle is the first software company to develop and deploy 100 percent Internet-enabled enterprise software across its entire product line, which includes databases, business applications, and application development and decision support tools. Oracle provides solutions divided by industry category and promises long-term support for customers of PeopleSoft, which was acquired in 2004. They have 40,000 professionals, working in more than 100 countries around the world. Their three business principles are Simplify, Standardize, and Automate. Oracle is headquartered in Redwood Shores, California (www.oracle.com).

INFOR   This company is the world's third-largest provider of enterprise software, with approximately $2.1 billion in revenue. It delivers integrated enterprise solutions in supply chain, customer relationship and supplier management, workforce, asset management, product life cycles, operational and business performance, and more. Headquartered in Alpharetta, Georgia, Infor is the tenth-largest software company in the world with 8,100+ employees, 70,000 customers, and offices in 100 countries worldwide (www.infor.com/infor).

MICROSOFT   Formerly Microsoft Business Solutions or Great Plains, Microsoft Dynamics (MD) is a comprehensive business management solution built on the Microsoft platform. MD integrates finances, e-commerce, supply chain, manufacturing, project accounting, field service, customer relationships, and human resources. The key benefit of MD is that users across your organization can use skills and products that they already know (e.g., a Web browser, Microsoft Office System products, and Microsoft SQL Server) to access and communicate information managed within the system. Another benefit of MD is vertical integration—Microsoft strategy is to provide an ecosystem of software on back office and front office for an end-to-end solution. In addition, MD is easy to deploy and configure (www.microsoft.com/dynamics).

LAWSON   Founded in 1975, Lawson provides industry-tailored software solutions that include enterprise performance management, distribution, financials, human resources, procurement, retail operations, and service process optimization. Lawson is headquartered in St. Paul, Minnesota, and has offices and affiliates serving North and South America, Europe, Asia, Africa, and Australia (www.lawson.com).

SSA GLOBAL   SSA Global acquired Baan in 2004 and doubled the company's size globally. They claim to offer solutions that accomplish specific goals in shorter time frames and are more efficient with time. SSA Global is headquartered in Chicago, Illinois, with offices all over the world (www.ssagt.com).

EPICOR   This company provides enterprise software solutions for midmarket companies around the world. The company claims to have solutions to a variety of needs, whether a customer is looking for a complete end-to-end enterprise software solution or a specific application. It provides solutions for a limited number of specific industries, including nonprofit, distribution, manufacturing, and hospitality. Epicor is headquartered in Irvine, California (www.epicor.com).

The ERP market has matured to a point where heightened competition has brought declining sales. As a result, ERP vendors are committed to bundling new functionality (e.g., CRM, SCM, and Compliance) to provide more value to their customers.

Software Extensions and Trends

In the mid-1990s, during the Internet and dot-com boom, many IT experts predicted the doom of ERP systems because virtual organizations, or *e-Business*, would eliminate the need for ERP. The focus of ERP has always been on supply chain management, and organizations were turning to Internet and Web-based technologies to accomplish this task. After the initial rush for Web-based supply chain software, however, with vendors like Siebel, i2, Ariba, and Commerce One, providers of best-of-breed point solutions that were powering SCM for *e-Business*, these new applications lost their luster due to lack of comprehensiveness of the applications. As *e-Business* firms started growing bigger with advanced needs in HR, accounting, and warehousing, the non-ERP vendors were not able to support their requirements. At the same time, ERP vendors were starting to expand their functionality to the Internet and *e-Business*. For example, SAP introduced mySAP.com and PeopleSoft introduced a three-tier Web-enabled client for accessing all their modules via the Internet. In addition, there were several third-party software integrators like Extricity and Neon that linked the Internet to ERP applications.

Intense competition and fluctuating sales have forced the ERP vendors to expanding their software functionality to add value and to support new organizational needs from compliance management, customer support, global supply chain, and such emerging technology platforms as open-source software (OSS) and service-oriented architectures (SOAs). Open source addresses a key concern in this instance. ERP vendors often pitch packaged applications to smaller enterprises that they can run as is, requiring little or no IT investment. It's a logical pitch in environments with scarce technological resources, but a substantial percentage of smaller companies want or need to customize the applications to fit their specific business needs, much like larger enterprises.

Another trend among big vendors has been the expansion of their software market for small to medium-size businesses. The saturation of the demand in big business and the lucrative nature of the small and midsized business markets have led vendors like SAP and Oracle to enter the small business market, which was originally the target of Microsoft and Epicor. For example, Oracle Corp. and its development partner NetLedger Inc. are providing hosted software suites for small and midsize businesses. NetLedger's NetSuite provides portal views into a suite of applications geared for smaller companies. SAP similarly launched its CRM on-demand solution for its small business customers. A Gartner Group study found that attracting and retaining new customers will be the No. 5 business priority for organizations.[8]

Similarly, SOA implementation will continue to grow as a factor in ERP purchase decisions because vendors are using creative marketing around product strategies versus buying what is currently available. Vendors are making their pitches with a subliminal message: "If you want to

---

[8] Peter Redshaw. (November 29, 2010). Case Study: First National Bank Boosts Customer Retention at SMBs Through Financial Management and Accounting Tool. http://www.gartner.com/DisplayDocument?id=1479927

stay current with the rush toward SOA, you need to be on our platform." Another shift is toward recurring and variable revenue models—with maintenance charges driving industry growth—companies like Oracle earn about 50 percent of their revenue from maintenance. Finally, the other major revenue shift is toward software as a service or hosted subscription-based applications. Although this strategy is causing difficult adjustments for the big vendors, they are adjusting their pricing models so that they can get incremental license revenue through higher levels of usage.

Looking ahead, social networking and open-source software solutions are poised for significant growth. For example, Facebook has become the number one social network software worldwide in 2010, with 500+ million users and growing. Soon, we may see an integration of social-networking system with ERP systems. Similarly, open-source software vendors, like Compiere (www.compiere.com) and OpenBravo (www.openbravo.com), have emerged by focusing on reducing the total cost of operations (TCO) of ERP implementation and by enabling high-level customization due to access to source code, which is not possible with traditional ERP software.

IMPLICATIONS FOR MANAGEMENT

Managers implementing ERP systems in their company should remember the following:

ERP systems implementation is a complex organizational activity. Mistakes will be made in any ERP system implementation, and these will usually not be on technology. It is important to evaluate and learn from the successes and failures. As described in the examples in this chapter, the difference between success and failure is sometimes very small. Managing risk is all about keeping project focus and clear communications throughout the organization. For example, ComAir had major problems with their merger with Delta Airlines because they had not upgraded their legacy customer and financial systems. Replacing legacy systems with a new ERP system is a very high risk, but, as Comair found out later, the cost of not replacing an aging system can be greater. The lesson to learn here is that managing risky endeavors is instrumental to business growth and success. IT systems are critical to a company's daily business. If Comair had clearly understood the problems they were facing, their decision to migrate to a new system would have saved the company customer service and financial problems. In the case of UMass Amherst, not fully testing the system under a heavy load created a great amount of confusion on campus.

ERP systems implementation requires strong project management oversight. ERP implementation projects must be continually evaluated for project status, effectiveness, and risks to the organization. Large ERP implementations often require external assessments done on a quarterly basis to help identify and address project risk areas and minimize failures. Older management styles and structures are not as effective in today's organizations. Current management styles need to be collaborative, creative, and flexible. Managers must be skilled in developing business models that can fully utilize the capabilities of an ERP. Successful managers will need to have skills both in facilitation and communication and in managing organizational change.

ERP systems provide improved and added functionality for an organization. ERP systems create an advantage by strategically cutting costs, increasing profit margins, and growing the enterprise. Integrated business processes and data also provide for improved strategic reporting for planning and decision making. The utilization of the Web creates access to new audiences and customers. Management must develop and communicate a long-term strategic business vision to determine how an ERP system will change or improve business. It will be difficult, if not impossible, to bring change to an organization without looking at the organization holistically.

ERP systems are set to proliferate globally. The globalization of commerce and the Internet bring the world closer, understanding how these systems work and the effects they will have on organizations is necessary. Today, even mid-market companies are increasing their international presence, often driven by major customers who have entered global markets. Every part of the organization is involved or affected by an ERP system, whether a technical staff person, functional analyst, or an end user. Small to midsize organizations are realizing the need for a single integrated system to adapt to the changing environments and needs around the globe. The proliferation of ERP system implementations continues and will continue at a rapid pace. New generations of systems will only capitalize on what has been accomplished already. Organizations successfully implementing an ERP system will not retreat to nonintegrated systems.

Summary

- This chapter provided an overview of information systems, ERP systems, and the history of how they started, where they came from, and why they exist. The components of an ERP system and the complexities involved in implementing and supporting the system were also discussed. Whereas the risks for implementing an ERP are greater, the payoff is very high for organizations.

- The integration of data helps an organization to better meet the demands of a fast and dynamic business world. As discussed in the examples, success or failure hinges on both the software and the implementation, organization, and planning. Management must be involved and support an ERP implementation, whereas project management and change management are the keys to successful implementations.

- Information systems have changed as information technology has changed. System models have moved from centralized to decentralized, and finally to the current state. As the models have changed, so also have the needs of organizations. The availability of ERP systems provides for integrated data and business processes, thereby creating opportunities for organizations to expand and change as their business changes.

- ERP components consist of hardware, software, information, process, and people to perform the fundamental phases of an information system: input, process, and output.

- ERP system architecture is a blueprint of the actual ERP system. There are two types of architecture: physical and logical. The logical architecture works to assist in implementing the organization's vision and business processes. The physical architecture highlights how the data, application logic, and presentations are integrated and installed in the IT environment.

- The ERP system benefits and limitations are discussed in Table 1-3.

- The business benefits and limitations of ERP systems are discussed in Table 1-4.

- There are several ERP vendors competing for an organization's business today. The current vendors include SAP, Oracle, Infor, SSA Global, Microsoft Dynamics, and Epicor.

- Before purchasing a vendor-developed ERP system an organization must identify and document its needs and its vision of the future. The selection of a system must be based on these needs and how well a vendor meets those needs now or in the future.

- There are many ERP system implementation success stories, but the ones that reach the news are often the ones that fail. It is essential to learn from both. A success or failure is sometimes based on something very small.

- To be successful in implementing an ERP system, an organization and its management must clearly understand the implementation process. The key to this is the application of an ERP life cycle and methodology throughout an implementation. A methodology brings about a process to arrive at well-thought-out decisions.

TABLE 1-3   System Benefits and Limitations of ERP

Benefits	Limitations
Integration of data and applications across functional areas of the organization. This means data can be entered once and used by all applications in the organization, improving accuracy and quality of the data.	Data conversion and transformation from an old to a new system can be extremely tedious and complex process.
Consistency of the user interface across various applications means less employee training, better productivity, and cross-functional job movements.	Consolidation of IT hardware, software, and people resources can be cumbersome and difficult to attain.
Maintenance and support of the system improves as the IT staff is centralized and is trained to support the needs of users across the organization.	Retraining of IT staff and personnel to the new ERP system can produce resistance and reduce productivity over a period of time.
Security of data and applications is enhanced due to better controls and centralization of hardware, software, and network facilities.	Complexity of installing, configuring, and maintaining the system increases, thereby requiring specialized IT staff, hardware, network, and software resources.

TABLE 1-4   Business Benefits and Limitations of ERP

Benefits	Limitations
Agility of the organization in terms of responding to the changes in the environment for growth and maintaining its market share in the industry.	Change of business roles and department boundaries can create upheaval and resistance to the new system.
Linking and exchanging information in real time with its supply chain partners can improve efficiency and lower costs of products and services.	Retraining of all employees with the new system can be costly and time consuming.
Efficiency of business processes are enhanced due to business process reengineering of organization functions.	High initial costs of purchasing software, consultant costs, and disrupting the work flow of employees.
Quality of customer service is better and quicker as information flows both up and down the organization hierarchy and across all business units.	To a degree, the company implementing vanilla (as-is) ERP may lose its competitive advantage when all businesses have the same standardized business processes.
Sharing of information across the functional departments means employees can collaborate easily with each other and work in teams.	
Reduction in cycle time in the supply chain from procurement of raw materials to production, distribution, warehousing, and collection.	

- People and organizations are an important part of the implementation process. Some organizations do not have the expertise or even the staff to implement a complex ERP system successfully. In that case, an implementation partner, either the software vendor or a third party, should be hired and used to assist or even to lead the implementation team.
- Whereas ERP implementations are costly in time and resources, the greater costs are in process change, system maintenance,

and remaining current. Organizations are often choosing to implement systems with minimal modification (i.e., vanilla) to ensure that the system can be upgraded on a timely basis and thereby remain current with industry.

With this high-level overview of ERP systems you will be prepared for the next few chapters, which will discuss the value of ERP systems and implementation complexities in greater detail.

Exercises

1. *Comparing ERP Vendors:* You have been appointed as a consultant to a small manufacturing company that is planning to select an ERP software vendor. The company has 300 employees spread across the United States, Canada, and Europe. Select five prominent ERP vendors and visit their Web sites to find information on the following:

   a. The business functional areas their product supports

   b. The product's industry focus and what size of business their product supports

   c. The average cost of the product or any license fees per seat

   d. How long the vendor has been in business

   e. Any other critical information on the vendor

   Use a spreadsheet to present the preceding information in a written report to top management of the company with your recommendation for a product. Please make sure to justify your decision.

2. *Software Functionality:* Download a demo application of Great Plains software and evaluate its accounts receivable and accounts payable functions. What

   features are supported by this software to improve accounting employee productivity and help the organization in their financial/accounting process?

3. *Application Service Provider (ASP):* Find an ASP for ERP software. Visit their Web site and write a report to your organization on how the ASP service works. For example, how will employees access the software? How will data be stored? What security and privacy safeguards are provided? In addition, compare the cost of renting the application versus buying and installing the ERP software on the company's servers.

4. *Careers in ERP:* Find the various career options available for a person who is thinking of a career in ERP. What are the starting salaries as well as the career opportunities? Compare the salaries with other IT areas. Present this information on a spreadsheet, graphs, or charts for a quick analysis. You may need to research in computer magazines like *ComputerWorld*, *CIO*, *Datamation*, or *e-Week*, and make sure to provide your references for the data presented in your analysis.

Review Questions

1. How is the role of ERP systems different from traditional TPS, MIS, DSS, and others? Can an ERP system support all levels of management?

2. Discuss the evolution of information systems in an organization. How can the use of ERP systems remove information or functional silos in organizations?

3. Among all the ERP components listed in the chapter, which component is most critical in the implementation process and why?

4. Discuss the role of ERP in organizations. Are ERP tools used for business process reengineering (BPR) or does BPR occur due to ERP implementation?

5. Why is the design and selection of ERP architecture crucial for the implementation project? What are the long-term implications of selecting a wrong architecture?

6. Discuss the criteria for selecting ERP vendors. Which is the most important criterion and why?

7. From the examples provided in the chapter on ERP success and failure stories, what are the critical factors of success and failures?

8. What are the critical steps of the ERP project cycle? Discuss the critical success factors.

Discussion Questions

1. Refer to the Hershey case. What were the goals and details of the Enterprise 21 project?

2. Refer to the Hershey case. What were some of the key problems that Hershey encountered when choosing, integrating, and implementing their new ERP system?

3. Refer to the Hershey case. What difficult lessons did Hershey learn from this entire process? Did Hershey ultimately achieve its original goals by implementing this new ERP system?

4. Provide examples of ERP components in an organization that you know of or where you are working.

5. If you had a choice between customizing an ERP application to meet the organization processes and modifying organization processes to meet the ERP functionality, which would you choose? Explain.

6. Where are ERP systems heading in the future? Do you agree or disagree with the trends discussed in the chapter? Explain.

7. Why is it necessary for the project triangle to be balanced at all times for project success? Discuss the implications of an unbalanced project triangle.

CASE 1.2
Real-World Case
Rolls Royce's ERP Implementation

Source: Based on Greg Sumner, Case Study Report, U Mass Lowell, 2006.

Rolls Royce (RR) is a global company with several divisions in more than 14 countries. It operates in four global markets: civil aerospace, defense aerospace, marine, and energy.[9] In 1996, Rolls Royce outsourced 90 percent of its IT functions to a contractor called Electronic Data Services (EDS), which meant that EDS was responsible for overseeing the existing IT structure as well as providing adequate IT solutions for the future prosperity of the company.[10] RR used more than 1,500 legacy (mainframe) systems that were inaccurate, expensive to operate, and difficult to maintain.

A need for an enterprise resource planning (ERP) system was noted during the late 1990s at RR to handle the volume of data being produced and processed from the new acquisitions and overall growth experienced by the company. In 2001, RR decided that SAP/R3, an ERP platform consisting of 12 functional modules, would be implemented at its aerospace division. There were multitudes of challenges that RR had to overcome in order for a successful implementation to occur.

---

[9] Rolls-Royce Web site. www.rolls-royce.com/index_flash.jsp (accessed October 2010).

[10] Kelly, L. (December 2003). Outsourcing Case Study: Rolls-Royce. *Computing.*

To conquer the challenges presented, RR had to have an excellent IT team in place with a viable implementation strategy. The ERP project consisted of a management team of specialists from EDS who in turn hired SAP consultants to provide specialized technical help with the implementation. Within the project team there were subject matter experts (SMEs) and staff that had vital knowledge of cross-functional business relationships and experience of the old legacy systems. In conjunction with this team there were operational business units (OBUs), each with its own ERP change management team, which was responsible for implementing working changes and training.[11] The ERP team at RR could be classified into three categories: cultural, business, and technical.

The cultural team's challenge was to overcome the problems that stemmed from whether or not SAP (1) would be accepted by users throughout the company and (2) would provide similar functionality as the prior legacy systems. The cultural team decided to illustrate the benefits to the company as a whole in order to quell concerns. They did so by training individuals throughout RR. Specialist users were trained, and they, in turn, trained expert users. Along with meetings and presentations, they allowed users fully to understand and utilize functionality.

The business team had to overcome the problems that stemmed from the fact that SAP required a rigid business process structure that necessitated a vanilla implementation. This meant that working practices at RR would have to change in order to meet the functional demands of SAP. The business team used process mappings of current procedures and remapped them to show how they would have to be changed organizationally in order to meet the demands of SAP. Overall, expensive modifications to the SAP software were avoided.

The technical team had to overcome problems mainly to avoid the possibility of inaccurate data. Their main challenge was cleaning data during the migration. Mr. Uwe Koch, the technical lead at RR, says: "We didn't achieve all our targets and still haven't finished cleaning the data. We are in a stabilization period. Making enough people available for these tasks has been difficult."[12] Data had to be screened and stored while avoiding duplication—a major concern for RR. RR built interfaces with the old legacy systems for some special circumstances, so some legacy systems weren't taken offline immediately. Interfacing required that data be retrieved from the prior legacy systems, which of course meant that it had to be accurate after being run into SAP. This was so because the reports generated from SAP had to be precise. This was accomplished by validating the data before putting it into the SAP data warehouse. The system required multiple weekly "runs" via a UNIX server, which bridged the data from the legacy systems.

The system rollout was another technical challenge. The ERP was designed in three phases, of which the third stage was actually the "implementation." The implementation was done in two waves. The first wave was focused around the replacement of the legacy systems. The second wave was done in order to implement such leftover elements as logistics and human resources that were not converted until wave one was completely successful.

The implementation team at RR, including EDS personnel and SAP consultants, identified problems that would be pertinent to the implementation of SAP as the ERP for

---

[11] Yusuf, Y., Gunasekaran, A., and. Abthorpe, M. S. (February 13, 2004). Enterprise in Formation Systems Project Implementation: A Case Study of ERP. *International Journal of Production Economics*, 87.
[12] Adshead, A. (May 13, 2003). Cheaper Field Staff Tracking Services. *Computer Weekly.*

the company before they could develop into issues that would impede and possibly cause the implementation to fail. Hence, a sound implementation strategy made the endeavor possible. This case is surely proof positive that having a solid and knowledgeable ERP implementation team that can anticipate problems during an implementation, while putting forth a solid strategy, is the key to success. RR continues to look into the future to adopt new technologies, methodologies, and processes to take them to the next level.

CASE QUESTIONS

1. What do you think of RR's ERP implementation project? Did they select the right implementation strategy?

2. Discuss the critical success factors of RR's implementation strategy and the role of SMEs in the project.

3. What advice can you give to RR's technical team on their approach of migrating legacy system with the SAP software?

2

Systems Integration

LEARNING OBJECTIVES
After reading this chapter, you should be able to:

- Understand the impact of organizational structure on information systems.

- Find out about the types of functional silos in organizations.

- Learn about the evolution of information systems technology generations and architectures and its influence on the silo environment.

- Know what systems integration is and why it is important for organizations.

- Understand the role of enterprise resource planning (ERP) systems in systems integration.

CASE 2-1
Opening Case
Air Cargo's e-Enterprise System

Source: Adapted from *Financial Executive's News*, June 2002, p. 8. www.Ioma.Com; Ed McKenna. (December 13, 2004). ACI Hits Stop Sign. *Traffic World*. Newark, p. 1.

Air Cargo, Inc. (ACI) is a logistics management company providing air cargo ground services to 17+ shareholder airlines and 53 associates, including a road feeder service that connects airports and cities in the United States and Europe, pickup and delivery of regular air cargo shipments, small package air cargo pickup, and delivery of flight-specific, time-definite shipments. A major system crash in the late 1990s caused ACI's revenue to drop from about $150 million to about $145 million; this served as a wake-up alarm for management and started their systems integration effort with their *e-Enterprise system*.

PROBLEMS WITH FUNCTIONAL SILOS

ACI runs various business applications for dispatching, invoicing, freight audits, and reconciliation. Before converting to ERP, ACI's accounting staff had to export and import text files to communicate across accounting and business applications. This took time and made even the most recent report slightly dated. ACI initially considered simply upgrading its existing accounting system to a new release; however, Jack Downing, ACI's IT director, decided this approach was not feasible because they had developed numerous custom procedures in their accounting and other business applications. "An upgrade wouldn't have been economical," he explained, "because we had made so many custom changes to the old software."

e-ENTERPRISE SYSTEM

ACI therefore implemented four *e-Enterprise* applications—its financial series, distribution series, customization series, and integration series—and integrated them with a database management system, Microsoft SQL Server, at the backend. In addition, ACI used the Microsoft transformation services. The immediate effect of this implementation was the integration of the accounting system with the line-of-business applications, thereby eliminating manual data reentry. This occurred because Microsoft SQL Server and the Data Transformation Services (DTS) software connected to ACI's line-of-business applications and delivered transaction data to the ACI *e-Enterprise system*. DTS software is an extract, transform, and load (ETL) tool which consolidates data from disparate sources to single or multiple destinations.[1] These data were used to update the financial records. Note that DTS runs in the background on a regular basis without requiring manual intervention. As a result, the accounting department no longer needs to export and import line-of-business records manually to generate its reports.

---

[1] See Microsoft Web site for more details: http://technet.microsoft.com/en-us/library/cc917688.aspx (accessed February 2007).

BENEFITS

The key advantage of the e-Enterprise system is that it links contracts managed in the line-of-business applications to financial records. "Once we agree on rates, terms, and hours of operation with a contractor, they are entered into our contracts administration system," says Sally Hartmann, ACI's CFO. "In the past, we had to reenter that information into the financial system manually and hope that we remembered to adjust it if there were changes in the contract. But now, we automatically move this information from the accounting system to the contract management system. And we have the ability to move that information in the other direction as well, which we didn't have in the past." The key benefit here is that if a contractor stops paying its bills, the warehouse system will immediately alert the dispatch people. Hartmann adds: "We are also completing a direct link from our human resources to our accounting system. This will eliminate another area of manual data entry and reduce the potential for errors."

Hartman ultimately sees three other advantages accruing to ACI from this ERP conversion. These are as follows:

- "Based on what I have seen so far, I am estimating that we will reduce our administrative workload by about 10 percent, primarily by reducing manual data entry."
- "With the ERP system, we will provide more accurate, complete, and timely information to decision makers."
- "We are moving heavily into e-commerce, and e-Enterprise provides the building blocks that enable two-way information flow between e-business and financial systems."

The ACI case highlights some of the problems with heterogeneous systems and how they can affect the various departments within the company from Accounting to Warehousing. The systems integration at ACI has introduced some benefits and drawbacks. *The question remains whether their benefits outweigh the drawbacks. What do you think?*

PREVIEW

In the Air Cargo case, you can see what happened to functional departments when a company moves from silo systems to an enterprise information system (EIS). The critical benefit from such conversions is usually the elimination of manual data re-entry (i.e., rekeying information from one functional application into another). Another benefit is the reduced dependence on spreadsheets to generate management reports and to answer special management queries. The drawbacks of implementing integrated systems can include the high cost of implementing an ERP system, the required process changes to benefit from the new system, and training the employees to use this new system.

In today's organization, integration of information systems (IS) is very critical for their survival and growth. Systems integration means that you allow a heterogeneous (hodgepodge) IS to communicate or integrate and share information (or data) *seamlessly* with one another. It is important to understand that the keyword here is *seamless* because systems have shared information with each other for a long time; however, they required a human link. Information generated from one system had to be re-entered manually by users into other systems, as illustrated in the Air Cargo case. This case also shows the typical problems faced by an organization with a manual data integration process. First, it takes much longer to get information into the system, there are errors and inaccuracies, and information sharing cannot happen in real time (or instantly as it's updated by others) between the various organization stakeholders. For example, the warehouse employee does not know the product sales cycle, and the customer service employee may not know the status of the shipped product. This breeds inefficiencies in the operations of an organization, which reflects poor customer service, and in the long term makes the organization ineffective in its competitive landscape. In fact, systems integration is a key issue for an organization for its growth; therefore, management needs to pay close attention to this issue. Enterprise information system plays a key role in systems integration, as discussed in this chapter. ERP systems are a major kind of enterprise information system that allows organizations to integrate the heterogeneous systems into one organization-wide application with an integrated database management system.

This chapter will trace the origins of how information systems have evolved into a heterogeneous collection of isolated systems or *silos* over the last 50 years—their relationship with an organizational structure, the value of systems integration, and the role of ERP in systems integration. Information systems have generally evolved around the needs of the organization. Before discussing evolution of IS, therefore, it is important to understand the evolution of organizations. This chapter takes a brief look at the evolution of functional silos in organizations, followed by a discussion on the evolution of IS in an organization. This is followed by a discussion on systems integration challenges, benefits of integrated systems, and the role of ERP in systems integration. The chapter will conclude with a set of challenges faced by management on systems integration and their role in resolving them.

FUNCTIONAL SILOS

According to Webster's dictionary, *silos* are *an airtight pit or tower* for preserving products. Silos are basically compartmentalized operating units isolated from their environment. Why have information systems and organizations evolved into functional silos? In order to understand the reasons, we first need to look at the historical evolution of modern organizations and the systems supporting their information requirements.

Horizontal Silos

Management theorists Huber and McDaniel[2] in their research study found that the complexity and turbulence in the organization's environment forces it to break complex tasks into smaller manageable units. If we take a closer look at the evolution of a modern organization, the early emphasis has always been on the horizontal or the functional paradigm. In the early 1900s, a management philosopher named Henry Fayol[3] was the first person to divide functionalized organization into five basic areas: planning, organizing, coordinating, commanding, and controlling. Fayol's classification was extended and conceptualized in the 1930s by Luther Gulick[4] into the functional model of POSDCORB (planning, organizing, staffing, directing, coordinating, reporting, and budgeting). The POSDCORB categorization (Figure 2-1) became very popular and led to a set of formal organization functions such as control, management,

---

[2] Huber, G., and McDaniel, R. (May 1986). The Decision-making Paradigm of Organization Design. *Management Science*, 572–589.
[3] Fayol, H. (1916). *Administration Idustrielle et Generale*. Paris: Dunod.
[4] Gulick, L. (1937). Notes on the Theory of Organization. In: *Papers on the Science of Administration*. New York: Columbia University Press.

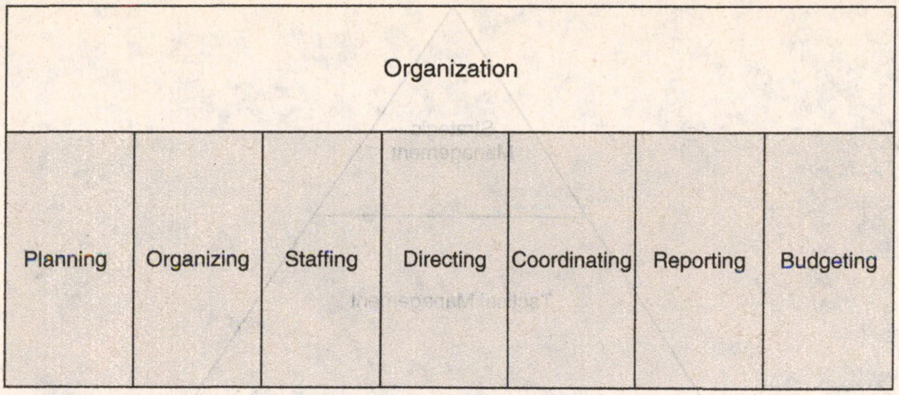

Organization						
Planning	Organizing	Staffing	Directing	Coordinating	Reporting	Budgeting

FIGURE 2-1 Functional Model of Organization (POSDCORB)   *Source:* Adapted from Bernard, C. (1938). *The Functions of the Executive*. Cambridge: Harvard University Press.

supervision, and administration starting in late 1930s.[5] Over the next 50 years the terminology of functions in organizations has changed, say from planning to management to strategy, but the concept of categorizing complex activities into organized functions has remained for control and coordination reasons. The current classification of organizations into divisions or departments like Accounting, Human Resources, Marketing, Management, and others reflects this evolution in organizations of breaking complex tasks into smaller manageable tasks that could be assigned to a group of people who could then be held responsible.

Vertical Silos

In addition to the functional or horizontal division, organizations have also seen a vertical or hierarchical layering of management functions. In the late 1960s, Robert Anthony,[6] an organizational researcher, at Harvard University, found that organizations also divided responsibility in hierarchical layers from strategic planning to management control and operation control. For example, most organizations have their top-level management like CEOs and presidents to plan the long-term strategy of organizations, whereas midlevel management (e.g., vice presidents or general managers) focuses on tactical issues and the execution of organizational policy to ensure that the company is accomplishing its strategic objectives. The lower-level management (e.g., supervisors) task is to focus on the day-to-day operations of the company. This vertical categorization, even though not discrete organizational functions, does involve a distinctive set of activities. The functional silos typically follow the scientific model for business and usually have hierarchical or multilayered reporting structures, formal leadership, management positions, or both with final authority on decision making. In this traditional functional (or silo) organization, maintaining command and control is usually critical for the overall functioning of the business organization.

Thus, when organizations get big and complex they tend to break functions into smaller units and assign one or more staff the responsibility for these activities. This allows the organization to manage complexity as well as the staff to specialize in those activities that enhance

---

[5] Barnard, C. (1938). *The Functions of the Executive*. Cambridge: Harvard University Press.
[6] Anthony, R. (1965). *Planning and Control Systems: A Framework for Analysis*. Boston, MA: Harvard University Graduate School of Business Press.

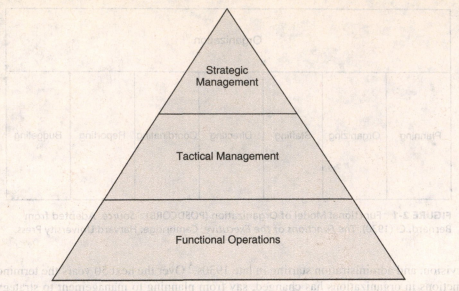

FIGURE 2-2 Hierarchical Model of Organization

productivity and efficiency. Work groups or teams with formal leadership or supervisors are part of this organizational structure as well. The quality of the products and services goes up, but the organization is divided into compartmentalized units that know very little of each other. Sharing of information occurs only at higher levels of management.

Despite attempts to break them, functional silos are alive and doing well. According to a survey by *Purchasing* magazine,[7] 96 percent of the respondents said their organization still maintains a functional structure but 86 percent also said they agree with their firm's decision to promote teamwork and integration of the functional areas in their organization. One reason for this is that information sharing and communications problems get worse as an organization spreads geographically and gets more virtual. The original purpose of functional division (i.e., efficiency and effectiveness) is defeated. The lack of information sharing at all levels of an organization often leads to problems with inventory management, such as overproduction of goods, when the sales department is not sharing current data on projected sales with the production department, or poor customer service, when a customer service representative does not know the status of shipped goods. The inefficiencies can creep from operations control all the way to the strategic planning level of the organization. With global competition and virtual organizations, the traditional functional organizational structure must change to process-oriented structure to allow easy integration of information and more flexibility for an organization to realign with its environment. In order to compete in a globalized economy, companies must take a business process view and utilize IT to integrate that business process.

BUSINESS PROCESS AND SILOS

The functional silo problem was felt by many organizations in the late 1980s and early 1990s, which gave birth to business process reengineering (BPR). The functional grouping often leads

---

[7] Purchasing. (November 4, 1999), 24.

to a shortsighted view of improving the division or department rather than the entire organization. This causes intraorganizational friction and is counterproductive toward an organization's overall goals. Business process focus led by such management gurus as Peter Drucker[8] and Hammer and Champy[9] reoriented management on improving an organization's efficiency and effectiveness by focusing on business processes (e.g., product development and order processing). The business process provides an alternative view of grouping people and resources focusing on an organization's activity, even if it means cutting across the traditional functional areas (e.g., order processing), which involves interactions between sales, warehousing, and accounting functional areas as the work progresses from initial sales order to collection of payment from the client. The cross-functional business process can involve people and resources from various functional departments working together, sharing information, if necessary, at any level of the organization. This business process focus has moved management thinking away from a functional department to business process view. The business process view flattens the organizational structure from a hierarchy to a matrix where people and resources from multiple functional units collaborated on such projects as new product development, procurement, or order processing in order to serve the external entities of the organizations better and quicker.

The cross-functional organizational structure breaks the traditional functional silos of an organization opening up the informational flows from one department to another. This opened the doors for more organizational changes because some organizations are moving from process orientation to customer orientation. A customer-centric organization focuses all its business processes around improving the relationship with its customers. For example, Dell Computers does not preassemble its computers for its customers; instead, Dell provides the configuration options to its customers via the Dell.com Web site. The customer designs the computer configuration based on his or her needs and then transmits the order to Dell. Dell then processes the order and ships it to the customer within two weeks. This customer-centric approach allows Dell to communicate and interact better with its customers and let them drive the organization's processes. Business process and BPR will be discussed in more detail in Chapter 9. This organizational evolution from functional silos to business process and customer-centric approaches has had a big impact on the evolution of information systems, as you will see in the next section.

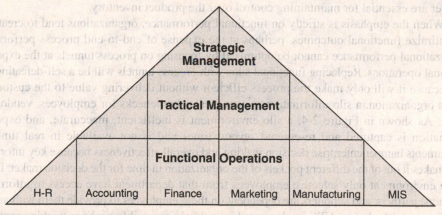

FIGURE 2-3 Matrix Structure of Organization

[8] Drucker, P. (1995). *Managing in a Time of Great Change*. New York: Truman Talley Books/Dutton.
[9] Hammer, M., and Champy, J. (1993). *Reengineering the Corporation*. New York: Harper Business Press.

EVOLUTION OF IS IN ORGANIZATIONS

As described earlier, the role of information systems has been and always will be one of supporting business activities and enhancing the workers efficiency. Over time, however, as business changes and expands, systems need to change to keep pace. The result is sometimes a wide variety of information systems and computer architecture configurations creating heterogeneous or independent nonintegrated systems. These systems ultimately create bottlenecks and interfere with productivity. These systems lack control and coordination. They become the breeding ground for inconsistent, inaccurate, and incompatible data and ultimately lead to mismanagement. The information systems that work independently and are grouped by the various functions and departments, or both, are known as silos. These systems cannot share data and therefore require users to access multiple systems to integrate the data manually. As a result, the chance increases for data errors and inconsistencies. Silo systems focus on individual tasks or functions, or both, rather than on a process and team. In addition, these systems make it very difficult for organizations to be customer-centric because data cannot be assimilated from different functional areas to address customer needs. For example, if a customer support process requires information to be pulled from the accounting and the shipping departments, the task requires access to two separate systems and then visually matching the shipping information with the billing information. This can be time consuming and prone to errors, resulting in poor customer support.

The essential problem with functional silos is that organizations design, manage, and reward their employees and managers by functional performance, yet they deliver value to customers via cross-functional processes. Today, many organizations reward employees on their performance on multiple areas that includes personal performance, business unit performance, and corporate-level performance.

Getting the right balance between functional management and process delivery is at the heart of organizational performance. Organizations have been designed around functions for a very long time and for good reason. The functions of an organization (e.g., sales, manufacturing, claims assessment, HR, and warehouse) are important. They provide a structure by which an organization functions smoothly. For example, the warehouse department and the warehouse manager are essential for maintaining control over the product inventory.

When the emphasis is strictly on functional performance, organizations tend to create silos that optimize functional outcomes, perhaps at the expense of end-to-end process performance. Organizational performance cannot be optimized by focusing on process tunnels at the expense of functional operations. Replacing functional silos with process tunnels will be a self-defeating function because it will only make the process efficient without delivering value to the customer. In today's organization, a silo information system creates bottlenecks for employees, vendors, and clients. As shown in Figure 2-4, a silo environment is inefficient, inaccurate, and expensive. Information is captured and re-entered several times and is not available in real time. Silo environments hamper enterprise decision making and overall effectiveness because key information never makes it out of the different pockets of the organization in time for the decision maker. In a silo system environment only selective employees from that department have access to information; customers, partners, and suppliers are dependent on these employees to provide them with answers.

For example, before UPS implemented its publicly accessible package tracking system for customers, partners, and suppliers, there were tremendous bottlenecks in finding the status of a package in UPS's vast distribution network. It was costing UPS millions of dollars to answer customer queries on package status. Implementing an integrated package tracking system was a

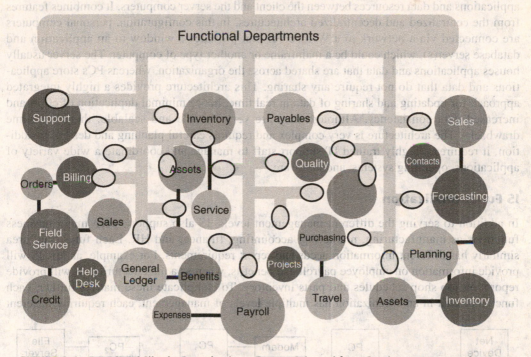

FIGURE 2-4 Functional Silos in Organization *Source:* Adapted from Oracle Inc. www.oracle.com

win–win for UPS and its customers, partners, and suppliers. UPS spent less on answering customer queries, and customers got their answers whenever they wanted to know. In an integrated system environment, all parties have access to the same data sources from a network in real time.

The evolution of IS, when observed from its hardware and software architectures to the various system generations, suggests that its role has generally been to support the organizations evolving information needs.

Information systems as we know them today have been used in business since the 1960s. The introduction of computers into business organizations by such vendors as IBM™ and UNISYS™ started to change how computer systems were used. The IS evolution is often viewed as a sociotechnical change process in which technologies, human factors, organizational relationships, and tasks change continuously. This sociotechnical process, often known as the systems life cycle for analyzing information system requirements, helps to analyze complex sociotechnical dynamics between information systems and organizations. By conceiving system evolution as a sequence of critical events and states within the sociotechnical system and its elements, process researchers can narrate explanations of processes and their outcomes.

IS Architectures

Today's IS can be configured using a wide range of system architectures depending on the information needs of the organization. The continuing rapid advances in computer and networking technologies, as well as changing organizational dynamics, drive the emergence of new information system models. Today's Web-based model will evolve and morph as business models change to meet the demands of customers and clients.

As with today's Web-based systems, using a *distributed* architecture allows sharing of applications and data resources between the client and the server computers. It combines features from the centralized and decentralized architectures. In this configuration, personal computers are connected via a network to a Web server that provides a window to an application and database server(s), which could be a mainframe or another type of computer. The server usually houses applications and data that are shared across the organization, whereas PCs store applications and data that do not require any sharing. This architecture provides a highly integrated approach for updating and sharing of data in real time, hence minimal duplication of effort and increased data consistency. Although they are very flexible and scalable, there are some drawbacks. The architecture is very complex and requires careful planning and design. In addition, it requires a highly trained IT support staff to manage and coordinate a wide variety of applications, operating systems, and hardware.

IS Functionalization

In addition to serving the different management levels, IS also supports such major business functions as manufacturing, marketing, accounting, finance, and HR. Each functional area similarly has different information needs and report requirements. For example, an HR IS will provide information on employee payroll and benefits, whereas a manufacturing IS will provide reports on job shop schedules and parts inventory. To complicate these matters further, each functional area in an organization has multiple levels of management, each requiring different

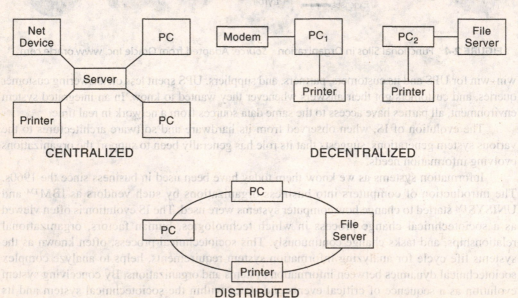

FIGURE 2-5 Information Systems Architectures

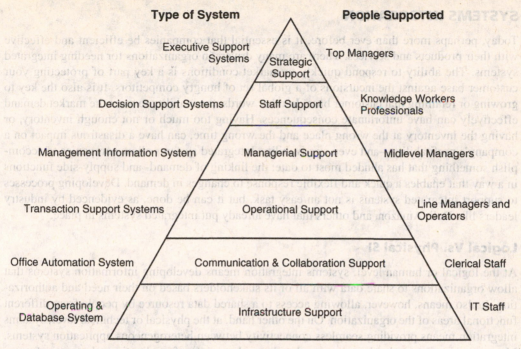

Type of System   **People Supported**

Executive Support Systems — Strategic Support — Top Managers

Decision Support Systems — Staff Support — Knowledge Workers Professionals

Management Information System — Managerial Support — Midlevel Managers

Transaction Support Systems — Operational Support — Line Managers and Operators

Office Automation System — Communication & Collaboration Support — Clerical Staff

Operating & Database System — Infrastructure Support — IT Staff

FIGURE 2-6   IS as Categorized by Functional and Hierarchical Models

levels of analysis and details of information. Figure 2-6 shows these various information systems by levels of management and functional areas of the organization.

Beyond the system infrastructure (e.g., operating systems, database, and networking) the lowest level of the IS pyramid consists of office automation systems (OAS), which support the activities of employees, and transaction processing systems (TPS), which are used to record detailed information in all the major functional areas and to create new information. TPS are the workhorses of the organization. They support the organization's operations and record every transaction, whether it is a sale, a purchase, or a payment. They are often categorized by the functional areas in the organization (e.g., sales, purchasing, and shipping and receiving).

Management information systems (MIS) are reporting systems that categorize and organize information as required by the midlevel managers. These reports can be sales by product for a quarterly period, or they can be production schedules by manufacturing plants. Decision support systems (DSS) are analytical systems that use mathematical equations to process data from TPS to assistant managers in conducting what-if analyses, in identifying trends, and in generally assisting in making data-driven decisions. It could be as simple as using spreadsheet software (e.g., goal-seeking, pivot tables) or something more sophisticated such as online analytical processing (OLAP) software.

Expert systems also assist managers in their decision making using qualitative analysis that captures problem-solving heuristics to identify solutions. It is a very useful tool for training novice managers in real-life situations by providing access to a knowledge base of experienced managers. Finally, executive support systems (ESS) provide a visual dashboard of strategic information to top-level management in real time (e.g., a snapshot of the organizational performance). These systems are typically customized for each functional area of the organization.

SYSTEMS INTEGRATION

Today, perhaps more than ever before, it is essential that companies be efficient and effective with their products and services. There are many drivers in organizations for needing integrated systems. The ability to respond quickly to market conditions is a key part of protecting your customer base against the incursions of a global set of hungry competitors. It is also the key to growing or retaining that customer base. In other words, the inability to meet the market demand effectively can have unfortunate consequences. Having too much or not enough inventory, or having the inventory at the wrong place and the wrong time, can have a disastrous impact on a company's profitability—and even survivability. Integrated systems allow companies to accomplish something that has alluded most to date: the linking of demand- and supply-side functions in a way that enables a quick and flexible response to changes in demand. Developing processes to support integrated systems is not an easy task, but it can be done, as evidenced by industry leaders like Dell, Amazon, and others that have already put integrated systems in place.

Logical Vs. Physical SI

At the logical or human level, systems integration means developing information systems that allow organizations to share data with all of its stakeholders based on their need and authorization. It also means, however, allowing access to a shared data resource by people from different functional areas of the organization. On the other hand, at the physical or technical level, systems integration means providing seamless connectivity between heterogeneous application systems. Most organizations today have accumulated a wide variety of applications that come from a variety of vendors and run on different operating systems and work with many databases. Some applications are old legacy systems that may need to work with the newer Web-based architectures. Having seamless connectivity in this heterogeneous computing environment is a complex task, but necessary for an organization to be efficient. This is where the term "Middleware" started. This software provides the appearance of seamless data presentation to the end user and maintains data integrity and synchronization within each application system database.

In order to achieve the logical integration and fit a company business model, organizational structures, processes, and employee roles and responsibilities need change. As mentioned earlier, business process reengineering goes beyond integrating heterogeneous technologies; it involves changing the mind-set of the employees in the organization, encouraging and enabling them to do their tasks in a new way. Before approaching the integration at the systems level, an organization has to overcome the people barrier, which involves educating and motivating employees to put aside their turf issues (or interdepartmental barriers) and work together as a team. Shifting the focus of employees from achieving the departmental goals to organizational goals is an essential task for management. In addition, changes will be required in the traditional hierarchical management structures that are purely functionally oriented. For example, in the cross-functional structure a budget analyst may work both for a financial manager and directly with a product manager. Thus, the product manager will be responsible for the hiring or performance appraisal for this budget analyst, who is reporting to the financial manager. This may sound very confusing and chaotic; however, this relationship complexity must be maintained for a flat and fluid organizational structure that can be easily adapted to the changing needs of the environment. *Teamwork* is essential if organizations want to break-up functional silos and have workers from all levels of management collaborate on solving organizational problems; furthermore, teamwork must be continually reinforced by having top management stress the achievement of organizational goals, rather than departmental goals, and team goals instead of individual goals.

Steps in Integrating Systems

In conjunction with systems integration, management has to work with the information technology group to come up with an approach for the seamless integration of data and services to support the new organizational structure and business processes. As mentioned before, organizations tend to add functionality to meet organizational demands. At times, application systems are added to the environment. These applications, while not encouraged, are developed on different platforms. Information system organizations often have to be able to support a variety of systems with multiple platforms and vendors. This could mean supporting multiple operating systems, databases, or development environments. Most IT organizations today support a Windows and flavor of UNIX. A database can be Oracle or MS SQL and even MySQL. Most important is the support of a development environment. This area continues to grow. At one point in time, C or C++ with SQL was the key development tool. That has somewhat given way to Java and SOAP with SQL. Integrating and supporting multiple platforms requires planning. System integration generally involves the eight steps in Table 2-1 (this is not an exhaustive list).

TABLE 2-1   System Integration Steps

Step 1	Resource categorization	Take an inventory of the various hardware and software resources focusing on vendors, operating systems platform, IS architecture used in these resources.
Step 2	Compliance and standards	Check whether the database and other technologies used in various applications are such supporting standards as JDBC/ODBC compliance for databases.
Step 3	Legacy systems support	Develop a policy in support of older legacy applications.
Step 4	Middleware tools	Think of middleware tools because most organizations will not dispose of their old system right away for systems integration. Middleware tools are essential for integration in the short term—if existing applications must be used by the organization.
Step 5	Authentication and authorization policies	Develop a single sign-on policy for application and data access because all employees and external partners will need access to an integrated system from anywhere, anytime.
Step 6	Centralized IT services and help desk support	Instituting IT support for an integrated systems environment is necessary to avoid support and maintenance problems with the integrated system. Centralization does not mean that they are all physically in one location. The IT staff can be all over the organization, but they need to be able to support all applications and platforms with a centralized IT help desk support.
Step 7	Backup, recovery, and security policies	Planning data and disaster recovery for organization's data in an integrated system IT is crucial for building the trust and confidence for the new system. A good backup and recovery system is essential if there is a system failure or a major disaster.
Step 8	Hardware and software standardization policies	Develop organization standards and policy on acquisition of new hardware and software which are aligned with organization IT strategy.

Benefits of System Integration

If done right, systems integration can produce tremendous benefits as shown in Table 2-2. Some of the key benefits of systems integration are as follows:

1. *Increased Revenue and Growth.* In general, one of the biggest benefits is reduction in inventory and personnel costs due to integrated systems. For example, Uvex Sports, Inc., a sports gear company, saw sales grow from $1.2 million to $5.2 million without additional costs and with the addition of only two extra employees.[10]
2. *Leveling the Competitive Environment.* Systems integration can make a small company behave like a big player because, with the help of integrated business-to-business (B2B) software, many of them can now compete with big companies to get orders from giant retailers like Walmart, Target, and others because they can provide the same level of service with enterprise systems.
3. *Enhanced Information Visibility.* The increased availability of information enables managers and employees to make informed decisions in a timely manner. For example, customer service representatives of American Express can now make credit approval decisions on the spot while talking with their customers due to better access to customer credit profiles.
4. *Increased Standardization.* A side benefit of integration is that it forces organizations to standardize on their hardware, software, and IT policy. This may initially cost some money, but in the long run companies easily recoup those costs.

Limitations of System Integration

Systems integration does have its drawbacks, as shown in Table 2-2. These are as follows:

1. *High Initial Setup Costs.* The initial implementation of integrated systems is high in terms of both hardware and software costs and human costs due to the re-engineering of business processes. Although these cannot be avoided, their negative influence on the implementation can be minimized by a long-term resource allocation plan and commitment from top management.
2. *Power and Interdepartmental Conflicts.* Systems integration often involves sharing of information across department and interdepartmental teams. This often creates power conflicts among the functional departments if they have not bought into the integration. Educating employees with a good change management strategy that communicates the long-term benefits from systems integration can minimize these conflicts.

TABLE 2-2   Benefits and Limitations of Systems Integration

Benefits of System Integration	Limitations of Systems Integration
Increased revenue and growth	High initial setup costs
Leveling the competitive environment	Power and interdepartmental conflicts
Enhanced information visibility	Long-term and intangible ROIs
Increased standardization	Creativity limitations

---

[10] Kempfer, L. (September 12, 2005). Integration Improves Throughput. *Materials Handling Management*.

3. *Long-Term and Intangible ROIs.* The return on investments (ROI) from systems integration often do not show up until several years after the implementation, and many of these returns come in intangible form and are therefore not recognized on the bottom line of the organization. Financial managers get very upset with this situation and can create pressures that will ruin the long-term impact of systems integration; therefore, top management's understanding and support for the long term are key ingredients for the success of systems integration.

4. *Creativity Limitations.* One of the drawbacks of standardization is that it restricts creativity and independence in the functional areas; however, this can be minimized with a better integration policy that provides flexibility and better communication from top management.

As you can see, the benefits generally outweigh the drawbacks when implementing systems integration projects, particularly in the long run. In industries with competitive markets, systems integration is very necessary regardless of the cost. For example, suppliers of automobile manufacturers (e.g., Ford or GM) or retailers (e.g., Walmart) do not have a choice for systems integration. If they skipped systems integration, they would not be able to do business with these large companies, which moved to electronic data interchange (EDI) systems in early 2000 with electronic commerce.

ERP AND SYSTEMS INTEGRATION

Enterprise resource planning (ERP) systems are integrated, multimodule application software packages designed to serve and support several business functions across an organization. An ERP system is a strategic tool that helps the organization improve its operations and management by integrating business processes and helping to optimize the allocation of available resources. These systems are typically commercial software packages that facilitate collection and integration of information related to various areas of an organization, including finance, accounting, HR, inventory, procurement, and customer service. By becoming the central information center of the organization, ERP systems allow the organization to better understand its business, direct resources, and plan for the future. ERP systems enable the organization to standardize and improve its business processes to implement best practices for its industry.

ERP's Role in Logical Integration

ERP systems play a very crucial role in enabling systems integration at various levels of the application architecture. At the logical level, ERP systems require organizations to focus on business process rather than on functions. ERP systems come with built-in processes for a wide variety of common business functions. An ERP system implements the best practices via specific built-in steps for processing a customer order in terms of how the order information is entered into the system, how it will be routed through various departments for actions or decisions, and how the output from system is communicated to the various parties, including the external customer and suppliers. While ERP systems can address data integration, if business processes do not change, an organization will not be able to take full advantage of the ERP capabilities. The term is *business process reengineering* (BPR). With the implementation of ERP business processes, organizational structures and even roles and responsibilities within an organization will change.

To revisit a previous example, when Dell computers receives an order from the customer, the order is divided by its major components and transmitted to the various units of the company, as well as to Dell's external partners, suppliers, or both. Each department is then regularly updated on the status of the order, as it moves through the various stages of the order-processing cycle. When the supplier delivers the parts to the manufacturing department, all parties will be notified of this process. When the computer is assembled and sent to the warehouse for shipping again all parties are updated on this information. Depending on Dell's company policy on sharing data, some of this updated information is sent to the customers to notify them of the progress. As the order is processed through the various stages of the order-processing cycle, any of the functional department employees responsible for this order can enter the ERP system and find out the current status of the order in real time.

The preceding example suggests that if a company has functional silos, either the silos will have to go or the ERP system implementation will be a failure. With their built-in bias for cross-functional business processes, ERP systems force organizations to abandon their silos. In the early days of ERP implementation projects, many organizations tried to implement ERP with their existing silos, which resulted in major ERP failures. For example, in 1997, Hershey Food's Nestlé division spent more than $200 million for implementing its ERP system without breaking the functional silos, which led to a system implementation failure.[11] Hershey had to face the wrath of its customers who did not receive the products they had ordered for Halloween. Instead of modifying their business processes, some organizations tried to modify the ERP functionality, which also led to implementation failures and additional costs for maintaining or upgrading the modified system. One key lesson to take from these early ERP implementation projects is that change in business processes and systems integration are the necessary precursors to ERP implementation. Some modifications to the ERP systems' built-in process functionality are fine as long as they are done for unique business processes; however, if these process changes are done to avoid user resistance even when they are inefficient or to support a silo organization, then ERP implementation could result in a costly failure.

ERP's Role in Physical Integration

In addition to the logical level, system integration is also necessary at the physical level. Before installing the ERP system, an organization may have to upgrade or install middleware and plan for the removal of their legacy system's hardware and software. Although it is possible to preserve some of the legacy systems and, if essential, integrate them via middleware tools, current-generation ERP systems do not work well with the centralized architecture on legacy platforms. As we will discuss later in the book, layered systems architecture must be adopted to integrate the systems into a common enterprise platform. Integration is also required at the *data level* (i.e., by transforming all the data resources into one database), *client level* (i.e., by standardizing on all the client platforms), and *application level* (i.e., via common user–interface design, back-end access to the system infrastructure, and backup and recovery plans).

ERP systems have therefore become a platform application for organizations to achieve the flexibility and fluidity to survive in the globally competitive world. A good ERP implementation improves operational efficiency with better business processes focusing on organizational goals rather than on individual departmental goals. Efficiency is also improved with a paperless flow within the organization and electronic data interchange or B2B commerce environment with its external partners. Organizations that want to implement a B2B e-commerce (or a supply chain management system) with its partners and suppliers will not be able to do a good job without a

---

[11] Worthen, B. (May 15, 2002). Nestlé's ERP Odessey. *CIO Magazine*.

robust ERP system in place. More discussion on this topic will follow later in the book, but suffice it to say that ERP systems provide a foundation for other advanced enterprise-level applications (e.g., customer relationship management, supply chain management, e-Business, and sales force automation).

Organizations can similarly achieve better fluidity with the help of ERP. By embedding the best business practices and technology standards (e.g., Web-based architectures, integrated systems platform, and distributed system access), ERP systems enable organizations to form quick alliances and partnerships with relative ease. Such companies as Amazon, Inc., can easily form and break alliances with other businesses (e.g., Toys R' Us, Walmart, and KBToys) to sell their products through Amazon's e-commerce Web site. This fluidity has helped Amazon to survive the dot-com bust by scaling its products and services with minimal costs. This would not have been feasible without an integrated system. ERP systems process the transactions for an e-commerce system, allowing it to scale without major bottlenecks in order fulfillment, customer service, and account administration.

IMPLICATIONS FOR MANAGEMENT

According to Robert Tucker,[12] author of the book *Driving Growth through Innovation*, one of the reasons that innovation has not become embedded as a key driver of growth and profitability in many organizations is that it has been limited by functional and divisional "silos" within companies. In other words, the responsibility for innovation has been limited to the R&D department, a special innovation SWAT team, or a senior-level strategic planning group. He points out that this is the way the innovation movement started out (i.e., with pockets of supporters in different departments), but it succeeded in gaining enough support that it is today a core operating value of the full organization in most successful companies. Thus, functional silos can have many unintended consequences that can harm an organization's growth and long-term competitive position in the industry. Some implications for management based on the above comment follow.

Silos do not work. Most organizations lose out in the long term when information is not shared in real time across the functional boundaries within the company. In today's globally competitive environment, organizations have to compete both on lower cost and by providing better customer service, through alliances and partnerships with competition, and from taking other agile strategies to survive. Silos will prevent organizations to take advantage of supply chain management and B2B e-commerce activity to introduce efficiencies in production and procurement. Along those lines information that is not accessible to customer service representatives when they are interacting with customers can spoil the relationships with the clients and have a negative impact on future sales. Integrated systems are a critical and basic foundation for such other information systems as customer resource management or sales force automation systems.

System integration has many hidden benefits. Management needs to understand the tangible and the intangible benefits of integrated systems. In addition to the immediate benefits of sharing organization-wide information, systems integration allows decision making to be cascaded to all employees in the organization. This can help the competitive position as employees at lower levels can make better decisions while interacting with clients or partners. This may make the

---

[12] Tucker, R. (2002). *Driving Growth Through Innovation: How Leading Firms are Transforming Their Futures.* San Francisco, CA: Berrett-Koehler.

employees feel more empowered and be more productive members of the organization. Of course, the organization has to change its business processes and policies to take advantage of better information sharing facilitated with integrated systems, but the potential of increasing the retention of employees exists; however, this is not a very obvious benefit when organizations decide to integrate systems.

System integration has many challenges. Most research on this topic tends to focus on the technological challenges of systems integration. There is considerable challenge and cost in integrating heterogeneous systems, including replacing old hardware and software with newer systems, working with IT consultants in developing middleware to facilitate seamless integration, or bottlenecks in data integration. The technical challenges are nothing, however, when compared with the human challenges that organizations face when integrating systems. The first challenge may be with people in the IT department who will have a major impact once the systems are integrated in terms of supporting and maintaining the new system. Other human challenges will come from the functional department heads who will lose control over the data produced from their areas. Another challenge is curbing the rumors and fears on job layoffs that accompany a systems integration project. Overcoming these fears and curbing the turf battles is critical for the success of a systems integration project. Getting employee buy-in on the systems integration project is very critical for the success of integrated systems.

Systems integration raises many new ethical issues. Systems integration raises several ethical issues for management (e.g., what information should be shared and how it should be shared). Integrated systems opens up new ways of sharing information, but it also brings the possibility of some employees exploiting this information for their personal advantage as well as illegal access of information that they can easily do from their desks. To avoid the unethical use of information, management needs to develop a policy on ethical usage of information as well as use proper security software and hardware (like firewalls) to prevent, track, and monitor information access and usage. In addition, organizations must allocate resources for training and educating of employees and external partners on how to access and use information and be aware of the ethical and security breaches possible with the integrated systems.

Summary

- Functional silos categorize an organization's tasks and activities into groups to improve efficiency and responsibility of work in the organization. They are generally represented as such departments as accounting or HR, each having its own goals and responsibilities. As organizations grow in size and complexity, they are divided into horizontal functions and vertical layers. Horizontal grouping is called functional divisions, and vertical grouping of management functions is called management hierarchy.
- Silos can improve productivity, but they often lead employees to achieve departmen-

tal goals rather than overall organizational goals. This can create interdepartmental conflicts and loss of competitive edge for the organization because the focus is not on the needs of the customers. Employees are valued and rewarded based on department achievements rather than organizational achievements.
- Information systems (IS) have always tried to support the needs of the organization; hence, in the early days, IS was developed to meet the needs of different functional areas of the organization. IS over the years have been divided horizontally by functions

and vertically by hierarchical levels. This led to the development of hodgepodge systems that could not share data across the various functional areas when organizations moved from silos to cross-functional teams focusing on business processes. This led to the major shift toward integrated systems.

- Global competition and business process re-engineering led to the drive of integrated systems since the late 1980s. In order for systems integration to be successful, organizations have to focus both on the human or logical level and on the physical or systems level. Focusing only on technical integration can lead to failure with high costs and employee-user frustration. Systems integration should be done in conjunction with business process re-engineering. There are lots of tangible and long-term benefits as well as short-term drawbacks for integrating systems.

- ERP systems have played a crucial role in systems integration because they have provided organizations with a single platform for integrating all of their functional systems. Organizations can simultaneously conduct both logical-level and physical-level integration because ERP systems come embedded with the best practices in business process for common functions from accounting to warehousing. ERP systems thus make the process of systems integration easier, but they are expensive and often require organizations to start from scratch.

- Management should not take the task of systems integration lightly or leave it for the IT staff. System integration involves and impacts the whole organization, requiring top-management support and resources for a long term. Human- or logical-level integration is necessary for the physical-level systems integration to work. Management must be ready to face the human and ethical challenges in a systems integration project.

Exercises

1. Locate a company that you know and contact the IT manager and HR manager.
   a. Find out what logical and physical integration issues were faced by this organization when they broke the functional silos and moved to integrated systems.
   b. Show the list of benefits and limitations mentioned in this chapter and find out which materialized after their systems integration implementations.
   c. Ask them for a few ethical or security violation examples that may have occurred in their organization. Also, how were they handled?

Review Questions

1. What are functional silos, and how did they evolve in organizations?
2. What is the relationship between organizational functional silos and IS functional silos?
3. Compare and contrast centralized, decentralized, and distributed IT architectures. Which do you think is most appropriate for ERP and why?
4. List the horizontal and vertical levels of systems that exist in organizations.
5. What is logical integration and how is it different from physical integration?
6. Describe at least five steps involved in systems integration.
7. What are the key benefits and limitations of systems integration?
8. What is the role of ERP systems in systems integration?
9. Summarize the role of management in systems integration.

Discussion Questions

1. Refer to the Air Cargo case in this chapter. Discuss the silo problem at ACI and how it was solved via the e-Enterprise system.

2. Refer to the Air Cargo case in this chapter. Discuss both short-term and long-term benefits of the e-Enterprise system.

3. Why do you think functional silos are not appropriate for today's organizations? Discuss your answer from organizational and technical perspectives.

4. What is the relationship between the logical and physical system integration? Why is it important for organizations to have both together?

5. Why is business process re-engineering needed for implementing an ERP?

6. Discuss the role of management in systems integration in terms of the ethical and other challenges they face during the systems integration process.

CASE 2-2
Real-World Case
Systems Integration at UPS Corp

Source: Adapted from Aimee Desrosiers. (2006). Case Study Report, U Mass Lowell; Emigh, J. (August 3, 2005). UPS Bolsters Online Shipment Tracking, Ziff Davis Internet; and UPS' Sutliff: Communication Key to Alignment, *CIO Insight* (January 28, 2003).

In the mid-1980s, United Parcel Service, Inc. (UPS) was struggling for market share with a relative newcomer to the shipping industry, Federal Express (Fed Ex). After only 10 years in business, Fed Ex was emerging as a formidable player largely due to the company's culture of embracing technology as a strategic competitive advantage in improving efficiency and customer service. In contrast, UPS studied their processes and employed less-technical changes (e.g., reducing physical motions in handling boxes) to shave time off their deliveries. Fed Ex started as an airfreight company and UPS as a truck delivery company, but the two increasingly desired market shares in the other's core business.

UPS faced the typical challenges of any shipping company. They knew that shipping errors due to the wrong address or loading the box on the wrong truck were expensive and time consuming. Errors happened frequently on systems that required manual data entry, and multiple systems required redundant processes to utilize the data. Much of the products UPS handles look similar, which allows for picking errors. UPS's phone-in customer service received an overwhelming number of phone inquiries each day that required time- and cost-consuming processes to locate approximate package status. They had also identified the Internet and integrated technology as global business drivers of the future. It was at this time that UPS decided to invest heavily in technology to drive growth.

UPS first identified their internal competencies and assets and looked for areas that could be improved through a strengths, weaknesses, opportunities, and threats (SWOT) analysis. They found that they had an extensive infrastructure and expertise in transportation. UPS next examined such external factors as their customers, the emerging business marketplace, and the competition. Traditional brick-and-mortar business and emerging e-Business all had similar requirements: integrated information and real-time connectivity. Their customers desired the power to buy, sell, and research on their own terms—not where and when business dictated. It was clear that UPS needed to bridge the gap between physical product or services and access to electronic information.

UPS developed an action plan that would be focused on the customer and enabled by technology. They offered a new variety of services integrated with core transportation functions to make UPS an invaluable part of the customer's business. They chose to centralize data in one of two large data centers (i.e., the hubs of their IT platform). Integration is the cornerstone of UPS's success. Since going public in 1999, UPS has acquired more than 30 other companies. They have more than 3,600 IT staff with two data centers in Mahwah, NJ, and Atlanta, GA. UPS has more than 14 mainframes, 2,755 mid-range computers, 260,000 personal computers, and 6,200 servers. According to the CIO of UPS, "We haven't made [these acquisitions] to gain market share. Instead, we've made them for very strategic (technology) reasons."[13] Each time, UPS integrates old and new services to add value to the delivery chain.

The IT department at UPS was a critical enabler and tried to integrate the systems from a business perspective.[14] They installed a couple of different ERP modules from Oracle: one for the HR functions and another for financials. By implementing the ERP UPS saved a tremendous amount of money for the goods and services purchased from hundreds of locations around the globe. In addition, the UPS logistics network, which is very extensive, is rigorous because it was built on well-defined technological standards. When UPS adds new applications, therefore, they fit into the rest of their interconnected IT infrastructure, which doesn't tolerate excessive waste. UPS makes sure all new technology fits in nicely over their architecture. In general, two factors have contributed to the successful integration of technology at UPS: a corporate culture of open communication and a commitment to training.

UPS now integrates information from more than 60,000 Web sites with more than 7.2 million customers making online tracking requests daily. The sophisticated UPS IT platform offers such new software as Package Flow12, which identifies the packages that should be loaded on the delivery truck first, second, and so on, so that the first deliveries are in the rear of the truck. Another software service is Trade Direct12, which now allows retailers, dot-com sites, and other enterprises to track the status of both small packages and large freight around the globe through a single Web-based system. Management is also committed to training whenever new technology is introduced and to providing an environment where all employees can contribute ideas for improvement.

From the customers' standpoint, systems integration translates to better services related to package shipping and tracking that can be easily accessed from the UPS Web site, or by using software provided by UPS. If an incorrect zip code is entered, an error message prohibits the user from continuing the process. The system provides "smart" data (e.g., identifying rural addresses that may require extra delivery time and allowing the user to change options). It is possible to save a database of shipping addresses to auto-fill fields for frequent receivers.

The UPS integrated system platform provides real-time communication links between packages shipped because the tracking number, date, and status are immediately

---

[13] Emigh, J. (August 3, 2005). UPS Bolsters Online Shipment Tracking. *Ziff Davis Internet*.
[14] UPS' Sutliff. (January 28, 2003). Communication key to Alignment. *CIO Insight*.

recorded. A client's customer service could respond to an inquiry instantaneously instead of having to acquire a tracking number manually from shipping, trace the package, and call the customer back. This puts the power directly in the customer's hands. UPS is the model for successful integration for all industries.

CASE QUESTIONS

1. What are some of the system integration challenges faced by UPS?
2. Discuss the systems integration solutions at UPS. How does it help UPS integrate new technologies?
3. Discuss the advantages of systems integration for UPS customers.

3

Enterprise Systems Architecture

LEARNING OBJECTIVES

After reading this chapter, you should be able to:

- Examine in detail the enterprise systems modules and architecture.

- Understand the effects of a well-designed architecture on ERP implementation.

- Know the various types of ERP architectures and the related benefits and drawbacks of each architecture.

- Learn about service-oriented architecture and its impact on ERP systems.

- Learn about cloud architecture and its impact on ERP systems.

CASE 3-1
Opening Case
Nestlé'S ERP Implementation

Source: Adapted from Worthen, B. (2002). Nestlé's ERP Odyssey. *CIO Magazine*. May 15; Aberdeen Group. (November 2005). Center-Led Procurement Organizing Resources and Technology for Sustained Supply Value; Weiss, T. (2002). Nestlé Shifts from HP to IBM in Data Center Pact. *Computerworld*, March 11.

Since market leader SAP introduced R3, the first ERP system with client–server architecture in 1992, thousands of companies worldwide have implemented this software. Many have been successful, but none has been without problems. Nestlé USA was one of them. Nestlé USA has seven business divisions: beverage, confections and snacks, food services, foreign trade, nutrition, prepared foods, and sales. Some of the popular brands sold in the United States by Nestlé are Alpo, Baby Ruth, Carnation Instant Breakfast, Coffee-Mate, Nescafé, Nestlé Carnation Baby Formulas, Nestlé Toll House, PowerBar, Stouffer's Lean Cuisine, SweeTarts, and Taster's Choice. Its annual revenue is around $8.1 billion with 16,000 employees.

The ERP implementation at Nestlé, code-named BEST (Business Excellence through Systems Technology), had an estimated cost of $210 million with an IT staff (including outside consultants) of 250, began in 1997, and was due to be completed in 2003. The project's main goal was to use common business processes, systems, and organizational structures across the autonomous divisions within the United States. These common systems across Nestlé USA would create savings through group buying power and facilitate data sharing between the subsidiaries.

Jeri Dunn, CIO of Nestlé USA, joined with executives in charge of finance, supply chain, distribution, and purchasing to form a key stakeholder's team for implementing the SAP. The stakeholder team made it clear to the top management that the SAP implementation would require business process reorganization and couldn't be done without changing the way Nestlé USA did business.

The stakeholder team, however, did not include any members from the groups that would be directly affected by the new business process. This caused a rebellion in the ranks and the employees resisted. Nobody wanted to learn the new way of doing things. Divisional executives were confused and angry. Morale sank and employee turnover reached 77 percent. Help desk calls reached 300 per day. The project team had overlooked the integration points between modules to account for the Y2K deadline. By the beginning of 2000, the rollout had collapsed into chaos and the project was halted. In its haste to unify the company's separate brands, the project team had essentially replaced divisional silos with process silos.

The company reconvened the stakeholder team and started the SAP implementation process from scratch. The group members eventually decided that to finish the project, they would need to start with the business requirements and then reach an end date, rather than trying to fit the project into a mold shaped by the predetermined end dates. They also made sure that they had support from the key divisional heads and that all the employees knew exactly what changes were taking place.

With SAP in place, Nestlé USA has already achieved a significant return on investment (ROI). The common databases and business processes led to more trustworthy demand forecasts for the various Nestlé products. This also allowed the company to reduce inventory and redistribution expenses. In 2003, Nestlé signed a $500 million, five-year deal with IBM for server hardware, software, and IT services, and integration of its mySAP.com e-Business software system, giving its workers access to mySAP.com via an internal portal customized for their individual jobs. Nestlé is attempting to solve the information management and systems challenge by standardizing on a common ERP system globally. As part of this initiative, they are rolling out a common e-procurement solution across its major regions and markets. Adoption of the solution, which is being licensed from SAP, has been accelerated by Nestlé's e-procurement rollout that does not conflict with its global ERP and data center consolidation efforts. (Nestlé will begin transitioning e-procurement system management to its own data centers in 2007–2008.) This approach also allows Nestlé to handle implementation and change management issues during the initial rollout, enabling simplified system setup and configuration when e-procurement system management moves in-house.

PREVIEW

Once ERP systems are integrated and implemented in a company, they become the cornerstone of the organization. With a successful implementation, every single transaction will now be processed through this system. The SAP-ERP implementation experience at Nestlé USA provides some very important lessons. In addition to systems integration, it is also necessary to focus on business process architecture, business requirements, budget, project management, commitments from top management, and continuous communication with employees informing them about future changes. If the ERP software is installed with a focus only on the system architecture, you may have a successful installation of software, but an unsuccessful implementation. An ERP implementation isn't just about the software. It's easy to install a new system. The hard part is changing the business processes of the people who will use the system. Nobody likes process change, particularly when they don't know what is coming. It is important to include the people in planning whose processes you are changing. Keep the communication lines open while the project is in the works and measure the level of acceptance before, during, and after the rollout. Remember the integration points. It isn't enough to simply install new systems; you need to make sure that both the system and people communicate efficiently and effectively with each other. Update your budget projection at regular intervals to stay on target for the project.

Why Study Enterprise System Architecture?

ERP system architecture provides a foundation for both the functional and the technical needs of the organization and adapts to future business challenges. It articulates the relationships among the complex information technology components, which include hardware, software, and data with such complex organization components as company structures, business rules, and people. For example, ERP hardware can range from multimillion dollar mainframe computer systems to complex networking and security equipment. ERP software similarly requires operating systems, a database, and other software in place for them to function properly. As mentioned in the Nestlé case, ERP systems require current and historical data and business rules from all parts of the organization to be embedded into the system during the implementation phase for a successful solution to business problems. This is a complex undertaking for any organization because it requires a good understanding of the enterprise systems structures, characteristics, behavior, and business operations.

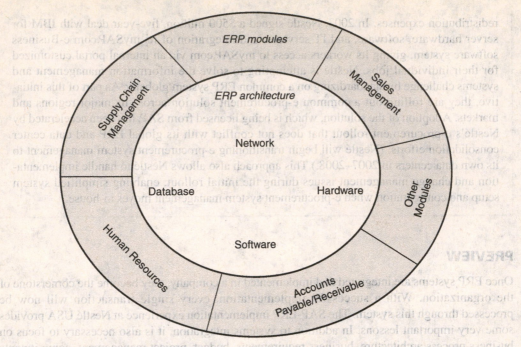

FIGURE 3-1 Enterprise Systems Architecture (ESA) Model

Understanding the enterprise system architecture is important for several reasons. First, it helps management and the implementation teams understand in detail the features and components of the enterprise system. Second, it provides a visual representation of the complex system interfaces among the ERP application and databases, operating systems, legacy applications, and networking. Finally, understanding the enterprise systems architecture, by clarifying the system infrastructure requirements, training requirements, change management requirements, and business process reengineering requirements, among others, can help management in developing a better IT plan.

The enterprise systems architecture (Figure 3-1) can be viewed from two different angles: (1) the functional angle that defines the *ERP modules* that support the various business functions of the organization and (2) the system angle that defines the *ERP architecture* through the physical components of hardware, software, and networking. In this chapter, you will learn more about the typical ERP modules, the system architecture and components, types of ERP architecture, and, finally, the role of architecture and its impact on the implementation stage of the project.

ERP MODULES

The key role of an ERP system is to provide support for such business functions as accounting, sales, inventory control, and production for the various stakeholders of the organization. Organizations often selectively implement the ERP modules that are both economically and technically feasible. ERP provides the same functionality to the users (e.g., the silo systems of the past), but the data are integrated or shareable across all the ERP modules. This means

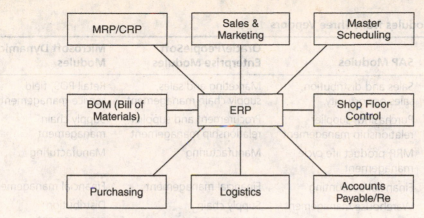

FIGURE 3-2 Typical ERP Modules

the data need to be entered into the system once, and, depending on the organization's business rules, they are made available to users either inside or outside the organization. In today's organization, teams are not limited to employees of the company; teams can include employees from various functional areas as well as employees of business partners and even customers. ERP systems, therefore, provide access to the data as defined by the organizations' business rules.

ERP vendors, including SAP, Oracle, and Microsoft, provide modules that support the major functional areas of the business (e.g., accounting, production, financial management, human resources (HR), sales order processing, and procurement). These modules provide the functionality to implement business policy and processes in accounting, production, finance, human resources, and so on. The ERP software embeds the best business practices into the software to allow organizations to implement their policies and procedures. ERP vendors often claim that these business practices will help improve organizations' productivity and performance. For example, a procurement module includes the best practices on purchasing (e.g., forms, routing, and methods of integrating with e-commerce application). Although the vendor claims are generally true, some business rules may conflict with the organization's policy. Customization or changes are therefore often necessary when implementing the ERP modules. Although this issue will be debated in more detail elsewhere in the book, suffice it to say that management needs to evaluate carefully when and how much modification is essential. ERP software provides different level of flexibility in modifying the system during implementation. Careful evaluation is therefore necessary when selecting the software to avoid problems later.

In general, ERP vendors provide a comprehensive range of enterprise software applications and business solutions to empower every aspect of business operations, identify new business opportunities, and enable the organization to respond to changing business realities. In addition, they include functionality to optimize business operations and resources to extend best practices to the entire value chain. Table 3-1 provides a high-level overview of the usual modules provided by major ERP vendors.

The functional and module list is not exhaustive and does not include all the enterprise software applications provided by these vendors. The following is a brief overview of some of these ERP modules.

TABLE 3-1   ERP Modules from Three Vendors

Function	SAP Modules	Oracle/PeopleSoft Enterprise Modules	Microsoft Dynamics Modules
Sales	Sales and distribution, sales opportunity	Marketing and sales, supply chain management	Retail POS, field service management
Procurement	Purchasing, supplier relationship management	Procurement and supplier relationship management	Supply chain management
Production	MRP, product life cycle management	Manufacturing	Manufacturing
Accounting	Financial accounting	Financial management	Financial management
Distribution	Warehouse management	Supply chain management	Distribution management
Customer services	CRM	CRM	CRM
Corporate performance and governance	Governance, risk, and compliance management	Corporate performance management	Analytics
Human resources	Human capital management	Human capital management	HR management
Miscellaneous	Banking	Campus solutions	e-Commerce, portals

Source: Adapted from Web sites of SAP Global, Oracle Applications, and Microsoft Dynamics. www.sapfans.com/sapfans/sapfmod.htm; www.oracle.com/applications/home.html; www.microsoft.com/en/us/default.aspx (accessed January 15, 2007).

Production Module

The production module helps in planning and optimizing the manufacturing capacity, parts, components, and material resources using historical production data and sales forecasting. Production modules have evolved from manufacturing requirements planning (MRP) II into ERP systems with the help of consulting firms who have accumulated vast knowledge of implementing a production planning module.

Purchasing Module

The purchase module streamlines the procurement process of required raw materials and other supplies. It automates the processes of identifying potential suppliers, negotiating price, awarding purchase orders to the supplier, and billing processes. The purchase module is tightly integrated with the inventory control and production planning modules. The purchasing module is often integrated with supply chain management software and business-to-business (B2B) Web software.

Inventory Management Module

The inventory module facilitates the processes of maintaining the appropriate level of stock in a warehouse. Inventory control identifies inventory requirements, sets targets, provides replenishment techniques and options, monitors item usages, reconciles the inventory balances, and reports inventory status. Integration of the inventory control module with sales, purchase, and finance modules allows ERP systems to generate vigilant executive-level reports.

Sales and Marketing Module

Revenues from sales are the lifeblood for commercial organizations. The sales module implements functions of order placement, order scheduling, shipping, and invoicing. The sales module is closely integrated with an organization's e-commerce Web sites. Many ERP vendors offer an online storefront as part of the sales module. On the other hand, the marketing module supports lead generation, direct mailing campaigns, and more.

Finance Module

The financial module benefits both for-profit organizations and nonprofit organizations. The financial module is the core of many ERP software systems. It can gather financial data from various functional departments and generate valuable financial reports (e.g., budgets, balance sheet, general ledger, trail balance, and quarterly financial statements).

Human Resource Module

The human resources (HR) module is usually the first model implemented by many companies. The HR module streamlines the management of human resources and human capital. The HR modules routinely maintain a complete employee database, including contact information, salary details, attendance, performance evaluation, and promotion. An advanced HR module is integrated with knowledge management systems to optimally utilize the expertise of all employees.

Miscellaneous Modules

Some vendors have started offering such nontraditional modules as business intelligence, self-service, project management, and e-commerce. For example, the business intelligence module offers tools and data warehousing capabilities to display real-time information through reports and to monitor historical trends. Furthermore, these reports can be viewed through the enterprise portal for decision making with executives who can be located around the globe and can collaboratively make decisions based on the same live data. Self-service is similarly an important module for present-day consumers because it satisfies their need for "instant gratification" in their everyday activities. It allows them to have more control over their purchasing, tracking, and research. Self-service also has many benefits for employees to include access to a company's intranet, 401Ks, leave and earnings statements, and so on. Employers are also discovering that there is cost savings associated with letting customers and employees take ownership of their inquiries and processing. In order for a company to take advantage of the cost savings, or for consumers and employees to take advantage of the freedom associated with self-service, an organization must focus on keeping the self-service capability as user-friendly as possible. This can be done by providing accurate information and a relatively easy method of database interaction.

Benefits of Key ERP Modules

The following details some of the key benefits touted by such ERP vendors as SAP and Oracle for the various application modules:

SELF-SERVICES

- Enable flexible support for employees' business functions with views of information tailored to their needs
- Empower employees and managers through simplified access to relevant information for HR management, financials, operations, and analytics, while boosting motivation, productivity, and efficiency

PERFORMANCE MANAGEMENT

- Improve business insight and productivity by delivering real-time, personalized measurements and metrics
- Provide executives, managers, and business workers with access to such information as business statistics and key performance measurements presented in the context of business tasks

FINANCIALS

- Ensure compliance and predictability of business performance
- Gain deeper financial insight across the enterprise and tighten control of finances
- Automate financial and managerial accounting and financial supply chain management
- Provide rigorous support for financial reporting and such corporate governance mandates as the Sarbanes–Oxley Act and Basel II

HR MANAGEMENT

- Attract the right people, develop and leverage their talents, align their efforts with corporate objectives, and retain top performers
- Increase efficiency and help ensure compliance with changing global and local regulations by using standardized and automated workforce processes
- Enable creation of project teams based on skills and availability, monitor progress on projects, track time, and analyze results
- Manage human capital investments by analyzing business outcomes, workforce trends and demographics, and workforce planning

PROCUREMENT AND LOGISTICS EXECUTION

- Sustain cost savings for all spending categories by automating such routine tasks as determining sources and converting requisitions into purchase orders and by allowing employees to use electronic catalogs to order products and services
- Reduce costs through process automation, integration of suppliers, and better collaboration
- Improve resource utilization with support for cross-docking processes and data collection technologies such as radio frequency identification (RFID) and bar codes
- Enhance productivity of all activities related to incoming and outgoing physical goods movements
- Reduce transportation costs through better consolidation and collaboration

PRODUCT DEVELOPMENT AND MANUFACTURING

- Shorten time to market through streamlined new-product development and introduction processes

- Deliver higher-quality products and ensure delivery of promised orders through optimal planning, scheduling, and sequencing on the factory floor
- Improve visibility and transparency in real time across all shop floor processes, including availability checking and costing

SALES AND SERVICE

- Increase the number of sales orders processed and reduce administrative costs through automation of sales order management and the use of such profitable Internet-based solutions as e-commerce
- Deliver greater customer satisfaction by providing easy access to accurate, timely information
- Streamline processes that facilitate cost-effective mobile access for field employees
- Improve the management of incentives and commissions to maximize productivity and boost sales
- Reduce travel costs by using online functions for planning, booking, and expense accounting while ensuring that company policies are applied to all processes
- Realize more effective real estate management, supported by tools that streamline and manage every stage of the real estate life cycle
- Adhere to environmental, health, and safety reporting requirements

ERP ARCHITECTURE

In today's business environment, ERP applications are most commonly deployed in a distributed and often widely dispersed manner. While the servers may be centralized, the clients are usually spread across multiple locations throughout the enterprise. ERP system architecture is organized in layers or tiers to manage system complexity in order to provide scalability and flexibility via a plug-n-play systems capability. This is highly essential in an enterprise-level system. Three-layer architecture is the most prevalent today and includes Web, application, and database servers. It is the most reliable, flexible, and scalable architecture. You can scale the number of users from 10 to 100 by adding servers. This is one example of simple hardware layering that has a significant impact on scalability. What if the layering is done at both the hardware and software environments? The scalability would have been 20-fold instead of just 10-fold. It is important to understand, therefore, that layering is merely a model of dividing the hardware and software in an information system. It is not limited to three tiers, but often supports many tiers. Hence, the term "N-tier client–server architecture" is often used to describe enterprise system architectures. In the term N-tier, N implies any number (e.g., three-tier, four-tier, or, basically, any number of distinct tiers used in your architecture).

Layered Architecture Example

An example of a layered ERP architecture is the Info.Net[1] architectures shown in Figure 3-3. This architecture generalizes the functional layers to allow it to change with newer technologies. This architecture provides a Web-based user interface (i.e., user can access the applications via the Internet through a PC). The PC needs to be capable of running a Java-enabled Web browser

---

[1] ERP Architecture. (2008). Intertul Web site: http://www.lamarsoftware.com/erp/index_architecture.html (accessed March 11, 2011).

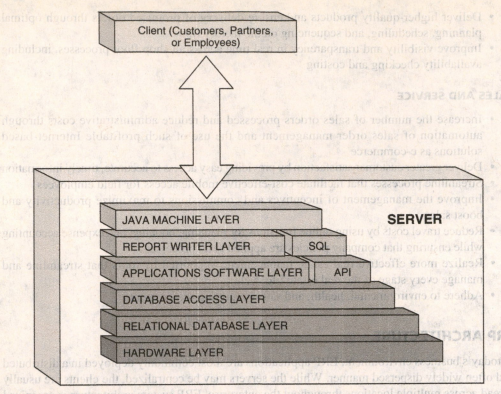

FIGURE 3-3 Example of Info.Net Architecture *Source:* Adapted from ERP Architecture Report, Intertul, Inc.

(e.g., Internet Explorer or Firefox). The PC is connected to both Intranet and Internet to be able to use one of Info.Net's servers. The user interacts with the Java Virtual Machine™ Interface layer to establish a secure connection via a secure socket layer (SSL) connection. The user is then communicating with the server through the applications software layer (ASL).

DATA TIER The data tier focus is on the structure of all organizational data and its relationships with both internal and external systems. Companies often change applications and data requirements incrementally, making it necessary for this tier to maintain flexibility. In the ERP architecture, this tier generally consists of the SQL Inquiry and Report Writer tools that are available for advanced users who have the authorization to filter, process, or filter and process the data from any table in the database. These tools allow users to develop complex SQL table joins for exception reporting on areas not covered by standard reports. The ASL is where all the business process logic and functionality resides for manufacturing, distribution, or service industries. This layer also determines where data will be stored. The relational database is where this information will be kept. This layer is what links together a sales order, items, delivery, and remarks on an order. The database access layer (DAL) extracts the data from the database for the ERP modules. It also includes a data dictionary that explains the different database functions for Info.Net applications.

APPLICATION TIER This tier is where data are entered and shared with other components of the system. It shields the business users from the inner workings of an ERP system, but still provides the information relevant to their job and business process. The users can download the data on their PC for any changes they may require that are relevant to their position and share information in real time within an extended enterprise. This seamless integration will allow for strategic decisions based on intelligence rather than on circumstance.

Through an application programming interface (API), ERP systems allow legacy and third-party applications the ability to integrate and share information. There are two basic architectures for integration. One is where an application will make a direct Java database connection (JDBC) and call another application's data tables directly. The second is the middleware-based integration. According to Abraham Kang King, "Middleware provides generic interfaces with which integrated applications pass messages to each other."[2] This architecture will allow for the support of numerous integrations, will require less maintenance, and perform a more complex set of operations. These types of integrations are common at a variety of layers such as the application layer and portal layer. The application layer, however, offers the richest integration, as all information is converted to a common standard for sharing across systems. These data can be analyzed along with information originated within the ERP system itself, allowing for reporting on both internally and externally derived information. Although applications integrated at the portal layer will be visible through the portal, it will not be fully integrated with the internal processes of these systems.

Around the industry, such standards as API have been developed to facilitate the integration and sharing of information across disparate systems. SAP has developed its own platform to facilitate the integration and sharing of information. The platform, called SAP Netweaver™ system, allows for easy integration of external applications through a Web services architecture that is based on an industry standard. SAP is able to integrate with such standards as .NET, IBM's Web Sphere, and any Java platform, including J2EE, which it utilizes as its internal standard. These standards allow for a common language to communicate. SAP's Netweaver platform and J2EE technology allow an extensive partnership of third-party technology vendors, system integrators, and applications providers a simple means to integrate and communicate. SAP continues to be a leader in many of the global organizations that promote the use of a common language such as the Organization for the Advancement of Structured Information Standards (OASIS) and the Java Community Process (JCP). Standards have been developed to help reduce the cost of integration and expedite the process. APIs such as SAP's Netweaver "cost generally between 25 and 40 percent lower than custom integration."[3] It is easy to understand from looking at this statistic why SAP has such a vast network of alliance partners.

WEB TIER   Employees rarely interact with SAP through an application tier. A Web-based self-service portal allows users the ability to access and analyze information through their Web browser. These portals allow the viewing of many independent systems (e.g., an ERP system), and external third-party applications. Integration is common at the portal layer, but as stated earlier, it is integrated only from the user-interface perspective, and not from a process perspective. Portals provide the ability to customize views for every function within an enterprise. Each function of an organization is able to see relevant data in real time and to alter and share information from within an extended enterprise. This collaboration, enabled by the Web, truly demonstrates the power of an ERP system. Information is shared instantaneously across oceans

[2] Kang, A. (August 2002). Enterprise Application Integration Using J2EE. www.javaworld.com/javaworld/jw-08-2002/jw-0809-eai_p.html (accessed March 15, 2011).
[3] Gartner Research. (September 16, 2002). High-Availability Networking: Towards Zero Downtime.

when a single user enters and saves a piece of data. Through this customization and sharing of content, experience is developed, reporting is made more strategic, and efficiencies are gained. For example, a sales manager will only be interested in information relevant to his or her role (e.g., how to increase sales and help project future revenue). For this reason, user roles are set up in the system to define access rights for each and every functional user of the system. The portals allow customization of the page such that a sales manager can monitor such information as sales revenue, representative performance, or any elevated support issues. This helps to eliminate time wasted sifting through useless data and facilitates the seamless transfer of information across job functions.

INFRASTRUCTURE REQUIREMENTS   An ERP system places tremendous load on the corporate network. Users form a wide variety of connections that access the network. According to AT&T's Web site, users can connect within the corporate local area network, whereas international or regional offices gain access through the wide area network. Partners or remote users gain connection through network cable or DSL connections to the Internet. All of these scenarios make the network and capacity planning for the network as crucial as the planning and deployment of the ERP system.

The implementation of an ERP system has its own infrastructure requirements that includes internal network and desktop requirements that a Web-based system requires. In addition, there are infrastructure requirements that provide anytime, anywhere access. This is where many implementations fail or not realize their benefits. Implementation of such an enterprise system as SAP requires more than just supporting the infrastructure requirements of these applications; it requires an extended enterprise that enables the sharing of this information. This is where the network comes into play. Leading up to the production rollout, network managers are provided with a very limited view from which they must size and estimate the required network. For example, there are times the implementation team is not aware that an interface on the application layer also requires bandwidth to support the sharing of data. According to Gartner Research, large companies in the Fortune 1000 lose on average up to $13,000 per minute every time their ERP system is down. The cost of downtime is extremely high. An important step in implementing an ERP is overall infrastructure planning. As is in most cases, traditional networks require upgrading prior to the deployment of ERP systems and must be a component of the overall budget. It is a "pay me now or pay me later" scenario. Up-front planning will provide for a stable and reliable environment, adding to the ERP implementations success.

If the network connection through which the end users access the application has problems, the user will experience poor performance. This poor performance leads to a loss of productivity; therefore, a high-availability network is a requirement for a fully functioning ERP system, especially one that can grow as the user population grows and support the continued expansion and integration of a supply chain. Some network analysts have estimated that network service failures caused by old infrastructure have increased threefold between 1998 and 2001, and this has impacted the corporate bottom line by more than $50 billion in lost revenues.

ERP system and its third-party integrations extend the benefit of an enterprise system to an organization's partners and customers. Integration with partner and customer systems allows "a company to manage important parts of the business such as order tracking, inventory management and replenishment, supplier interaction, customer services, and HR management."[4] As discussed earlier, this integration can be done through either the application layer or the portal layer,

---

[4] AT&T Point of View/Networking in ERP. (June 10, 2006). www.peoplesoft-planet.com/POINT-OF-VIEW.html (accessed June 10, 2006).

thereby extending the value and benefit of the deployment and these systems. Even though it is pretty easy to understand the benefit of integration, the additional value is derived from the business intelligence compiled through the sharing of data across partner, customer, and internal systems.

Finally, online analytical processing (OLAP) is the foundation of the business intelligence module in ERP. It provides the ability to access, present, and analyze data across several dimensions (e.g., time, place, and product line). Through a comprehensive platform of knowledge management and data warehousing, executives are able to base decisions on the most relevant information in real time or through analyzing trends that incorporate a variety of intelligence gathered from an extended value chain. This is one of the true realized benefits of an ERP system: the seamless transfer of data and information across an extended enterprise allowing for a strategic advantage in decision making.

ERP architectures have evolved over the years with the IT infrastructure. As noted in Chapters 1 and 2, the IT infrastructure in organizations has moved from centralized to distributed systems. Current IT infrastructure's focus is on integrating the corporate architecture with the Web and extending it well beyond the organization to suppliers, clients, and customers via the service-oriented architectures (SOA). The ERP architecture has similarly evolved from two-tier to three-tier, N-tier, Web, and SOA. This section will review, in detail, the three-tier architecture.

THREE-TIER ARCHITECTURES   Most of the current ERP implementations follow a *three-tiered architecture*, which consists of a *Web tier*, an *application tier*, and a *data tier*. The segmentation of these tiers allows for the system as a whole to be more scalable and reduces resource utilization. It also provides higher security due to the separation of resources.

The *Web tier* includes the Web servers that a client interacts with for application access. This is where the graphical user interface (GUI) applications reside and data get inputted, requests for information are submitted, and the data satisfying these requests are presented. These systems can be located and accessed within the organization's internal network or externally on the Internet. For servers within the Web tier, it is important to accurately forecast how many users are expected to use the system concurrently and what the peak loads will be. The data the application sends back to the user also need to be considered, especially if video or other multimedia components will be used. The network portion of the Web tier will need to be designed around these expectations. If the system is for internal use only, it might be connected to a network with ample bandwidth available to it. However, if the application is Internet facing, the bandwidth available externally might be much lower. The same will be true if the application needs to be accessed across the organization's WAN, since bandwidth varies among these types of connections.

Network security within the Web tier is extremely important as this is the front door to an organization's ERP system. Whether the system lives internally or externally, there is a risk of someone breaching the system. The first line of defense should be a firewall that is located between the Web tier and the connection to the rest of the network. Management will need to dictate policies for the type of traffic that is allowed to enter the Web tier. Traditionally, this would be http and https traffic. For further granularity, the Web tier could restrict access to specific networks within the organization, for example, the network HR or accounting utilize. The next piece of security that should be implemented within the Web tier is an intrusion detection device. This device will examine traffic entering the Web tier and determine if it is malicious in nature based on predefined patterns. If the device determines there is malicious activity, it can either take action by blocking a user's connection or notify IT.

The *application tier* provides components to apply the business logic of the functional modules. It acts as the intermediary between the client applications and the database. This tier includes components that have function-specific logic but are not self-contained (or silo'd). Instead, they are reuseable objects of business process rules that can be reassembled, Lego™ style, into many functional applications.[5]

The application tier is where most of the processing for the ERP system occurs. It is located between the Web tier and the database tier. The application tier handles users' request, retrieves data from the database tier, and processes data as needed. The systems that live in the application tier are most likely more powerful than the systems in the Web tier. The network for this tier should provide adequate bandwidth to both the Web tier and database tier. If not enough bandwidth is provided, there will be a risk of congestion on the network. This congestion might cause delays between the tiers, causing the end user to experience slow performance. Like the Web tier, system utilization needs to be forecast to properly design the network portion of this tier. Today most servers are connected to the network via very high speed Ethernet.

Security for the application tier should be as stringent as in the Web tier. The application tier sits between the Web tier, which may have a high risk of being compromised, and the database tier, which holds the organization's most valuable data. Firewalls should be deployed on both sides of the application tier, implementing policies for the type of traffic and systems allowed in the application tier. Intrusion detection systems should also be deployed, and for added safety logging and periodic auditing of all switches and routers in the environment should be preformed.

The *data tier* is responsible for data management. This layer provides the central repository for all of the data that are shared between the functional modules and maintains the integrity of data transferred to and from the clients and servers. System components at this level include Sequel (or SQL) manager and other interface components to the database management system of the organization. The amount of data that will traverse between this tier and the application tier will most likely be higher than any other tier. The network should be designed to properly handle large data transfers with minimal delay. Like the application tier, scalability for future bandwidth needs is crucial in the database tier. Servers today should utilize gigabit or even 10 gigabit Ethernet connections within this tier.

Security in the data tier is just as important as in the other tiers. Firewalls, intrusion detection systems, and logging all activity should be deployed. With proper security in place, organizations should be better protected in the event there is a breach. With tiers isolated by firewalls, the chance of more than one tier being compromised is reduced. Logging and periodic auditing of systems help detect malicious attempts into the system that can be missed by an intrusion detection device. Many of today's compliance certification such as PCI and SOX require this type of security for many different types of environments. Adding these types of control into the design at the early planning stages will eliminate the need to return to them in the future.

The three-tier architecture can be expensive for an organization to deploy. If not planned and implemented properly, it can cost the business time and money. For example, when an application is performing slowly, the first group that is contacted is the network group. Most often the problem is that a process on an application or database server is using up system resources. Sometimes it can be related to network congestion due to inadequate provisioning of network

---

[5] Adapted from Robinson, S. (December 10, 2004). A Developer's Overview of ERP. www.developer.com/design/print.php/3446551 (accessed March 15, 2011).

resources. If this is the case, IT must now go back to management and explain the problem and the solution, which is often either a replacement of network switches and routers or more band-width for WAN and Internet-facing connections. Proper design, planning, and fund allocation are key to a successful ERP deployment that will be scalable for the future.

The three-tier client–server architecture, seen in Figure 3-4, has been shown to improve performance for groups with a large number of users (in the thousands) and improves flexibility when compared with the older and somewhat obsolete two-tier approach. One way to help ensure scalability is to reduce some of the burden of processing and database access from the users' client computers. This is at the heart of the three-tier approach. With this approach, which is sometimes also referred to as application partitioning, the bulk of the complex business processing is performed on separate computers called application servers. Because the application servers do the complex processing and report generation, the amount of data that must be passed from the database server to the (many) client computers is greatly reduced, as is the amount of computing work each client computer must perform. This processing conservation reduces the load on the network, which is a key consideration for applications with large numbers of users. It also reduces the hardware requirements for the client computers. For this reason, mainframes have found their new role as servers in three-tier architectures.

Benefits and Limitations

Three-tier applications provide several benefits over traditional client–server applications including the following:

- *Scalability.* Three-tier architecture allows easier architecture to add, change, and remove applications because the user interface and database are not affected by upgrades to applications.
- *Reliability.* Three-tier architecture makes it easier to increase reliability of a system by implementing multiple levels of redundancy. In addition, scheduling and prioritization of jobs can be managed better from a central location.
- *Flexibility.* By separating the business logic of an application from its presentation logic, three-tier architecture makes the application much more flexible to changes. Flexibility in partitioning can be as simple as "dragging and dropping" application code modules onto different computers.

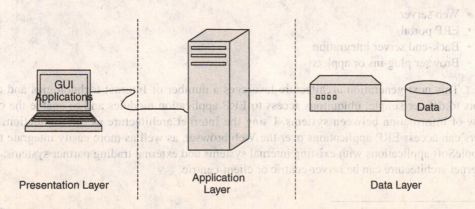

Presentation Layer   Application Layer   Data Layer

FIGURE 3-4   A Three-Tier ERP Architecture

- *Maintainability.* Support and maintenance costs are less on a single server than it would be to maintain each installation or upgrade on a desktop client because the middle layer adds scheduling and prioritization for work in progress.
- *Reusability.* Separating the application into multiple layers makes it easier to implement reusable components.
- *Security.* Three-tier architecture provides higher security because there is less software on the client machines, which means the IT staff has more control over the ERP system.

Three-tier applications also have some limitations, including the following:

- *Economics.* Three-tier applications require additional hardware and software infrastructure to support the middle layer, which can increase the overall platform costs.
- *Complexity.* A key limitation with three-tier architectures is that the development environment is reportedly more difficult to use than the visually oriented development of two-tier applications.

The benefits of three-tier architectures outweigh the limitations in the long run and are more commonly used in many large-scale distributed systems and enterprise applications including a large number of e-commerce solutions. Component technologies such as Enterprise Java Beans (EJB) and CORBA Component Model (CCM) support the middle tier of three-tier architectures. They provide frameworks for component development and deployment. Many Web services based on hypertext transfer protocol (HTTP) and extensible markup language (XML) similarly make use of three-tier architectures. Even though no two three-tier systems may be alike, they share similar requirements and consequently similar system designs.

Web Services Architectures

In the last decade, many ERP vendors have introduced Web (or Internet)-based architecture for their systems. This is often described as a fourth tier where the Web tier is split into services tier and browser tier.[6] The ERP systems focus on the Internet to provide a powerful new functionality for Internet-based access and integration. This architecture leverages a number of Internet technologies and concepts to deliver simple, ubiquitous access to ERP modules and enable the open flow of information between systems. This functionality is primarily supported through the following Internet access technologies:

- Web server
- ERP portal
- Back-end server integration
- Browser plug-ins or applets

This next-generation architecture leverages a number of Internet technologies and concepts to deliver simple, ubiquitous access to ERP application modules and to enable the open flow of information between systems. Using the Internet architecture as the foundation, end users can access ERP applications over the Web browser, as well as more easily integrate their PeopleSoft applications with existing internal systems and external trading partner systems. The Internet architecture can be server-centric or client-centric.

---

[6] Sandoe, K., Corbitt, G., and Boykin, R. (2001). *Enterprise Integration*. New York: John Wiley & Sons, 79–81.

In server-centric environments, clients only need access to the Internet and a standard browser (e.g., Internet Explorer or Firefox) with a few plug-ins (e.g., Java Virtual Machine and others). There are no other user interface applications required on the client; therefore, the client can be any Internet device that uses such standard Internet technologies as hypertext transport protocol or hypertext markup language (HTML) for user access, or extensible markup language for back-end communication between an application and a third-party system with the Internet application server. The latter falls more under system-to-system integration and is covered in a later section.

In client-centric environments, client devices will need installation of software development kits (SDKs) and proper configuration and integration with client devices for the application to work properly. This is practically disappearing from PC-based clients due to the advantages provided by server-centric environments as well as due to higher network bandwidth and reliability. Client-centric platforms are popular in such other devices as personal digital assistants (PDAs), Blackberries, and mobile phones that are increasingly used to access information from the enterprise systems.

BENEFITS AND DRAWBACKS   The key benefit of using the Internet platform as the foundation is that organizations are able to provide a wide range of end users with access to ERP applications over the Web as well as more easily integrate their ERP applications with existing internal systems and external trading partner systems.

The Internet architecture can be server-centric or client-centric. The server-centric architecture, like the one shown in Figure 3-5, enables secure end-user access to ERP application

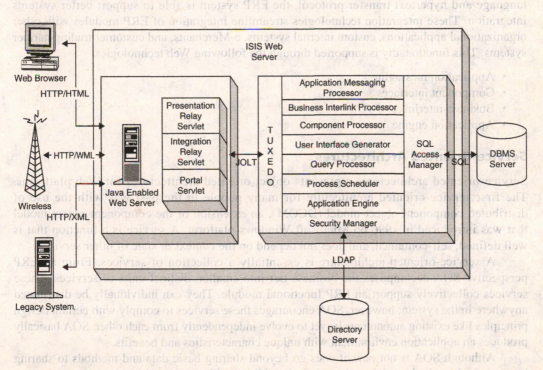

modules from any Internet-enabled device (e.g., a Web browser running on a PC or a cell phone) that uses such standard Internet technologies as HTML, XML, and HTTP(S), which can access and execute ERP applications. The benefit of the server-centric architecture is that there is no complex, expensive client software installation. The Internet client device accessing the Internet architecture already has all the software and configuration it needs. No additional software need be installed on the client for interaction with ERP applications (i.e., no Java applets, Windows DLLs, or browser plug-ins are needed). Simple, open architecture creates easy, inexpensive access and is a big reason why the Web has been such an enormous, fast-growing success.

On the other hand, the client-centric architecture requires the applications and data to be downloaded from a server and executed from a client workstation. Each architecture has its benefits and drawbacks. Although the server-centric architecture has better security and controls because all the applications and data are on the server and clients do not need any specific configuration, it does tend to have slower response time because all user requests are processed on the server. The client-centric architecture similarly has better response time because user requests are mostly processed on the client's computer; however, they can lack security and require all client workstations to be set up according to the standard specifications.

In addition to improving end-user access, Internet-based architectures also allow better system-to-system integration, which is often considerably more complicated and costly. The Web system platform fundamentally supports a better and more open flow of information between systems. By leveraging such ubiquitous Internet technologies as extensible markup language and hypertext transfer protocol, the ERP system is able to support better systems integration. These integration technologies streamline integration of ERP modules with other organizational applications, custom internal systems, e-Merchants, and customer trading partner systems. This functionality is supported through the following Web technologies:

- Application messaging
- Component interfaces
- Business interlinks
- Application engine

Service-Oriented Architectures

Service-oriented architectures represents object-oriented architectures for Web platforms. The first service-oriented architecture for many people in the past was with the use of distributed component object model (DCOM), an extension of the component object model that was introduced in 1996 on Microsoft Windows platform. A service is a function that is well defined, self-contained, and does not depend on the context or state of other services.

A service-oriented architecture is essentially a collection of services. From an ERP perspective SOA decomposes the business tier into smaller, distinct units of services. These services collectively support an ERP functional module. They can individually be distributed anywhere in the system; however, SOA encourages these services to comply with certain design principles like existing autonomously, yet to evolve independently from each other. SOA basically produces an application environment with unique characteristics and benefits.

Although SOA is not new, it does go beyond sharing basic data and methods to sharing business logic and other advanced services. In addition, object-oriented architectures of the past allowed interactions only within the corporate firewall. SOA allows message interaction between any service consumer and service provider. It could also involve two or more services coordinating some activity, as long as they follow SOA standards.

The SOA standard includes a description language for all functions or services that have active programming services that are called on to perform business processes. Each interaction is independent of each and every other interaction and the interconnect protocols of the communicating devices with different infrastructure components. Because services are independent of the operating system platform, a consumer from a device using any operating system in any language can use this service. SOA is similar to Web services, but it is not the same. Web services is an application of SOA with such Web-based technologies as SOAP and XML. SOA is more than a set of technologies; it is a standard that runs independent of any specific technologies.

SOA is a software development model based on a contract between a consumer (client) and a provider (server) that specifies the following:

- Functional description of the service
- Input requirements and output specifications
- Precondition environment state before service can be invoked
- Postcondition environment state after service has been executed
- Error handling when there is a breakdown

Figure 3-6 illustrates basic components of service-oriented architecture. It shows a consumer sending a service request message to a provider. The service provider returns a reply message to the consumer. The request and subsequent replies are defined in a service-level agreement that is understandable to both the service consumer and service provider.

In short, SOA consists of several best practices that permit an organization to conceal the complex nature of technology while supplying agile resources for the business. It rearranges the capabilities of different business applications and turns them into business services. These services are then converted into business processes. It can then be said that SOA permits the business flexibility and agility.

Agility and flexibility allow an organization to do many things that will better serve their business. These things include, but are not limited to, the following: improving business visibility, reducing the cost of integration, increasing the business' agility, and increasing the reuse of services. Depending on the type of problems the organization is trying to solve with SOA, these benefits and others not listed can provide a monumental return at several different levels. In enterprise content management, SOA can connect dissimilar systems and integrate enterprise content management into areas where it did not have a presence.

BENEFITS AND DRAWBACKS   The main characteristic of an SOA is that of a loosely coupled, document-oriented interaction model. The key benefits of SOA, therefore, are scalability,

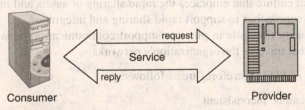

Consumer   Provider

FIGURE 3-6   An SOA Architecture

reusability, and flexibility. SOA offers the following benefits over traditional approaches to distributed computing:

- Business-level software services across heterogeneous platforms
- Complete location independence of business logic
- Services can exist anywhere (i.e., any system and any network)
- Loose coupling across application services
- Granular authentication and authorization support at service unit level
- Dynamic search and connectivity to other services

Short-term benefits of SOA:

- Enhances reliability of the architecture
- Reduces hardware acquisition costs
- Leverages existing development skills
- Accelerates movement to standards-based server and application consolidation
- Provides a data bridge between incompatible technologies

Long-term benefits of SOA:

- Provides the ability to build composite applications
- Creates a self-healing infrastructure that reduces management costs
- Provides truly real-time decision-making applications
- Enables the compilation of a unified taxonomy of information across an enterprise and its customers and partners

Business value benefits of SOA:

- Increases the ability to meet customer demands more quickly
- Lower costs associated with the acquisition and maintenance of technology
- Empowers the management of business functionality closer to the business units
- Leverages existing investments in technology
- Reduces reliance on expensive custom development

SOA also has its drawbacks. It brings changes in architectural style, programming models, best practices, patterns, testing, and management approaches, and the collective learning cycle will take some time. SOA focus is on business process with an underlying assumption that not everything in technology can be the same, so standard methods and processes must be defined to enable disparate technologies to communicate, regardless of manufacturer or language. For example, SOA requires:

- System environment consisting of numerous complex structures for integration
- SOA implementations, which are costly and time consuming
- Maintenance environment to support rapid integration capability within these structures
- Organizational culture that embraces the rapid sharing of assets and information
- Management approaches to support rapid sharing and integration
- Complex security firewalls in place to support communication between services across applications that traverse the organization's networks

The key limitations of SOA, therefore, are as follows:

- Performance can be inconsistent
- Requires enterprise-level focus for implementation to be successful

- Security system needs to be sophisticated
- Costs can be high because services need to be junked very often

According to Gregor Hohpe, enterprise integration practice leader at Chicago-based ThoughtWorks, Inc., and coauthor of the book *Enterprise Integration Patterns,*[7] "the SOA architecture is a different approach to distributed services. It provides simple messaging-based interactions. Messages are more self-contained, lack object-oriented complexities, and better accommodate asynchronous communications."

SOA and Web Services

Web services play an important role in the SOA approach. That is because Web services precede SOA. While the concepts are associated in some form, they're also quite different. Web services basically are interfaces that allow different software applications and components to be operated together. Web services are necessary because different applications operate in dissimilar ways.

One special feature of Web services is that the IT industry reached a consensus on certain standards concerning the communication of applications to other applications. These standards are passed down from organizations like W3C and OASIS. Thanks to these standards, different applications can interact with each other without concern for communication problems.

There are several important characteristics of Web services to consider. First, the only method of interaction by Web services is by receiving and sending messages. Because of the nature of Web services, the programs that activate them can simply be changed without worrying about interference with their communication ability. Second, these services are developed using open standards. Such standards include, but are not limited to, WSDL (Web Services Description Language), UDDI (Universal Description, Discovery, and Integration), and SOAP (Simple Object Access Protocol). Finally, the protocols used in Web services are XML based. The behavior of the respective Web services is documented in what is known as a contract. These contracts describe the interaction between services and the applications that invoke them.

Enterprise Content Management and SOA

Enterprise content management deals with enterprise software products. These products usually store, preserve, manage, and deliver any documents or content that is connected to business processes. Meanwhile, enterprise content management strategies and tools mainly concentrate on managing any unstructured information that exists in an organization. Nevertheless, enterprise content management is also about supporting business goals, not just managing content itself.

Until recently, enterprise content management solutions were supplied by vertical applications. The problem with that is it made developing new applications for content management a process that is more expensive, longer, and more complicated. The business would have to deal with integrations that were problematic to maintain and develop. Integrating Web services to enterprise applications were made quite simple. However, they lack efficiency.

Now due to SOA, the software market for enterprise content management is being overhauled. Vendors have come to an understanding that content management takes advantage of technology and information assets across the business and is no longer application specific. Where enterprise content management is concerned, utilizing the SOA approach consists of

---

[7] Hohpe, G., and Woolf, B. (2003). *Enterprise Integration Patterns.* Boston, MA: Addison-Wesley.

extracting the features of the enterprise content management platform as services across the life cycle of the content. This way, businesses can take advantage of enterprise content management resources in a manner that is flexible and reusable.

As business process management and enterprise content management systems cross over many departments and, as a result, many systems, the SOA approach works well with them. Therefore, the point of SOA in enterprise content management involves extracting functionalities from legacy systems, developing applications, and incorporating enterprise content management into areas where it didn't exist previously.

Cloud Architecture

Cloud computing (CC) has recently emerged as a powerful platform to support the growing needs of many organizations that do not want to own and maintain complex software systems for the enterprise. There are high costs and headaches with software purchasing, installation, and maintenance today; IT staff have to contend with networking, technical support, security, privacy, compliance and other issues, which makes it very expensive to own software. The cloud computing platform provides a great alternative for these organizations as they do not have to purchase, install, or maintain the software applications, nor do they have to worry about security, privacy, and legal issues associated with data storage (assuming they choose to store their data bases on the cloud environment). Of course, the cloud computing platform is risky for organizations as it forces them to rely on cloud computing vendors for reliability, security, and continuity of enterprise applications. However, as the cloud computing platform settles down in near future and with large vendors like Microsoft, Oracle, and SAP starting to integrate their applications and services on this platform, more and more organizations will adopt this platform.

BOX 3-1 Microsoft and SOA

For developers interested in creating new SOA-based applications, Microsoft developed a new series of services that utilizes the company's BizTalk server technology.

BizTalk Services offers a merged identity, access control, and verification, which are all based on WS-Trust standards. BizTalk Relay Services connects physical networks, allowing links between systems so cross-organizational messages can be sent behind firewalls. The Internet Service Bus offers a straightforward message bus. The BizTalk Workflow Services allows applications to be created graphically by developing flowcharts.

Some analysts believe these BizTalk services will increase efficiency and performance while cutting down on infrastructure and operation costs. Additionally, it is believed that these services will reduce the production of infrastructure software within the company. At the same time, the development team will be more capable of crafting and developing secure services.

BizTalk Services is intended to fix problems concerning low-level infrastructure. This is something that is utilized in projects in order to expand their capabilities. Also, the services are capable of handling complex infrastructure. A major benefit is that they can be incorporated into Windows Communication Foundation (WCF). As a result, it will be easier for developers to tend to their infrastructure concerns and focus on business goals.

All in all, BizTalk Services promotes Microsoft's maxim of providing software plus services, which is viewed as a hybrid approach. On top of its other products, this gives Microsoft an edge over its competition. From a technical point of view, the company's approach provides better performance for the end user.

Cloud computing has been defined or interpreted in many different ways. Some define cloud computing as "on-demand access to virtualized IT resources that are housed outside of your own data center, shared by others, simple to use, paid for via subscriptions, and accessed over the Web."[8] Others have a much wider and fuzzier definition: "virtual servers available over the internet". The following is the most comprehensive definition of cloud computing: "What makes cloud computing so powerful is that it is based on a system of modularity. The use of virtualization and a cloud platform allows organizations to break down services and systems into smaller components, which can function separately or across a widely distributed network. Servers can be located almost anywhere and interfaces can be changed and customized on the fly. These services and software are only as far away as an Internet or mobile phone connection."[9]

Based on the definitions above, cloud computing is basically a software service provided over the Internet, securely, by a service provider on a monthly or yearly lease. CC is similar to your ISP, which for a monthly fee provides you access to the Internet. The CC service provider provides for a monthly fee storage space for your data and access to an increasing number of software applications. Companies leasing CC services save money by replacing their purchased software that requires a license fee per seat. For example, if a company finds that it is spending too much money on Microsoft Office suite (software, licenses, and upgrades), they can replace it with an online version of the suite or similar suite for a fixed monthly fee without worrying about installation, maintenance, or security. Microsoft, Google, and Zoho are three vendors who offer Office applications suites, each with its own benefits and liabilities (Foyle, 2010).

Some cloud computing providers also let you build your own applications using their engines and then they would host those applications for you as part of the service. For example, Google offers the Google App Engine, which enables users to build Web apps for their companies. The Google App Engine offers fast development and deployment and simple administration. Google promises to deliver a 99.9 percent uptime SLA, which eliminates concerns regarding servers performing up to standard. The cost to create your own application using the Google App Engine is $8 per user, per month (with a maximum $1,000 a month), which means that you pay for what you use. Paying depending on the amount of usage can save companies money, because in the traditional model, companies would have to pay a fixed price for a system whether 5 people used it or a 100 people used it (Google App Engine). Google is updating this engine with a new service that will be offered later this year with a hosted SQL database service and a Secure Socket Layer (SSL) service on their client's platform for secure communications. But Google is not the only company out there that allows you to do these things; there are other companies like Amazon who also offer the flexibility of programming your own application and host it on their servers with the subscription. In addition, Amazon offers services to creating iPhone and Facebook applications (AWS Solutions). It seems that there is no limit on the software services that are being offered on the cloud computing platform, and ERP systems are heading in their direction.

There are several enterprise applications, like e-mail, customer relationship management (CRM) software, sales automation software, accounting, procurement systems, online meeting spaces, Web site and domain hosting, and others that are being offered on the CC platform. VMware, a CC vendor, offers a solution that utilizes a virtualized version of SAP system for

---

[8] Brynjolfsson, Erik, Hofmann, Paul, and Jordan, John. (May 2010). Cloud Computing and Electricity: Beyond the Utility Model. *Communication of the ACM*, 53 (5), 32–34. DOI=10.1145/1735223.1735234, http://doi.acm.org/10.1145/1735223.1735234.

[9] Greengard, Samuel. (May 2010). Cloud Computing and Developing Nations. *Communications of the ACM*, 53 (5), 18–20. DOI 10.1145/1735223.1735232.

testing, development, Q&A, training, and production environments. The implemention of virtu-alized SAP solutions allows clients of VMware to reap multiple categories of cost savings; when calculating the total cost of ownership (TCO): savings come from downtime (30 percent of TCO), operation (40 percent of TCO), administration (10 percent of TCO), and hardware and software (20 percent of TCO).

Similarly, Oracle is offering a CRM solution for the cloud. Oracle offers sale, service, marketing, contact-center operations, and real-time and historical analysis and helps integrate business processes with prebuilt Web services. Oracle calls this cloud computing service as *Oracle CRM On Demand*, which offers its clients the power to break down their departmental silos. The service is offered at a (subscription-like) per-user, per-month price. Therefore, the companies using this service need not worry about paying maintenance and upgrade costs.[10]

In general, the greatest attraction for cloud architecture is cost, particularly as the services are free for the first 3–5 users and the cost is not very high for more users. Other benefits of cloud computing include the ease of access, which means that all you need is a computer with Internet access and an Internet browser and you will be able to access your cloud service. Also the costs of money and resources related to owning those software and hardware can be saved and spent in other areas of the business as the cloud service provider takes care of the server, installation, security, and maintenance for the applications. CC allows IT staff and management of companies to sleep at night knowing that your servers and applications will be working the next day because of the provided reliability of the company hosting your applications (Cusumano, 2010).

However, everything is not perfect in the world of cloud computing. Just like other solutions, there are some risks that are associated with keeping your applications and data outside of the company. As mentioned before, there is a great concern about data security and vulnerability. Not having the physical control over who accesses the data and how well the data are protected, most companies are not comfortable or ready to store information, especially sensitive information, outside the company's firewalls. Further, not knowing where the data are being stored and processed discourages companies from accepting cloud computing as a viable business option (Nicholson, 2009).

Sometimes there are potential conflicts of interest when the company that is hosting your application also has its own application that is similar to yours. For example, a CC ven-dor like Google or Amazon could decide to create an application that is similar to yours and offer it to their clients and who could possibly be your competitors. This would create a big conflict between Google and their customers, as well as between two competing clients that now have access to similar technology. These issues are a big reason why many companies are staying away from cloud computing as an answer to the traditional expensive in-house IT solutions.

Network vendors today are realizing that most applications will be housed either internally or externally on a CC platform. Whether they live in an organization's data center or off site in another vendors cloud, the network is now becoming more important than ever. Networks need to be designed to handle larger amounts of data than ever before. They are also expected to be highly redundant and never require any downtime. Vendors are responding to these demands and introducing network equipment that not only fills these requirements but also scale as requirements change while keeping costs nominal.

---

[10] CRM on Demand, Oracle (2010).

Cisco, for example, is one vendor who is taking steps to stay ahead of the curve and has introduced a product line that meets the requirements for a virtualized data center. Their Nexus product line is a data center solution, which provides the capability to combine both network and storage traffic over a single connection, reducing the need for multiple connections per server. The Nexus platform is a 10-gigabit platform scalable in the future to 100 gigabits. It is also capable of providing in-service upgrades which allow for the network to stay up while the network switch is upgraded to fix bugs or add features. As more systems are virtualized and storage network becomes more prominent, the need for higher bandwidth becomes critical. The Nexus platform is clearly built for these requirements and the future. ERP systems of the future can utilize this type of platform to provide users a richer experience while reducing costs through virtualization on the back end. The initial costs of this type of network device will be high, but the long-term benefits should help offset the cost.

BENEFITS AND DRAWBACKS   *Benefits of cloud computing:*

- Pay for subscription, not for licenses and upgrades
- Reduced capital and operating expenditures for IT equipment and support personnel
- Accessed from everywhere, as long as you have an Internet connection
- No need to install anything on the user's computer
- Dynamic scalability available on demand
- No maintenance fees for software or hardware
- Promotes green computing environment as servers in cloud run on clean energy
- Guaranteed reliability.
- *Drawbacks to cloud computing:*
- Data security
- Vulnerability
- Possible conflict of interest, if the company who stores your applications decides to create a similar application to what you created on their servers
- Not suited for all highly competitive industries like biotech where intellectual property cannot be protected easily

IMPLICATIONS FOR MANAGEMENT

Managers implementing ERP systems should remember the following advisories.

Enterprise architecture is an important technology for the long-term functioning of the organization. It provides the information system foundation on which all the employees and other stakeholders of the company will depend for critical information and for the decision-making process. Enterprise architecture identifies the main components and how these components interact and function together to achieve defined business objectives. It is also important to remember that the enterprise components extend beyond technology into organizational culture and business processes. Enterprise architecture is supposed to communicate, inspire, and lead the company to design good systems that produce quality information for critical business decisions.

ERP architecture decisions are complex because their impact goes beyond systems and technology to people, organizational policy, and business processes. Management, therefore, must not leave these decisions for the IT department, and instead work together with IT staff in selecting the architecture. Management involvement must also be at both the functional and physical levels of the architecture. Management's role is to look at the different types of ERP architectures and see what is most appropriate for their organization in terms of people, business process, and overall fit of the architecture with their organizational policy and culture. At this stage, managers need to stay away from specific vendor solutions in order to avoid any bias.

ERP architecture must be flexible to support a diverse set of hardware and software platforms. From a systems' perspective, management first needs to be aware that in order for diverse technologies to operate smoothly the IT group must have standards and policy for technology decisions. Today's organization requires real-time support from anywhere and anytime for business processes, regardless of the management level of the user in the organization. From CEOs to customer support personnel, people in the organization need live access to data, anywhere and anytime. In addition, organizations today have customers, suppliers, and other external entities accessing information from the ERP system.

Do not get carried away with ERP technology hype. With new technologies and architectures constantly touted by vendors and consultants, it is very easy to end up with a very sophisticated architecture and system, and yet have a major implementation failure. As discussed earlier in the Nestlé's case, when the people and organization's processes are not in tune with the architecture, then even a good system will not be able to achieve success in improving the bottom line. Management must learn how to filter out the *hyped* technologies that do not provide value to their organization. For example, SOA may not be appropriate for a company that has a small-scale ERP used mainly for internal operations by its employees. On the other hand, SOA may be appropriate for a company with e-commerce applications that has B2B relationships with several of its partners and vendors.

Summary

- System architecture provides answers to such questions as, what will the system look like? How will the system work? How will it be developed? Do we have the required infrastructure to support the system? Can the system be used for any business function, or just for a specific business function like human resources? This chapter has provided answers to these and other questions related to the enterprise systems architecture and revealed why it's important to have a good architecture before implementing an ERP system in an organization.

- System architecture includes ERP modules and ERP architecture. Major vendors provide modules to support such basic business functions as accounting, finance, marketing, and HR to such advanced business functions as self-service, compliance management,

and business intelligence. This functionality is constantly evolving as needs of organizations change. The focus today is on supporting enterprise-wide needs of the company. This means ERP systems are accessible by a wide variety of people and departments, making them complex and vulnerable from management and maintenance perspectives.

- ERP architectures are generally organized in tiers or layers. This provides tremendous flexibility and scalability for ERP systems, which have traditionally been organized in three tiers: data, application, and presentation. The separation of data from application or application from presentation makes the ERP implementation very flexible because an organization can change the presentation layer (i.e., user interface) without affecting the business logic or database system. Changing the database similarly will not affect the other layers. This can lower maintenance and future upgrading costs of the system.

- There are various types of layered architectures. The simplest and somewhat obsolete is a two-tier architecture, but it has limitations (e.g., it supports only a small number of users and is not flexible for new versions of ERP software). Three-tier architectures separate application from the presentation layer, thereby increasing the flexibility and scalability of the system. ERP systems currently have expanded to Web-based architectures to facilitate better integration with the Internet technologies.

- Another architecture that is gaining popularity is service-oriented architecture. SOA separates the service provider from the service consumer by making them sign a service-level agreement contract that specifies how the consumer requests the service

and what information and services will be provided by the provider. This is similar to object-oriented system architectures with a higher degree of separation with a clear communications agreement between the two objects. SOA benefits include faster application development and reuse of software modules. Major ERP vendors are now supporting SOA in their newer versions of their software.

- Management should not leave the enterprise systems architecture decisions to the IT department. ERP architecture is quintessential to a successful integration and implementation of an ERP system, and it has a wide and long-lasting implication on the organization. Top management must therefore be involved in designing the architecture from the very beginning of the ERP implementation project. ERP systems embed organizational policy and are costly to implement, so any errors can bring down the organization.

Exercises

1. Search the Internet for SOA support from the three major ERP vendors: SAP, Oracle, and Microsoft Dynamics. Compare the SOA features in a table format.
2. Locate a company that you know and contact the IT manager and the HR manager.

   a. Find out what ERP or enterprise architecture they have in their company.

   b. Find out how the architecture helped them in the ERP implementation.

   c. Does their ERP implementation support Web integration and SOA?

   d. Write a one-page summary and include a diagram or figure of their architecture.

Review Questions

1. What is necessary for the ERP implementation to be successful?
2. What is ERP system architecture?
3. Why is it important to have good enterprise system architecture?
4. What is the role of architecture in ERP implementation?
5. List five of the major functional modules of ERP.
6. Discuss the different types of ERP architectures.
7. List benefits and limitations of one ERP architecture.
8. What is service-oriented architecture and how is it different from Web services architecture?
9. What are the key benefits and limitations of systems integration?
10. What is the role of management in designing enterprise systems integration?

Discussion Questions

1. Discuss the objective of ERP implementation at Nestlé USA. Did they achieve these objectives?
2. Refer to the Nestlé case in this chapter. What problems were faced by Jeri Dunn, CIO, and what do you think would be the right systems architecture for Nestlé?
3. Discuss the benefits and limitations of ERP implementation at Nestlé USA.

4. Why should ERP architecture include a discussion on organizational structure, business processes, and people, instead of just information technology and systems?
5. Why is server-centric architecture better than client-centric architecture?
6. Discuss the benefits of service-oriented architecture over the traditional three-tier architectures.

CASE 3-2
Real-World Cases
Wipro and MBH

Source: Adapted from Navarre, E., Price, B., and Reimer, S. (2006). Case Study Report, University of Massachusetts, Lowell; and Wipro Technologies (2001). Employee Self-service, Collaboration and Community Framework; A Journey by HR Team of Wipro.

Even though a self-service can be used in any aspect of a company, many companies such as Wipro Technologies, SAP, and MBH Solutions have implemented self-service as an HR function. The main theme driving this HR design in each company is to improve service offerings to employees. This is a critical move in today's market because many companies can't afford to lose talented employees.

WIPRO TECHNOLOGIES

Wipro Technologies'[11] key objectives of HR self-service are "to improve services to employees and managers . . ." and " . . . to focus on becoming more strategic by expanding services, aligning HR activities with business strategies, and attracting and retaining key talent to support the business direction." The avenue that Wipro used to obtain these objectives was a strategy labeled Channel [W]. Prior to using Channel [W], Wipro analyzed their organization to understand their employees' needs and wants, as well as how well these were handled. Their research led them to identify two patterns that accompanied the information flow within their organization, one pulled and sorted information ("infotainment"), whereas the other pushed and thrust the information on the employee by the organization itself ("intellectual"). The way in which bonding took place was another important aspect identified within Wipro (i.e., inward to outward and outward to inward). A graph showing these quadrants helped Wipro establish a strategy for each quadrant (Exhibit 3-1). These strategies followed their objectives by promoting a "bonding" atmosphere in which employees felt comfortable and were encouraged to build relationships. From these various inputs Wipro devised a solution with Channel [W], a television-like desktop program for

---

[11] Wipro Technologies (2001). Employee Self-Service, Collaboration and Community Framework; A Journey by HR team of Wipro.

Magnet
(Random choice, personal enrichment, and personal productivity focus)

Neural Networks
(Connectivity for goals, structured choice, and corporate productivity focused)

Inward –
Outward
Branding

Outward –
Inward Branding

WIPRO Self-Service Solution

Channel W
(unlimited choice of personal enrichment and fun at workplace)

Camp W
(Corporate cause, forced set of choices, structure fun)

EXHIBIT 3-1   Wipro: Self-Service Strategies

their employees that provided various personal and organizational programs normally found on a company's Intranet. Wipro's solution used two main drivers: bonding (as mentioned earlier) and employee focus.

The implementation of Channel [W] was important to Wipro because, in an effort to eliminate steps, approvals, forms, and the like, Wipro would be able to free up time for their employees, which in today's market is a very valuable resource. In order to implement this capability an ERP self-service design was needed. Wipro identified their self-service objectives as: (1) increase information access; (2) enable strategic HR; (3) reduce administrative costs; (4) eliminate process steps, approvals, and forms; and (5) improve service to employees and managers. On the technical side of things, Wipro's software solution for Channel [W] was Web-based: HTML, JavaScript, JSPs, Oracle 8i, and Netscape Enterprise Server 4.0 or 4.1. In addition, the implementation process has been gradual since its genesis in 2000.

Wipro considers the Channel [W] self-service strategy a success because they methodically achieved the following self-service success factors: (1) collaboration among HR and IT; (2) adequate budgeting or funding; (3) CEO/high-level executive commitment; (4) strategic plan that prioritizes applications; (5) process design or reengineering; (6) marketing–employee communications; (7) corporate standards for technology solutions; (8) business case; (9) any time and any place access; (10) metrics; (11) consistent look and feel; and (12) consistent interface across media. These success factors, however, are not the only method of measuring Channel [W]'s worth. Wipro has also been evaluating the quantitative business side by measuring costs, returns, cycle time, and so on to understand the complete value of this project. Even though this is a self-evaluation of Wipro's internal self-service implementation, their report seemed thorough and objective, especially toward the conclusion when tables identified various IT applications used to show their progress.

MBH SOLUTIONS

MBH Solutions[12] acknowledges the need for self-service as a function of HR and has broken down self-service as both a separate entity and a layer of a much larger ERP solution. They have outlined various aspects of self-service that they feel companies should take into consideration prior to implementing a Web-based self-service solution. First, MBH recognizes that implementing a self-service architecture must be a gradual step-by-step process versus a big bang scenario. A company realistically must integrate their existing architecture and information into a self-service design. MBH identifies these as two vastly different aspects to consider. Self-service is primarily focused on information and data workflow, whereas the existing architecture, information, and data, which MBH labels "back office processing," is tailored for a different purpose: data gathering and processing with little focus on the ease of use or workflow. Companies currently use new self-service concepts with their existing architecture in an attempt to increase information flow without losing their original capabilities or back-office processing.

With the implementation of Web-based self-service architecture, MBH identifies many challenges inherent to this transition: (1) Real-time access to back office through the Web-based self-service architecture is subject to the time constraints of the current back-office server. (2) Complex modifications to the existing data can be costly. (3) Back office may have unique patterns or habits that may be projected to the user interface on the Web, thereby decreasing user satisfaction. (4) Each company has its own back-office processing technology that is extremely difficult to duplicate at another site. This can cause one self-service solution to be completely different from another from the same company. (5) Last, upgrades are needed to the back office in order to integrate into the Web application. This upgrade may constrain priority objectives from previous upgrades. There are numerous challenges facing the implementation of any new ERP architecture. Self-service is extremely challenging because success depends on many factors, with the largest factor being user satisfaction.

MBH identifies the need for upgrades in the future as the biggest concern for companies implementing self-service architecture. Vendors can release upgrades annually or biannually, with a long implementation process that pulls many resources from the company. In an attempt to establish a stable baseline after each upgrade implementation, a company can run into a bottleneck with their back-office data processing driving the schedule. There is an irony here: A company may be put in a situation of taking its resources from doing business, potentially decreasing user satisfaction, to focus on maintaining and upgrading its self-service architecture, which is designed to increase user satisfaction. So what is MBH's solution? They proposed decoupling the self-service architecture from the back-office data processing and gathering. In short, unlink the Web-based self-service tool from the back office and provide a methodical schedule for the back-office and self-service tool to share information. Whereas this cuts down on real-time data, it can prevent many of the problems associated with integration and implementation of a self-service architecture onto an existing system.

Wipro's internal self-service implementation, their report seemed thorough and objective, especially toward the conclusion when tables identified various IT applications used to show their progress.

---

[12] MBH Solutions, Inc. (2006). Considerations for Deploying ERP Self-Service Technology. www.mbhsolutions.com/peoplesoft.htm (accessed October 23, 2006).

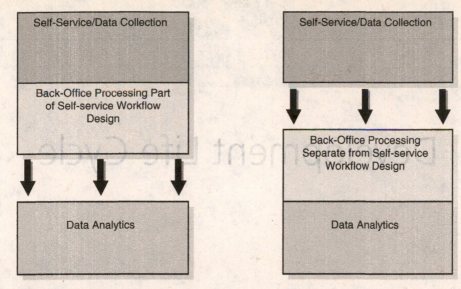

EXHIBIT 3-2 MBH Solutions: Self-Service Recommendation

Self-service is a very valuable tool. HR departments can use an integrated ERP self-service design to provide employees and consumers with a user-friendly interface for Web-based interactions. These can provide much needed information like 401Ks, order processing, basic intranet functions, and so forth. Although self-service is currently a popular HR solution, MBH Solutions recommends careful analysis and design of the interactions between existing back-end data processors and front-end Web-based workflow management.

CASE QUESTIONS

1. Compare and contrast the self-service implementation between Wipro and MBH. Which company did a better job? Explain.
2. Are the measures used by Wipro (i.e., costs, returns, and cycle time) appropriate for evaluating their self-service implementation?
3. What would happen to the self-service implementation at MBH if the company decided to adapt the SOA model? Does self-service implementation make it easier or more difficult to implement SOA? Explain.

Development Life Cycle

LEARNING OBJECTIVES

After reading this chapter, you should be able to:

- Review the systems development life cycle (SDLC).

- Examine the problems and alternatives with SDLC.

- Know the key issues in ERP implementation strategy.

- Understand ERP implementation life cycle.

- Examine the rapid implementation methodologies.

- Compare and contrast SDLC and ERP life cycles.

- Examine the role of people like top management, consultants, and subject matter experts (SMEs) in the ERP life cycle.

- Understand the importance of the project management office and the project organization to a successful ERP implementation.

- Know the components of a project organization and the roles and responsibilities of each.

CASE 4-1
Opening Case
Of Men and Mice: An ERP Case Study

Source: Based on the article by Katz, D. (2001). Of Men and Mice: An ERP Case Study, *CFO.com*, March 21.

Jackson Laboratory is a nonprofit, independent, world-renowned genetic research institute founded in 1929. Located in Bar Harbor, Maine, it had a budget of $80 million and 1,200 employees, including 32 in IT. Jackson Laboratory decided to install an ERP system with a $5 million budget and a one-year time frame. Despite the installation challenges, the project's actual cost was close to the budget and took only about six months longer than expected.

Jackson Lab's major installation challenge was the integration of its unique mouse-development functions into Oracle's ERP system. One of the problems faced by Jackson stemmed from an internal HR issue (i.e., the risk that the action or inaction of the software provider would hinder the implementation). Jackson Lab coped with these challenges by modifying the ERP system to accommodate its business process, placing special emphasis on training, seeking a fixed-fee contract with Oracle, and purchasing a surety bond to reduce project risk. The surety bond was issued by an entity on behalf of a second party, guaranteeing that the second party would fulfil an obligation or series of obligations to a third party. In the event that the obligations are not met, the third party would recover its losses via the bond. Every year about $3 billion worth of surety bonds are generated by construction projects compared with a mere $8 million for IT (mostly for governmental contracts); however, there is insufficient commonality and standardization in the IT industry on the bonds. A surety bond works well only for a fixed-fee contract because it provides the benchmarks needed to frame a bond price.

Jackson Lab selected an integrated ERP suite from Oracle rather than a best-of-breed option. The Oracle applications suite included modules for process manufacturing, accounting, e-procurement, and HR, among others. Their biggest challenge was modification of the Oracle Process Manufacturing (OPM) module to accommodate the lab's unique business processes of raising and distributing mice. The OPM module was designed for companies that mix ingredients together to produce such products as bread or beer, not for a lab environment.

The implementation team chose a phased-implementation approach instead of a big bang approach. The first phase initially went live in February, including the management of production capacity, accounts receivable, some general-ledger functions, and the purchasing of manufacturing material; in April, they launched other modules including accounting for research grants, the rest of general-ledger functions, accounts payable, and fixed assets. For the second phase, which began in June, the remaining modules including process management, human resources, payroll, labor distribution, and a grant filing application were installed.

Jackson faced personnel problems during ERP installation when the best and brightest employees were involved in the implementation process, leaving them short-handed to do the everyday work. In addition, Jackson's IT staff lacked experience with

ERP, only one person had some experience in installing an ERP. Further cost overruns resulted from training, an especially big-cost item. The time-and-materials basis contract would have increased the risk of overtime and going over budget because vendors and consultants have an interest in quoting low and seeing the work grow as the project proceeds. There is a natural competitiveness between the buyer and the ERP vendor. The vendor benefits by placing a "veil of complexity" over their work; the buyer wants to get the system up and running with the least amount of work and customization. The service-level agreements generally tend to be very complex because a much clearer definition of roles and responsibilities between client and service provider is needed. From a consultant's and vendor's perspective, a high (>25 percent) contingency is quite reasonable depending on the nature of the work, whereas this is too much from the buyer's perspective.

PREVIEW

This chapter will discuss the systems development process as it applies to ERP applications. As you saw in the opening case, organizations like Jackson Lab can spend significant dollars beyond their initial estimates to purchase and implement an ERP—and in addition change their business processes to fit the mold of the purchased system. The ERP implementation's success depends significantly on redesigning processes rather than customizing the technology to fit that process. Customization is expensive. Overall it increases the support fees paid for upgrades and prevents organizations from taking advantage of rapid implementations. To overcome these problems, Jackson Lab used several strategies to reduce the risk. First, they negotiated a *fixed-fee contract* with Oracle rather than use the more commonly used *time-and-materials contract.* Second, they bought a *surety bond* from Gladwyne, a risk management consulting firm. This strategy protected Jackson Lab from the project's cost overruns caused by IT staff being forced to solve the technological challenges with "out-of-the-box thinking." Third, it spent considerable time and effort on *changing the business processes and training* its employees with the new processes. Finally, they got better *cooperation from the vendor*, Oracle, by negotiating a fixed-fee contract and a favorable service-level agreement. One additional strategy was that Jackson Lab should have built a time buffer into their ERP implementation life cycle to avoid the pressure of delivering the system on a predetermined timeline.

In general, there are various technical and organizational challenges in implementing ERP depending on the organization, scope of implementation, business processes, and skill level of the people using these applications. The purpose of this chapter is to make you knowledgeable about the ERP life cycle process and to alert you to the implementation challenges by looking at the experiences of other organizations. The chapter begins with a brief overview of the system development life cycle (SDLC). SDLC provides useful guidelines to the ERP implementation process. Next, it discusses the key phases of the ERP life cycle with emphasis on roadblocks in each phase and solutions available to overcome these roadblocks, surveys the different life cycle methodologies and accelerators for ERP implementation, and discusses the key differences between SDLC and ERP life cycles. Throughout the discussions, the chapter provides hints on what roles you should play as an end user and discusses the implications for managers.

SYSTEMS DEVELOPMENT LIFE CYCLE

The process of developing new information systems is often called the system development life cycle. It basically includes a systematic process of planning, designing, and creating an information system for organizations. Even though the process of developing a system for individual or personal use can be simple, the task can become very complex when the system has to support thousands of business processes for several hundred users both inside and outside an organization. For complex systems development projects (e.g., ERP), it is often better to have a structured methodology to avoid mishaps and coordinate the design and development tasks properly among the members of a large systems development team.

SDLC uses a *systems approach* for problem solving that basically states that complex problems need to be broken up into smaller manageable problems using a systems' hierarchy, and then developing a solution for each problem within the hierarchy. It provides a structured top-down problem identification and bottom-up solution process for managing complex problems. The structured or phased approach is designed to catch problems at an early stage before they become a major risk to the system implementation process. The SDLC process requires both technical and nontechnical problem-solving skills; therefore, the development team must understand technology, as well as the organization's business processes, culture, and people (or potential end users of this system). For example, a component of an HR system must capture organizational policy on health care benefits and retirement and the process of deducting the premiums from the payroll checks. Every organization will have some variations that need to be accurately captured and processed by the new system. Capturing these processes and then implementing them in a new system can be difficult for a person with an IT background only; therefore, the development team must be composed of people with a wide variety of IT and business skills for the project to be successful.

Traditional SDLC

In the early days of systems development, very few of these projects were successful in the first attempt. There were many reasons for the early failures, chief among them being lack of experience. This led to the systems approach, which we described earlier, and a structured SDLC methodology. The SDLC consists of tasks that are divided into phases or stages as shown in Figure 4-1. Please read systems analysis and design books for complete details on SDLC.

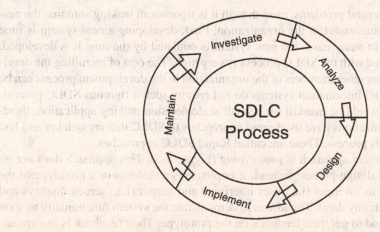

FIGURE 4-1 Traditional SDLC Methodology

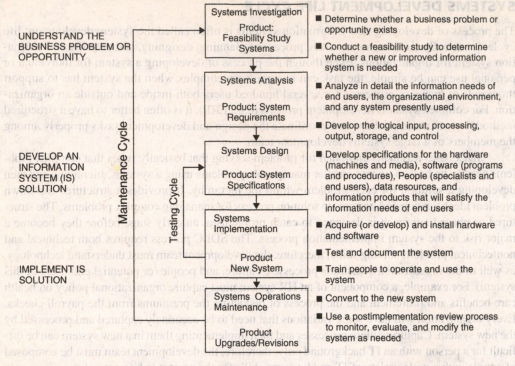

FIGURE 4-2   SDLC Approach

Figure 4-2 provides a summary of the traditional SDLC methodology. The SDLC process begins when someone in the organization identifies a need, or investigation phase, for a new system and ends the implementation phase where the new system is installed and running in the organization.

Rapid SDLC Approaches

The SDLC process has several problems, even though it is rigorous in making sure that the new system is complete and successful in the organization. First, developing a new system is time consuming and tedious. In many cases the new system is outdated by the time it is developed. Second, the cost associated with the SDLC process is very high. The cost of recruiting the development team and involving other members of the organization in the development process can be very expensive. Finally, all information systems do not require such a rigorous SDLC process. For example, the SDLC would be overkill for a small-scale decision-making application; therefore, over the years organizations have used rapid approaches to SDLC that are quicker and less expensive shortcuts to this process. These are called Rapid SDLC approaches.

One rapid development approach is *prototyping* (Figure 4-3). This approach does not go through the analysis and design phases; instead, it implements a skeleton or a prototype of the actual system with a focus on input (i.e., user interface) and output (i.e., screen displays and reports generated with dummy data). The idea is to demonstrate the system functionality as soon as possible to the users and to get their feedback on the prototype. Their feedback is incorporated into the new system and demonstrated back to the users. This approach has proven to be very

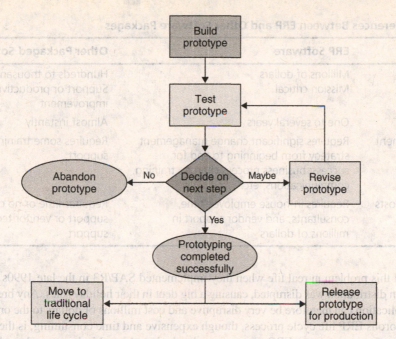

FIGURE 4-3 Prototype Development

effective with user-interactive systems because the prototype is eventually converted into a full-scale system. In ERP implementations, many companies install a sandbox system to expose users to the system functionality. ERP sandboxes replicate at least the minimal functionality needed to get user feedback before implementing a full-scale system. The goal of sandboxing is similar to that of prototyping.

Another rapid development approach is *end-user development* (EUD), which lets the end users create their own applications. This process became popular in the 1980s with the advent of personal computers (PCs). In this process the users are trained by the IT staff or professional trainers to develop customized applications (e.g., a small decision-making application with an Excel spreadsheet or a departmental employee tracking system with an Access database). Several other customized approaches have similarly been developed over the years to circumvent the exhaustive SDLC. EUD is applicable in ERP for designing custom reports from the ERP system.

ERP IMPLEMENTATION LIFE CYCLE

ERP applications are prepackaged software developed by commercial software vendors and custom installed for organizations to automate and integrate the various business processes. Although an ERP is packaged software, it is very different from PC-based software packages (e.g., Microsoft Office or other software) that you may have purchased for personal use as shown in Table 4-1. These are complex software packages costing millions of dollars to develop and maintain that automate hundreds of business processes in an organization. Furthermore, these applications are mission critical (i.e., if they fail or break down, the organization will stop functioning). For example, without these systems a bank would not be able to service its customers for withdrawals or deposits, and a manufacturing company would not be able to assemble and ship their products. Hershey, Corp.,

TABLE 4-1   Differences Between ERP and Other Software Packages

	ERP Software	Other Packaged Software
Software Cost Significance to Organization	Millions of dollars Mission critical	Hundreds to thousands Support or productivity improvement
Installation Time	One to several years	Almost instantly
Change Management Strategy	Requires significant change management strategy from beginning to end for success; business process change, training, communications, etc.	Requires some training and support
Implementation Costs	Requires in-house employee time, consultants, and vendor support in millions of dollars	Requires little or no consulting support or vendor technical support

experienced this problem in real life when they implemented SAP/R3 in the late 1990s when their supply-chain distribution was disrupted, causing a big dent in their holiday sales. Any breakdown of an ERP application can therefore be very disruptive and cost millions of dollars to the organization.

A rigorous ERP life cycle process, though expensive and time consuming, is therefore recommended to ensure success. ERP systems can be deployed in a big bang or phased approach, either of which initiates the stages of a system development life cycle. According to the staged system implementation model,[1] the life cycle consists of four phases—adaptation, acceptance, routinization, and infusion. Adaptation is similar to system investigation, whereas acceptance is similar to system analysis where user requirements are analyzed and accepted by the team before proceeding to design and implementation. Additionally, routinization is where the ERP system is either customized or business processes are changed to assimilate the system in the organization. Once operational, the infusion or maintenance and evaluation phase gets started where recurring problems are fixed and new features are sought for next implementation life cycle.

ERP Implementation Plan

An ERP implementation plan is used to create a roadmap or blueprint to meet cost, scope, and time constraints of an implementation. There are many different ERP implementation methodologies promoted by different vendors and consultants. The appropriateness of the plan depends, in part, on the project, the company, and the reasons for the implementation.

Following are three major implementation plan choices:

1. *Comprehensive.* A comprehensive ERP integration plan is the most expensive, lengthy, and costly approach. It involves implementation of the full functionality of the ERP software in addition to industry-specific modules. Implementing the full functionality requires a high level of business process reengineering (BPR) with major changes in the business processes and customization of legacy systems.

---

[1] Kwon, T. & Zmud, R. (1987). Unifying the Fragmented Models of Information Systems Implementation, in: R. J. Boland & R. A. Hirschheim (Eds.), *Critical Issues in Information Systems Research* (pp. 227–252z). Chichester, UK: Wiley.

2. *Middle of the Road.* A middle-of-the-road ERP implementation plan involves some changes in the core ERP modules and a significant amount of BPR. The middle-of-the-road approach is not as expensive as the comprehensive approach or as straightforward as the vanilla approach.

3. *Vanilla.* A vanilla ERP implementation plan utilizes core ERP functionality and exploits the best practice business processes built into the software. A company following a vanilla implementation will have to simply align their business processes to the ERP system, rather than modify the software. By eliminating or minimizing the required BPR, the project's costs and time required for the implementation are minimized.

ERP Implementation Methodology

Methodology refers to a *systematic* approach to solving a business problem. ERP methodology builds on the theory that an enterprise can maximize its returns by maximizing the utilization of its fixed supply of resources. Information technology, with its increasing computer power and the ability to correlate pieces of information, has proven to be the best tool for business problem solving. Like SDLC, an ERP development life cycle provides a systematic approach to implementing ERP software in the changing but limited-resource organizational environment.

There are many different vendor-driven methodologies or approaches that use traditional ERP development life cycle or rapid ERP life cycles (e.g., Total Solution, FastTrack, Rapid-Re, Accelerated SAP (ASAP), and business integration methodology (BIM)). Implementation methodologies are similar in their overall approach with the differences coming primarily in the staging of the process steps and formality of structure. The traditional ERP life cycle accomplishes one stage at a time and requires formal milestone approvals prior to moving to the next stage. In a rapid ERP life cycle, once a company commits to the implementation, employees are empowered to make the decisions to keep the project moving forward. They also allow flexibility and quicker feedback loops to accommodate rapid corrections as shown in Figure 4-4.

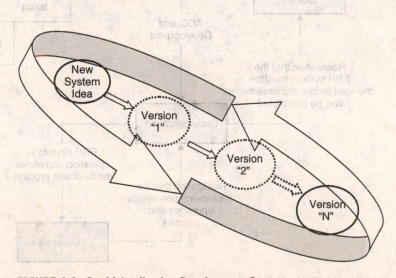

FIGURE 4-4 Rapid Application Development Process

Traditional ERP Life Cycle

Like the traditional SDLC, which we discussed earlier, the traditional ERP life cycle approach has a deliverable at the end of each stage (e.g., a report with supporting documents) that is reviewed by management and upon which a decision is made either to continue with the project or not. End-user or people involvement is critical in both SDLC and ERPLC; however, there are other variations to the traditional SDLC process. The emphasis in ERP implementation is on customizing the software as well as on changing the organization's business processes, rather than determining the user requirements for developing new applications (as in the traditional SDLC). This may seem like a small deviation, but it requires a major change in the thinking process as well as team composition and skill level of people involved in the development process. Furthermore, the ERP life cycle, as shown in Figure 4-5, iterates at a much faster pace than in the traditional SDLC.

The traditional ERP life cycle includes the following major stages:

Stage 1. *Scope and commitment stage.* This is similar to the investigation stage in SDLC discussed earlier. In addition to conducting the feasibility study, however, one of the first steps is to develop a scope of ERP implementation within the resource and time requirement. A number of task parameters or characteristics of the ERP implementation

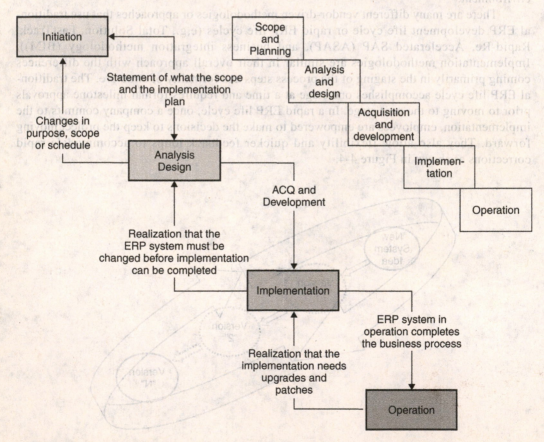

FIGURE 4-5 Traditional ERP Life Cycle

need to be defined at the planning stage. How large will the ERP system scope be in terms of departmental or functional coverage? Develop a long-term vision for the new system and a short-term implementation plan and top management's commitment for both the vision and implementation plan. The composition and the structure of the implementation team, the role of external consultants both in terms of time and scope, and the role of internal employees, including the subject matter experts (SMEs) who will provide the knowledge to embed business rules and input for interface and report design, are other key factors to be considered at this stage. Vendor selection is another key activity toward the end of this stage. Although no decisions should be made on the ERP software, vendor information must be reviewed and choices could be narrowed by testing alternative software and developing a business case for the project. A number of items need to be assessed and established to create the boundaries and scope. Table 4-2 lists the key decisions to be made for each type of scope.

Stage 2. *Analysis and design stage.* In addition to analysis of user requirements, the ERP team has first to make a decision on the software and decide on consultants and SMEs. Another key activity is to map the differences between the current business process and the embedded process in the ERP software or gap analysis and to develop a long-term plan on whether to change the business processes of the organization or to customize the ERP software to support existing processes. Using the gap analysis, the team must develop a design that among other things includes a change management plan, a list of embedded processes, user interface screens, and reports in the ERP software that will need customization, design of these changes, and a process of involving subject matter experts in the design. Other activities include creating plans for data conversion, system conversion, and training. For a system to be successful, the team must develop a detailed change management strategy and plan for the release of the new system. By the end of this stage, the team usually has a sandbox or prototype of the ERP software installed that is accessible to the entire implementation team, consultants, and SMEs.

Stage 3. *Acquisition and development stage.* This stage is similar to the acquisition and testing stage of traditional SDLC. The organization has to purchase the license for the production version of the software and build the production version of the system, which

TABLE 4-2   List of Scopes and Commitments

Scope Type	Description/Key Decision Points
Gap Analysis	Gap analysis is the evaluation of the functions provided by the ERP system compared with the operational processes necessary to run your business
Physical Scope	Establishes which sites will be addressed, the geographical locations of the sites, and the number of users.
BPR Scope	Will the current processes be refined, replaced, or eliminated. What users, departments, sites will be affected?
Technical Scope	How much modification will be done to the ERP software? What processes will be utilized as is and which will be customized?
Resource Scope	How much time and budget is allocated for the project?
Implementation Scope	Which modules should be implemented? How should the modules be connected to the existing system?

is eventually to be made available to the end users. The entire production platform must be configured and built with the necessary hardware, network, security, software, database, and real production data. The tasks identified in the gap analysis are executed at this stage. These include customization of embedded software rules, data in the database tables, input screens, and reports that come with the ERP system. While the technical team is working on the installation, the change management team works with end users on implementing the changes in business processes and preliminary training with the sandbox version of the software. The data team similarly works on migrating data from the old system to the new system. This can be an extremely difficult task when the old system is a legacy application using a nonrelational database. Data mapping, missing data, and data dictionary design are the major tasks for data conversion. Finally, the ERP system needs to be configured with proper security, implement the authentication and authorization policy for accessing the system, and contain other modifications as recommended by the design plan.

Stage 4. *Implementation stage.* The focus for this stage is on installing and releasing the system to the end users (i.e., "Go-Live") and on monitoring the system release to the end users. This production platform is a mirror of the development version of the system. Errors found in the production version have to go through the help desk or support staff. Any changes made to the development version are then retested and migrated to the production system as regularly scheduled updates. System conversion is a major activity for the new system and needs to be managed carefully. There are four basic conversion approaches, which are visually represented in Figure 4-6. The first

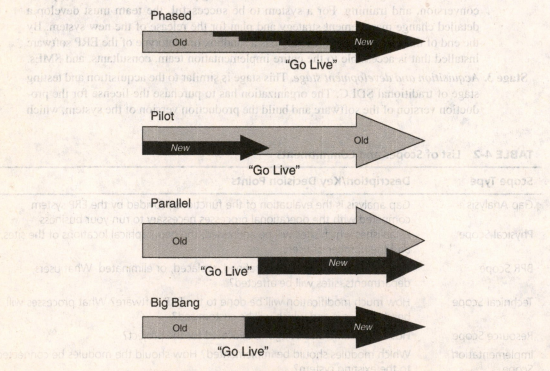

FIGURE 4-6 ERP Conversion Approaches

approach, *phased*, is a gradual movement of the company from the existing legacy system(s) to the ERP implementation. This approach can take a significant amount of time, but can also be the least disruptive to the company. The second approach, *pilot*, implements a small version of the final system. This pilot system is used to ensure that the final system is appropriate. It is the equivalent of a test drive in that the system is used, but only by select areas, and its impact can be managed more closely. The third approach, *parallel*, has the most up-front cost because the ERP system is implemented and used in conjunction with the legacy system. This approach is best used when risk of ERP failure is of significant concern. The final approach, *direct cutover* or big bang, is the highest-risk approach but the most straightforward and clean. The company moves from the legacy system directly and immediately to ease the ERP system. This approach has the least amount of up-front costs because systems are not duplicated or run concurrently for any length of time. Training end users on how to use the new system is another important activity. Training is generally part of the change management strategy designed to ease the transition to the post-implementation environment. Feedback received from system usage needs to be funneled to the post-implementation team for ongoing system support, including upgrades and patches, as well as to make adjustments to the change management strategy.

Stage 5. *Operation stage.* This is often managed by the operation team with assistance from the implementation team. Knowledge transfer is the major activity as support for the new system is migrated to the help desk and support staff. Some implementation team members are very often hired as support staff. The other major activities are ongoing training of new users to the system as ERP modules are released, as well as to take a fresh look at the change management strategy. The team has to monitor user feedback from training and actual system usage carefully and make the necessary adjustments to the change management approach. Another key activity is management of new releases of the software, installation of patches and upgrades to the system, and managing the software contract with the ERP vendor.

A summary of ERP life cycle phases is shown in Figure 4-7.

ROLE OF CHANGE MANAGEMENT   Change management (CM) plays an important role throughout the ERP life cycle. System failures often occur when the attention is not devoted to this from the beginning stages. A vision for CM needs to be articulated from the first stage and then revised, monitored, and implemented on a constant basis. A major role of the SMEs and other internal users working with the team is to guide the implementation team on all the activities of change management, including guidance on what processes need changing, customization of business rules in ERP software, input screen design, report design, and training and communications plan for the end users affected by the new system. Support of the top management as well as skills of the change management team are essential for successful implementation. Change management strategy and activities are discussed in detail elsewhere in this book.

Rapid ERP Life Cycles

ERP implementations are usually very long. They usually start with a long requirements-gathering phase, followed by designs, and implementations. That means that significant amounts of time (months to years) could go by between the time the requirement is given and the time it is

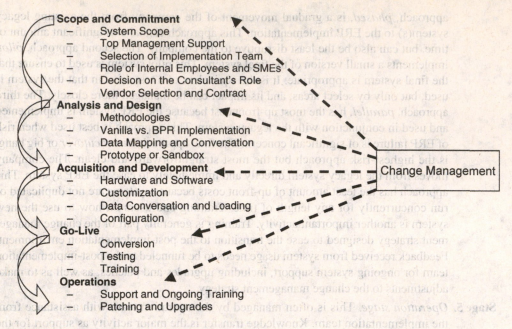

FIGURE 4-7   ERP Life Cycle Phases Summary

actually implemented. As businesses grow and move quickly, there is a high chance that the requirement will change during those months or years of time that pass.

Consultants play an important role in rapid implementation of ERP systems. They provide different methodologies and techniques for rapid or accelerated implementation. This is an area where the use of experienced consultants can best be leveraged as they bring knowledge of techniques and approaches that have worked well with other organizations. Scripts and wizards provided by consultants can help automate some of the more common tasks that occur during an implementation. These include migration of data, identification of duplicate data, and other standard tasks.

This section will give you a sample of methodologies offered by ERP consulting firms. The appropriate implementation model may vary based on company, culture, software, budget, and the purpose of the implementation, but previous implementation experience of the program management and consultants will likely be the largest driving factor in determining the best approach. With that said, the high commitment of resources required in the first stages of the implementation and the time and cost saving claimed by rapid implementation approaches have drastically increased the number of rapid implantations. Some examples of methodologies used in implementing ERP systems follow.

TOTAL SOLUTION   ERP packages have increasingly become indispensable to run businesses; yet, ERP implementations often fail because these solutions are highly integrated, demand cross-functional collaboration, and require significant change management. Although ERP solutions have matured and stabilized over the years, they are still difficult to implement and manage. Ernst & Young, LLP, have developed a systematic way of approaching systems reengineering called the *Total Solution*. The Total Solution approach has five components:

1. *The value proposition.* Building the business case for an ERP solution. The key decision to be made before any process can begin is to make sure that the ERP solution makes sound business sense. The following questions should be answered before the process is started:
   - Is the investment in new technology justified?
   - Does the ERP solution match the company's objectives?
   - Does management understand what change means, and does that change have full support?
   - What is the framework for making decisions?
   - What milestones will measure the project's progress?
   - Is value being delivered throughout the process?

2. *Reality check.* Assessing an organization's readiness for change. Since many people oppose change, it's something that needs to be anticipated. Status quo is easy. Change is not. The following questions therefore need to be asked:
   - Is the organization ready for change?
   - Are there any "hidden agendas?" If so, how will they be managed?
   - Is everybody on board with the nature, scope, and pace of the change?
   - What are management's expectations?

   The answers to these questions will adjust the implementation approach. Knowing the answers up front helps to avoid a possibility that the change is incompatible with the client's expectations.

3. *Aligned approach.* Setting the right expectations that deliver both short-term and long-term value. Short-term as well as long-term benefits are equally important to any project's success. Even if change is discomforting for some, it is easier to accept when progress is visible. In this approach, the following tasks are performed:
   - Evaluate alternatives to a comprehensive reengineering project.
   - Craft a "best-fit" approach that allows the implementation to proceed in well-defined modules.
   - Communicate expected results to management. Keep communicating throughout the project so no surprises surface at the end. This approach helps keep the entire project on time, on budget, and on management's agenda for success.

4. *Success dimension.* Getting the right blend of people, skills, methods, and management in the team. The key to any project's success is having the right mix of people, skills, methods, and management (i.e., people with diverse skills in process management, change management, knowledge management, and industry skills). Teamwork is very important to a project's success.

5. *Delivering value.* Measuring results and celebrating success. A project that does not show measurable results throughout the process is going to flounder. People will lose enthusiasm and the expectation of a new way of doing business becomes just another broken promise. Total Solution methodology makes sure that every project pays continuous "value dividends" all along the way and helps to minimize the risk of change.

FASTTRACK   Whether your business objective involves global reengineering, process improvement, or software replacement, Deloitte & Touche Consulting Group's FastTrack implementation methodology can enhance and accelerate ERP software implementations. The *FastTrack* approach developed by Deloitte & Touche is based on a matrix of five phases and five focus areas:

Phases   Designed to reflect and integrate decisions regarding business redesign, organizational change and performance, training , process and systems integrity, client–server technologies and technical architecture.

Stage 1. *Scoping and planning:* Project definition and scope. Project planning is initiated.
Stage 2. *Visioning and targeting:* Needs assessment. Vision and targets identified. As-is modeling.
Stage 3. *Redesign:* To-be Modeling. Software design and development.
Stage 4. *Configuration:* Software development. Integration test planning.
Stage 5. *Testing and delivery:* Integration testing. Business and system delivery.

Areas   In addition, it identifies five areas (groups) as an individual thread to be woven into a cohesive fabric through its five-phase work plan. The areas and a list of the functions performed are as follows:

Stage 1. *Project management* (project organization, risk management, planning, monitoring, communications, budgeting, staffing, quality assurance).
Stage 2. *Information technology architecture* (hardware and network selection, procurement, installation, operations, software design, development, installation).
Stage 3. *Process and systems integrity* (security, audit control).
Stage 4. *Change leadership* (leadership, commitment, organizations design, change readiness, policies and procedures, performance measurements).
Stage 5. *Training and documentation* (needs assessment, training design and delivery for project team, management, end users, operations, and help desk. Scripting of end-user and operations documentation).

Rapid-Re   Gateway, a consulting firm in New York, has developed an ERP life cycle methodology called *Rapid-Re.* The five-stage, 54-step modular methodology is customized to the needs of each project because that is what happens in practice. Individual projects skip, rearrange, or recombine tasks to meet their needs or give greater or lesser emphasis to some tasks.

Stage 1. *Preparation.* Mobilize, organize, and energize the people who will perform the reengineering project.
Stage 2. *Identification.* Develop a customer-oriented process model of the business.
Stage 3. *Vision.* Select the processes to reengineer and formulate redesign options capable of achieving breakthrough performance.
Stage 4. *Solution.* Define the technical and social requirements for the new processes and develop detailed implementation plans.
Stage 5. *Transformation.* Implement the reengineering plans. In an ideal project, stages one and two consider all key processes within a company and conclude with a step that sets priorities for the processes to reengineer. The other stages are executed repeatedly for each process selected for reengineering.

ACCELERATED SAP (ASAP)   The ASAP roadmap is a detailed project plan by SAP that describes all activities in an implementation. It includes the entire technical area to support technical project management, and addresses such concerns as interfaces, data conversions, and authorizations earlier than do most traditional implementations.

The ASAP roadmap consists of five phases—project preparation, business blueprint, realization, final preparation, and go-live—and supports continuous change.

Phase 1. *Project preparation.* Proper planning and assessing organizational readiness is essential. Determine if there is a

- full agreement that all company decision makers are behind the project
- clear project objectives
- efficient decision-making process
- company culture that is willing to accept change

ASAP's project estimator can be used to guide the project team through a series of predefined questions and to drive interviews with senior executives and key operating managers about their expectations of R/3 and the speed of its deployment.

Phase 2. *Business blueprint.* The engineer delivers a complete toolkit of predefined business processes. During the business blueprint phase R3's broad scope is narrowed to fit the industry-specific processes. Using questionnaires and the models from the business engineer, the business processes are documented to reflect the future vision of the business. Industry templates further accelerate the process by predefining industry best-business practices. The result is a comprehensive blueprint of the business. During this phase, training begins on R3's integrated business systems. Level 2 hands-on training provides a step-by-step education of R3 business process skills. The business blueprint is a visual model of your business' future state. It will allow the project team to define the scope clearly and only to focus on the R3 processes needed to run the business.

Phase 3. *Realization.* Based on the business blueprint, a two-step process is begun to configure the R3 system. First, the baseline system will be configured. Second, the system is fine-tuned to meet all of the business process requirements. Because the initial configuration is based on the blueprint, the baseline system gives a real-worldview of how the business transactions will actually run.

Phase 4. *Final preparation.* In this phase, the R3 system is fine-tuned. Necessary adjustments are made in order to prepare the system and the business for production start-up. Final systems tests are conducted, and end-user training is completed. Initial audit procedures are developed.

Phase 5. *Go-live and support.* In this phase, procedures and measurements are developed to review the benefits of the R3 investment on an ongoing basis. SAP support and services are provided to ensure that the system continues to run smoothly. The online service system (OSS) provides electronic support using a remote connection. The implementation assistant provides answers for most of the questions that may arise. It is an easy-to-use repository of information defining what to do, who should do it, and how long it should take.

ASAP provides examples, checklists, or templates as samples for things such as a cutover plan. They are used as a starting point to avoid "reinventing the wheel." ASAP calls these things "Accelerators."

BUSINESS INTEGRATION METHODOLOGY (BIM) The BIM, developed by Accenture Systems in the 1990s, is targeted for full-scale ERP projects that diagnose business integration needs, design business strategies and architectures, deliver one or more business capabilities to meet those needs, and ensure that the value of those capabilities can be sustained over time. This includes the strategic planning, delivery, and operation of technologies, processes, facilities, and human performance. To achieve business integration, a team must define and implement a comprehensive set of changes to an organization, spanning improvements to business processes, technology, and human performance, all aligned with an organization's overall strategy.

This methodology is best suited for full life cycle projects where organizations expect to involve either custom-built solutions or a blend of custom and packaged components. In addition, it is intended for use on medium to large projects that implement a full life cycle custom-built BI solution and comprises the BIM content areas that are relevant to custom solution planning, delivery, and operations:

The planning phase. The objective of this phase is to help an organization define appropriate strategies and approaches for achieving an enduring competitive advantage and building stakeholder value. The planning phase defines new and improved business capabilities to support the organization's strategies and creates detailed plans to help the organization effectively and efficiently implement changes—and realize and sustain value—during the delivering and operating phases.

The delivering phase (aka the standard or custom route). This phase translates the business architecture into a specific business capability. A business capability is the combination of human performance, business process, and technology that collectively creates value by improving business performance. The delivering phase defines a cross-competency approach for taking each business capability from blueprint to deployment.

The managing phase. This phase directs, coordinates, and monitors the activities outlined in the other three phases, in order to achieve improved business results. This phase determines whether the proposed business values were achieved; the projects and change journey were effectively managed; there was an ongoing alignment of context, content, and course of action; the necessary levels of ownership, sponsorship, commitment, and leadership were achieved; and the program sponsor or stakeholder expectations were met or exceeded.

The operating phase. This phase operates the new business capabilities that were created in the delivering phase. Operating is based on the definitions of sourcing strategies, service providers, and customers, which were established in the planning phase. The work in this phase must meet the formal service targets and metrics established in earlier phases, and it must provide feedback for improvements based on measurements of actual performance against those targets.

AGILE DEVELOPMENT   The agile development methodology has gained popularity over the past decade for traditional software development. This success has helped this methodology migrate to ERP implementations. Here is a key reason for this success:

> *At the core of any agile approach is an assumption that whatever the requirements might be at the beginning of a project, they won't be the same at the end of the project. The longer the project, the more truth there is in this assumption. To mitigate this situation, agile methodologies start with smaller sets of requirements, they start small and deliver functionality incrementally in a series of releases. No single release covers all requirements, but every release delivers more than the previous one.*[2]

---

[2] *Is agile ERP implementation possible?* (March 11, 2009). Retrieved on October 2010 from http://community.dynamics.com/product/nav/navnontechnical/b/navigateintosuccess/archive/2009/03/11/is-agile-erp-implementation-possible-63.aspx

Therefore, the key problem that agile methodology tries to solve is changing and unclear requirements. By developing smaller portions of the ERP system and releasing them to users, the users will be able to provide feedback quickly on how this system meets their needs. This also means that if a requirement is missing or wrong, it can be corrected quickly (often in one iteration, which may be between two and six weeks), rather than requiring a long and expensive process. Another key aspect is that new components are not built upon building blocks that are wrong. In a traditional waterfall implementation, if the first requirement implemented is wrong, an entire ERP system could be implemented upon that basis. This means that if one thing needs to be changed, it could cause the entire system, or at least a large portion of the system, to be changed. This is very expensive and time consuming to undertake and should be avoided at all costs.

An agile methodology has many different types of implementations. Two of the most popular implementations are Scrum and extreme programming (XP). In Scrum, the methodology states the following: "Instead of providing complete, detailed descriptions of how everything is to be done on the project, much is left up to the team. This is done because the team will know best how to solve its problem."[3] The Scrum methodology works in an agile iterative methodology; however, it empowers the team (including a Scrum master, product owner, and team members) to make decisions that will help deliver a successful product deliverable. "Extreme Programming (XP) is successful because it stresses customer satisfaction. Instead of delivering everything you could possibly want on some date far in the future this process delivers the software you need as you need it."[4] In XP, an agile iterative approach is valued because it gives working software to the customers quickly and incorporates their feedback quickly to build the best product possible.

OTHERS   There are industry-specific rapid implementation approaches (e.g., those available from the Cobre Group's consulting firm called *Implementation Accelerator*). This accelerator facilitates conversions and upgrades by providing a tool to use for data mapping, workflow analysis, project planning, and end-user training.

Another example is from the Chemical Industry Data Exchange. They have an implementation accelerator that is divided into phases: plan, assess, enable, test, and go-live. Each phase has specific tools, templates, and real-world suggestions contributed by members.

ERP Life Cycle Vs. SDLC

Because of their prepackaged nature, ERP applications generally do not require the traditional SDLC process; however, that does not mean they can be bought from the vendor, installed (i.e., a PC-based software package), and used *as is* immediately. ERP packages are complex with embedded business processes in all major functional areas of business. In addition, they represent best practices by industry or area of business. These processes and functional activities are generic in nature and must therefore be adapted for the specific requirements of the company. This is not an easy course of action. It requires a thorough understanding of the business process of the company, data requirements, informational flows, system access and security, integration with existing software applications, and compatibility with current hardware systems of the company. The ERP life cycle is often therefore as rigorous as is the traditional SDLC life cycle;

---

[3] *Introduction to Scrum—an agile process.* (2010). Retrieved on October 2011 from http://www.mountaingoatsoftware. com/topics/scrum
[4] Wells, D. (September 29, 2009). *Extreme Programming: A Gentle Introduction.* Retrieved on October 2010 from http:// www.extremeprogramming.org/

TABLE 4-3 Comparing and Contrasting SDLC with ERPLC

	SDLC	ERP Life Cycle
Goal	Develop a new system to support the organization requirements	Implement a packaged system to support the organization requirements
Analysis	Evaluate user needs through observations and interviews and create system specifications	Vendor analysis and evaluation of business process changes due to the implementation
Design	Develop new system architecture, user interface, and reporting tools	Installation and customization plan of ERP software, data conversion, and change management strategies
Implementation	Acquire hardware, software, develop applications, installation, testing, training, and conversion	"Go-Live" conversion or releasing the system to the users, training, and support
Consultant Role	Technical support mainly during design and implementation	Change management, process change, and technical support from beginning to end
Management Role	Some oversight and support	Significant oversight and involvement—especially in change management
End-User Role	Focus group providing input during the various stages with most involvement during implementation stage	Multiple groups such as SMEs, advance users, and self-service users are part of implementation team with continuous involvement
Operations	Maintains, updates, and provides technical support	Maintains, updates, upgrades, and monitors change management strategy

however, there are also differences due to the prepackaged nature of the software as shown in Table 4-3. Some of the key differences are as follows:

- SDLC does not mention software acquisition until the fourth stage, whereas in the ERP life cycle, the ERP software must be selected at a very early stage of the implementation process. One of the key early decisions in the ERP life cycle is software or vendor selection. ERP vendors have traditionally embedded the best practices and business rules in their software. Some vendors specialize in certain industries. Understanding the ERP software's functionality and the embedded business processes are therefore crucial for successful implementation. A good match between the company's business process and software's embedded functionality means quicker implementation and millions of dollars saved in implementation costs.
- In SDLC the new application is custom designed based on the user requirements as determined from the feasibility study and analysis. On the other hand, in the ERP life cycle the new application is bought by the organization and users are asked to change their business process and policy to take advantage of the best practices embedded in the ERP software. The emphasis in ERP life cycle is more toward reengineering organizational process and change management to improve productivity and create efficiencies with the help of embedded functionality of the ERP software.
- Another difference is in the role of external consultants in the ERP life cycle. In traditional SDLC, the consultant's role is limited to IT hardware, software, and training. Most of the team is made up of people from inside the organization. Consultants play a very important role right from beginning to end during ERP installations advising the organization on software vendor selection, business process reengineering, software installation, and change management.

There are similarities between the ERP life cycle and SDLC. For example, the feasibility stage in the ERP life cycle is similar to the SDLC. ERP implementation requires scoping the project requirements and conducting a proper feasibility study from operational, economic, technical, and strategic perspectives like any other system. The new ERP system must be strategically aligned with an organization's long-term strategy and vision. Top management support will be available only when the new system fulfills the long-term vision of the company. With top management support there is also a long-term commitment of resources for the project. The ERP implementation life cycle is an expensive long-term investment for the company with a return on investment that is intangible and spread over a long period of time. In addition to the feasibility, other similarities occur at the conversion stage. The company can either go for a phased approach or a big bang conversion that replaces the old system with the new on a fixed date and time. ERP implementations similarly require extensive data conversion, proper software testing and quality assurances, end-user training, and post-implementation IT support in terms of installing software patches and product upgrades.

PROJECT MANAGEMENT

ERP projects take on their own organizational duties and job functions separate and apart from the day-to-day business functions. A clear project plan and reporting structure will better ensure that the project receives the attention and accountability needed to be successful. Figure 4-8 shows a sample organization structure for an ERP implementation.

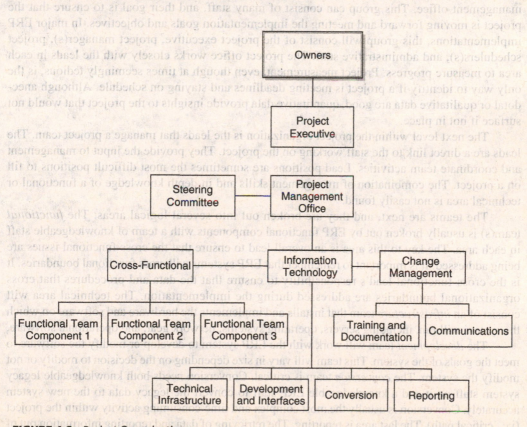

FIGURE 4-8 Project Organization

The organizational structure must coincide with the project governance. The project owners, a project steering committee, and project executive must develop the hierarchy and determine who is responsible for each system implementation component. A number of staff is most often assigned to the implementation from existing business organizations. It is recommended that organizational structures for the functional and technical staff on the project report to project leads and not to their home departments. The ERP implementation project should provide "backfill" staff to departments that have assigned staff to the project to ensure business can continue without interruption and free up staff assigned to the project to work full time on the project without also having to continue with duties from the home department.

As is often the case, ERP implementation project organizations are created just for the project; however, this is changing. Companies are finding more and more that a modified project organization is needed to support the ERP and ensure ongoing progress. Many businesses now have a project management organization within IT to provide the project management necessary for company projects. The functional, technical, and change management staff for the project will likely consist of existing staff from the business, new hires, and consultants. The creation of the project organization and having them work together as a team takes effort and should not be overlooked. The staff in each area must be skilled to accomplish the tasks assigned to them and to develop a strong sense of project teamwork for the overall success of the ERP implementation. The development of the team is the responsibility of the project management office along with the leads in each area.

The organization structure is divided into several areas, the first of which is the project management office. This group can consist of many staff, and their goal is to ensure that the project is moving forward and meeting the implementation goals and objectives. In major ERP implementations, this group will consist of the project executive, project manager(s), project schedulers(s), and administrative staff. The project office works closely with the leads in each area to measure progress. Project measurement, even though at times seemingly tedious, is the only way to identify if a project is meeting deadlines and staying on schedule. Although anecdotal or qualitative data are good, quantitative data provide insights to the project that would not surface if not in place.

The next level within the project organization is the leads that manage a project team. The leads are a direct link to the staff working on the project. They provide the input to management and coordinate team activities. Lead positions are sometimes the most difficult positions to fill on a project. The combination of management skills and in-depth knowledge of a functional or technical area is not easily found.

The teams are next, and they are broken out into several logical areas: The *functional* team(s) is usually broken out by ERP functional components with a team of knowledgeable staff in each area. The key to this area is an overall lead to ensure that the cross-functional issues are being addressed. It is important to remember that ERP systems will cross functional boundaries. It is the cross-functional lead's responsibility to ensure that the data and procedures that cross organizational boundaries are addressed during the implementation. The technical area will consist of an *infrastructure* team that installs and implements the hardware and software on which the system will run, including servers, operating systems, network gear, and operational software.

The *development* team will work with the ERP system to develop or modify the software to meet the goals of the system. This team will vary in size depending on the decision to modify or not modify the system. The *conversion* team is critical. Conversion needs both knowledgeable legacy system staff on it and a knowledgeable ERP staff to convert the legacy data to the new system accurately. Conversion is usually the most complex and time-consuming activity within the project (i.e., critical path). The last area is reporting. The retrieving of data and reporting information out of the new system has a steep learning curve. The *reporting* team will need to develop a reporting framework and initial set of reports that need to be included in the system implementation. As with most conversions from a legacy system to an ERP there will be hundreds, sometimes thousands, of reports that have been written for a variety of purposes. Identifying and prioritizing the reports is a job in itself. You will find that many of the reports will not be necessary in the ERP system so prioritizing reports and even eliminating reports from the inventory for a Go-live is essential to ensure that the company's needs are being met with the implementation. As the implementation progresses, the reporting team will need to continue to develop reports and/or provide the tools and training necessary to easily retrieve data from the system.

Last, the *change management* team will be the glue that provides the link back to the company and keeps the project in the forefront. Change management will develop both the training plan and a communications plan for the project. Their role is to provide project implementation information to key areas within the organization. Change management should use all communication methods available to them to ensure the message is getting out. This includes e-mail, Web, letters, and presentations. Presentations are especially helpful because they are much more interactive.

PROJECT ROLES AND RESPONSIBILITIES

Identifying and describing roles and responsibilities for project staff is necessary to ensure there is accountability within the project. Project staff will be made up of a variety of people from different parts of the organization along with external staffing (consultants). Defining roles, often used as job descriptions on a project, will be the responsibility of the project management office. Each member of the project team will need to know what is expected of them, who they will report to, and what they will be evaluated on. Table 4-4 is an example of project roles along with the defined activities for each and the skills to fill that role. Note that there will be more detail to the information in the table in Appendix A in this chapter.

IMPLICATIONS FOR MANAGEMENT

ERPs are becoming more and more ubiquitous in the business landscape as they become critical to the long-term positioning and success of today's businesses. As companies look to ERP systems, there is a steady stream of painful and, more times than not, unsuccessful attempts at implementations. The strategy used for the implementation along with the ancillary decisions as to what implementation accelerators to use and which, if any, third-party applications to select all factor into the overall approach. There are several areas that positively increase the chances of implementation success.

First and foremost, it is critical to have solid top management commitment. ERP implementations typically address fundamental business operations. If senior management is not committed to the project, it will eventually lose backing and fail.

Given the complexities of ERP implementations, it is also important to have strong and experienced program management. Program management is the glue that keeps the project together and provides leadership. If the project does not have a strong leader, it can flounder and not achieve goals within the boundaries of scope, schedule, and cost. Along with experienced program management, it is important to have experienced ERP consultants. By using people who have previously implemented the technology, the project leverages the knowledge gained and starts further up the learning curve.

TABLE 4-4 Summary of Roles for ERP Implementation

Project Role Title	Role Definition
Owners	The owners will consist of senior management in the company. The chair is empowered to make decisions when the owners cannot reach consensus. The owners determine overall policy, budget, and scope of the project. The owners meet when needed at the call of the chair.
Project Executive	The project executive oversees project activities, provides broad project oversight, resolves policy level issues, and ensures that the project stays within scope. The project executive also builds consensus on business process changes that impact the business and provides project status updates (as needed) to the owners. The project executive works with the application steward and project manager(s) to establish overall project direction, review and evaluate project progress, and ensure appropriate user involvement for the duration of the project.
Project Manager(s)	The project manager manages the day-to-day aspects of the project, ensures that the project plan is being followed, and keeps both team members and the project executive aware of the status of the project. This responsibility includes overall management of the project to ensure that all tasks are completed on a timely basis, in a quality fashion, and in accordance with the approved project plan. The project manager serves as the primary liaison between the project team and project executive.
Functional Module Leads	The module leads provide leadership and overall direction for the implementation at the module level, ensuring the quality of deliverables and adherence to the project plan and milestones.
Technical Infrastructure Team Lead	The technical infrastructure lead is responsible for overall technical infrastructure implementation including organizing and directing the efforts of the team, coordinating technical team meetings, and reporting on progress to project executive and project manager(s). The technical infrastructure lead must understand all of the technologies well enough to ensure that there will be no "gaps" in the solution and that all of the technologies will be integrated.
Development Lead	The development lead is responsible for managing the development team in the design and implementation of all modifications including reports, interfaces, online changes, and batch programs.
Change Management Lead	The change management lead coordinates the overall change management effort, including training, communication, and campus readiness activities. The change management lead is responsible for developing strategies and detailed work plans, monitoring progress, and resolving change management issues.
Conversion Lead	The conversion lead coordinates the overall conversion effort. The conversion lead is responsible for developing strategies and detailed work plans, monitoring progress, and resolving issues.

TABLE 4-4   Continued

Project Role Title	Role Definition
Reporting Lead	The reporting lead coordinates the overall reporting effort. The reporting lead is responsible for developing strategies and detailed work plans, monitoring progress, and resolving issues.
System Test Lead	The system test lead coordinates the overall system testing effort. The system test lead is responsible for developing strategies and detailed work plans, monitoring progress, and resolving issues.
Module Team Members	Module team members are responsible for analyzing requirements and converting them into solutions. Module team members provide direction and application knowledge with respect to business process design, configuration, testing, training, and implementation. Module team members are composed of the functional and technical resources from the project and campuses and report to the module leads.
Technical Infrastructure Team Members	The technical infrastructure team members are responsible for supporting the module teams throughout the design and implementation of the ERP software. The technical infrastructure team members are responsible for designing and building the necessary architecture components to supplement the delivered ERP technical solution.
Development Team Members	Development team members are responsible for developing the designed solutions necessary to meet business requirements. Development team members provide direction and ERP technical knowledge to the client team with development of modifications and interfaces.
Change Management Team Members	Change management team members are responsible for completing the tasks related to the training development and delivery.
Conversion Team Members	Conversion team members are responsible for designing and developing conversion programs (temporary and permanent) necessary to convert the legacy system data into the ERP database.
Reporting Team Members	Reporting team members are responsible for designing and developing the reports needed to support the system.
System Test Team Members	System test team members are responsible for completing the tasks related to system test effort.
Subject Matter Experts (SMEs)	Subject matter experts are responsible for ensuring that business-specific requirements are addressed in the design, built, and the system is tested. SMEs provide coordination and facilitation of communications between the project team and the organization. SMEs coordinate and prioritize functional requirements. SMEs provide leadership and functional expertise in support of the implementation with specific knowledge in one or more business processes.
Project Administrative Support	Project administrative support is responsible for providing administrative to the project.

In order to reduce the chances of unexpected and unpleasant surprises, it is a good heuristic to minimize the type and number of customizations that are implemented. Any change is a chance for unexpected and unwelcome surprises and increases the chance of risks becoming reality. It is also important to empower team members. The more each member of the team can do, the greater the amount of work that is performed. As part of empowerment, however, it is important to keep a focus on processes to ensure that the right activities are occurring, the right groups are involved, and a methodology is being followed.

Along with the actual implementation, it is critical to emphasize training and change management. The implementation is not successful if the system is not used to its fullest extent. It is also important to have significant and strong post-implementation support. The job is not done once the system goes live. ERP applications, when updated and upgraded regularly, can last for a long time and provide enormous benefits and returns for the entire organization. Finally, effective and frequent communication will keep everyone on the same page and give the greatest chance of issues and problems being identified early, one hopes, along with preventing problems before they are allowed to affect the project.

Summary

- This chapter reviews the systems development life cycle—both traditional and alternative approaches—and points out the benefits and limitations of the traditional and the newer approaches. Reviewing the five phases of the SDLC approach (i.e., investigation, analysis, design, implementation, and maintenance) provides the necessary background to understand the ERP life cycle methodologies and see why the SDLC approaches cannot be used without changes for ERP implementation.

- The ERP life cycle has variations from the SDLC process due to various reasons; however, the key reason is that organizations buy ERP as prepackaged software and then have to customize them as well as change their company's business processes to implement these systems. Because ERP systems are complex systems that impact a large number of users in the organization, the implementation team will need a proper installation and change management plan.

- One of the first steps is choosing an appropriate implementation strategy. There are three routes for the company: comprehensive, vanilla, or middle-of-the-road strategy.

- Comprehensive will take longer and require more resources as opposed to vanilla, which can be quick but may or may not help improve the company's operations. Most organizations may choose a middle-of-the-road strategy because it will allow them to maximize their returns on the ERP investment.

- There are various ERP methodologies. In addition to the traditional ERP implementation life cycle there are rapid implementation methodologies developed by ERP consulting firms. These are Total Solution, FastTrack, Rapid-Re, ASAP, BIM, and others. These implementation methodologies are similar, in the sense that they allow you to choose from among the implementation strategies discussed earlier, with the differences coming primarily in the staging of the process steps and formality of structure.

- Consultants play an important role in rapid implementation of ERP systems. Rapid or accelerated implementation approaches are very popular and require the use of experienced consultants to leverage the knowledge of techniques that have worked well with other organizations. Scripts and wizards developed by consulting firms can help to automate some of the more common tasks that occur during an implementation. These include migration of data, identification of duplicate data, and other standard tasks.

- Because of their prepackaged nature, ERP applications generally do not require the rigorous traditional SDLC process. The emphasis on the ERP life cycle is whether to customize the software or to change the organization's processes to match those embedded in the software. Change management strategy therefore plays a very important role in the ERP life cycle.
- ERPs are becoming more and more ubiquitous in the business landscape as they become critical to the long-term positioning and success of today's businesses. Management should not take a hands-off

approach and leave the implementation entirely in the hands of the IT staff. ERP software is mission critical, has a major impact on the organization business processes, and impacts a lot of people in the organization. They also cost a lot of money during the implementation period while their returns are spread over a long period of time.

- The sense of team and teamwork is paramount to the project. It is the role of the project management office to address teamwork initially and throughout the project.
- It is important that each person on the project understands his or her role and responsibility. By doing this, it helps to create teamwork and makes individuals and the project organization accountable to the project and the project's success.

Exercises

1. Search the Internet for any new (2006 and beyond) ERP implementation methodologies. Provide the overview of the consulting firm, the details of the methodology, and case studies of the use of this methodology. Provide URLs, references, and an e-copy of the articles used for this project.
2. Locate a company that you know (or work at) and contact the ERP team project manager and some members.

   a. Find out what ERP life cycle approach they used in their ERP project.
   b. Find out what were the benefits and drawbacks of this approach.
   c. Would they recommend their ERP implementation approach to others?

Write a one-page summary and include diagrams/figures of the methodology in the appendix.

Review Questions

1. What is the role of the systems approach in the SDLC?
2. Briefly discuss the key phases of the SDLC methodology.
3. Discuss the alternate approaches of SDLC and the benefits of these alternatives.
4. Compare and contrast the three major ERP implementation categories.
5. What is ERP implementation methodology? Give examples.
6. List the major tasks in the scope and commitment phase of the ERP life cycle.
7. List the major tasks in the analysis and design phase of the ERP life cycle.
8. List the major tasks in the acquisition and development phase of the ERP life cycle.
9. What is the role of change management in the ERP life cycle?
10. List the major differences between the ERP life cycle and SDLC.

Discussion Questions

1. Is a surety bond an effective means to establish true accountability for IT implementation, as presented in the Jackson Lab case?
2. Was the phased implementation a good approach for an organization like Jackson Lab that deploys an ERP solution for the first time? Would it allow focus on a critical area, stabilization of the system usage, and quicker visible benefits?
3. What do you think about the modifications in a unique business process at the Jackson Lab (e.g., raising and distributing the mice)?
4. Discuss the risks and benefits of going for a big bang conversion versus using the phased or parallel approaches.

5. How should organizations approach the change management strategy to manage their people problems that usually cause many mishaps and are the main reason of failure in ERP implementation projects?
6. Pick any two rapid implementation methodologies of ERP. Discuss the benefits and limitations of each in a table format.
7. What do you think should be the role of consultants in the ERP life cycle? Explain.
8. Discuss why top management support and involvement is important for the ERP life cycle.

CASE 4-2
Real-World Case
Two Short Cases: OilCO & ExploreCO

Source: Based on article by Parr, A., and Shanks, G. (2000). A Model of ERP Project Implementation. *Journal of Information Technology*, 15, 289–303.

The first company, OilCO, is a refiner and marketer of a broad range of petroleum products in Australia and 11 countries in the Pacific. As one of Australia's major industrial companies, OilCO directly employs more than 2,000 people and owns assets valued at approximately $2 billion. OilCO is the Australian subsidiary of one of the world's largest multinational oil companies. It has a nationwide network of 1,800 locations, is one of the four major oil companies in Australia, and enjoys a substantial market share. When the global oil industry underwent significant restructuring and increasing competition, OilCO decided to implement a new system to achieve full process integration and automation, improve customer service, and facilitate planned business restructuring. To meet these complex business requirements the company selected a mainframe-based ERP solution. With 1,600 users in Australia, New Zealand, and the Pacific Islands, this ERP system became one of the largest and most complex mainframe implementations in the world. It processed 25,000–35,000 transactions per hour and handled more than 1,000 orders per day across the country.

The implementation of the system at OilCO involved major change to the company's business processes, so they matched the ERP's processing methods. Even though they recognized that some existing business process changes were necessary, OilCO aimed to maximize the integration benefits of the ERP while simultaneously streamlining the company's existing processes. The implementation also involved the development of an oil industry–specific module. The ERP (referred to here as ERP-1) implementation resulted in substantial business benefits for OilCO. They included better sales forecasting, fully automated ordering and delivery processes, real-time financial data, improved data quality, and streamlined business processes. Like any other ERP project, however, ERP-1 went significantly over budget and over time.

The second company, ExploreCO, is an oil and gas exploration and production company in southwest Australia. ExploreCO is an affiliate of OilCO. The company is involved in offshore gas and oil exploration and production. When OilCO acquired another oil exploration company that had an operational resource system it became the ExploreCO operational system; however, there was substantial dissatisfaction with this system within the ExploreCO system. ExploreCO had to decide either to rework and upgrade the existing system or to replace it. They chose a new system and conducted a feasibility analysis of several ERP systems. For budgetary reasons and, because it suited their exploration business, they decided to implement an ERP system (referred to here as ERP-2). The budget and project scope were considerably more modest than the OilCO implementation, so they planned to implement and "Go Live" with the system in 11 months.

Documentation on the existing system indicated that an understanding of the requirements was already advanced, but they took the opportunity to renew and reengineer the system, particularly given the level of dissatisfaction with the old system. Moreover, they needed to align the new system (ERP-2) with OilCO's existing ERP (ERP-1). The implementation project was driven by OilCO's head office, which performed cost analysis, set the scope, made recommendations, and provided leadership on the steering committee. System goals were set via performance indicators. For example, the indicators included the number of check runs in a given period, a measured reduction in off-system payments, and a reduction in suppliers from 6,000 to 600. Given the lessons learned in the OilCO implementation, the steering committee insisted that the best people be released full time for the life of the project and a "project champion" (that was the official title) placed on the steering committee.

The project was completed on time and on budget and was described by the highly experienced project manager as the "easiest implementation" he had "ever been involved in" (from an interview with the project manager in December, 1999). The business benefits of the ERP-2 system were significant. These include (1) a measured reduction in manual processes, manual transactions, and the number of suppliers, which has led to improved procurement and inventory systems; (2) streamlined, real-time accounting systems; (3) a reengineering of processes that involved a devolution of responsibility back into the hands of the operators; and (4) improved time accounting (to 15-minute intervals). This last benefit has been particularly important since this company had many joint ventures. The critical success factors (CSFs; Table 4-5), identified in ERP-1, were used to augment the second project.

Tabular summary of the importance of each CSF is then presented in Tables 4-6 and 4-7. Table 4-6 represents the OilCO case study findings and Table 4-7 the ExploreCO findings. The tables show the CSFs in a particular phase. The number of *dots* in each cell represents the strength of the participants' consensus that that particular CSF was necessary in that phase. *Four dots* indicate that the particular CSF was considered to be of major importance in that phase of the PPM. *Three dots* indicate that the CSFs were considered very important. *Two dots* indicate that the CSFs were considered important. *One dot* indicates that the CSFs were considered to be of minor importance. *No dots* indicates that the CSFs were considered to be unimportant. We have not included "smaller scope" as a CSF in Table 4-7 because one implementation was clearly large in scope and the other smaller in scope.

TABLE 4-5   CSFs for ERP Implementation

Critical Success Factors	Description
Management Support	Top management advocacy, provision of adequate resources, and commitment to project
Release of Full-Time Subject Matter Experts (SME)	Release full time on to the project of relevant business experts who provide assistance to the project
Empowered Decision Makers	The members of the project team(s) must be empowered to make quick decisions
Deliverable Dates	At planning stage, set realistic milestones and end date
Champion	Advocate for system who is unswerving in promoting the benefits of the new system
Vanilla ERP	Minimal customization and uncomplicated option selection
Smaller Scope	Fewer modules and less functionality implemented, smaller user group, and fewer site(s)
Definition of Scope and Goals	The steering committee determines the scope and objectives of the project in advance and then adheres to it
Balanced Team	Right mix of business analysts, technical experts, and users from within the implementation company and consultants from external companies
Commitment to Change	Perseverance and determination in the face of inevitable problems with implementation

TABLE 4-6   OilCO—ERP Implementation Incorporating CSFs

	Phase Project					
Factor	Planning	Setup	Reengineering	Design	Configuration Installation and Testing	Enhancement
Management Support	∙ ∙ ∙					
Champion						
Balanced Team	∙ ∙ ∙					
Commitment to Change	∙ ∙ ∙					
Vanilla ERP						
Empowered Decision Makers						
Best People Full Time						
Deliverable Dates	∙	∙		∙		
Definition of Scope and Goals	∙	∙		∙		

TABLE 4-7	ExploreCO—ERP Implementation Incorporating CSFs					
	Phase Project					
Factor	Planning	Setup	Reengineering	Design	Configuration Installation and Testing	Enhancement
Management Support	. . .	. .	. . .	. . .	. . .	. .
Champion	. . .			.	.	.
Balanced Team		. .	. . .	. .		.
Commitment to Change	. . .	.			.	
Vanilla ERP	. . .					
Empowered Decision makers	.		. . .		.	
Best People Full Time	. . .	.			.	
Deliverable Dates	. . .			.		.
Definition of Scope and Goals	. . .	. .		.		. .

Even when both companies identified what appeared to be the same CSF, they differed in that ExploreCO devised a process and structures in order to facilitate its achievement. The starkest example of this concerns their recognition that a project champion was crucial. In ExploreCO the champion was actually known by that title, was allocated to the project for its duration, had defined responsibilities, and, most importantly, was a member of the board (called the leadership council) of the company. This level of seniority, plus the daily hands-on approach, proved to be invaluable. In contrast, in OilCO this person was not officially recognized and the person in the role changed over time. The drive for the system initially came from a U.S. managing director who promoted the ERP as a global strategy. The venture manager (brought in from the United Kingdom) subsequently became the de facto champion, and there later was an in-house senior ERP "convert." There was no defined role, nor were there processes or structures via which his influence could be conveyed.

There is considerable variation in the pattern of CSFs between the two companies. Both companies adopted a policy of minimal customization and deliverable dates; however, OilCO was forced to commission an oil industry–specific module, and they generated endless reports because it was often possible rather than desirable (according to the project manager). These changes were accompanied by extensive company restructuring, and it is unclear which of these caused them to go years beyond their projected end date. ExploreCO adhered to the principles of minimal customization and deliverable dates until their project was well advanced in the configuration and testing phase, when it became clear that the interfaces were unacceptable to the users, at which time they brought in Lotus Notes and wrote the necessary interfaces. This meant they ran two weeks past their "rock-solid end date."

CASE QUESTIONS

1. Compare and contrast the implementation of OilCO and ExploreCO. What were the similarities and differences between the two implementations?
2. Why do you think the projects were successful? Was it the articulation of CSFs? Was it their strategy of minimal customization? Or something else? Explain.
3. What can we learn from this case? Also, provide suggestions for improvement.

APPENDIX A

DETAILED DESCRIPTIONS OF ERP ROLES AND RESPONSIBILITIES

Project Role/Title	Owners
Role Definition	The owners will consist of senior management in the company. The chair is empowered to make decisions when the owners cannot reach consensus. The owners determine overall policy, budget, and scope of the project. The owners meet when needed at the call of the chair.
Responsibilities	• Approve major scope changes.
	• Provide funding to complete the project.
	• Maintain financial integrity of the project.
	• Review project financials on a quarterly basis or as requested with the project executive.
	• Provide strategic policy and procedure direction.
	• Monitor project progress against milestones and timeline.
	• Commit appropriate resources to the project, reassigning resources when necessary.
	• Publicly demonstrate support and commitment to the project.
	• Provide final resolution on key project issues.
Skills	• Executive level management and communication skills.
	• Thorough knowledge of the organization.
Reports To	Owners

Project Role/Title	Project Executive
Role Definition	The project executive oversees project activities, provides broad project oversight, resolves policy level issues, and ensures that the project stays within scope. The project executive also builds consensus on business process changes that impact the business and provides project status updates (as needed) to the owners. The project executive works with the application steward and project manager(s) to establish overall project direction, review and evaluate project progress, and ensure appropriate user involvement for the duration of the project.
Responsibilities	• Resolve project issues escalated by project manager(s).
	• Ensure that project goals and scope stay aligned with the project objectives. Make recommendations to the owners regarding any major scope changes.
	• Review, approve, and consolidate project work plans, staffing plans, project milestones, and transition plans.
	• Monitor project financials and timeline.
	• Ensure that an appropriate process is used for issue identification and resolution.
	• Ensure project meets key campus expectations.
	• Provide expectations and performance feedback to project manager(s).
	• Publicly demonstrate support and commitment to the project.
	• Confirm project roles, responsibilities, and reporting relationships.
	• Approve all project resources.
	• Work with project manager(s) and implementation partner staff to ensure that knowledge transfer to personnel is facilitated.
	• Review and approve training approach and strategy.
	• Review and approve testing approach and strategy.
	• Participate in all hardware and software selections and contracts with vendors related to the implementation.
	• Communicate project status and other critical communication messages to the team and owners.
Skills	• Excellent project management skills.
	• Excellent leadership skills. Ability to keep a large team focused on the objectives.
	• Issue resolution skills. Ability to obtain resolution by team consensus when differences in business processes are discussed.
	• Excellent communication and negotiation skills. Ability to keep a wide audience informed of goals, expectations, progress, and issues.
	• Solid knowledge of large-scale system implementations.
	• Thorough knowledge of the company organization.
Reports To	Owners

Project Role/Title	Project Manager(s)
Role Definition	The project manager manages the day-to-day aspects of the project, ensures that the project plan is being followed, and keeps both team members and the project executive aware of the status of the project. This responsibility includes overall management of the project to ensure that all tasks are completed on a timely basis, in a quality fashion, and in accordance with the approved project plan. The project manager serves as the primary liaison between the project team and project executive.
Responsibilities	• Establish project planning guidelines and methodology.
	• Developing project objectives, scope, policies, procedures, milestones, schedules, and budget. Work with project executive to report progress and status against project plan to the team, company, and owners.
	• Work directly with the project executive in defining and establishing an organizational and governance structure that is effective and efficient.
	• Confirm project roles, responsibilities, and reporting relationships; communicate them to project team members.
	• Determine resource needs meet project expectations. Determine appropriate mix of resources.
	• Work with consultants to facilitate knowledge transfer to company personnel.
	• Manage resources deployed to ongoing production operations.
	• Review and approve training plans: formal ERP training and internal user training.
	• Monitor the completion of performance evaluations for each staff member assigned to the project.
	• Identify and incorporate best practices into new system and business processes.
	• Define and enforce standards for deliverables. Ensure deliverables are completed on time and within budget.
	• Manage the change control process used to inform, document, and elevate changes to project scope.
	• Manage the issue resolution process. Work to expedite issue resolution, ensuring a minimum loss of development time due to conflicts. Address issues that cannot be resolved by module leads.
	• Coordinate the decision-making process. Ensure appropriate parties are involved and make timely and informed decisions.
	• Review and approve the development of test plans and test scenarios: application/unit test, integrated test, performance/stress test, Go-live, readiness.
	• Coordinate Go-live planning and execution of readiness plan. Prepare implementation/rollout plan.
	• Recommend and facilitate space assignments and allocations.
	• Determine necessary audit requirements.
Skills	• Excellent project management skills.
	• Excellent leadership skills. Ability to keep a large team focused on the objectives.

Project Role/Title	**Project Manager(s)**
	• Issue resolution skills. Ability to obtain resolution by team consensus when differences in business processes are discussed.
	• Excellent communication skills. Ability to keep a wide audience informed of goals, expectations, progress, and issues.
	• Solid knowledge of large-scale system implementations.
	• Solid understanding of technical processes and relevant business processes.
	• Solid technical expertise.
	• Thorough understanding of company and ERP applications.
	• ERP implementation experience preferred.
Reports To	Project executive

Project Role/Title	**Functional Module Leads**
Role Definition	The module leads provide leadership and overall direction for the implementation at the module level, ensuring the quality of deliverables and adherence to the project plan and milestones.
Responsibilities	• Communicate the objectives, scope, policies, procedures, status, and project issues clearly to the module team.
	• Develop and manage module work plans. Prepare status reports documenting progress against plan.
	• Assist the business in controlling project scope and minimizing customizations to the software. Help to determine acceptable workarounds, and use the software as delivered.
	• Elevate project risks and scope issues to the project manager(s).
	• Ensure that the deliverables created by the module team provide quality, add value, and contribute to the project's success. Implement and enforce standards for deliverables.
	• Ensure that all project-related activities are thoroughly documented.
	• Identify staffing requirements at the module level. Communicate requirements to project manager(s).
	• Request the necessary resources (e.g., equipment and facilities) to support the module team.
	• Supervise and control the activities of their teams. Assign tasks to team members.
	• Mentor and coach project team members.
	• Provide performance feedback to team members.
	• Collaborate with change management team to provide information and timing for training materials, communications, and other change management efforts.

(Continued)

Project Role/Title	**Functional Module Leads**
	• Collaborate with the help desk to identify and resolve issues.
	• Participate in or develop designs, or do both, for conversion, interfaces, reports, and modifications, and ensure that these are implemented as planned.
	• Manage development of configuration and business procedures.
	• Coordinate batch job scheduling with operations and system users and monitor job execution.
	• Provide security administration including request processing, authorization, and maintenance of user security levels. Lead the development of a system security matrix.
	• Develop test plans and scenarios ensuring that all aspects of the module are fully tested: application/unit test, integrated test, performance or stress test, software upgrades, and releases. Execute tests.
	• Develop and document implementation or rollout plans at the module level.
	• Provide module support including problem analysis and resolution, on-call support, and end-user support.
Skills	• Excellent project management skills.
	• Excellent leadership skills. Ability to keep a large team focused on the objectives.
	• Issue resolution skills. Ability to obtain resolution by team consensus when differences in business processes are discussed.
	• Excellent communication skills. Ability to keep a wide audience informed of goals, expectations, progress, and issues.
	• Solid knowledge of large-scale system implementations.
	• Solid understanding of technical processes and relevant business processes.
	• Solid technical expertise.
	• Knowledge of all aspects of the system development life cycle.
	• Thorough understanding of business and ERP applications.
	• ERP implementation experience preferred.
Reports To	Project manager(s)

Project Role/Title	**Technical Infrastructure Team Lead**
Role Definition	The technical infrastructure lead is responsible for overall technical infrastructure implementation including organizing and directing the efforts of the team, coordinating technical team meetings, and reporting on progress to project executive and project manager(s). The technical infrastructure lead must understand all of the technologies well enough to ensure that there will be no "gaps" in the solution and that all of the technologies will be integrated.

Project Role/Title	**Technical Infrastructure Team Lead**
Responsibilities	• Responsible for supervising the design and implementation of the technical architecture.
	• Design and implement a stable and secure development, test, and production environment.
	• Manage technical project work plan, schedule, resources, budget, issues, expectations, and external forces.
	• Develop a comprehensive technology vision that is compatible with the overall goals of the information technology plans and the needs of the functional units.
	• Ensure the functional teams are appropriately supported (in terms of both people and hardware and software).
	• Manage the technical resources and develop the technical organizational structure. Define internal and consulting resource requirements.
	• Ensure tech team staff possess, or develop, the right skills for maintaining the system throughout the project and beyond.
	• Establish standards and standard procedures for such technical areas as software customization and development, application maintenance and administration, security administration, technical documentation, and system and database administration. Communicate standards to the project team.
	• Schedule rollout activities and coordinate work with appropriate operations teams and other tech personnel (e.g., connectivity, hardware and equipment installation).
	• Communicate with campus department or unit technical staff about support requirements and changes to their technical environment.
	• Report technical status and issues to the project executive and project manager(s).
Skills	• Excellent project management skills.
	• Thorough knowledge of the organization's technical infrastructure and policies.
	• Solid knowledge of trends in technology and the ability to apply the knowledge to the business objectives.
	• Excellent negotiating and communication skills.
	• Solid understanding of technical processes and relevant business processes.
	• Knowledge of all aspects of the system development life cycle.
	• Strong leadership skills.
	• Issue resolution skills. Ability to obtain resolution by team consensus when differences in business processes are discussed.
	• Solid experience in large-scale systems implementations.
	• Thorough understanding of the business organization.
	• ERP implementation experience preferred.
Reports To	Project manager(s)

Project Role/Title	**Development Lead**
Role Definition	The development lead is responsible for managing the development team in the design and implementation of all modifications, including reports, interfaces, online changes, and batch programs.
Responsibilities	• Manage development project schedule, resources, budget, issues, and expectations.
	• Supervise the development effort for all modifications.
	• Responsible for documenting and ensuring that all development and coding standards are followed.
	• Perform all design, code, and unit test reviews with each programmer for all modifications. Sign off on all modifications.
	• Analyze the development impact to other ERP modules, related tables or views and panels or panel groups.
	• Analyze the development impact to fixes and subsequent system upgrades.
	• Establish standards for development code.
	• Utilize existing development and version control procedures.
	• Estimate development work efforts.
	• Provide expertise and leadership to the various development teams.
	• Lead effort to develop module interface program specifications: interfaces to or from other ERP modules and interfaces to or from legacy systems.
Skills	• Excellent project management skills.
	• Excellent negotiating and communication skills.
	• Solid understanding of technical processes and relevant business processes.
	• Knowledge of all aspects of the system development life cycle.
	• Strong leadership skills.
	• Issue resolution skills. Ability to obtain resolution by team consensus when differences in business processes are discussed.
	• Solid experience in large-scale systems implementations.
	• Thorough understanding of the business organization.
	• Experience with EDI and real-time or batch interface development.
	• Strong technical development skills.
	• ERP implementation experience preferred.
Reports To	Project manager(s)

Project Role/Title	**Change Management Lead**
Role Definition	The change management lead coordinates the overall change management effort, including training, communication, and campus readiness activities. The change management lead is responsible for developing strategies and detailed work plans, monitoring progress, and resolving change management issues.
Responsibilities	• Manage overall change management effort including training design. • Manage work plans and budgets for overall change management effort. • Work with project manager(s) and module leads to identify appropriate training and organizational readiness initiatives for their areas. • Coordinate strategies for communication, campus readiness, and training development or delivery. • Work with project executive and project manager(s) to resolve issues and confirm direction and support for training and organizational readiness activities. • Review training materials for quality, consistency, and adherence to standards. • Oversee documentation management. • Serve as "change agent" to actively endorse and support changes at all levels of the organization. • Promote cross-team and cross-functional collaboration and knowledge sharing. • Coordinate the training database development and testing process. • Ensure training rooms are operational, stocked, staffed, and monitored. • Track evaluation results from training and user support activities and funnel the results back into continuous improvement efforts. • Plan for transition activities from the implementation project to an ongoing training program.
Skills	• Excellent project management skills. • Excellent negotiating and communication skills. • Strong leadership skills. Ability to lead cross-functional, multicampus efforts. • Issue resolution skills. Ability to obtain resolution by team consensus when differences in business processes are discussed. • Solid experience in large-scale systems implementations. • Thorough understanding of the business organization. • Excellent written and verbal skills. • Solid and current understanding of training methods and trends. • Experience managing a large training effort across multiple sites. • Experience delivering training. • ERP implementation experience preferred.
Reports To	Project manager(s)

Project Role/Title	Conversion Lead
Role Definition	The conversion lead coordinates the overall conversion effort. The conversion lead is responsible for developing strategies and detailed work plans, monitoring progress, and resolving issues.
Responsibilities	• Provide expertise and leadership to the team regarding data mapping specifications (e.g., tools, formats, default values, fillers). • Work with development lead to ensure program code, new tables, panel modifications, and the like are added to the system. • Work with each campus to determine unique conversion requirements. • Manage conversion project schedule, resources, budget, issues, and expectations. • Supervise the conversion development effort for all modifications. • Responsible for documenting and ensuring that all development and coding standards are followed. • Perform all design, code, and unit test reviews with each programmer for all modifications. Sign off on all modifications. • Estimate conversion work efforts. • Provide expertise and leadership to conversion team.
Skills	• Excellent project management skills. • Excellent negotiating and communication skills. • Solid understanding of technical processes and relevant business processes. • Knowledge of all aspects of the system development life cycle. • Strong leadership skills. • Issue resolution skills. Ability to obtain resolution by team consensus when differences in business processes are discussed. • Solid experience in large-scale systems implementations. • Thorough understanding of the business organization. • Solid understanding of business legacy systems. • Solid understanding of data management, data conversion, and mapping. • Strong programming skills. • ERP implementation experience preferred.
Reports To	Project manager(s)

Project Role/Title	**Reporting Lead**
Role Definition	The reporting lead coordinates the overall reporting effort. The reporting lead is responsible for developing strategies and detailed work plans, monitoring progress, and resolving issues.
Responsibilities	• Lead effort to prepare report inventory. Development module reporting specification. Determine best approach for reporting (e.g., delivered, custom, query). • Integrate efforts of all reporting teams (across modules). • Analyze the impact of application changes on the reporting infrastructure. • Work with each campus to determine unique reporting requirements. • Help determine reporting architecture and report distribution process. • Manage reporting project schedule, resources, budget, issues, and expectations. • Supervise the reporting effort. • Responsible for documenting and ensuring that all development and coding standards are followed. • Perform all design, code, and unit test reviews with each programmer for all modifications. Sign off on all modifications. • Estimate work efforts. • Provide expertise and leadership to the reporting team.
Skills	• Excellent project management skills. • Excellent negotiating and communication skills. • Solid understanding of technical processes and relevant business processes. • Knowledge of all aspects of the system development life cycle. • Strong leadership skills. • Issue resolution skills. Ability to obtain resolution by team consensus when differences in business processes are discussed. • Solid experience in large-scale systems implementations. • Thorough understanding of the business organization. • Experience with reporting tools (e.g., SQL, SQR, Query/Crystal). • Strong programming skills. • ERP implementation experience preferred.
Reports To	Project manager(s)

Project Role/Title	**System Test Lead**
Role Definition	The system test lead coordinates the overall system testing effort. The system test lead is responsible for developing strategies and detailed work plans, monitoring progress, and resolving issues.
Responsibilities	• Manage system test schedule, resources, budget, issues, and expectations. • Develop and maintain test approach. • Plan and conduct kick-off information meeting for entire project team regarding testing phase. • Coordinate test planning activities. • Manage test effort. • Manage issues. • Coordinate testing-related change control process. • Coordinate internal or external dependencies. • Coordinate sign-off activities with users. • Conduct status and planning meetings with team members. • Coordinate adjustments to test approach with appropriate personnel. • Measure and monitor progress to ensure testing and validation are completed on time and within budget and meet project and quality standards. • Ensure results meet entry and exit criteria. • Provide expertise and leadership to the system test team.
Skills	• Excellent project management skills. • Excellent negotiating and communication skills. • Solid understanding of technical processes and relevant business processes. • Knowledge of all aspects of the system development life cycle. • Strong leadership skills. • Issue resolution skills. Ability to obtain resolution by team consensus when differences in business processes are discussed. • Solid system test experience in large-scale systems implementations. • Thorough understanding of the business organization. • ERP implementation experience preferred.
Reports To	Project manager(s)

Project Role/Title	**Module Team Members**
Role Definition	Module team members are responsible for analyzing requirements and converting them into solutions. Module team members provide direction and application knowledge with respect to business process design, configuration, testing, training, and implementation. Module team members are composed of the functional and technical resources from the project and campuses and report to the module leads.

Project Role/Title	Module Team Members
Responsibilities	• Employ a deep understanding of functional business policies, processes, and procedures.
	• Review, test, and understand delivered ERP capabilities.
	• Create business procedures and process flows and descriptions, based upon ERP system.
	• Work with functional areas to translate business needs into software solutions. Provide alternative solutions and recommendations to complex problems and issues allowing the teams to decide on the best approach. Provide estimates (effort and time) to implement enhancements.
	• Identify, document, and prioritize potential modifications.
	• Create, review, and revise functional software designs.
	• Define and document configuration tables.
	• Lead effort to manage module interface program specifications: interfaces to and from other application modules and interfaces to and from legacy systems.
	• Lead effort to manage report inventory. Determine module-level reporting specifications. Determine best approach for reporting (i.e., delivered, custom, query).
	• Provide functional data conversion information to conversion team.
	• Lead effort to develop testing plans and scenarios ensuring that all aspects of the module are fully tested: application and unit test, integrated test, and performance and stress test. Execute test plans.
	• Define, establish, and test security profiles.
	• Identify and plan activities needed to complete task assignments.
	• Troubleshoot and resolve functional issues.
	• Provide status updates to the module lead.
	• Provide ERP functional knowledge and expertise to team.
Skills	• Thorough knowledge of systems functionality and navigation.
	• Solid understanding of technical processes and relevant business processes.
	• Team leadership skills. Ability to work effectively across university campuses.
	• Issue resolution skills. Ability to obtain resolution by team consensus when differences in business processes are discussed.
	• Excellent communication skills.
	• Experience in all phases of the project life cycle: design, prototype, construction, and deployment.
	• Solid understanding of the business organization and infrastructure.
	• ERP implementation experience preferred.
Reports To	Module lead

Project Role/Title	Technical Infrastructure Team Members
Role Definition	The technical infrastructure team members are responsible for supporting the module teams throughout the design and implementation of the ERP software. The technical infrastructure team members are responsible for designing and building the necessary architecture components to supplement the delivered ERP technical solution.
Responsibilities	• Install, configure, and support ERP application software required to support module teams, including application of patches and fixes and migration of modifications.
	• Install, configure, and support peripheral products required, including report distribution, security, and batch scheduler.
	• Conduct performance tuning for identified online and batch transactions.
	• Design, build, and test the technical architecture (i.e., development, execution, and operations architectures).
	• Perform security administration troubleshooting.
	• Understand ERP data structures.
	• Identify and escalate technical issues to technical lead.
	• Work with developers and other appropriate resources to research and resolve technical issues.
	• Collaborate with functional analysts as needed to resolve technical issues.
	• Provide ERP technical knowledge and expertise to the team.
	• Provide status updates to technical lead.
Skills	• Solid understanding of technical processes and relevant business processes.
	• Team leadership skills. Ability to work effectively across business organizations.
	• Issue resolution skills. Ability to obtain resolution by team consensus when differences in business processes are discussed.
	• Excellent communication skills.
	• Solid understanding of the organization and infrastructure.
	• ERP implementation experience preferred.
	• SQL, SQR.
	• ERP application server architecture.
	• Windows 95/98, Windows 2000 and NT, NT scripting.
	• UNIX, UNIX scripting.
	• Knowledge of database structures.
	• Report distribution.
	• Batch controls.
Reports To	Technical infrastructure lead

Project Role/Title	**Development Team Members**
Role Definition	Development team members are responsible for developing the designed solutions necessary to meet business requirements. Development team members provide direction and ERP technical knowledge to client team with development of modifications and interfaces.
Responsibilities	• Review, test, and understand delivered ERP capabilities.
	• Understand ERP data structures.
	• Inventory current data sources.
	• Inventory current interfaces.
	• Identify and document potential interfaces.
	• Develop general and detailed designs for modifications and interfaces.
	• Receive sign-off and approval on designs.
	• Perform code modifications based on approved designs.
	• Develop and perform unit tests (i.e., test data, test scenarios, expected results).
	• Utilize knowledge of ERP tools, SQL, and other development languages and tools.
	• Utilize existing version control procedures and tools.
	• Document all customizations and modifications completely, per established standards.
	• Identify and plan activities needed to complete task assignments.
	• Work with functional analysts to understand business needs related to modifications and interfaces.
	• Identify and escalate technical issues to the technical infrastructure team.
	• Assist with production troubleshooting
	• Provide status updates to development lead.
Skills	• Solid understanding of technical processes and relevant business processes.
	• Team leadership skills. Ability to work effectively across business organization.
	• Issue resolution skills. Ability to obtain resolution by team consensus when differences in business processes are discussed.
	• Excellent communication skills.
	• Experience in all phases of the project life cycle: design, prototype, construction, and deployment.
	• Solid understanding of the business organization and infrastructure.
	• Software design and development experience.
	• Experience with interface programming.
	• ERP implementation experience preferred.
Reports To	Development lead

Project Role/Title	**Change Management Team Members**
Role Definition	Change management team members are responsible for completing the tasks related to the training development and delivery.
Responsibilities	• Review, test, and understand delivered ERP capabilities.
	• Develop performance objectives for training courses.
	• Create course descriptions for the training courses.
	• Create participant and instructor guides.
	• Populate and test training database.
	• Facilitate pilot training sessions.
	• Deliver or assist, or both, with instructor-led training.
	• Assist with training registration and tracking.
	• Develop and report on training evaluation.
	• Identify and plan activities needed to complete task assignments.
Skills	• Thorough knowledge of systems functionality and navigation.
	• Team leadership skills. Ability to work effectively across business organizations.
	• Issue resolution skills. Ability to obtain resolution by team consensus when differences in business processes are discussed.
	• Solid understanding of the business organization and infrastructure.
	• ERP implementation experience preferred.
	• Excellent written and verbal skills.
	• Solid and current understanding of training methods and trends.
	• Experience managing a large training effort across multiple sites.
	• Experience delivering training.
	• Excellent presentation skills.
	• Good rapport with people.
	• Ability to explain complex functions in a concise manner.
	• Ability to keep to the agenda.
Reports To	Change management lead

Project Role/Title	**Conversion Team Members**
Role Definition	Conversion team members are responsible for designing and developing conversion programs (temporary and permanent) necessary to convert the legacy system data into the ERP database.

Project Role/Title	Conversion Team Members
Responsibilities	• Understand ERP data structures.
	• Inventory current data sources.
	• Design and develop programs to extract data from legacy systems.
	• Design and develop load programs for loading data into ERP.
	• Receive sign-off and approval on designs.
	• Develop and perform unit tests (i.e., test data, test scenarios, expected results).
	• Utilize existing version control procedures and tools.
	• Document all customizations and modifications completely, per established standards.
	• Identify and escalate technical issues to the technical infrastructure team.
	• Support the data cleansing process.
	• Develop tools to automate the testing process.
	• Identify and plan activities needed to complete task assignments.
	• Provide status updates to conversion lead.
Skills	• Solid understanding of technical processes and relevant business processes.
	• Team leadership skills. Ability to work effectively across business organization.
	• Issue resolution skills. Ability to obtain resolution by team consensus when differences in business processes are discussed.
	• Excellent communication skills.
	• Experience in all phases of the project life cycle: design, prototype, construction, and deployment.
	• Solid understanding of the business organization and infrastructure.
	• Solid understanding of business legacy systems.
	• Solid understanding of data management, data conversion, and mapping.
	• Software design and development experience.
	• Experience with data conversion efforts.
	• ERP implementation experience preferred.
Reports To	Conversion lead

Project Role/Title	Reporting Team Members
Role Definition	Reporting team members are responsible for designing and developing the reports needed to support the system.
Responsibilities	• Review, test, and understand delivered ERP capabilities.
	• Understand ERP data structures.
	• Inventory current data sources.

(Continued)

Project Role/Title	Reporting Team Members
	• Identify and plan activities needed to complete task assignments.
	• Work with functional analysts to understand business needs related to reporting.
	• Translate business requests for information into technical report specifications. Develop new reports according to technical specifications using identified reporting tools.
	• Develop unit tests scripts (i.e., test data, test scenarios, expected results).
	• Follows all development and documentation standards and best practices as defined.
	• Identify and escalate technical issues to the technical infrastructure team.
	• Modify existing or build new summarized reporting tables as needed.
	• Modify existing or build new reporting table data refresh programs.
	• Provide status updates to reporting lead.
Skills	• Thorough knowledge of systems functionality and navigation.
	• Solid understanding of technical processes and relevant business processes.
	• Team leadership skills. Ability to work effectively across business organization.
	• Issue resolution skills. Ability to obtain resolution by team consensus when differences in business processes are discussed.
	• Excellent communication skills.
	• Experience in all phases of the project life cycle: design, prototype, construction, and deployment.
	• Solid development experience.
	• Relational database experience.
	• Experience with reporting tools.
	• Solid understanding of the business organization and infrastructure.
	• ERP implementation experience preferred.
Reports To	Reporting lead

Project Role/Title	System Test Team Members
Role Definition	System test team members are responsible for completing the tasks related to system test effort.
Responsibilities	• Review, test, and understand delivered ERP capabilities.
	• Define test conditions based on functional requirements that the testing should satisfy and group them logically into test cycles, subcycles, or cycles and subcycles.
	• Prepare test scripts based on the test conditions, cycles, subcycles, or cycles and subcycles.
	• Create test data and expected results.
	• Execute the test cycles or subcycles, or both.
	• Check the actual results against the expected results.
	• Log any unexpected results in the system investigation request (SIR) database. Analyze these unexpected results (SIRs).

Project Role/Title	**System Test Team Members**
	• Obtain sign-off of testing activities from the project manager(s).
	• Make sure that final testing components (i.e., conditions, cycles, subcycles, scripts, test data, expected results) are accurate, complete, and documented in such a way to make them repeatable and reusable.
	• Identify and plan activities needed to complete task assignments.
	• Work with functional analysts to understand business needs related to testing activities.
	• Identify and escalate technical issues to the technical infrastructure team.
	• Provide status updates to the system test lead.
Skills	• Thorough knowledge of systems functionality and navigation.
	• Solid understanding of technical processes and relevant business processes.
	• Team leadership skills. Ability to work effectively across business organizations.
	• Issue resolution skills. Ability to obtain resolution by team consensus when differences in business processes are discussed.
	• Excellent communication skills.
	• Experience in creating test scripts preferred.
	• Solid understanding of the business organization and infrastructure.
	• ERP implementation experience preferred.
Reports To	System test lead

Project Role/Title	**Subject Matter Experts (SMEs)**
Role Definition	Subject matter experts are responsible for ensuring business specific requirements are addressed in the design, build, and test of the system. SMEs provide coordination and facilitation of communications between the project team and the campus. SMEs coordinate and prioritize campus functional requirements. SMEs provide leadership and functional expertise in support of the implementation with specific knowledge in one or more business processes.
Responsibilities	• Provide expertise on functional business processes. Identify opportunities to streamline business processes to best leverage the ERP system.
	• Work with organization to translate business needs into software solutions.
	• Assist business in controlling project scope and minimizing customizations to the software. Help to determine workarounds and to use the software as delivered.
	• Participate in the conference room pilot (CRP) process and provide content and business process expertise.
	• Work on general and detailed design tasks as required.
	• Participate in the development of reporting requirements.
	• Participate in the development of conversion and interface requirements. Ensure results meet expectations.

(Continued)

Project Role/Title	**Subject Matter Experts (SMEs)**
	• Review and approve training and performance support designs and deliverables.
	• Review issue resolutions and recommend approaches.
	• Review and sign-off of functional deliverables, including configuration, procedures, and test plans.
	• Collaborate with other SMEs to develop common processes across the business organization.
	• Publicly demonstrate support and commitment to the project.
Skills	• Thorough knowledge of systems functionality and navigation (both legacy and ERP).
	• Solid understanding of relevant business processes.
	• Team leadership skills. Ability to work effectively across businesses.
	• Issue resolution skills. Ability to obtain resolution by team consensus when differences in business processes are discussed.
	• Excellent communication skills.
	• Solid understanding of the business organization and infrastructure.
Reports To	Module lead(s), campus PMT

Project Role/Title	**Project Administrative Support**
Role Definition	Project administrative support is responsible for providing administrative support to the project.
Responsibilities	• Support team with general administrative needs.
	• Procure supplies (e.g., office supplies, computer equipment) for the project team.
	• Serve as liaison with business support functions (e.g., phones, architect's office).
	• Assist in procuring space for the project team.
	• Maintain project team rosters and e-mail distribution lists.
	• Assist in taking meeting minutes as requested.
	• Provide word processing, spreadsheet, and graphics support.
	• Assist in the preparation and distribution of project documents.
	• Coordinate copy and duplication requirements.
	• Maintain ongoing files for all purchase orders and invoices related to the project.
	• Maintain a record of project team member roll-on and roll-off dates.
Skills	• Ability to handle multiple tasks simultaneously.
	• Ability to prioritize tasks.
	• Excellent organizational skills.
	• Excellent communication skills.
Reports To	Project executive, project manager(s)

APPENDIX B

BONUS REAL-WORLD CASE

Overstock.com

Overstock.com executives had to reinstate earnings for a five-and-a-half-year period, dating back to 2003. Overstock incurred accounting mistakes during that period, which led to a $12.9 million reduction in revenue and a $10.3 million increase in cumulative net loss. CEO Patrick Byrne explained the $14.2 million third-quarter loss to investors this way: "My bad." This was all due to an overly aggressive CEO and a problematic Oracle ERP rollout that started back in 2005. Overstock had previously used a homegrown system and rushed the Oracle implementation project in order to get the new system live before the fourth quarter of 2005 and the busy shopping season. "Honestly, it didn't have anything to do with Oracle per se, it was the implementation," Overstock stated. "We had consultants and we had help, but it was all driven by Overstock. We set the timelines." The problems with the rushed implementation manifested itself in strange ways. "Some things were going through okay and a lot weren't," CEO Patrick Byrne said. "It was just spraying orders. Sometimes customers might not get a ship confirm. Sometimes the order might not flow through the system. Sometimes the order got misrouted." After the restatement and delivery of the third-quarter financials, The Motley Fool financial Web site named it as one of five stocks in a tailspin.

As part of their accounting module upgrade they changed from recording refunds to customers in batches to recording them transaction by transaction. After the implementation, in the instance of some customer refunds, this reduction wasn't happening, and Overstock didn't "catch it." Overstock uses internal "reason codes" that show why various customers get refunds. Under the new system, not all reason codes were automatically recorded; some customer refunds required manual entry in the financial system. Unfortunately, Overstock missed some of the manual customer refunds and, as a result, did not record all that were occurring. Over time, this error built up and, on a cumulative basis, eventually became material. In addition, the company learned that the system failed to "reverse out" shipping revenue for cancelled orders, "and these $2.95 charges also added up over time. Overstock had been under-billing its fulfillment partners for certain costs related to product returns over the past two years, they weren't recording some customer refunds and we weren't recouping some costs from partners on some returns. The combined result was that the returns costs looked reasonable. One observer said problems like those cited by Overstock.com can happen on any ERP project without the proper care and planning." The ERP system will do what you design it to do, which is why we often say it's very important to spend time on design and mapping. As you can see by these cases, not properly preparing and setting realistic time lines can lead to a disastrous implementation. It only takes one module to be corrupt to affect the entire organization. "Our 1st Commandment is 'maintain a bullet-proof balance sheet,' but while the spirit is strong, the flesh made a mistake," Overstock.com CEO Patrick Byrne said in an October 24 letter to shareholders. "The short version is: when we upgraded our system, we didn't hook up some of the accounting wiring; however, we thought we had manual fixes in place. We've since found that these manual fixes missed a few of the unhooked wires."

QUESTIONS

1. Would a rapid SDLC approach have been a better implementation choice for Overstock? Explain.
2. Which SDLC phase(s) should not have been rushed? What phase(s) could have corrected Overstock's errors?
3. Even though this project was driven by upper management and had experienced Oracle consultants, it still failed. Where would you put the blame?
4. It seemed they used a big bang approach. Would a phased approach have been the better choice? Why?

5

Implementation Strategies

LEARNING OBJECTIVES

After reading this chapter, you should be able to:

- Acquire a greater knowledge base of ERP components and how they work together to support business.

- Learn why third-party products are needed to operationally round out ERP system functionality and the issues involved in using them.

- Appreciate the impact of an ERP implementation on platform components

such as data security, system reliability, and sustainability.

- Understand implementation approaches, the differences between vanilla (minimal or no system modifications) and chocolate (modifying the system) implementations, and the short-term and long-term impacts on the system and company.

CASE 5-1
Opening Case
Aquatech International Corporation

COMPANY OVERVIEW

Aquatech International Corporation was established in 1981 and specialized in pure water systems for the power industry. The company diversified its products in the late 1980s and developed a worldwide presence in the 1990s.

The headquarters of Aquatech is in Canonsburg, Pennsylvania, and the company has offices across the United States and all around the globe, including Canada, China, and India. Aquatech provides water treatment solutions, including design, engineering, project management, manufacturing, turnkey installations, and commissioning and field troubleshooting for several types of water treatments. With these technologies and services, Aquatech has clients in the power generation, semiconductor, petrochemical, automotive, chemical, pharmaceutical, pulp and paper, fertilizer, microelectronics, and steel industries.

The existing Aquatech information systems had begun to hinder the company's growth. Most of the company's data were on paper. As the company grew and expanded, it became a time-consuming and often a very complex process to develop strategic reports on business and personnel processes. To remedy this, the company decided to replace their legacy systems with an ERP system that would automate and integrate business processes and data to produce key management reports.

ERP IMPLEMENTATION

Aquatech chose SAP as its ERP to implement. An external consultant evaluated the different ERP systems on the market. Aquatech initially believed that SAP was not a good fit, but as the company went through the evaluation process, with help from an external consultant, they decided SAP actually was the best system for them.

The implementation took one year, and, similar to other implementations, issues were discovered as they went through the implementation process.

"We thought we'd have a really easy time because we had no legacy system," said Devesh Sharma, Aquatech's vice president of products and services. "We were wrong."

The implementation suffered from not enough skilled and dedicated resources, a lack of project sponsorship and accountability, institutional resistance, less-than-adequate communications, and a lack of clear goals. Even with these issues, the system went live and the implementation one year later was a success.

At this time, Aquatech has a regular set of reports and data on virtually every aspect of the company's operations, including manufacturing and finances. The company now makes decisions based on current information.

CONCLUSION

Even though Aquatech did a very good job in evaluating the fit of SAP, they did not assess their readiness to start the implementation. If they had evaluated their readiness, they would have understood that more buy-in from the users and senior management was needed and that they lacked overall implementation experience.

PREVIEW

ERP implementation start-up planning is all about managing risk and creating a strategy that will position a business to succeed with the implementation of an ERP. This was not the case with Aquatech. After the selection of SAP, the company immediately started the implementation without developing a strategy. A start-up process involves assessing the business environment, culture, and skills of the staff and "readiness" of the company. At this time, early in the project, open and honest assessments are critical to project planning. Self-assessment, which was not done at Aquatech, is often difficult and inaccurate, so it is not unusual for businesses to hire consulting companies to make these complex assessments. The amount of time, effort, and money spent on an ERP implementation makes one ask, "why not have an accurate assessment of a business's ability to implement an ERP successfully?"

In this chapter, you will learn about the infrastructure components that make up an ERP system. It is often said that the ERP software is the inexpensive component of an implementation. The reality is that all the other surrounding systems components and resources cost more. With any ERP implementation strategy, all the implementation components need to be identified and planned. This chapter focuses on the components and then works to address the implementation strategy. Software selection and the process of "Go-live" and operational needs are separately addressed in Chapters 6 and 7, respectively.

In addition, you will learn about the risks and impacts of an implementation on a business and what it means to implement a vanilla system. In contrast, you will also learn what it means to modify or customize a system, along with the corresponding risks and business impacts in doing so.

You will also begin to learn the importance of project governance, project management, communication, teamwork, work groups, and charters and how they are used to better ensure the project's success. A key factor in every ERP implementation is creating clear expectations and communicating those expectations to the business during the planning process.

ERP COMPONENTS

Hardware

Hardware includes all computer devices and peripherals used by an ERP system. An ERP system will specifically require a powerful set of servers for development, testing, and production environments.

The following are the key hardware resources necessary for an ERP system (Figure 5-1):

- **Servers.** ERP systems are very hardware intensive; hence, they require high-end multi-processor systems with, for now, 64-bit processing. In addition, they need several gigabytes of main memory or RAM, and several terabytes of secondary storage, which includes hard drives for data storage and system backup and recovery.
- **Clients.** People accessing ERP systems (e.g., end users, IT support staff, and developers) use personal computers (PCs) to access the ERP system. These PCs could be desktop computers, laptop computers, or personal digital assistants (PDAs). The current generation of ERP systems uses Web clients and therefore does not require more than a Web browser for clients to access the ERP system. IT support staff and developers will require secure connections (i.e., virtual private network or VPN) to access the ERP administration and development environment.

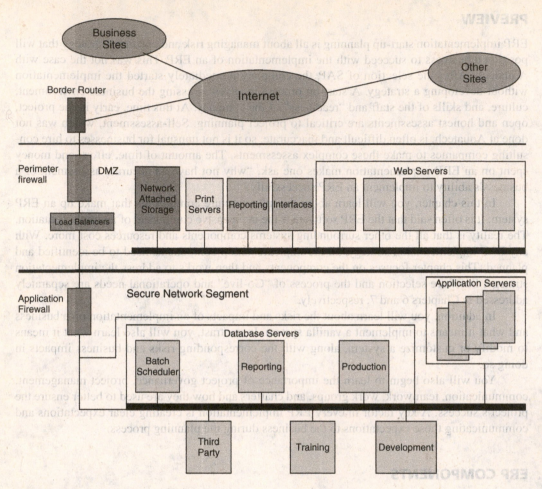

FIGURE 5-1 Typical ERP Architecture.

- *Peripherals.* ERP systems also require media for long-term archiving of all business transactions, backup and recovery RAID and/or network-attached storage devices, and the like. In addition, they will require e-mail servers, printers, backup power supply equipment, and networking hardware to support a multiuser access over the Internet.

Software

The traditional definition of software is a set of operating instructions and logic called *programs* that control and direct the computer hardware to perform its functions. The more contemporary definition also includes a set of information-processing instructions called *procedures* to assist people in their work. Software today can be visual (e.g., Microsoft Office) or embedded in the control systems (e.g., in automobiles).

The key software components for ERP systems are as follows:

- *System software.* This is the operating system (OS) platform that is essential for any application software to work efficiently with the hardware and IT personnel. Similar to

TABLE 5-1 Software Components with Oracle/PeopleSoft ERP

Vendor	Software
Oracle	Database management
BMC Control-M	Batch run control
Cobol, C++, Java	Software compilers
Informatica PowerCenter	Extract, translate, load tool for creation of reporting database
Oracle Advanced Security Option (ASO)	Data and network encryption
BEA WebLogic Express	Web software
Quest—Stat	Software control system
Quest—Toad	SQL development tool
McAfee PGP	Security
SMTP	E-mail communications
Adobe Output Designer	Letter development and generation
Merkur Fax Software	Faxing documents

other application software, ERP work on a wide variety of server platforms (e.g., Microsoft Windows Server and Linux). One of the key requirements for the OS platform is multiuser and multitasking capabilities with good security, backup, monitoring, and recovery systems.

- *Database management system (DBMS).*   A reliable multiuser DBMS with good authentication, authorization, security, backup, and monitoring functionality can serve as a strong foundation for the ERP system. Most ERP systems today can work with a variety of DBMS (e.g., SAP/R3 works with IBM-DB2, Oracle, Microsoft SQL); however, some of the smaller ERPs (e.g., Microsoft's Great Plains) work only with Microsoft SQL.
- *Application software.*   These are programs or software utilities that help in the development, monitoring, and integration of ERP software. Even though they are not as critical, many ERP implementations will require project management software, development software, remote access software, and automated software for monitoring system traffic, virus protection, and other software utilities to enhance the quality of experience with the users.

Table 5-1 illustrates some of the software used with an Oracle/PeopleSoft ERP implementation. As with most technology in the world today, Oracle is developing its ERP software using a newer set of software development services that is more current with the open-source software direction.

People Resources

For the implementation and operation of ERP systems to be successful, a knowledgeable staff is necessary. This includes end users, IT specialists, and project manager(s).

End users can be employees, clients, vendors, and others who will ultimately use the system for their work. The success or failure of an ERP implementation is ultimately in the hands of these people. It is very important to understand the needs, skills, and abilities of this group very early in the implementation process.

IT specialists are staff members of the ERP implementation team. They consist of database administrators, IT operations support, developers, change managers, trainers, and others in the IT group that are involved with the development and operation of the ERP system.

The *project manager* plays a very important role in the success or failure of the ERP system. A good project manager is one that can put together a harmonious team, work with top management in getting support and resources for the project, and champion the system implementation and communicate its benefits to the end users.

The ERP implementation team will include various subteams from business or functional areas, change management, development, data migration, and system support. For example, the functional team determines the fits or gaps between the ERP functionality and the business processes requirements. During the implementation process the functional team must chart out a customization and configuration plan for the development team. The development team customizes the systems functionality and forwards the changes to the quality assurance (QA) team, which is responsible for testing and assuring that the system functions according to requirements set out in the implementation plan. Along the way, the change management team works with end users on training, communications, and support activities.

ERP AND VIRTUALIZATION

In recent years, virtualization has been gaining momentum in the information technology world. The concept of virtualization is not new, but due to new technological advancements, it has become possible on industry-standard servers.[1] An infrastructure's availability, standardization, and usability are all very important for any ERP implementation, and virtualization technology can serve as the foundation for standardization and integration in enterprise architectures.[2]

The purpose of this chapter is to demonstrate that a virtualized organization will improve the efficiency and availability of its ERP system. This chapter will explain what virtualization technology is, what virtualization options are available for the major ERP software vendors, and the benefits and implications of a virtualized environment. This chapter will then present both a case study proving that a virtualized environment initiative can successfully be integrated alongside an ERP implementation and a brief outlook on the future trends of virtualization.

Kamoun describes virtual machine (VM) server technology as providing a "technique to run multiple and isolated virtual servers on a single physical device, thus optimizing hardware usage." Each virtual server that is installed in the same physical server operates under its own OS independently of the other VMs present. Having multiple VMs installed in one physical server is not the same as having one operating system with multiple applications installed, where the behavior of one application can have an adverse effect on other applications and the stability of the entire operating system. Each VM behaves as if it were the sole operating system configured in the server such that each VM can be powered on or off without affecting the others.

While other virtualization architectures exist, the two more common models used for mission critical application are known as hardware virtualization and paravirtualization. Hardware virtualization is the better, well-known architecture and includes products from VMWare and Microsoft. With this approach, the server virtualization technology is placed directly on the server hardware, sometimes referred to as "bare metal." It uses hypervisors, modified code or APIs, which facilitate faster transactions with hardware devices. The benefits are that virtualization (1)

---

[1] Kamoun, F. (2009). Virtualizing the Datacenter Without Compromising Server Performance. *Ubiquity*, 009.9, Print.
[2] Daniels, J. (2009). Server Virtualization Architecture and Implementation. *Crossroads*, 16 (1), 8–12, Print.

supports multiple types of operating systems on a single server ("Top Ten Considerations For Choosing A Server Virtualization Technology"), (2) is relatively easy to install and use, (3) offers true isolation of each virtual OS instance, and (4) the operating systems serving as VMs do not need any modifications. This approach has the potential of creating significant overhead, especially for I/O-intensive workloads such as a database.[3]

Paravirtualization is similar to hardware virtualization in that it is designed to support multiple types of OSs on a single server, while providing isolation from other OS instances running on the server. A benefit of paravirtualization is that it provides more efficient processing and lower overhead. The net result is better performance than hardware virtualization ("Top Ten Considerations for Choosing a Server Virtualization Technology"). The drawback is that its extra software layer exists and is complex to both install and administer. The server OS must be modified to run with paravirtualization; some OSs may not be readily available for this solution.[4]

The virtualization method chosen will depend on the ERP system. Some ERPs limit the choices of potential virtualization vendors. To retain full vendor support for Microsoft Dynamics GP 2010, for instance, the two virtualization choices available are Microsoft Virtual Server and Microsoft Virtual PC ("System requirements for Microsoft Dynamics GP 2010"). If another virtualization vendor is chosen, Microsoft's policy states that "Microsoft does not test or support Microsoft software running together with non-Microsoft virtualization software" ("Support policy for Microsoft software running in non-Microsoft hardware virtualization software").

Oracle is utilizing the same model as Microsoft. In November 2007, Oracle released its own virtualization software called Oracle VM. Oracle VM uses paravirtualization architecture based on the Xen open-source technology that brings with it both Linux and Windows support ("Oracle Virtualization introduction guide"). In early 2009, Oracle expanded its virtualization portfolio by acquiring Sun Microsystems and Virtual Iron Software Inc ("Guide to Oracle's virtualization strategy"). In November 2009, Oracle announced it would only support applications running on its own virtualization software. In practice, however, Oracle is supporting applications that run in other virtual environments.[5]

SAP has taken a different approach to virtualization. SAP's strategy does not dictate what software customers can use to virtualize their applications. SAP's strategy for virtualization has been to provide customers with the tools, code tweaks, and support they need to make sure their SAP virtualization projects go smoothly. This strategy has helped SAP emerge at the front of the virtualization pack. The company's focus has been to remain strictly an application vendor as opposed to a platform or infrastructure software provider. If a customer running SAP on a dedicated virtualization platform confronts an issue, that customer only needs to contact SAP, and SAP will work with those vendors to identify and resolve the issue.[6]

Today's marketplace contains many hardware and software companies offering virtualization solutions for ERP systems. The major hardware vendors offering them are Dell, Fujitsu-Siemens, HP, and IBM. Some of the major virtualization software vendors from VMWare, Microsoft, Citrix,

---

[3] Berman, J. (January–March 2009). Red Hat Delivers with Integrated Virtualization Capabilities. *SAP Insider,* 13–14, Print.

[4] Stafford, J. (2007). Server Virtualization: Three Top Methods, Plus Pros and Cons. *Techtarget.com.* http://itknowledge exchange.techtarget.com/server-virtualization/server-virtualization-three-top-methods-plus-pros-and-cons/ (accessed July 14, 2010).

[5] Beal, B. (2008). What Does Virtualization Mean for SAP Managed Hosting? *SearchSAP.com. TechTarget.*

[6] Wartenberg, R. and Gunther S. (January–March 2009). SAP Virtualization: Partnering to Increase Flexibility, Improve Scalability, and Reduce TCO. *SAP Insider,* 19 (12), Print.

and Red Hat Linux. Each vendor has specific solutions for specific ERPs. The following will examine solutions for the SAP ERP systems.

A key and unique advantage that IBM has over the competition is that they were the originators of virtualization systems in the 1970s. IBM has also been one of the earliest supporters of the x86 server virtualization solutions offered by VMWare, Microsoft, Citrix, and others ("IBM Bottom Line Impact for Enterprise Infrastructures"). IBM's model is called the IBM Dynamic Infrastructure. By applying the disciplines of this model, companies can improve their services to the business functions, reduce the cost of IT, and effectively manage their SAP infrastructure, including all applications, databases, servers, storage, and networks.

Fujitsu-Siemens virtualization solution is called the FlexFrame platform. FlexFrame provides an operating environment with a holistic approach to data center management that enhances the way customers set up, operate, and maintain their data centers and resources.[7] FlexFrame is worldwide the first to support full virtualization, allowing companies to run physical and virtual servers within the same single shared environment ("FlexFrame for SAP").

In 2003, Microsoft entered the virtualization business with the acquisition of Connectix, a software vendor of virtual machine technology. Microsoft packages its virtualization software within its server operating systems. Similarly, Red Hat Linux is also packaging its virtualization software within its Linux server OS. The advantages claimed are first lower cost, but having the OS and virtualization layer tightly coupled benefits applications that have high demand for network and storage traffic. Both companies offer robust high-availability clustering options for redundancy. Microsoft claims to have a robust centralized management tool that works with other VM vendors such as VMWare, with the ability to intelligently place virtual machines in the right hosts.[8]

Since 1999, when VMWare introduced virtualization to x86 systems, the company has held the dominant position in the virtualization market space, with more than 150,000 customers globally (Davis). Additionally, since VMWare became a SAP partner in December 2007, a staggering 89 percent of SAP customers who use virtualization in their data center use VMWare virtualization ("EMA Impact Brief").

VMWare solutions include the following:

- *VMWare High Availability,* which automatically restarts virtual machines on servers that have spare capacity when there is a physical server failure.
- *VMWare VMotion,* which enables the live migration of virtual machines from one physical server to another without scheduling system downtime.
- *VMWare Site Recovery Manager,* a disaster recovery process that can be implemented without investing in an exact replica of the hardware.[9]

Benefits:

1. *A main benefit of virtualization is enhanced hardware utilization.* Virtualization allows an organization to consolidate underutilized servers. For Windows based servers, estimates indicate that the average capacity being used on each server is 8–12 percent; UNIX servers are using 25–30 percent. Instead of purchasing more servers, new virtual machines can be created on existing

---

[7] Friess, B. (January–March 2009). Coping with Growing Demand and a Shrinking IT Budget? *SAP Insider*, 3–5, Print.
[8] Vu, D. (January–March 2009). Want Higher ROI and Increased Agility from Your SAP Infrastructure? *SAP Insider*, 15, Print.
[9] Reisbeck, C. (January–March 2009). Open Up New Possibilities for Your SAP Landscape. *SAP Insider*, 9, Print.

hardware. Maintenance costs are avoided on the idle servers and floor space is freed up. For example, virtualization saved Bowdoin College the $2 million it would have cost for a new data center. The college had run out of room in its 500 square foot data center. Instead of increasing the physical size of the data center and the number of servers, consolidation through virtualization meant that the number of physical servers went from 101 to 46. The project cost $150,000 for 16 HP blade servers and $50,000 for the virtualization software.[10]

2. *Virtualization makes provisioning and deploying more agile.* Each OS instance can be cloned and reused to deploy additional servers. This feature allows the provisioning of a new virtual server on an existing physical machine with no hardware, software, or reconfiguration requirements.

3. *Through consolidation, virtualization can lower total cost of operations TCO at the data center.* Info-Tech research group studies maintain that server consolidation results in hardware cost improvements of about 30 percent due to reduction in physical resources ("Operate and Optimize"). Lower TCO is achieved through the following: (1) the deferred purchase of new servers, (2) a smaller data center footprint, (3) lower maintenance costs, (4) lower power, ventilation, cooling, rack, and cabling requirements in that every server that is virtualized saves 7,000 kWh of electricity and four tons of carbon dioxide emissions each year ("The Environmental Impact of Right-Sizing IT"), (5) lower disaster recovery costs, and (6) reduced server deployment costs.

4. *Virtualization technology also enhances business continuity and availability.* Each OS instance is unaware of the underlying hardware, which makes it easy to transfer a virtual machine from one physical host to another. Virtualization makes disaster recovery procedures simpler because there is no need to duplicate the exact server hardware at the DR site from the main site. Virtualization technology has matured to be very reliable. Two years ago, Futurecell, a manufacturer of biofuels and organic chemicals virtualized its mission critical SAP application using VMWare. The results—"for the past two years, it has worked well," according to Lance Wehrung, senior systems engineer for the company. "It's really run smooth. We haven't had any outages of this system due to anything [with] VMWare."[11]

Drawbacks:

1. *Although virtualization technology is beneficial, it can create some challenges.* There may be a tendency to try to squeeze more performance out of a physical server by creating too many virtual machines. This strategy will lead to significant concerns when the server is operating at peak loads. Before organizations migrate from physical servers into a virtual environment, a proper assessment of their computing, storage, and performance requirements must be done to ensure the performance of the applications running in the VM is up to acceptable user standards.

2. *Another concern with virtualization is security.* The fact is that if a hacker compromises the security of the hypervisor, he or she might get access to all virtual machines running on the host server. It is important to design the right security perimeters and policies, intrusion prevention systems, and access controls and incorporate the best VM security practices. The key organizations need to understand is that the old way of securing servers will need to be modified once a virtualized infrastructure has been decided on.

---

[10] Gaudin, S. (May 29, 2006). Virtualization Delivers A Cost-Saving Lesson. *InformationWeek.com*, 30–33.
[11] Bjorlin, C. (2009). SAP Virtualization Becoming More Prevalent, Even with Mission-critical Apps. *SearchSAP.com. TechTarget.* http://searchsap.techtarget.com/news/1353296/SAP-virtualization-becoming-more-prevalent-even-with-mission-critical-apps (accessed July 9, 2010).

THIRD-PARTY PRODUCTS
What Are They and Why Are They Needed?

What are third-party products? Third-party products are add-on software components either to make the system operational or to add missing functionality not offered by the ERP system. These products are often purchased or developed. System operational software may allow the new ERP system to distribute reports, permit a single-user ID and password, enforce a higher level of security, or improve system performance monitoring. Although these systems are not necessarily integrated with the ERP system, they need to work with the system on a regular basis, and they must work seamlessly.

The other type of third-party product is one that adds missing functionality within the ERP. This is sometimes thought of as a gap in functionality. This type of product, whether purchased or developed, will need to work in conjunction with the ERP system. It will need to be integrated with the system. How often and when the third-party system is updated depends mostly on the requirements between the system components. Some third-party functionality has a real-time update requirement, and others may only need to be updated daily to effectively provide the function needed within the organization. A good example of this type of product is an imaging system to scan and save documents (i.e., signed receipts, checks, invoices) associated with information in the ERP but not a part of the application.

Impacts of Integration with ERP

When using third-party products, the decision to integrate or interface needs to be addressed. *Integration* is defined as the sharing of data and data elements directly with the ERP system without data redundancy or copying of data to another table or database. An *interface* is a process by which data or data tables are copied or updated to or from, or both to and from, the ERP system. Both processes are similar to an implementation, but they also have distinct issues that need to be addressed. Integrating a third-party product can be complex and requires a technical skill set within the IT organization to incorporate it into the system. Interfacing a third-party product is less complex and requires a less technical set of skills to develop and support the product.

Component integration should not be taken lightly. To integrate a component successfully, a staff person with a particular technical skill set is often needed. This is a person that fully understands the ERP system's internal data and coding structures. Staff must understand specifically how and when the system components and data will be updated. As described earlier with third-party products, each time the ERP is upgraded, the third-party product's impact on the upgrade must be researched and estimated. If the ERP and third-party products are both purchased, the vendors will sometimes only allow authorized staff to modify the system, thereby creating a dependency on both vendors each time either of the systems are changed or upgraded.

Interfaces are sometimes easier to implement, but the downside is that the data will not be as timely as they would be if they were integrated. In general, interfaces should be one way, either from the ERP to a third-party component or from a third-party component to the ERP. Entering or changing data in one location will save time and reduce data and reporting errors. Two-way interfaces are sometimes required and should be addressed only after exhausting a one-way interface approach.

Support

Third-party product support will vary on level of technical expertise and the timing of upgrades that coincide with the ERP vendor upgrades. This will need to be addressed as upgrades are available and tested against the other products that make up the operational environment. The key to this whole process is to develop a thorough testing plan and to execute it. This testing plan will better ensure that upgrades to any component of the operational environment meet the production needs of the business.

Overcoming Third-Party Integration Issues

STRATEGIC PARTNERS   ERP vendors have recognized third-party products and integration can cause problems. To remedy that, ERP vendors have developed relationships with third-party software vendors in the industry to assist in addressing integration and interface issues. This generally means that the third-party product vendor will receive early versions of ERP system upgrades to allow for time to test and change the third-party product to work with the upgraded ERP version. Over time these partnerships have proven to be very beneficial and have expanded beyond early releases to developing coding standards and more elaborate system validation processes. In looking at third-party products, a business should work with the ERP vendor to identify the vendor's strategic partners and to fully understand the meaning of a strategic partner. Third-party product vendors need to display a high standard of coding and to validate their product with the ERP vendor to ensure system integrity and reliability.

Middleware

Interfacing and integration are recognized as problematic to ERP systems. The development of middleware is an attempt to solve this issue. Middleware can assist with the development of reporting databases that use extract, translate, and load (ETL) tools and with newer middleware systems that act as the arbitrator between an ERP and other systems or products. The ultimate goal for middleware is to create a seamless process between two or more systems without needing to modify either system. This type of middleware continues to evolve and will mature with time.

DATABASE REQUIREMENTS

Understanding Transactional and Reporting Needs

Relational databases have come of age and are used throughout the industry. There have been many iterations of relational databases since they were first introduced back in the 1970s. They have matured as products. In addition, hardware infrastructures have grown and are better suited to sustain the environment. This was not always the case: It often took a large number of specialized technical staff to ensure that the database environment was available and functioning well.

For an ERP system to perform up to expectations, the update or transactional component and the reporting component must respond in a timely fashion. The transactional component requires a quick response time to individual pieces of information for updating or inquiring. All ERP systems are initially set up to provide as rapid as possible a response time for single transactions as possible; however, this works in contrast to strategic reporting, which generally requires retrieval of large amounts of data for summarization or large-volume output. These two components, transactional and report generation, do not work well with a single database instance and this has led to the development of data marts, data warehouses, and ETL middleware. These reporting environments currently import data from the transactional environment and arrange them in such a way as to be able to produce reports without having to write complex programs to retrieve the desired data. In most instances, a "user-friendly" reporting tool can extract data and arrange what is needed in a report without having to develop complex programs.

Selecting the Database

Large ERP system implementations require a robust relational database system. There are only a few vendors today that can support a large ERP system. Oracle, DB2, and Sybase are predominant in the market, with Microsoft SQL gaining more and more support. There is more variety with a medium-size system, with approximately 8–10 database systems.

In selecting a relational database a number of factors need to be considered, including taking into account the availability of software applications using the relational database, the availability of skilled and trained technical staff to implement and maintain the database environment, and the overall functionality of the database itself. If a business is purchasing an ERP system, it is best to work with the selected vendor to address this issue. As a general rule, the ERP vendor will not commit totally to one database or the other, but they can convey how many businesses have chosen a specific relational database, which ones they develop system functions for first, and which ones get early releases. This is all good information to consider, but the ultimate decision resides with the IT staff and how a relational database will best fit with the overall IT infrastructure.

Staffing and Database Administration

It is a steep learning curve for staff to develop the expertise to maintain a relational database. Over the years skilled consultants in relational database technology have made a lot of money by helping companies install and maintain a relational database. There is not enough database expertise in the industry today, and developing organizational expertise requires a significant amount of training and hands-on use to maintain the ERP database environment effectively. If they do not have expertise in-house, businesses should be prepared to hire from the outside the organization or to develop a database group from within the existing IT staff. The hiring of consultants for long-term engagements is usually very costly. It brings in immediate expertise, but it also has the potential for not developing the knowledge base within the business.

ERP IMPLEMENTATION ORGANIZATION AND APPROACHES

To successfully implement an ERP, a temporary organization needs to be defined and staffed and an overall implementation strategy decided and communicated. The temporary organization must have rules of engagement or governance. This governance will provide a framework for decisions, escalation of issues, and involvement of company staff at all levels of the organization. Implementation strategy is how the temporary organization will accomplish the implementation. Two key aspects include an implementation methodology or the process steps from the beginning of the implementation to the end (Go-live). And the second aspect is the guiding principles for the implementation, often called the implementation approach. A decision on whether or not to modify the system needs to be made from the beginning and used as a guiding principle throughout the implementation. Where there are gaps in the ERP functionality, a decision will need to be made on the business process or the system modified to fill the gap in functionality.

Governance

Governance is critical in any project that transforms an organization. In an ERP system implementation, governance should outline and define committees and workgroups that are responsible for the different components of the implementation, how the different groups interact, and the decision-making process, including escalation procedures. The components of governance should include, but not be limited to, such project organization as technical development, hardware and software installation, functional components, communications, change management, reporting, project management, project owners and sponsors, budget management, and the issue escalation process.

It is critical in any ERP implementation that governance be defined and communicated to all involved in the process. The ERP implementation will involve a vast majority of a company's users and require a commitment of IT staff along with senior management and end users. A well-defined governance structure, with a clearly understood organization in place, helps to create a comfort level for all involved as to how the project decisions and priorities will be addressed. The governance structure must be communicated to all involved and fully understood before the project begins.

SAMPLE GOVERNANCE

I. Purpose

Governance is a framework of processes and underlying accountabilities that guide the management of the project. This framework defines the leadership, organization structure (i.e., roles and responsibilities), and processes that align decision making with strategies and direction. Leadership provides clear and consistent direction, organization structure creates the infrastructure to support the implementation of decisions, and process alignment defines the activities that turn ideas into action.

II. Roles and Responsibilities

Owners   The owners will consist of the senior management. The chair is empowered to make decisions when the owners cannot reach consensus. The owners determine overall policy, budget, and scope of the project. They will meet when needed at the call of the chair.

Owners:	Senior management functional areas
	Senior management IT
	Project executive

Project Executive   The project executive oversees project activities, provides broad project oversight, resolves policy-level issues, and ensures that the project stays within scope. The project executive also builds consensus on business process changes that impact the company and provides project status updates (as needed) to the owners. The project executive works with the steering committee and project managers to establish overall project direction, review and evaluate project progress, and ensure appropriate user involvement for the duration of the project. The project executive works directly with the implementation partner (if one is being hired) and the steering committee to resolve appeals of decisions made by project managers, the cross-functional team, or both. The project executive will represent the project at the project steering meeting, project management office meeting, and team leads meeting.

Project executive:	person ultimately responsible for the success of the implementation
Advisory:	implementation partner if necessary

Steering Committee   The steering committee will oversee the project's efforts and ensure appropriate leadership. The committee will link business leaders with the project to assure that high-level direction, resource commitments, and timeframes are consistent and support business priorities and strategies. Members will include business owners, information technology leaders, and project management staff.

Application Steward   The application steward is appointed by the owners cabinet. This position may rotate periodically. The steward will work with the other business owners to develop an overall business direction of the system, developing consensus, and resolving functional issues raised to the steering committee. It is important to understand that the application steward, in the absence of consensus, is expected to make the decision in the best interest of the whole.

Chairperson   The chair will oversee the activities of the steering committee, ensuring that the committee functions in accordance with the overall project oversight. This includes budget, resources, deliverables, risk, and expectations management.

Members:	business owners
	information technology
	project manager(s)
	project executive

Project Management Office   The project management office (PMO) consists of the project executive, business and technical project manager(s), and the implementation partner (if hired). The project managers manage the day-to-day aspects of the project, ensure that the project plan is being followed, and keep both team members and the project executive aware of the status of the project. This responsibility includes overall management of the project to ensure that all work tasks are completed on a timely basis, in a quality fashion, and in accordance with the approved project plan. The project manager(s) will represent the project at key weekly meetings with the teams.

Project Teams   The project teams consist of functional teams (i.e., functional leads, core functional team members, and subject matter experts (SMEs)), technical team, development team, change management team, conversion team, reporting team, and the system test team. Project team members provide direction and ERP application knowledge with respect to business process design, configuration, conversion, testing, training, reporting, and implementation.

The following (module or project) teams will exist:

- Cross-functional component team
- Functional component teams
- Technical infrastructure team
- Development team
- Change management team
- Conversion team
- Reporting team

Project Team Leads   The project team leads provide leadership and overall direction for the implementation, ensuring the quality of deliverables and adherence to the project plan and milestones. The project team leads will inform the project managers of any and all issues that are identified by their respective project team, including those that are specific to their module or team, or have cross-module, cross-team, or cross-campus impacts. The project team leads are empowered to make decisions on behalf of their team should the team be unable to reach consensus on its own.

The project team leads will represent the project at the component or project team leads meeting, component or project team status meeting, issues meeting, and integration meeting.

Cross-Functional Team   The integration team will consist of the module or project team leads from the business modules and the development leads. This group will meet as needed to discuss and resolve cross-module issues. When a module or project team identifies a cross-module issue, the lead notifies the integration team. The issue(s) and the impact(s) on the other module or project team(s) should be documented, along with possible solutions. The integration team will discuss each issue and determine the recommended approach. The solution will then be communicated back to the module or project team, including SMEs, for their input.

SAMPLE SET OF MEETINGS

Project Sponsors Meeting
Led by: owners chair
Who: owners cabinet, project executive, implementation partner
When: at the discretion of the owners cabinet chair

Steering Committee Meeting
Led by: chair
Who: business owners, information technology, project manager(s), project executive, implementation partner
When: monthly (biweekly, if needed)

Project Management Office Meeting
Led by: project executive
Who: project executive, project manager(s), implementation partners
When: weekly

Module or Project Leads Meeting
Led by: project managers
Who: project executive (1), project managers, conversion lead, development lead, infrastructure leads, functional lead, reporting lead, change management lead
When: weekly

Module or Project Team Status Meeting
Led by: module or project team lead
Who: module or project team lead(s), core team member(s), SMEs
When: at the discretion of the module or project team leads

Issues Meeting
Led by: project manager
Who: project manager(s), conversion lead, development lead, infrastructure lead, module leads, reporting lead, change management lead
When: weekly

Cross-Functional Module Meeting
Led by: project manager
Who: project manager(s), functional leads, and development lead, change management leads
When: at the discretion of the project managers—follow-up to the issues meeting.

Database Planning Meeting
Led by: technical infrastructure lead
Who: project manager(s), functional leads, change management leads
When: monthly

Implementation Methodology

System implementations are complex, time consuming, and resource intensive. As with any system, no ERP system is perfect, "bug free," or meets all the user requirements. ERP systems, however, will grow and change to provide the business with a new way of looking at business processes and decision making. A business will need to grow, change, and adapt to ERP systems whether vendor purchased or developed internally.

Understanding ERP system life cycles from inception to operations and the effects on today's organizations is fundamental to fulfilling the long-term investment in an ERP system. The key to a successful implementation is to use a proven methodology. When a system implementation does not have a well-defined methodology, deadlines will likely be missed, budgets overspent, and the functionality not meet the client's requirements. In other words, the results will be less predictable. ERP system implementations are very risky, but a well-defined project methodology will assist in managing those risks.

There are many methodologies documented and used in system implementations. There is nothing complex about methodologies, but they need to be well understood and proven. A proven methodology will better ensure a successful implementation. Implementation risks will be reduced as the technology improves and the information technology and functional staff gain more experience in ERP systems. Until that time you should consider a robust ERP system methodology as critical to the project's success in terms of time and budget. A sample methodology appears in Figure 5-2.

When selecting a methodology, make sure it addresses all components for the entire project. This includes project start-up through system stabilization. If an implementation partner is involved, be sure to review their methodology. The implementation partner's expertise in functional areas of the system is important, but the most important reason for using a partner is the knowledge base and process of how to design and implement systems successfully.

In the past, it was considered Nirvana when a business deployed a single database instance from a single ERP vendor that provided the functionality a company needed to do their business. This type of implementation has been contemplated and discussed for years with few successes. It did not become feasible to address this until the mid-to late 1990s. The Internet and Web allowed connectivity anywhere at anytime, cheaper and faster servers improved

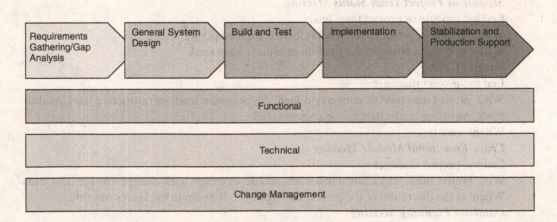

FIGURE 5-2   Sample Project Methodology.

response time, and significant increases in storage capacities made it feasible. It was difficult to provide the connectivity and the hardware to support the software technology fully to realize the goals in an ERP implementation prior to using this newer generation of IT infrastructure. The process to reach those goals, however, is complex. As previously described, there are many components that need to be planned and implemented for a successful ERP implementation. It is a significant amount of work. That being said, a company should analyze whether or not the system is going to be modified or not. It is sometimes termed a "vanilla" implementation when modifications are not allowed.

What Is a Vanilla Implementation?

A vanilla implementation is the decision to implement an ERP *as is* and modify business processes to match the system or to modify the ERP to match business processes. It is fundamental to make this decision prior to starting an implementation. A vanilla implementation is when the company chooses not to modify (i.e., customize) the system but instead to change business practices to fit the system.

Why Would You Consider a Vanilla Implementation?

In the global business world of today and with added scrutiny and tighter regulations in the area of financial reporting, modifying a system can be costly. Several factors need to be considered before customizing an ERP:

- Businesses with relatively straightforward business practices that are not unique should consider a vanilla implementation.
- Businesses that are not skilled or experienced at building or changing systems should consider a vanilla implementation.
- In vanilla implementations, all of a company's branches run the same system in a single instance and enter and retrieve data in a similar fashion, thereby reducing hardware, software licensing, implementation, and training and support costs. This is a cost-control factor.
- For a company using a purchased ERP system where the financial component is critical for reporting, a vanilla system will more than likely pass the Sarbanes–Oxley audits in a timely fashion.
- Last, for a competitive advantage, it is important to know the ability of what and where things are around the world with your business in terms of parts inventory, maintenance agreements, and processes. Again, and as an example, if everyone is entering and retrieving the same information, the ability to know inventories and what is needed in a timely fashion without needing to contact others around the world creates a competitive advantage for a business that needs to react to information in a timely manner.

When Should You Consider Modifying an ERP?

Even though there are many reasons to implement a vanilla ERP, many businesses choose to customize or modify the system to meet business needs (i.e., add in some chocolate) and are very successful. Businesses that have highly skilled IT developers and a proven process for managing modifications can certainly choose to change the system in areas where a business already has a competitive advantage. In a situation like this, an ERP system is too generic to fit the specialized business or specialized process.

Benefits and Drawbacks

A single-system instance is easier to maintain and support in today's worldwide market. System modifications are not one-time changes. If a system is modified, each modification will need to be analyzed in light of the upgrade to see if it needs to be incorporated in the upgrade or removed. The modifications will need to be looked at, validated, and possibly added back into each upgrade, which is paying for a modification several times over.

Vendors sometimes supply a tool to identify conflicts between a modification and the current release. Those areas identified need either to be rewritten or removed from the system and tested by IT and the business analysts to ensure proper functionality. If an ERP is highly modified, an upgrade can sometimes turn into a reimplementation, which requires more resources and time to implement the upgrade. Customizations can take up to one-third of the total upgrade time.

When there are problems or bugs with an upgraded ERP system, it is often the modified code that is the issue.

As with most implementations organizational change is difficult. Assessing organizational change along with modifying the system to meet the needs of the business will help to minimize risk. In any case the decision to modify or not to modify is critical and should be discussed at the very beginning of the implementation. It will have an effect on change management, training, and system sustainability.

ERP IMPLEMENTATION EXAMPLES

There are many examples of ERP implementations in business today. Many are implemented to replace aging legacy systems, whereas others are to make use of new technology. All are meant to improve services, provide better data for decision making, or increase profit margins. Some are successful, and some fail. A few examples of types of implementations follow.

Piggly Wiggly   (*CIO Decisions,* June 2005): Grocery stores these days operate on slim profit margins. It is a highly competitive marketplace with businesses working to distinguish themselves from their competitors. Piggly Wiggly franchises 600 stores in 16 states, mostly in the southern United States. They compete with such chains as Food Lion and Wal-Mart. Piggly Wiggly is constantly working to improve profit margins and gain customer loyalty. Over the last few years the company implemented a payment system using biometrics. The use of biometrics allows customers the ability to check out using their telephone number and a finger scanner (Pay By Touch) as a method for identifying and paying for items from the grocery store. This implementation has improved the speed of customer checkout and increased market share in a business with thin profit margins. The belief at Piggly Wiggly is that stores of this type have just scratched the surface of using technology.

Celanese   (*CIO Magazine*, January 15, 2003): Celanese, a worldwide chemical product maker, is a holding company for five business units. One such product is a sweetener for Pepsi One. The dilemma Celanese faced was the use of multiple SAP systems. A business case was made to integrate several SAP systems into one over a four-year period. They called it "OneSAP." The project was considered technically feasible, with the culture change being the most risky aspect. The culture change was to fit the business into one SAP system and to standardize all business processes. The change in business process was complex and very time consuming. If the project succeeded, it meant the decommissioning of more than a dozen systems and a savings for the company of 30–50 percent in operational costs. The implementation approach was to minimize the tailoring of SAP and to require the business to conform to the software.

University of Massachusetts-Amherst   As the competition for students increases, universities are looking at ways to improve services to students and increase levels of support that address retention and graduation rates. Some of the ways that ERP systems can be utilized to improve services to students are as follows:

- Expand access of student data for students
- Increase the functionality of online learning through the Web
- E-payments
- Online advising

The University of Massachusetts-Amherst replaced its nonintegrated legacy systems with the integrated Oracle/PeopleSoft Student Administration ERP. This included Web access to applicants, students, faculty, and staff. It simplified student administrative functions that allowed students to do most of their requisite administrative processes through the Web, including registering, paying or billing, housing, financial aid, and advising services. The student administration ERP is successfully installed in more than 700 institutions around the world. With that said, short-term success and failure are sometimes determined by a single event. That event at UMass-Amherst happened when 24,000 students needed to access the system for the fall registration cycle to add and drop classes. The volume of students crashed the system, bringing the process to a standstill. In addition to not being able to add and drop classes, students could not look up the building and room where their classes were being taught. There were long lines everywhere and much confusion. The problem was eventually resolved and fixed, but the timing of the downtime hurt what was otherwise a successful implementation.

Comair   (*CIO Magazine,* May 1, 2005): Comair is a regional airline operating in 117 cities that carries approximately 30,000 passengers on 1,130 flights per day. The decision to replace aging systems is sometimes difficult. It requires vision, a thorough analysis, and the creation of a business case. In Comair's case the investment in replacing aging legacy systems did not occur. Their 20-year-old legacy system failed during a merger with Delta, creating a number of customer service and financial problems. Replacing legacy systems with a new ERP system is very high risk, but as Comair found out, the cost of not replacing an aging system can be greater. The lesson to learn is that managing risky endeavors is instrumental to business growth and success. IT systems are critical to a company's daily business.

PLATFORM ISSUES

As stated earlier, ERP systems are complex and difficult to implement; however, the risk is worth the long-term benefits if approached properly. The ERP system implementation is high-risk, as is the installation of the IT infrastructure. Most ERP systems are Web based, which provides for anytime, anywhere access, and the IT infrastructure must be prepared to address this level of access. The Internet has brought the business world closer and made it more accessible. Today, a business must be able to operate 24 hours a day, seven days a week if it has to compete. The infrastructure platform needs to be both available and secure and reliable. The number of components that need to work together is numerous, and maintaining them is strategic to the long-term ERP success. Any ERP implementation must address issues related to connectivity, network and system bandwidth, security, transaction volume, user load, backup, and recovery. PC configurations, including Web browsers, need to be addressed. Each of these areas needs a full analysis and validation before the system can "Go-live." The IT infrastructure team must be involved in discussions on how the system will be used and when. Documenting and communicating usage expectations will assist in the installation of the IT infrastructure platform.

Servers

The selection of servers is often based on input from the ERP vendor, which is similar to the relational database selection. Servers that make up the infrastructure will need to grow as the system grows and expands. The planning for an expanding infrastructure is another critical component to a successful implementation. The infrastructure team is responsible for selecting the right-size database, as well as the application and Web servers, with enough storage to ensure that data are quickly retrievable.

Network

Most businesses today have a reliable and secure network in place. Network connectivity and speed from the end user to the server environment needs to be assessed. Some businesses outsource the server and the database environment. In that case, providing connectivity to the outsourced site should be a part of the outsourced contract.

Security

To ensure that the ERP system is secure from unauthorized access, several technical and not-so-technical components must be installed and implemented. Desktop PCs must be set up to ensure that viruses, Trojan horses, spyware, and any other type of PC infiltration tools can be arrested before they take hold in the environment. Businesses have often developed standard PC configurations for users that ensure the desktop PCs are well protected.

This does not fully prevent security exposures and breaches. Security awareness is critical to any system's reliability and integrity. The majority of serious breaches of access to systems are through user error including writing down passwords, choosing passwords that are easily guessed, and the sharing of user IDs and passwords. All of these security issues should be a part of end user implementation training.

Disaster Recovery and Business Continuity

Last, and it does not happen very often, but planning for a disaster and providing business continuity is a part of every ERP implementation. There have been instances where this kind of planning was valuable and was put to use. The 9/11 terrorist attacks in New York and Washington DC, in addition to Hurricane Katrina, brought the importance of disaster and business continuity planning for businesses to the forefront. A plan essentially needs to be developed and tested based on several types of disasters. Business managers and senior management must identify mission critical transactions and make them available as quickly as possible after a disaster. Although it might initially appear that disaster recovery and business continuity is just an IT issue, it is not. It involves both IT professionals and functional users and senior management to put together an effective plan. There are many documented processes for developing a disaster recovery or business continuity plan that a business can use. The main concern in this book is that this type of planning must be addressed with the implementation.

IMPLICATIONS FOR MANAGEMENT

An implemented ERP system can create opportunities for a business to grow and change for the better. The risks and rewards for a company depend both on the system selected and on all the surrounding components as well as the methods and processes involved during the implementation. Decisions around the hardware, software, governance, methodology, and level of modifications need to be based on the goals set out for the purchase of the ERP system. Management must be sure that all the components for the implementation are going to be planned and managed throughout the implementation process. Even though the ERP system selected is the key component for the company, there are a significant number of third-party products that can have a large impact on an implementation's success or failure.

There are two initial decisions, however, that will have a large effect on the implementation that are neither hardware nor software based. First is the use of an implementation methodology and whether or not to modify the system. There are a number of proven implementation methodologies available. If the company has a methodology with which they are familiar and can scale it to a complex ERP system implementation, then it should be highly considered. Management must have confidence in the methodology and trust that all things considered will help to ensure all the components and steps for an implementation are in place and followed. This will help to reduce implementation risks.

The second decision is whether to implement the system with or without modifications. Modifying an ERP system is costly from the programming side, but not modifying the system is costly in that business processes are changed to meet what the system is set up to do. Both can be costly in terms of resources and sustainability. Management must decide on the approach prior to the start of the implementation process, and it must be communicated to all on the project. The direction must be clear to all involved; otherwise, it will hinder or slow down the implementation process and possibly undermine the implementation altogether.

Summary

- Many components make up an ERP system. The software as well as the surrounding operational software and third-party software are needed to ensure that the business can accomplish its goals.
- In addition to software there are a myriad of hardware components and devices.
- The table below shows some of the hardware and software components.
- It is more important in the overall project organization and methodology to implement the ERP system. ERPs are all about change, both to business flows and, more importantly, to employees. This makes an ERP system implementation a very high risk.
- Managing the risk throughout the project is key to being successful.
- A robust and proven implementation methodology and a clear and understood

governance structure will enable the project staff to manage risk and implementation progress.
- A number of fundamental discussions and decisions need to be made even before the ERP system is taken out of its wrapper. One key decision is whether or not to modify the system, change business processes, or use some combination of modification and business change. Vanilla implementations are becoming more and more common.
- Senior management does now look at ERP systems as large investments that need to be protected, so modifying the code in these very complex systems jeopardizes that investment. Setting this expectation early, whatever the decision, will better guarantee the adoption of the system.

Hardware	Software
Application servers	Operating system
Database servers	Database management system
Web servers	ERP system
Personal computers	Software development
Storage devices	System performance
Printers	Virus protection
Networking equipment	Report distribution
Uninterruptible power supply	Batch run control
	Software version control

Exercises

1. Many companies that implement ERP systems are worldwide. Research two companies that have implemented an ERP system: one in a central fashion and the other in a decentralized fashion. Compare and contrast the implementation issues as they relate to risk, access, costs, and data consistency.

2. There are several different methodologies for implementing an ERP system. Research two companies that used different methodologies and find out the following:
   a. Why they used their methodology?
   b. How they chose their methodology?
   c. The level of success they had with it.

Review Questions

1. What are the components of an ERP system?
2. Why would a company choose to implement an ERP?
3. What are third-party products and why are they needed?
4. What is an implementation methodology and why is it important in ERP implementations?

5. What are the pros and cons of implementing a system without customization?
6. Why are there differences between a transactional and reporting database?

Discussion Questions

1. Governance and methodology are important for ERP implementations. Discuss the merits of each and how each of them was implemented in the U.S. Army case.

2. When ERP implementations are addressed, the infrastructure also needs to be addressed. Describe the infrastructure components and what is involved in choosing and installing the components.

CASE 5-2
Real-World Case
United States Army

Source: From U.S. Army Web site on ERP Implementations.

GOAL

The army's ability to see, anticipate, and respond to the rapidly changing operational environment is possible through the management of information and knowledge from a One Army and One Enterprise perspective. The capability to employ, deploy, and sustain responsive combat capability can only be realized through knowledge superiority provided by systems that provide a common view of the environment as well as the ability to rapidly affect combat operations by anticipating change and providing decisive and dominant combat capability where and when required. It is the institutional army's transformation of business systems, processes, and practices that will produce the streamlining necessary to reallocate the resources (i.e., personnel, dollars, and time) required for this transformation across the business mission capabilities designated by the BMMP:

- Acquisition
- Financial management
- Human resource management
- Installation and environment
- Logistics

The operational army will be represented in the three other mission areas:

- Warfighting mission area
- Intelligence
- Enterprise information environment mission area

Each of these business mission capabilities and mission areas must work together to eliminate boundaries, to synchronize transformation between the institutional and operational army. They will identify opportunities to optimize the army at the enterprise level. The army must transform from end to end: One Army, One Enterprise, and so on.

The army has recognized that an ERP implementation is high risk and high reward. With that in mind they have developed standards and guidelines for any ERP implementation they undertake.

KEYS TO SUCCESS
Change Management

Most major business transformation efforts historically fail. The failure rate is often as high as 65–75 percent. The primary cause of failure is most frequently the failure to anticipate and effectively manage cultural and organizational change.

Table 5-2 identifies five transformation management (TM) considerations, along with the specific challenge for the army and strategies to overcome these challenges.

Table 5-2 offers several considerations. These will now be looked at more closely.

TABLE 5-2   Change Management Considerations

Consideration	Army Challenge	Strategy to Overcome
Sponsorship or Leadership	Rotation	Engaged leadership
		Comprehensive transition
Stakeholder Alignment	Enterprise view	Enterprise-level governance
Cost	Hard to justify $$ (10–15percent)	Make the case for change
		Justify based on lessons learned
Project Life Cycle	When to start	Communications
		Iterative process
Culture	Resistance to change	Sponsorship from within
		Education
Communication	Number of stakeholders	Communication strategy that includes tactical methods of disseminating program information

Sponsorship. ERPs require sustained leadership, but army leaders rotate often, and one ERP implementation could span two or even three sponsors. Sponsors need to be *engaged*, not just brought in. They also need to convey the importance of continued engagement to their successors during transition.

Stakeholder Alignment. The army has traditionally been "stovepiped" (i.e., operating in silos). The ERP model requires making trade-offs in some domains for the greater good of the enterprise. These decisions require governance above the mission area and the domain level.

Cost. Transformation management can cost as much as 15 percent of the program budget and is one of the first areas to get cut when budgets are trimmed. This is a big mistake, as the Gartner quote earlier in the chapter shows; therefore, the case for TM and its value must be made. TM is an investment in the success of the program and must be portrayed as such.

Project Life Cycle. TM is often left as an afterthought, started just before Go-live. It needs to start at the outset of the project and continue throughout.

Culture. The army is an organization with a lot of history and tradition. As such it can be resistant to change. This is not true of everyone, and not of every part, but it is an issue in the army just as it is in most large organizations. The solution to this issue is sponsorship from within the army (i.e., it cannot be outsourced). A system integrator or other consultant can bring experience, tools, and methodologies, but sponsorship has to come from within. A leader from the inside has to say, "I recognize we need to change, I am going to change, and I want you to change with me for the good of the army."

Communication. Communication is a key implementation consideration because there are so many stakeholder groups impacted by an ERP program both internal (e.g., soldiers, business mission area personnel) and external to the army (e.g., legislators, taxpayers). A communications strategy that includes tactical methods of disseminating ERP program information both top–down and bottom–up via diverse communication channels is an effective approach that contributes to program success.

GOVERNANCE

Governance of any major change in an organization is critical to the success of the change effort, but governance of ERP programs is even more critical because of the size and scope of the programs. They change both technology and business processes and job content. This level of change requires that the organization understand the implications and be prepared to make tough decisions. These types of decisions require executive sponsorship and governance at the most senior level of the organization.

PERFORMANCE MEASUREMENT

Performance measurement of ERP generally includes two components: the ERP implementation itself and the operational or business results, or both. For the implementation itself, the traditional measures of cost, performance, and schedule can be used. In terms of operational or business results, or both, types of measures should include effectiveness, efficiency, and customer satisfaction (i.e., the customer category can include internal and external customers). An example of measuring business results is reducing the average cycle time of vehicle parts restocking from 10 days to 4 days. All performance measures must have a baseline. If there is not a baseline, there is nothing against which future performance can be compared; therefore, there are no valid results.

CUSTOMIZATION AND CONFIGURATION

The decision to customize ERP software core functionality is not one to be made lightly. The decision to modify ERP software is traditionally made to avoid painful and necessary business process change and should be strongly questioned by senior leadership. The benefits of ERP software, including the ability to take advantage of vendor updates to functionality, are negated by customizations. There are huge dollar amounts and resource hours involved, often in ACAT 1 programs, so it benefits the army to ensure that the investment is appropriately realized.

In addition to the benefits of ERP implementations as detailed in the ERP overview, there are specific benefits to not customizing ERP software:

- Proven industry business practices can become embedded in the enterprise if effective change management is conducted.
- Maximizing investment in ERP software by minimizing the cost of upgrades and maintenance of software.
- Integrating processes and information systems on a DoD-wide level is significantly less complicated and costly if multiple components have the same application and version of an ERP module without modifications.
- Reducing the need for scarce technical resources because the army would be able to leverage the vendor's support organization and realize the full value of the ongoing support and maintenance fees charged by software vendors.

The common argument for customizing ERP software is that it is not possible to run the army using commercial processes because army processes are too dissimilar and vary due to specific mission or organizational objectives. Even though that can be a true statement based upon statutory and regulatory constraints, this is not usually the case. The statement is usually made by stakeholders or team members who either do not think they are empowered to make decisions about process changes or want to avert change to maintain the status quo.

If the organization is committed to changing business processes to match those inherent to the software package, customization of ERP software should be rare. The effort involved to reengineer business processes to fulfill this commitment cannot be understated. There are various DoD statutory and regulatory rules that are not accommodated by ERP software; however, this does not have to be a barrier to using the delivered ERP functionality. Sometimes these regulations can be changed to accomplish the same goal using the delivered software. Blueprinting, which includes comprehensive pilots on a live system of proposed business processes using delivered ERP functionality, is key to developing an effective and accurate process. The result of these rigorous pilots should be a list of valid customizations mainly based upon statutory and regulatory rules that cannot be changed in the foreseeable future or cannot be accommodated by changing a current business process.

The first line of defense if major business requirements cannot be met by delivered ERP software functionality is acquisition of a bolt-on, whether it's a product of the same ERP vendor or a third-party software vendor. Bolt-on provides similar benefits to those of ERP software. It can also provide process innovations necessary for specialized industry needs. The additional cost of support and maintenance of an additional software license would need to be evaluated versus the magnitude of the customization required to meet the necessary business requirements. Table 5-3 contains the type of customizations that could be candidates for bolt-on versus minor customizations to meet a requirement that cannot be met by the ERP software or a process change. If a requirement is historically too industry specific, even bolt-ons may not meet the need. The next priority should be changing a business process or, as a last resort, customization of ERP software.

There are two potential methods for customizing ERP software, but only one method should ever be used. The method that should be prohibited by project leadership is modification of delivered software code from the vendor. The accepted method is the creation of a new code base, also called an extension, which is derived from a clone of a delivered software routine. The modified code is then referenced by core application components. This approach requires that all the references to the delivered code be changed to reference

TABLE 5-3   ERP Approach to Meet Requirement Gaps

	Major Customizations	Minor Customizations
Approach	Bolt-on product	Clone and modify ERP code
Description	Processing engines	Simple processing routines
	End-to-end processes	Reports
	Security structure	Web pages
		Menus

the new code, creating a potentially costly modification from a time and budget perspective. If a major business requirement needs to be met, a bolt-on is the preferred approach. Table 5-3 lists the development platforms that could be cloned and modified in the major ERP packages to create an extension.

An extension retains the delivered vendor's code in the database, but the original code is no longer used. Subsequent ERP upgrades will update the delivered code, and the modified code can be integrated into the upgraded application if the underlying technology remains the same. The following must also be considered:

- The upgrade process for a customized ERP implementation is more time consuming than an upgrade of an ERP implementation with no customizations.
- The time frame and cost of upgrades increase exponentially with the number of customizations due to validation and testing.
- Customizations are not supported by the vendor and must be maintained and updated by army or contractor staff.
- If the army's customization is one used by multiple clients, there is the possibility that the ERP vendor can be persuaded to include this customization in their next product release, but this could require significant negotiating leverage and is uncertain.
- Depending upon the magnitude of the required customization, a bolt-on can be more cost-effective, less susceptible to defects, and enable the team to meet project timelines.

The measurement of the level of customization of a particular installation of an ERP system is difficult to judge. There is currently no industry measurement baseline or metric for this type of analysis. Objective measurements would ideally involve a determination of the amount of customized code as a percentage of the vendor's delivered code. In order for this measurement to be meaningful across industries, and even within the army, there would need to be a common metric for delivered code and a common method for determining the means to parse and quantify the amount of customized code. These measurements would be further complicated by the fact that implementing an ERP product often does not include implementing full functionality. ERP modules are often implemented over a period of time in a phased approach that leads to the need to refine further the definition of the baseline delivered code versus customized code. Finally, this analysis also presumes that a common baseline would be applicable across ERP packages, leading to a comparable assessment of the levels of customization of, for example, a SAP versus an Oracle implementation. This task is not without merit, but it will require industry and organizational alignment to reach fruition.

A final consideration related to this discussion is the configuration of ERP software. Configuration is *not* customization or modification; it is the entry of customer-specific data into the tables delivered in ERP software. A standard, simple or pre-configuration, however, may allow faster processing speeds and easier queries. A more complex configuration may cost more in terms of user training, processing speed, and data access. Complex configurations may better support current or legacy business processes. They may not, however, represent best practices or changed business processes. Table 5-4 provides a summary of the configuration and customization approaches along with some pros and cons.

TABLE 5-4 **Comparison of Customization and Configuration Approaches**

Attribute	Customize	Configure
Functionality	Custom coding or modification	Choose from out-of-the-box processes and functions
	More control over functionality	Set parameters
		Less control over functionality
Cost	Higher	Lower
Upgrades	More difficult	Easier
	Longer cycle	Shorter cycle
Support	Reduced vendor support	Full vendor support

INTERFACES AND INTEGRATION OF EXISTING OR THIRD-PARTY SYSTEMS

Additional issues that must be considered when planning ERP implementations are the costs and time associated with developing interfaces and integration with existing systems. Even though the ERP database becomes the central, authoritative data source, most organizations are not able to eliminate all existing databases. As a result they must build interfaces between the ERP system and existing systems that will not be retired immediately. Not all systems will be retired by implementing an ERP.

CASE QUESTIONS

1. What were the key goals in the army using an ERP system?
2. What were the key implementation considerations that were addressed as part of the planning process, especially related to using an integrated ERP and transforming the culture?
3. How was the change management process incorporated into the implementation?
4. Discuss the pros and cons to customizing the system.

6

Software and Vendor Selection

LEARNING OBJECTIVES

After reading this chapter, you should be able to:

- Understand the initial steps in the process for the successful purchase and implementation of an ERP system.

- Understand why the first steps in the purchase of an ERP are critical to the change management process.

- Determine the total cost of ownership and what it is to partner with an ERP vendor.

- Identify the steps involved in negotiating a contract with a vendor.

CASE 6-1
Opening Case
Oracle Wins Out Over SAP at Welch's

Source: Based on article written by Robert Westervelt, News Writer, March 3, 2004, *Search SAP.com*

In March 2004, Welch Foods chose Oracle over SAP. The international juice maker with sales close to $600 million purchased the Oracle Corporation ERP system to implement companywide. The plan is to implement the e-Business suite over the next several months.

The leader of Welch's ERP selection committee, Larry Rencken, said the competition between the two software vendors was close. Oracle won the contract when it discounted its initial price significantly, Rencken said, and after committee members became convinced that Oracle would be less difficult to implement on a large scale.

"It was a consensus vote from the selection team, and that selection team looked at functionality, ease of implementation and flexibility—in addition to TCO," Rencken said. "While functionality was very close between the two products, ease of implementation and flexibility was won fairly handily by Oracle."

Both SAP and Oracle, vying for the purchase, entered into a sort of bidding war for the project. Welch's was able to leverage each of the offers to the betterment of the company. The competition lasted for several weeks, but by the time SAP submitted a competitive bid, the decision had been made, Rencken said.

"In the end, SAP did come back with a counteroffer that was a very close, competitive counter, but we [had] already made our decision," Rencken said. "They were not as competitive as they could have been in the initial rounds."

The Welch's deal proves that no single vendor owns the ERP market, said Joshua Greenbaum, who owns Daly City, California–based Enterprise Applications Consulting.

"This proves to me that there is still a lot of competition in the marketplace and, particularly, that SAP does not have a lock on the market," Greenbaum said. "What this says is that there are a lot of issues in a competitive deal and that the market system still works for enterprise software." The new reality, Greenbaum said, is that many software buyers can negotiate deals that weren't possible before the large ERP market became saturated and the economy became so tight.

Bill Wohl, SAP's vice president of public relations, called the decision by Welch's a "disappointment." "What happened at Welch's essentially flies in the face of what is a clear track record of customer success," Wohl said. "The reality is that what we have is strong competition in the market."

Rencken said that Welch's is using IBM Global Services to help implement Oracle's software suite. IBM is working with Oracle Consulting on part of the implementation, he said. "We certainly had an infrastructure with a lot of spaghetti code keeping it together, and now we have a desire for one fully integrated enterprise," Rencken said. The project consists of two phases: Oracle Financials and HR in the first phase, and then Oracle Order to Cash, Warehouse Management, Inventory Management, and Production and Purchasing.

PREVIEW

The selection process for Welch's Foods shows that there is good competition and value in going through an elaborate evaluation process to determine what ERP best fits the company needs. The vendor is often blamed for an unsuccessful implementation. This chapter will discuss how that is usually not the case and how, from the beginning, to best position a company to implement an ERP successfully. Once the decision or case has been made to replace the existing application system(s), the initial step involves the purchase of an ERP system. The selection of a vendor that best meets the needs and long-term direction of the company is a critical first step in a successful implementation.

In selecting a vendor, a well-understood selection process needs to be utilized. Depending on a given company's experience in purchasing an ERP system, that company may want to bring in a specialized consulting firm to assist in the selection process. In any event the steps involved in selecting a vendor generally are based on best fit of an ERP to business functions and the overall ERP vendor's product performance in the market.

VENDOR RESEARCH

The first step in selecting an ERP system is generally to research vendor ERP systems on the market and to identify a short list of vendors who will help to shape business requirements. This process is especially helpful for companies moving from aging legacy systems and technology to current and state-of-the-art technology. A state-of-the-art ERP system

---

BOX 6-1   High-Level ERP Purchase Process

1. Vendor research and information gathering
2. High-level vendor demonstrations and evaluation
3. Needs and requirements assessment using current legacy systems, business process reengineering analysis, or both
4. Development of request for bid or proposal (if needed or desired)
5. Release request for bid to vendors
6. Analysis and selection

   Evaluation of bids

   Functional evaluation

   Technical evaluation

   Vendor-detailed demonstrations

   Contact references

   Develop a total cost of ownership

7. Vendor(s) negotiation

   Contract review and change

   Pricing—software, maintenance, and consulting support

8. Purchase system (let the fun begin)

purchase will likely mean the replacement of the current hardware and software infrastructure. Identifying and researching all aspects of a vendor package and the platform that the hardware and software runs on will assist companies in determining the total cost of ownership (TCO).

In general, identifying vendors today is not overly difficult. Using current Web search engines is a good starting point. It also helps to know what packages the competition uses. An exhaustive list of vendors, even if you do not research them completely, is important for a successful implementation. Another strategy to identify vendors is to ask department managers and subject matter experts if they know of vendors that should be considered. It will be said many times, "the process is important," so including end users will help with change management issues later in the project. It will also help to gain and secure trust for later in the implementation.

The following should be considered when researching vendors and gathering information:

- Other businesses using the vendor
- The vendor's financial position
- The vendor's implementation philosophy and support issues
- The hardware and software infrastructure used to support the ERP
- The vendor's direction and currency of software
- The vendor's release and upgrade strategies
- The vendor's user-base involvement in defining future functional changes
- The vendor's development and maintenance resources

Some ERP vendor systems (e.g., SAP) are designed for and can scale to a large number of users, whereas other systems (e.g., Great Plains) are geared for a small number of users. Many ERP vendors have similarly geared their application for a *specific industry*. For example, PeopleSoft has historically focused on government and educational organizations, whereas SAP has focused on the manufacturing industry. Oracle PeopleSoft is also known for human resource (HR) applications, whereas SAP is well known for production and supply chain management (SCM) applications. In recent years these large vendors have tried to diversify their systems by expanding their application modules through acquisition of other software companies. Oracle now owns the Peoplesoft ERP along with its own e-Business Suite. Nonetheless, they still focus on certain industries and are known for applications in certain functional areas of business. It is therefore important for businesses evaluating ERPs to pay close attention to these criteria before selecting the software.

The *IT infrastructure* criterion is important because a company not having the resources to invest in new infrastructure may want to acquire an ERP application that will work on an existing platform. Some ERP vendors have structured their applications to work on specific platforms with specific database and third-party software. In that case, having the vendor install a "sandbox" application for demonstration purposes on the company's existing infrastructure can be very helpful. Finally, the *resource question* is the most important issue that has to be resolved before moving to the next phase of ERP implementation. That is, what organization resources will be needed to implement and support the product? Senior management must be involved in making this decision. If they are not committed to the project for the long run, both in terms of resources and time commitment, the implementation is doomed for disaster. The majority of ERP vendor relationships with organizations are long term. Vendors are constantly upgrading or releasing new applications requiring a business to remain close to what is happening with the system. This requires long-term resource commitments from the organization.

ERP System Research Table

Item	Description
User Base	How many companies are using the system and for what purposes. Identify competitors using the system.
Financial Position	If publicly traded, this information is fairly straightforward. If not, the ERP vendor information may not be available until such time later in the purchase process. It should include sales revenues, profits, growth, research and development, and any outstanding debt.
Implementation Issues and Support	This can be accomplished through calls to companies using the software or IT researching companies that survey and collect this type of information on a regular basis. Be sure information is current. What may have happened three or four years ago may not be accurate.
HW/SW Infrastructure Fit and Scalability	ERP vendors usually support more than one platform. Identifying and documenting the platforms will provide a better understanding of the scalability of the system and ultimate fit with the company's direction.
Vendor Direction	This information should be tracked through the vendor history of change and upgrades to the system along with a statement of direction from each vendor. The ability to implement a stated direction is important; hence, knowing the history is critical to understanding the hype versus the reality.
Currency of Technology	Like legacy systems, a vendor's software is often written in older technology. In some sense every vendor goes through this because technology is changing rapidly, but the ability to migrate to new technology must be understood and documented during the research process.
Release Strategy	How often are there releases to the system, and what is included in the releases? Are fixes timely and minor upgrades included periodically? What is the timing for major releases, and are there defined upgrade paths? Are there vendor costs related to upgrades?
Development and Maintenance Staff	This is an area that sometimes requires some exploration. It is difficult to compare apples to apples because the "size" of the ERP vendor system will have an effect on the development and maintenance staff. One should really look for a disproportionate number within an ERP vendor and across ERP vendors.
System Update Process	This is a key area. It helps to understand how much your company's direction and long-term needs will be met by the vendor. A company's involvement in further defining the functional direction of an ERP system is important to understand and document in the vendor research process.

BOX 6-2   Short List of ERP Vendors

SAP—Founded in 1972, SAP is the recognized leader among ERP vendors, currently claiming the largest market share. Its solutions are for all types of industries and for every major market. Headquartered in Walldorf, Germany, with 12 million users, 88,700 installations, and more than 1,500 partners, SAP employs more than 32,000 people in more than 50 countries. Its products include mySAP Business Suite, SAP NetWeaver, and solutions for small and midsize companies (e.g., SAP Business One and SAP All-in-One) (www.sap.com).

(continued)

(continued)

Oracle/PeopleSoft—Oracle technology can be found in nearly every industry around the world and in the offices of 98 of the Fortune 100 companies. Oracle is the first software company to develop and deploy 100 percent Internet-enabled enterprise software across its entire product line: databases, business applications, and application development and decision support tools. Oracle provides solutions divided by industry category. The company promises long-term support for customers of PeopleSoft, which it acquired in 2004. They have 40,000 professionals, working in more than 100 countries around the world. Their three principles are as follows: simplify, standardize, and automate. Oracle is headquartered in Redwood Shores, California (www.oracle.com).

Lawson—Founded in 1975, Lawson provides industry-tailored software solutions. Lawson's solutions include enterprise performance management, distribution, financials, human resources, procurement, retail operations, and service process optimization. Headquartered in St. Paul, Minnesota, Lawson has offices and affiliates serving North and South America, Europe, Asia, Africa, and Australia (www.lawson.com).

SSA Global—By acquiring Baan in 2004, SSA Global effectively doubled the company's size. They claim to offer solutions that accomplish specific goals in shorter time frames and that they are more efficient with time. Headquartered in Chicago, Illinois, SSA also has offices all over the world (www.ssagt.com).

Great Plains—Great Plains offers integrated capabilities for financial management, distribution, manufacturing, project accounting, HR management, field service management, and business analytics. Part of the Microsoft Business Solutions group of products, its solutions can be tailored according to business needs (www.microsoft.com/businesssolutions/greatplains/).

Epicor—Epicor focuses on enterprise software solutions for midmarket companies around the world. The company claims to have solutions to a variety of needs, whether a customer is looking for a complete end-to-end enterprise software solution or a specific application. It provides solutions for a limited number of specific industries including nonprofit, distribution, manufacturing, and hospitality. Epicor is headquartered in Irvine, California (www.epicor.com).

Infor Visual—This ERP software is a flexible, fully integrated, and easy-to-use ERP suite that is widely deployed across many different types of industries from aerospace to biomedical, capital equipment, precision tools, and more. Infor Visual ERP is a scaleable solution with powerful technology to deliver real-time information, streamline operations, and increase profitability and customer satisfaction. With state-of-the-art advanced planning and scheduling, quality management, customer relationship management, time and attendance, business intelligence, and warehouse management system capabilities built in, Visual appeals to manufacturers and distributors with a combination of affordability, depth of functionality, and ease of use.

Plex Online—Plex Online's full suite of enterprise resource planning, manufacturing execution system, and supply chain management features let you eliminate the need for costly, time-consuming software and hardware installations. You gain the flexibility to meet the unique needs of your enterprise. A continuously improved ERP system means you avoid disruptive updates and the hassle of version control. You'll better manage and streamline your operations and realize key achievements such as the following:

- Increased productivity
- Reduced inventories
- Reduced scrap
- Reduced lead time
- Full compliance with ISO, QS-9000, TS-16949, Honda, and other mandates
- Improved decision making through timely and accurate information

IFS—This global enterprise applications company provides software solutions that enable organizations to become more agile. Founded in 1983, IFS pioneered component-based enterprise resources planning software with IFS Applications, now in its seventh generation. IFS's component architecture provides solutions that are easier to implement, run, and upgrade and that give companies the flexibility to respond quickly to market changes, new business opportunities, and new technologies.

IFS has a solid, growing presence in the North American business software market. IFS North America serves medium-size to large companies in a variety of key industries, including aerospace and defense, industrial manufacturing, automotive, high-tech, construction, and process industries such as food and beverage.

IFS combines a global product and organization with local support for its customers. IFS North America is headquartered in Chicago, with major offices in Milwaukee; Raleigh, North Carolina; San Jose, California; Tucson, Arizona; Toronto; and Mexico City. IFS also has a large virtual organization to bring the company even closer to its customers while providing a better quality of life for its employees.

Other successful large vendors include I2, Intentia International, QAD, IFS, Sage, Glovia, Syspro, Macola, Solomon Software, Visibility, and Flexi, among others.

MATCHING USER REQUIREMENTS TO FEATURES

There are two approaches to matching requirements to an ERP system. The traditional approach is to meet with departments and groups in the organization to define requirements taking into account legacy system functionality and BPR. A newer approach that has historically been addressed after the ERP was purchased is a format fit/gap process.

Traditionally, the identification and documentation of user and system requirements can be done as an exercise by documenting current legacy system functionality and using business process reengineering to address "best practices" in the industry. This process will provide the company with the functional requirements on which to select an ERP system. A key component of the document will need to be how the integrated ERP system cross-functional data flow will affect departments within the company. In all likelihood this will be very new to the subject matter experts and needs to be understood fully by them as the project moves forward. This process will assist in selecting an ERP based on facts and documented needs.

Two major documents are often a result of the functional requirements process. The first is a data and functional flow of departmental or business processes, including any changes to those processes; the second is a table or description of functions in each department and the level of importance of each function. Some functions are absolute requirements, whereas others are "nice to have."

With departmental functions and business processes documented, the company can now perform a high-level evaluation of the vendors identified. A request for information (RFI) is sometimes used to get this information from the ERP vendors. This is a written request to vendors asking for ERP system information only and is not part of the bid process. In gathering and reviewing the information it will quickly become apparent how close the company's business processes match a vendor's system. This will also help the company assess if the documented processes are rational and reasonable. Again, identifying vendor system functionality based on documented processes will help to purchase a system based on facts.

As with most processes, the data from the RFI will raise questions. This becomes an opportune time to bring in several of the vendors and have them answer questions related to functionality and even to demonstrate the system. Seeing a system visually will be important. It will add a level of believability to the process and start to create more of a sense of momentum to the project.

The second approach to identifying ERP functionality with organization requirements is by conducting a fit/gap. Fit/gaps is a step in the implementation process but has been usually completed after the ERP has been purchased. While some vendors will charge for fit/gaps, some organizations today have made this part of the vendor selection process and found it very beneficial in selecting the best vendor for their business. The fit/gap process has the vendor walking the organization through the ERP functionality. The organization can then see what works for them, what business processes will need to change, and what changes are necessary for the ERP to work for the organization. Time-consuming organizations have found that they know just what they are buying and what changes are necessary before the implementation is in full swing. With this information, the organization can decide on what changes will be made to the system, if any, and get an estimate on how much they cost. A benefit of this process is the organization will know up front what changes will be made to the ERP and a cost estimate in addition to the ERP purchase.

REQUEST FOR BIDS

The bid process in private industry is not required, but in public institutions it almost always is. It is an expensive and time-consuming process for both the company and vendor(s), but it can yield significant software savings when done right. In addition, one of the benefits of bidding is a more detailed understanding of the ERP system functionality and a willingness of the vendors to work with the company better to ensure a successful implementation (see Appendix A for a sample bid layout).

The request for bids (RFB), which is sometimes called request for proposals (RFP), should include the type of ERP system the company wants with specific functionality, along with a specified hardware and software infrastructure, training requirements, and any specific contract issues required by the company. If the company has an infrastructure in place it should be clearly stated in the request. A format to respond to the bid, including a pricing sheet and a clear description of the selection process and a timeline for selecting an ERP vendor, should also be a part of the RFB. The goal will be to evaluate bids from vendors, comparing "apples to apples" to determine which system will work best in the company's current and future environment.

VENDOR ANALYSIS AND ELIMINATION

The task of evaluating ERP system bids will take organizing and planning. There will be many components to a bid that require many different skill sets. Office staff will need to evaluate functionality, IT staff will evaluate the technology requirements, and contract staff will need to evaluate the contract and pricing of the system. All of this will need to be coordinated to select the top one, two, or three vendors with which to start negotiating a purchase. If there is clearly only one vendor that meets the needs with no close second, the negotiation should only include that vendor. If there is more than one, however, be sure to negotiate with each of them. If needed, bring the vendor(s) in to clarify any questions and answers.

The bid evaluation and any vendor discussions should focus on the best fit. It is important to understand that no vendor will meet all the requirements. Further evaluation is needed if the number of vendors is not reduced to one. One must evaluate both the functionality, as well as any other additional components needed to make the ERP operational, and the expansion capability of the ERP system if growth occurs within the company. It is appropriate to check references of the vendors looking for issues related to functionality and implementation. It is helpful to learn from others' experiences where possible.

Last, develop and analyze the total cost of ownership. This can be difficult, but it should be inclusive of all costs. The largest cost of the system occurs after the implementation in the system maintenance and upgrades. The actual software purchase will likely be less than 15 percent of the overall cost.

TCO was developed in the 1980s as a result of PC hardware and software proliferation. In moving computers to the desktop, many companies were evaluating what it would take to maintain all of the PCs that were showing up on staff desktops. TCO, which is essentially for ERP systems, provides a financial framework for evaluating and comparing products. It proved to be a good evaluation tool that was adapted and used in many other areas of IT. Its accuracy in ERP systems has been marginal, but it is a worthwhile exercise in the selection process.

CONTRACT MANAGEMENT AND LICENSE AGREEMENTS

It is very appropriate to enter into contract negotiations for the product, services, and maintenance after evaluating ERP vendors based on fact and narrowing the number of possibilities down to one or two. If there are two vendors, it is best to help understand the value of each product and create a competition between the competing vendors. The goal of this phase is for a company and vendor to end up with the best licensing agreement and prepare for a successful implementation. The vendor with the best ERP fit and successful track record must be the one to "win" the bid.

In discussions with the vendor(s), the talks should center on the products included in the purchase and maintenance terms of each product. Terms and conditions will be a significant part of the contract and will be addressed by the buyers, contract attorneys. Professional services for the implementation or installation can be included or bid separately. There are many professional consulting companies with much experience in system implementation that may be used. This has more recently been the preferred method because software vendors do not necessarily have the best experience in implementing an ERP system.

During discussions with the vendor(s), contract life cycle management will need to be addressed. There are certain aspects that should be present in every ERP contract that will increase the chances of a successful purchase and implementation. The first is that all deliverables must be clearly identified. They must be identified, and they must have delivery dates associated with them. Next, you must ensure that you, the customer, have acceptance authority. This may seem to be common sense, but an unsatisfactory deliverable can halt an entire implementation while parties squabble. It is much more difficult for a vendor to cut corners if the customer has a clear acceptance contract for each deliverable. Finally, the contract should identify those responsible on both sides for contract management and those who have the authority to authorize changes to the contract. With these things in place, contract management will be much easier for both sides.

There will be more of a focus on the program manager and the change management process after the purchase of an ERP system. This is preferable to ensure the ERP implementation success and highlight the importance of a contract manager. The program manager must appoint a contract quality manager or contract monitor. It will be this person's responsibility to become an expert on the contract terms and conditions. They will have primary responsibility for making sure both sides abide by the terms and conditions of the contract. The emphasis here is that they will monitor *both* sides. As important as it is for the monitor to keep the vendor honest, it is vitally important to monitor the buyer's program manager to keep the company implementing the system within the terms of the contract. A program manager or other employee involved in the implementation could unintentionally wander beyond the bounds of the contract, thus violating the agreement, which may not matter when things are going smoothly but if something goes wrong, this could be used against the buyer resulting in negotiations or court actions.

There are times when unforeseen circumstances force changes to the contract, and this can happen even with strong contract relationships. Again, it is important that you are aware of all terms and conditions of the contract to ensure differences do not fundamentally change each party's position in the contract. The intent of changes should not be to renegotiate major price and performance guidelines; rather, changes should only be made when necessary due to unforeseen circumstances, mutually beneficial reasons, or unintended mistakes. The discovery of missing hardware intended to support the vendor's software is an example of unforeseen circumstances. The vendor may offer a change to the contract to offer this hardware at a negotiated price so only the specifications affected by this circumstance are changed in the contract. The use of an inaccurate count of system users in negotiating the original contract is another example that could affect the contract. It is beneficial here for both parties to readjust the contract price based on the new accurate user count.

Finally, contract negotiations can take a significant amount of time to finalize, so expectations management is very important during that time. Senior management and end users have all been through the process and are anxious about the purchase. Communicating progress—including the next steps—keeps all involved and will also help to maintain momentum. It is best to over-communicate during this phase.

IMPLICATIONS FOR MANAGEMENT

Management must play a role in choosing the right system that will meet the company's needs and requirements. An open process based on realistic needs in selecting a vendor sets the stage for the implementation. System needs or requirements can be based on the legacy system, a business process reengineering analysis, or both. Most companies choose the latter because ERP systems are such different systems from the majority of legacy systems.

Management must remember that the vendors are very skilled at selling their systems. There must be enough time allocated to evaluate the system, observe a complete and comprehensive demonstration, and communicate to references and others using the system. In addition to how the system currently works, discussions with the vendor about future improvements and direction must be scheduled. This will allow management to understand how the vendor will be able to address the growing needs within the company and not feel like they are limited in direction and scope.

Last, if at all possible, it is best to have a couple of vendors that can meet the company needs for an ERP system. Negotiating with two vendors is time consuming, but it will yield a better purchase price. If the company has little or no experience in negotiating software contracts, there are consultants that can help. Remember that vendors have a staff of skilled negotiators and do this on a regular basis. In the negotiations be sure to address total cost of ownership. The ERP software is a small percentage of the overall implementation costs. There will be additional software products, hardware, and implementation support that should be a part of the overall equation.

Summary

- The majority of ERP systems today are purchased.
- There are a significant number of steps involved in purchasing a system that require organization and management. In this chapter, you learned the steps, including vendor research, defining

business requirements, requesting information, matching requirements to system functions, request for bids, analyzing vendors, meeting business needs, determining total cost of ownership, and finally, negotiating a contract and license agreement.

- A business must deal in facts with every step of purchasing an ERP system. The purchase decision will be made based on data by gathering information, researching vendors, documenting business processes, and reviewing vendor bids.
- Knowing detailed information on ERP system functionality and business requirements

is the basis for setting implementation expectations. This is very important during the implementation phase. During a project you will often find yourself going back to the original documents for clarification, support, and reviewing decisions.

Exercises

1. Research two recent purchases of ERP systems, the processes used to select a vendor ERP, and the level of implementation success for each.
2. Identify the components of an ERP license and why each is needed. Contact a company that

recently purchased an ERP, and review with them the components and how well they addressed each area.

Review Questions

1. What are the steps in purchasing an ERP?
2. Who generally needs to be involved in the ERP selection process and why?
3. What is total cost of ownership (TCO), and why should it be a part of the ERP selection process?
4. What are the key components in the contract negotiation and licensing?

5. Why is it important in the request for bid process to make the vendors reply in a specified format?
6. Why is communication important in this phase?
7. What is the difference between an RFI and RFB?
8. What are the benefits of a bidding process to purchase an ERP?

Discussion Questions

1. As Welch's Foods narrowed down the vendors in their quest to purchase an ERP, discuss the steps Welch's Foods took to get the best price.
2. Describe the components of TCO and why it is difficult to use in comparing ERP systems.

3. Defined and documented functional requirements are a part of the bid process. Discuss why this would be beneficial in the selection of an ERP system even if a bid is not required.

CASE 6-2
Real-World Case
Enterprise Solutions for Fruit and Vegetable Beverage Manufacturing

THOMAS R. CUTLER

Fruit and vegetable beverage manufacturers face a set of unique issues from all other beverage sectors. From safety to organic technology, solutions rarely address the gamut of the idiosyncratic requirements.

VARIABLE INPUTS/CONSISTENT OUTPUTS

The challenge for most fruit and vegetable manufacturers is that ingredients come out of the ground and can have various characteristics (an orange picked in June may have different characteristics than an orange picked in August), while customers require the finished product to be consistent. To manage variable characteristics of lots, enterprise resource planning (ERP) solutions must track lot attributes; few offer this capability. Typically, fruit and vegetable attributes are captured such as Brix/percent solids, pH/acidity, and other similar characteristics. When a lot is issued to a production batch, systems such as escape velocity systems (EVS) calculate the expected chemistry of the finished product and compare it to the specifications defined for the finished good. If the batch is out of the required specifications, the system warns the production manager.

PURCHASING CITRUS

In the citrus industry, most juicers do not purchase pounds, gallons, tons of fruit; they purchase "pound solids." Essentially juicers are purchasing the sugar that is in the fruit, not the water content. Sometimes a trailer of oranges can be 5,000-pound solids; sometime the same volume can be 4,000-pound solids if the fruit has more water and less sugar. The difficulty is they will issue the fruit into a batch by weight or volume. The relationship from pound solids to weight or volume is not a linear relationship; therefore, the technology solution must have the capacity to facilitate multiple, nonrelated units of measure on a lot basis. The O2 ERP system is one of the very few technologies that provide this capability for juicers.

CUSTOMER/ITEM SPECIFICATION

According to Evan Garber, President of EVS (www.evs-sw.com), "Many times a customer will have specifications for a juice that is different than the company's specification for the product . . . the company manufacturers orange juice with between 30 and 40 percent solids, a client may require that the orange juice that they get be 37–40 percent solids. ERP solutions must allow a fruit beverage company to manufacture to the company's specification, the customer's specification or when picking for a sales order, perform a "best-fit" of existing products to meet the customer's requirement."

GROWER ACCOUNTING IS COMPLEX

Sometimes fruit and vegetable manufacturers purchase from growers. The accounting process is often complex and must produce settlement sheets (based on when finished goods made by the material purchased is actually sold), including charge backs and commissions. Additionally, the technology solution must be able to keep vendor-specific information about purchased items, such as whether they use pesticides, fertilizers, acreage, and other pertinent data.

QUALITY CONTROL: FOOD SAFETY INCLUDING HACCP

The usual quality control and food safety issues apply to fruit and vegetable beverage with some additional concerns. Some of the Hazard Analysis Critical Control Points (HACCP) are for sterilizing the fruit upon receipt (such as bleach concentration, temperature on the pasteurizer, and metal detection on the finished goods).

LINE SCHEDULING

Fruit and vegetable beverage manufacturers deal with allergens. Allergen tracking is important, as well as color/product scheduling issues. Production scheduling must optimize a production schedule based on attributes of the formula; apple products should be run before blueberry products and nonallergens before allergens. The ERP functionality must capture the cost-saving benefit of minimizing changeover time.

KOSHER/HALAL CERTIFICATION

Some juice manufacturers make Kosher and Halal beverage products. Garber suggested, "Any technology solution must indicate whether a formula is Kosher or Halal. O2 is one of the few batch or recipe process manufacturing ERP systems that allow a user to indicate formulas that are Kosher or Halal. Whether Muslim in the case of Halal certification or a Rabbi in the case of Kosher certification, both will typically review formulations as well as historical production to verify that Kosher or Halal products have been used. The ability to print and view all formulas and ingredients that have a designation is vital and must be true of historical production batches."

Other ERP functionality for these two designations include the requirement of "source of ingredients" because of the direct relationship to lot tracking of raw materials from procurement through production to finished goods. The requirement of "status of production equipment" relates to machines that only run Kosher or Halal items (given the cleaning specification of both food designations). Garber also noted, "Production planning (finite capacity) rules can be set to state that a section of formulas are only run on certain machines. If a planner tries to run on another line, the schedule board will prohibit it from moving. Production history can be updated for the machine indicating that a batch was actually run and received the required verification that batches were run on proper equipment. Indicators that the needed blessing has been made to a particular batch, item, or lot can be indicated."

PRIVATE LABEL

Many times a manufacturer will produce private label products—the juice is all the same, however it is packaged in multiple unique packages for different clients. An ERP system must allow for the manufacture of coproducts and define different packaging based on each SKU.

EXPIRY DATES AND SELL-BY DATES

Fruit and vegetable beverage manufacturers use ingredients that have very short expiration dates. Some industries (like citrus) squeeze all the fruit right away, package some, and make the rest concentrate and freeze; others store the fruit in coolers until they are ready to use them. The latter process is constantly in a race against time to use the fruit before it spoils. ERP systems must track lot expiry dates; when creating picks for production batches, it is best if the technology selected can suggest the oldest lot (or first to expire) for the batch.

LANDED COSTING

The cost of shipping of materials can be a significant portion of the material cost. Many fruit and vegetable manufacturers need to have the total cost of receiving an item included in the cost of material; this requires landed costing functionality.

THE ORGANIC ELEMENT FOR FRUIT AND VEGETABLE BEVERAGES

Throughout the grocery industry, affluent shoppers are attracted to organic fruit and vegetable beverage choices; this marketing strategy creates a required organic authentication process for all who provide these products.

A high-ranking executive of the Soil Association suggested to Chris Mercer, editor of BeverageDaily.com, that organic food could capture around 30 percent of the food market. Mercer suggests, "Organic food sales are rising . . . surely that only suggests that people are dissatisfied with the quality of food they ate before." While consumers may want better tasting, healthier, and locally grown products, safety and quality issues must validate the perceived benefits of organic food products.

Some of the essential characteristics of organic systems include design and implementation of an "organic system plan" that describes the practices used in producing crops and livestock products; a detailed record-keeping system that tracks all products from the field to point of sale; and maintenance of buffer zones to prevent inadvertent contamination by synthetic farm chemicals from adjacent conventional fields.

According to the U.S. Agriculture Department, "organic" food is produced by farmers who use renewable resources and conserve soil and water; animals are given no antibiotics or growth hormones. Additionally, there cannot be any conventional pesticides, petroleum-based or sewage sludge-based fertilizers, and genetic engineering or radiation. "Natural" does not mean "organic"; natural usually means a product is minimally processed and contains no artificial ingredients or added color.

Organic food must have at least 95 percent organic ingredients and list which ingredients are organic in order to use the USDA seal, and it must list the certifying agent. "Made with organic ingredients" means at least 70 percent organic ingredients are contained in the food product, and it must list which ingredients are organic, yet are not permitted to use the USDA seal.

Some question the safety of organic food. It is a common misconception that organic food could be at greater risk of E. coli contamination because of raw manure application (although conventional farmers commonly apply tons of raw manure with no regulation). Organic standards set strict guidelines on manure use in organic farming: It must be either first composted or applied at least 90 days before harvest, which allows ample time for microbial breakdown of pathogens.

THE CONTROLS REQUIRED FOR ORGANIC QUALITY

Garber insisted "ERP vendors must support organic producers in food processing and manufacturing, as well as full distribution management throughout the entire supply chain."

Indeed the record keeping required to authenticate "organic" status is significant, costly, and comprehensive. Some of the key features technology solutions must provide to ensure organic standards include the following:

- Record keeping for organic raw material purchases
- Country of origin tracking of purchases
- Organic supplier tracking
- Separate organic product storage to prevent product comingling
- Hazardous chemical tracking and reporting to prevent contact with prohibited substances
- Online processing procedures to ensure adherence to compliance standards
- Online record keeping and audit trails for fast compliance reporting

The few technology solutions providers who understand the range of these special needs recognize that one size does not fit all when it comes to fruit and vegetable beverage manufacturers; the unique issues of this beverage sector requires unique solutions.

Thomas R. Cutler, President and CEO of TR Cutler, Inc. (www.trcutlerinc.com), Fort Lauderdale, Florida, is the founder of the Manufacturing Media Consortium of 3,000 journalists and editors writing about trends in manufacturing. It is the largest manufacturing marketing firm worldwide. Cutler is also the author of the *Manufacturers' Public Relations and Media Guide.* He is a frequently published author within the manufacturing sector with more than 300 feature articles authored annually; he can be contacted at trcutler@trcutlerinc.com.

CASE QUESTIONS

1. What are some of the tracking issues a fruit and vegetable manufacturer must utilize in an ERP to better ensure success?
2. What is an "organic system plan," and what are some of the key features an ERP must include?
3. Why are some manufacturing systems specific to a product?

APPENDIX A

Sample RFB

STATEMENT OF OBJECTIVES

Describe the overall business objectives for purchasing an ERP system.

BACKGROUND

General description of company or institution and the purpose of the RFB.

BID PROCESS

Bidders' Responsibilities

Preparation of Bids

a. All bids must be sealed and submitted on the *bid form* enclosed (see specifications). Telephone or fax bids will not be accepted.

b. Bids must be *signed in ink* and cost *typewritten* or in *ink*. Facsimile signatures are unacceptable. Bids that are priced or signed in pencil may be rejected as nonresponsive. Bidders are cautioned that errors, alterations, or corrections on the submitted bid must be initialed by the person signing the bid proposal or his or her authorized designee. Failure to do so may result in rejection of the bid for those items erased, altered, or corrected and not initialed.

c. *"Certification of Tax Status"* Pursuant to "State Law," the bidder certifies under penalties of perjury that to the best of the bidder's knowledge and belief, they have filed all state tax returns and paid all state taxes required by law.

d. *"Certification of Noncollusion"* Pursuant to "State Law," the bidder certifies under penalties of perjury that their bid is in all respects bona fide, fair, and made without collusion or fraud with any person, joint venture, partnership, corporation, or other business or legal entity.

Bidder's Representations

Each bidder by making its bid represents the following:

1. The bid document and specifications have been read and understood by the bidder.
2. The bid is based upon the items described in the bidding documents and specifications without exceptions.
3. The bid has been arrived at independently and is submitted without collusion.
4. The contents of the bid have not been disclosed by the bidder nor to the best of its knowledge and belief, by any of its employees or agents, to any person not an employee or agent of the bidder, and will not be disclosed to any such person prior to the opening of the bids.
5. No attempt has been made or will be made to induce any other person or firm not to submit a bid or proposal.

Conflict of Interest

The "institution or company" may, by written notice to the bidder or vendor, terminate the right of the bidder or vendor to proceed under the agreement if UMass determines that gratuities in the form of entertainment, gifts, or otherwise were offered or given by the bidder or vendor, or agency or representative of the bidder or vendor, to any officer or employee of "institution or company" with a view toward securing the agreement or securing favorable treatment with respect to the awarding or amending of the making of any determinations with respect to the agreement and as set forth in "State Law."

Bid Documents

(Public agencies must be specific with vendor as in the example below.)

One (1) original, one diskette (electronic MS Word or Excel), and (#) additional hard copies of the proposal should be submitted in a sealed envelope to:

Name and Address

Attention: director of procurement

Outside of envelope should be marked with the following information:

Proposal for: (name of bid)

Bid opening date: (date)

Proposal number: (bid #)

Attention: director of procurement

Bid Opening

Proposals will be accepted until [date and time of Bid opening] at the procurement department, when they will be publicly opened and made available for inspection. Proposals received after that date and time will not be considered. It is the bidder's responsibility to see to it that this condition is met. Receiving at our central mailroom or receiving dock is *NOT* acceptable. Please allow for possible internal mail delays in getting your bid to Procurement. No award will be made at time of bid opening. If sending proposals via FedEx, UPS, etc., please send Direct—Desk-to-Desk delivery.

The bid opening will be held at [Location].

QUESTIONS

All questions a bidder may have concerning this "Request for Proposal" document should be directed to [name and title]. All questions should be submitted electronically to [e-mail address] prior to [date and time].

Amendments

The "institution or company" reserves the right to amend, alter, or cancel the bid at any time prior to the deadline for submissions of bids. If such action is necessary, all potential bidders who have received or requested a copy of the bid will be notified of the changes to be made in writing and whether the bid opening date will be extended.

Modifications or Withdrawal of Bids

Any bid may be withdrawn or modified prior to the date and time stated in the bid for the opening of bids. Such withdrawal or modification may be either in writing and signed by an authorized representative of the bidder or made in person at the Procurement Department provided in the latter case that adequate identification is shown by the bidder or his authorized representative. Telegraphic withdrawals, but not modifications, will be accepted, provided written confirmation by the bidder is mailed and postmarked on or before the date and time set for the bid opening.

Contractual Terms

Enclosed herein please find a copy of the actual "State" Standard Contract for Services that will be used to finalize the contract process with the chosen vendor. Additional paperwork is included that is required by the bidder in order to do business with the "State." Failure to accept these documents may deem the bidder as nonresponsive.

Late Bids

Late bids will not be considered. Bids must be in the Procurement Department before the date and time specified. Postmarks are not considered in determining late bids; however, should a late bid be the only response and if the bid is also postmarked prior to the date and time of bid opening, Procurement may choose to make award to the bidder if it is determined that acceptance of the late bid is in the best interest of "institution or company." When no bids are received, or no qualified bids are received, in urgent circumstances the Procurement Department may make an award based upon informed competition and without advertising.

Award

   a. Award shall be made to the vendor(s) who most closely meets the needs of the "institution or company" based upon its selection criteria.
   b. A review committee has been established consisting of administrative personnel who will review all proposals and select the vendor that offers the cost and capabilities that are in the best interest of the "institution or company."
   c. The right is reserved to reject any and all bids, to split bids between vendors, to omit an item or items, or to accept any proposal deemed best for the "institution or company."
   d. The "institution or company" reserves the right to waive technicalities, irregularities, and omissions, if in the opinion of the Procurement Department they are insubstantial and to do so will serve the best interest of "institution or company."
   e. The Procurement Department reserves the right to make an award within one-hundred and twenty (120) calendar days from the date bids are opened, unless otherwise specified in the bid.
   f. Generally, notification of award to the successful vendor is accomplished by means of a purchase order. However, the vendor receiving this award will receive written notice and be required to enter into a formal contract.
   g. If the awardee fails to sign the proffered contract after award, the Procurement Department may determine that the awardee has abandoned the contract and shall be free to make an award to another vendor. In such a case, the Procurement Department may also choose to debar the awardee from bidding on future requirements of "institution or company."

Debriefing

Any Vendor may request a debriefing within one (1) week after receiving notification of award, to discuss the Selection Committee's evaluation of its bid proposal. Request for debriefing shall be made in writing to the Procurement Director. Debriefing shall not include discussions of any competing bids.

Freedom of Information (only required if state has this law)

All proposals received are subject to "State Law" regarding public access to such documents. Statements or endorsements inconsistent with those statutes will be disregarded.

References

The "institution or company" reserves the right to contact by phone or to arrange a site visit, with any or all of the respondent's clients, which are of the same size and scope, and contact may be made without the assistance of the respondent.

Prebid Conference

The "institution/company" will hold a nonmandatory prebid conference on [date, time, location].

APPENDIX B

Standard Contractual Terms and Conditions

Terms and Conditions (Need to contact Procurement for standard terms and conditions but T&Cs usually include the following sections)

> Contractor's certification
>
> Liability
>
> Compliance with laws and indemnification of university
>
> Term

- The term of the initial contract will be for (length of time)
- Renewal terms are possible for a period of (#) months each.
- A maximum of (#) renewal terms are possible under this RFP/agreement.
- A vendor review will occur quarterly based on the service-level agreement. A vendor evaluation will occur annually. A negative evaluation will be sufficient reason for the university to invoke contract termination as described in the following section.

TERMINATION

> Conditions and timing
>
> Options in event of termination

Below is a partial list of items that may be a part of terms and conditions

> Assignment by contractor and subcontracting
>
> Notices and invoices
>
> Governing law
>
> Tax exemption

Nondiscrimination in employment and affirmative action

Record keeping, audits, and inspection of records

Confidentiality

Publicity, publication, reproduction, and use of contract products or materials

Political activity prohibited, antiboycott warranty

Protection of property

Insurance

EVALUATION OF PROPOSALS

Each proposal will be evaluated by a screening committee against the following criteria to determine which vendor(s) are most capable of meeting requirements.

- Ability to meet listed conditions
- Demonstrated ability and past experience to provide the services requested
- References
- Cost

ABILITY TO MEET REQUIREMENTS

Is your company able to meet all listed requirements and conditions listed within this RFB, especially **Mandatory Requirements**?

YES _____   NO_____

VENDOR INFORMATION

Vendor Overview

Please provide the following:

- The name and location of your company.
- A brief general description of your business.
- How many years has your company been in business?
- Is your company a subsidiary of another corporation? If so, what is the name of the parent company?
- Please explain your strategy for developing new products and product enhancement, including information on the current status of your product, upcoming planned enhancements, and release dates for future releases.
- How many personnel are employed by your company? Please describe the breakdown by functional areas in your company.

    Sales:

    Software support:

    Software development:

    Other:

- Please provide any certifications relevant to this RFB.

CLIENT BASE

Provide specific reference information for three organizations currently using a configuration similar to the one being proposed to include the following:

- Organization name and location
- Starting date of service
- Relevant volume statistics
- Contact name, title, and telephone number

List total sales made in the last 36 months, number of unique clients, applications purchases, and purchase date.

SCOPE OF PROJECT

General Requirements

Describe general requirements for the system component by component

Specific Requirements

Describe in detail, by component, specific requirements that must be addressed in the bid and how the requirement will be met. It is important to note that not all requirements need to be described in detail. Only those deemed by the institution or company to be vital to the success of the implementation are important.

Equipment Capabilities

Vendor must describe the types of equipment needed and any sizing information available.

Additional Capabilities

Other specific capacities the system has that are not identified in the General or Specific requirements section that is or are a part of the system.

Ongoing Support

Vendor must describe ongoing support processes available to the institution/company.

Documentation

Description of documentation included with the purchase of the ERP.

Costs

Basic system

Please specify what is included in the basic system cost. For example:

- Hardware
- Software
- Installation
- Maintenance
- Training
- Documentation
- Any other (please specify)

Please specify the timeframes for acceptance and warranty of products and services.

Maintenance costs

Please specify any maintenance costs. For example:

• Upgrades
• Documentation
• Technical support
• Any other (please specify)

Options and services

Please specify any options and services available at an additional cost. For example:

• Training (please indicate on site and/or at your facility)
• Consulting
• Customization
• Data conversion
• Any other (please specify)

References

The vendor must provide three references for essentially similar installations. Reference information must include the name, address, and telephone number of a person knowledgeable about the system installation as well as a brief statement of the scope of the installation.

Acknowledgment form should be included in bid document.

RETURN THIS FORM IMMEDIATELY!

Acknowledgment: Receipt of Request-For-Bid Documents
Bid Number:
Title:

Please take a moment to acknowledge receipt of the attached bid documents. Your compliance with this request will help us to maintain proper bid follow-up procedures while ensuring that all vendors have the opportunity to bid.

Date Issued: _____
Date bid received: ____/____/____
Do you plan to attend the Bidders Meeting
to be held on _____?   Yes_____ No_____
Please indicate who will be attending:
Do you plan to submit a proposal?   Yes_____ No_____
_____

Print or type the following information:
Company name: _____
Address: _____
City or Town: _____
Phone: _____
Fax: _____
Received by: _____

Note: Faxed acknowledgments are requested! FAX #
A cover sheet is NOT necessary.
IMPORTANT: DO NOT FAX BIDS.
BIDS MUST BE SUBMITTED IN SEALED PACKAGES!

BIDDER'S CHECK LIST

This form need not be returned with your bid. It is suggested that you review and check off each action as you complete it.

—— 1. The bid has been signed by a duly authorized representative of the company (unsigned bids are automatically rejected).

—— 2. The bid prices you have offered have been reviewed and verified.

—— 3. The price extensions and totals have been checked. (In case of discrepancy between unit prices and total prices, the unit price will govern the bid evaluation).

—— 4. Any errors, alterations, corrections, or erasures to unit prices, total prices, et cetera, are initialed by the person who signs the proposal or his designee. Such changes made and not initialed will automatically reject the bid.

—— 5. The payment terms are net 30 days. Net terms for periods less than 30 days may result in bid rejection. (You may offer cash discounts for prompt payment.)

—— 6. Any technical or descriptive literature, drawings, or bid samples that are required have been included with the bid.

—— 7. Any addenda to the bid have been signed and included.

—— 8. The envelope has been addressed to: RFB – Name, Number, and Address

—— 9. The envelope has been clearly marked with the bid number and bid opening date.

—— 10. If additional copies are required as part of your response, make sure the original is clearly marked.

—— 11. The bid is mailed or hand-delivered in time to be received no later than the designated opening date and time (usually 2:00 P.M.). Late bids are **NOT** accepted under any circumstances. Faxed responses are not accepted. Please allow enough time if mailing or delivering your proposal.

7

Operations and Postimplementation

LEARNING OBJECTIVES

After reading this chapter, you should be able to:

- Describe all the components to a successful "Go-live" and determine their readiness.
- Understand what is involved in stabilizing the system after "Go-live" and how to track and address problems and issues on a daily basis.
- Value the transition from developing a system to supporting it in a production environment.

- Understand the process of transferring knowledge to operational staff and its importance to long-term system success.
- Realize the value of training before and after "Go-live."

CASE 7-1
Opening Case
Hugger-Mugger ERP Implementation

Source: Based on Stafford, Jan (Ed.). (2006). Hugger-Mugger fixes goofed Open Source ERP Implementation, *SearchOpenSource.com*, July 5.

Hugger-Mugger is based in Salt Lake City, Utah, with revenues of about $5 million. The company produces yoga accessories (e.g., yoga mats, bags, and shorts) (www.huggermugger.com). The company is more than 20 years old and had implemented a number of standalone systems over those years. These systems were proving to be out of date with the needs of Hugger-Mugger, so they decided to implement an integrated ERP.

Hugger-Mugger went through a selection process for midsized ERPs and selected Compiere. The company chose the package based on its needs coupled with the cost of the software. Compiere is an open-source ERP system (open-source software (OSS) that required free distribution applications with the source code. There was no warranty or liability with the product (i.e., there usually is a cost for support and services). After the selection of Compiere, the software was installed and implemented in very short period of time. The IT staff made most of the decisions on how the software was to work. No documentation was created on the implementation. User training was minimal at best, and a true understanding of the system was not achieved by "Go-live"—a recipe for disaster. They did use a well-documented or well-understood project methodology, and users were not involved enough in the implementation process. Users actually knew very little of how to use the system, nor did they understand its complexity. Data entry was slow and incorrect, which resulted in orders and customer information that made no sense. To make matters worse, IT staff left after the implementation. The new company president, Tom Chamberlain, quickly realized there was a major problem with the implementation and set about to fix many of the oversights made during the process. A consulting company, which had implementation experience with Compiere and used a well-documented project methodology, was hired to address the problems. Two dedicated IT staff, and the inclusion of users in the process, have improved the system performance immensely. "A customer can place an order in the afternoon of one day, and it will be on the dock to ship at 9 A.M. the next morning," Chamberlain said.

CONCLUSION

As ERP implementations go, this one was not well organized, and it lacked a good methodology for moving through the phases of an implementation. The new president wisely brought in an implementation partner to work through the problems and stabilize the system. The training and readiness for "Go-live" were almost nonexistent.

PREVIEW

The ERP implementation phase, just before going live, is one of the most critical points in a project's success. It is the culmination of a number of planned tasks, activities, and resources brought together to implement the system based on the goals of the organization. Even though there were a number of issues that can be identified in the Hugger-Mugger case, it was clear they were not ready to "go live." In assessing an ERP project's readiness for Go-live, it is vital to focus the efforts of the teams to ensure that task and activities are completed before going live. This allows project management to address any outstanding issues that may jeopardize the Go-live date. An elaborate readiness process is considered a "best practice." The readiness assessments must be conducted and communicated to the team and organization, and they should begin well in advance of the Go-live date. This readiness process needs to include as many team members, appropriate users, and managers as possible because it helps the overall organization to understand that the implementation is near and changes will be taking place. This is also good for the change management process. During a project it seems like the system will never be implemented. There is so much work needed to be done, and getting through it all is very overwhelming. A good readiness process cuts through all that and lets the different teams and organization know that Go-live is not too far off.

Although it may seem like a lot of work to get to go live, much of the success of the implementation lies with the stabilization and postproduction support processes. Stabilization is the time from Go-live to about 90 days after, or until the number of issues and problems has been reduced to a small, manageable number. During the stabilization period, development within the system should cease. All resources should be focused on ensuring users understand how to use the system and that issues and problems are resolved as quickly as possible. How well the teams respond to stabilization will somewhat determine how well the system is accepted by the end users and management. Daily and continual monitoring of the implementation issues will provide a basis for moving from stabilization to postproduction support. In the case of Hugger-Mugger, the stabilization process brought into focus a number of problems with the implementation methodology prior to going live. This will always be the case.

Training also gears up during the readiness process and continues through stabilization and postproduction support. A successful ongoing training component will be important to the long-term success of an ERP implementation, beginning just before Go-live. Training needs to address all the different processes for the users because the new system will seem overwhelming. In addition, training should be a continual, ongoing process that will allow the end users to know that there will be help if required. Users will even want and need to take refresher courses to better understand how the system works better. Figure 7-1 depicts the areas of focus for this chapter.

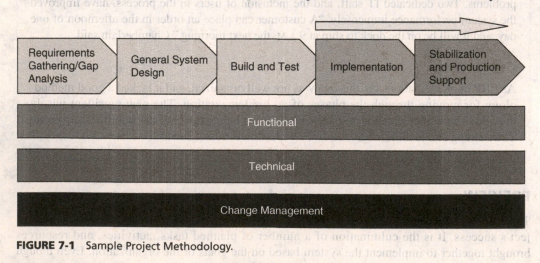

FIGURE 7-1 Sample Project Methodology.

GO-LIVE READINESS

Several tasks and activities need to fall into place to Go-live, and determining the level of readiness is a challenge. If an elaborate readiness checkpoint is not in place, steps will be missed and the Go-live will be very bumpy or, worse, have to retreat back to the old legacy system. Assessing the level of readiness should start several months before the actual Go-live date. For some time the teams will have been working to finish a variety of tasks and activities throughout the project. The Go-live readiness process will clarify the progress toward completing the activities and identifying the major issues on which to focus before going live. All implementation areas must be assessed in the readiness process. These include the infrastructure, development, configuration, conversion, testing, training, communications, operations, command central, reporting, and users. Input from the project teams, users, and team leaders needs to be gathered and summarized for review.

With the first readiness review many tasks and activities will not be completed or look close to completion. The conversion team may not have had a successful conversion, and testing will likely be problematic, especially if development is not complete. Training documentation and course objectives may not be finalized, and reporting may be totally up in the air. This is okay. The first readiness checkpoint gives management and the project team a very good idea of what remains to be done before going live. It raises issues of what needs to be accomplished for Day one and creates a focus for the teams. Management will be able to address issues with additional staff or project management. Only after several months or years of working through an implementation will the readiness process let the teams know just how much more needs to be completed before going live.

Go-live readiness is at best tedious and time consuming. Most staff and users will be frustrated with the process during the first round of review. Teams often get caught up in the emotion of day-to-day problems and issues. Readiness will clarify for them what needs to be done and move the teams and staff from dealing with the anxieties of the project to the tasks at hand to prepare for Go-live. It will help the project management office (PMO) to address areas that are not ready and to notify senior management on the project progress toward going live.

Go-live readiness reviews need to be documented and communicated to the project team and the company. Readiness involves documenting the current metrics related to what remains to be completed. These data, along with input via discussions with all team members, need to be reviewed and verified for accuracy. This process will allow team members to express concerns about project readiness and bring to light the facts of what is truly complete and what remains before going live. The project management office evaluates data and progress based on input from the project leads and a few other team members. This process allows for all involved to provide input and keeps the teams centered on what is truly complete and what is not as complete as one believes.

The first readiness review will bring several issues to light on which to focus and, one hopes, not too many surprises. From the first to the last review, the teams will see significant project progress toward going live. The Go-live date needs to be evaluated with each review. Unless there are a significant number of new issues or changes in the reported project status, the Go-live date should not be changed with the first Go-live readiness review. There should be at least three readiness reviews, about one month to six weeks apart, with the last one to two weeks before the Go-live date to decide ultimately on going live. With the second and subsequent readiness reviews the Go-live date should be assessed as to whether the date can be met. As with any project there should be a Go-live date with at least two other alternative dates. These Go-live dates, along with the readiness review status, will help the project management office decide on the actual Go-live date. The readiness review status and Go-live date must be communicated to all involved. This will be important to the credibility of the process.

A detailed report needs to be available, along with an executive summary for senior management. It is important to meet with senior management to review the readiness status for a couple of reasons: It will inform senior management on the status of the project and allow them to ask questions related to moving forward. It also gives the project management office another opportunity to discuss with senior management the successes and issues with the project. Even though senior management should generally be up to date on what is going on, the Go-live readiness meetings create a higher level of awareness of how this implementation will affect the company. Finally, there needs to be an abbreviated readiness review just before Go-live to assess any of the outstanding issues brought to light in the previous review.

The Go-Live Readiness Review and Status Report is often a table that shows the status of each area at a glance, with the key activities that need to be completed or a workaround agreed to before going live.

Sample Go-Live Readiness Review and Status Report

Category	Criterion	Criticality	Site 1	Site 2	Group 1	Group 2	Key Measures	Contingent Workaround(s)	Decision Owner	Task Contact	Minimum "Pass Status"	Current Actual Status	Assessment Assessment Date

Category: Technical infrastructure readiness
Operational readiness
Testing readiness
Conversion readiness
Training readiness
Communications readiness
Production support readiness
Audit readiness
Risk readiness
Corporate management readiness

Criterion: What activity or component needs to be ready?

Criticality: High, medium, or low

Site or Group: Area, location, or group that must be ready

Key Measurement: What activity or task needs to be completed?

Workaround:	If the task or activity is not complete before Go-live, is there an acceptable workaround?
Decision Owner:	Name of the person responsible for making this decision.
Task Contact:	Name of the person responsible for working on the task and can address the actual status of the task or activity.
Minimum Pass:	Usually a percentage of task or activity that must be completed before going live. This can be anywhere from 100 to 85 percent complete.
Current Status:	This is the status as of the readiness assessment
Assessment:	This is usually a red, yellow, green indicator. Red means that, given the current assessment, this activity will not be ready before the Go-live date. Yellow indicates that in all likelihood the task or activity will be completed. Green indicates the activity is complete.
Assessment Date:	Date on which the task or activity was assessed.

Source: Developed and used at UMass for Peoplesoft ERP implementation with Accenture as the implementation partner.

There needs to be a list of tasks and activities identified for each category. This information is usually taken from the project plan and incorporated into the readiness document. The PMO and team leads are key contributors to setting up the initial document. The process for determining readiness consists of a series of meetings and discussions on the status of each area's tasks and activities. The meeting will be with each of the team leads, team members, and the subject matter experts (SMEs). It must be conducted by the PMO with the goal toward gathering input on project activities. Listening is the key skill for the PMO during these meetings. The PMO will assess the overall implementation readiness after each meeting. As previously stated, the PMO should see a lot of *red* items the first time through. It does not mean the Go-live date is in jeopardy; rather, it will help to focus the project teams on what needs to be accomplished in the time period between the assessment and Go-live (see sample readiness assessment in Appendix A). The readiness assessment must be reviewed by the teams and with senior management for consensus once it is ready and documented.

ERP TRAINING

It is important to discuss the value of training and the training concept on ERP implementations as an organization is going live. Training must be provided to everyone who will be using the system and should use real data and examples that will be performed once the system is "live." Training does not need to be completed before going live, but providing training in the essential transactions is important, although it is best for the other processes (i.e., those that are periodic and take place once a quarter or yearly) to be taught at the time they are going to be used. The focus for training must be on how the organization is going to use the system and transactions for daily processing. Users will at best be very concerned about making mistakes. They will be using the system with real transactions, some that they did not encounter during training. If done correctly, training will capture about 90 percent of what users will see on a daily basis.

A training program must be available with predictable results that follow the training guides and show examples. The program must also provide a practice environment for those who have been trained that has real data with all security and configuration in place so users can practice in the system without worrying about what happens to the data. The practice instance should be available in the training labs as well as on user desktops. The availability of these data will help users to try transactions and processes with a variety of data and input to see how the system will work. The practice instance often becomes the place where users try things out if they do not know exactly what will happen in the production system. Over time, the practice instance has proven to be very worthwhile.

Many organizations are using training as a validation of the users' understanding of how to use the system. This is sometimes called a "certification" process. It ensures that users know and understand how to use the system before going live. It is an effective tool for identifying staff who need more training or some additional practice on the system. This has become highly effective and a part of successful ERP implementations. Training will not be a one-time process. Continual training must be provided on a regular basis for the users to utilize the system fully.

With regard to operability, approximately 10–15 percent of ERP implementations have smooth introductions that deliver the anticipated benefits.[1] The counter to that is poor training, which is considered to be one of the main contributors to such widespread ERP implementation failure. A well-thought-out training plan, with good training materials, is a significant component of a successful ERP implementation.

ERP training can be delivered by several different methods and a variety of personnel. The different personnel could include trainers who work for the software vendor, in-house staff who often don't have that much experience with the ERP system, or third-party trainers that have specific experience in ERP systems (i.e., SAP, Oracle, Peoplesoft). The training is generally conducted either on-site where the client uses the ERP or in a classroom away from the client's workstation or work environment. There are multitudes of training formats available (e.g., Web-based virtual classrooms, computer-based training, knowledge warehouses, video courses, self-study books, and pop-up help screens) with an almost endless menu to suit every need of any sized company with small or huge budgets. A variety of these methods must be available to be effective at training simply because not all users learn the same way. Developing a variety of ways to train will better ensure the effectiveness of training and the overall success of the implementation.

ERP training has become a giant business, and it is usually independent of the ERP applications themselves. There seems to be a train of thought that the better the training the faster you

---

[1] Wheatley, M. (June 1, 2000). Enterprise Systems. ERP Training Stinks. *CIO Magazine.*

will see the business metrics move in the direction you're seeking.[2] Most people in the IT field, however, now believe that the training component that matters most to success is not showing clients where to point and click. This has historically been called "training," but it is now viewed as inadequate. Truly valuable training must focus on the underlying flow of information through the business.

John Conklin, the CIO of World Kitchen (formerly Corning), said he "separates training into two parts: education and training." He asserts that "education is the why, who, and where issues, while training is the how part of the equation." ERP implementations were historically considered purely technical, but today most issues during and after an implementation are people and culture related. The human element of the training process is so important because the users must understand how the relationships of processes and people in different departments affect each other. For example, users must understand how poor data entry processes from an operational standpoint can adversely affect other parts of the business. If the sales department inputs questionable data into the ERP, it is entirely possible that it will have a waterfall of negative consequences down the line (e.g., invoices not getting sent or, worse, not being paid).

As previously stated in many ERP implementations, training is not given very much consideration in the overall process. Training is the first thing to cut when it comes to budget. Even though training should be conducted just in time, it usually comes as a postimplementation concern when deadlines are already missed and timeframes are being compressed to fit the schedule. Thus, it gets put into the postimplementation schedule as a last-minute activity and is usually problematic.

With regard to business process, training must be put forth to middle management because decisions that once had no negative effect on the business (e.g., circumventing system inputs in order to get product to customers expediently) may in fact be catastrophic in an ERP postimplementation environment. Although trained in operating, the system managers will not see far enough down the road to decide to forego the short-term benefits of conducting a bad business process. Only a broad education in the company's ERP-mediated business processes will do that.

Overall, training needs to be endorsed by senior management early in the implementation process so that adequate funding and scheduling are utilized for business processes and technical training.

STABILIZATION

The stabilization process begins when the ERP system software is in production, initial training is complete, and conversion of critical data is done. It has taken a lot of time and effort by the project teams to get to this point. There have been many difficult and challenging issues, but the implementation itself is not the goal—it is merely the means that helps an organization to get to the predefined goals (e.g., labor savings, better customer service, and process improvements). In any case, it is a major accomplishment to get to this point.

After the ERP system goes live, the organization will need to shift into a stabilization process. This process can take anywhere from 60 to 90 days, depending on the number of issues.

[2] Ibid.

This stabilization time frame must be used to let the users get familiar with the system and the new processes and to fix problems or bugs in the system. There should be very little development addressed during this phase. There should also be tracking and communication of problems in place. In all likelihood there will be a significant number of questions and issues that arise (i.e., how the system is working, incorrect data conversion, and system stability). It will be important to log all issues and track them to resolution. Users must be aware on a daily basis of what has been resolved and what is still outstanding. During the stabilization process the teams and users will likely meet once in the morning and in the late afternoon to discuss problem resolution and upcoming cycles just to be sure everyone understands what is being done. This would include any batch cycles or reports that will be run overnight.

During the stabilization period, the IT staff will be monitoring the infrastructure for response times and ensure that backups are taken appropriately for all hardware and software; hence, they are often simultaneously researching and fixing problems. As previously discussed, there are many components to an ERP implementation, and all of them need to work together for a successful implementation. Any one component that does not work correctly can impact the system performance, trigger problems that were not discovered before, and flood the IT support center with many calls. Likewise, the subject matter expects should be prepared to help many users from their departments operate the system in the correct way and support them while they are making the first steps in the system.

Stabilization is a demanding and frustrating period, which is characterized by long hours, many problems, and lots of anxiety. Users are often not very sure of themselves, which may or may not be a result of insufficient training but will mostly be of human nature (i.e., confusion, excitement). Some user issues and activities that arise during stabilization are as follows:

- Customizations add to the complexity if they are not documented and communicated appropriately.
- Not being able to perform ad hoc activities is another issue in stabilizing the ERP system. It is not so much that the system is not capable of ad hoc activities; rather, it is more about learning how to accomplish the activity that seemed so simple in the legacy. This is often frustrating to users or managers, and it sometimes leads to low morale or motivation.
- Another issue is that one of the reasons for implementing the system is business process reengineering. Business processes are new to users, and they make mistakes as they use the new process for the first time.
- If the organization opts for a parallel implementation approach, the ERP system is operated concurrently with the old legacy system, which is labor intensive, confusing, and frustrating. In addition, determining whether a reported problem is a real problem or not is time consuming. Finally, reconciliation has to be done between the new ERP system and the old legacy system to validate the inputs and outputs.

There are strategies that the company can apply to minimize business disruptions due to stabilization problems. Some of them can be applied in advance, whereas others have to be applied in real time. The ERP implementation team can identify not only problematic processes but also a workaround for them. Rigorous testing during the implementation phase should uncover many errors and bugs that can be fixed or documented. During the stabilization period, the implementation team can provide frequent communications with its suppliers and customers, which will facilitate their support in this difficult time and understanding in case of errors that result from running the new software. The company can opt for the parallel approach (i.e., maintaining the old legacy system while going live with the ERP); however, this strategy can introduce a problem, as well as double the effort and cost required to operate the system. Training users for change management is critical and can prevent many problems that result from frustration and confusion. Changing business processes to match the system functionality can help, although it can also introduce business process issues. There is the opposite approach, which is to customize the software to match the business process; again, this can introduce software bugs.

POSTPRODUCTION SUPPORT

The development of a postproduction support plan and process is as important as any set of activities outlined during the development phase. In the past many project managers used Go-live as their final and primary milestone in the implementation process. Getting to the Go-live point is actually just one part of a successful implementation (Figure 7-2). In fact, if the postproduction process is inadequate, then the implementation may be considered a failure. It is that important!

Managing the daily system operations and ensuring that the system is doing what it needs to do is really the purpose of postproduction support. Many new processes must be understood and communicated to gain the benefits of the ERP implementation fully. It becomes very relevant very quickly after Go-live. Key measurements need to be in place to understand the effectiveness of the new system fully. Without the data, users and management will question and even complain about how much has changed and that the system is ineffective. It is important to know the effect the new system has on the organization. Are people using the system effectively? Is the software making the business more efficient (e.g., through improved reporting or time to distribution)? Is it adding value to the organization?

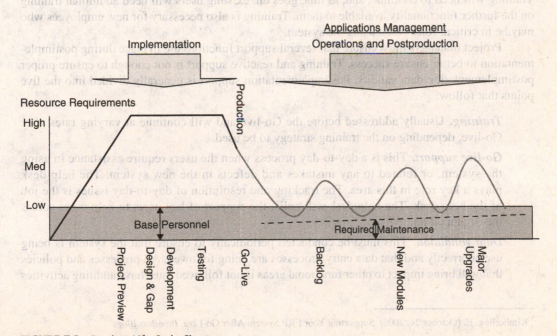

FIGURE 7-2 Product Life Cycle Chart.

These are many questions that go unanswered until well after Go-live, which is why it is important to have a solid user support program in place to supplement your technical cutover activities.[3]

Many of the risks associated with cutting over to the new ERP can be reduced by appropriate pre–Go-live and end-user training, but additional support is needed after the system is put into production. Subject matter experts and core project team members should be used to provide general support to answer simple process and system questions. The vast majority of user problems are attributable to the lack of understanding of the system and how business processes interact with the system. This will be the case more often than not; usually, it is not a bug or problem of the ERP system not working correctly. Subject matter experts will need to provide ongoing support for people who encounter difficulties. The support process is divided into tiers. Tier 1 is considered triage and is usually the help desk or call center. This group will attempt to address very straightforward problems or questions. The calls are often related to password problems or resets or general access issues. Beyond that, the help desk will forward the question or problem to Tier 2. Tier 2 support is where the subject matter experts are used. The subject matter experts must be available to answer system process questions or provide resolution on how to maneuver through the system to complete processes. This will initially include basic navigation and, as time goes by and the users become more knowledgeable, the questions will be more about processes and data flow. If Tier 2 subject matter experts cannot resolve the issue or problem within a short period of time, then the issue should be bumped to Tier 3. Tier 3 can be a combination of technical staff along with vendor or implementation partner support. These are often complex problems that will require the technician to research and fix.

There are numerous ways to add support to users in addition to in-person support. This includes Web-based frequently asked questions (FAQs), job aids that are printable that describe how to access and complete a function within the system, short videos on using the system, and complete training documentation that shows and describes step by step how to use the system. Training will need to continue, and, as time goes on, existing users will need additional training on the further functionality available to them. Training is also necessary for new employees who may be in critical roles when using the system.

Project managers must ensure that several support functions are in place during postimplementation to better ensure success. Training and reactive support is not enough to ensure proper postimplementation data validity. Postimplementation support is generally divided into the five points that follow:

Training. Usually addressed before the Go-live and will continue at varying rates after Go-live, depending on the training strategy to be used.

Go-live support. This is a day-to-day process when the users require assistance in using the system, or related to any mistakes and defects in the new system. The help desk plays a key role in this area. The tracking and resolution of day-to-day issues is the job of the help desk. The help desk will enlist the support of key users to help users across the organization.

Data validation. This must be conducted periodically to ensure that the system is being used correctly and that data entry processes are being followed. All processes and policies that will bring impact to other functional areas if not followed must have auditing activities

---

[3] Kimberling, E. (October 24, 2006). Supporting Your ERP System After Go-Live. *Ittoolbox Blogs.*

until they are stabilized. This is mostly accomplished through the development of detail reports that identify data problems within the system.

Data correction. The system is sometimes implemented, but the data are not converted correctly or automated interfaces update the system incorrectly. The ability to identify bad data and correct it will be a part of the stabilization process. In cases where there are large amounts of data to be corrected, an automated mass update process needs to be available and used to correct the data; however, it is not something that should be used often. Correcting data in such large quantities can lead to other data and systems issues if not done carefully.

Patches and fixes. All during the implementation process and even while in production, software errors/bugs will be encountered and reported to the vendor for a solution. Vendors have a support group that will work to reproduce the error in an unmodified environment to ensure the error is of their doing. If the error is reproduced, the vendor will research the best way to resolve the error. Once the error is resolved through coding changes or other means, the vendor will distribute the patch/fix to the software for testing and implementation. The patch/fix will need to be added to the software and regression tested and moved to production. A well-defined process will need to be in place since patches/fixes are very much a part of an implementation and production support process.

New features/upgrades. No system is ever complete: Businesses change or grow, and with that the system must keep pace to remain current. The change control process must be managed and addressed with the implementation. It is very important to ensure that resources are available to incorporate the evolution of the solution that was already implemented. This approach also increases the level of confidence of the users toward the system because they begin to understand that the system will continue to evolve as the ERP is better understood. In addition to patches/fixes vendors will release upgrades to the product. These upgrades will incorporate new and updated features to the system. All upgrades need to be evaluated to determine if or how the feature will be implemented within the business. This process will need to be planned and managed as upgrades are released. Scheduling the best time to implement upgrades will need to be discussed with the users. Oftentimes meetings with the users are needed to communicate the changes to the product and how they will be implemented (minifit gap). While upgrades are not as elaborate as an implementation, they must be planned and managed using an implementation methodology to ensure the upgrade is implemented effectively.

By clearly defining and communicating Go-live and the ongoing support processes as part of the overall ERP implementation, you will better set the overall expectations and leverage the ERP to realize measurable business benefits and return on investment from your ERP project.

KNOWLEDGE TRANSFER

You need to concentrate on the visible key issues in an ERP implementation, but a good project manager must work at all issues including those that are much less obvious and yet still important to the long-term ERP system success. This is exactly the case with knowledge transfer. Some problems related to knowledge management are loss of knowledge due to an employee who leaves the company, high learning curve for new users, forgetting system features, and misuse of the system. These problems often surface in the postimplementation phase when the system is in production and is being used extensively by the company; however, if the implementing organization makes sure there is a knowledge management plan in place, the company can prevent the pitfalls and missteps that would otherwise occur. A study of more than 100 SAP customers[4] concludes that there are four areas businesses should focus on when they implement an ERP system. One of the four areas is training and knowledge development (the other three are vision and strategy, structure and decision making, and management processes).

The ERP implementation process can be divided into major phases: Requirements Gathering and Definition, Build, Go-Live, Stabilization, and Ongoing Support. Knowledge is gained and lost during any of these phases, and the most problematic time frames are moving from one phase to another. More often than not, there are changes in personnel during those time frames as both internal and external resources leave or join the ERP implementation team or users. The project team must therefore ensure that there is a well-defined process in place during those time frames in order to transfer the knowledge and skill to new or existing staff or team members. Knowledge and skill transfer should be an integral part of the implementation plan, starting from Day one. If you are using an implementation partner or external consultants, then be sure that they have defined the roll-on and roll-off process and that it includes knowledge transfer.

Multiple aspects of the implementation process must be documented during the Definition and Build phases. From the project management perspective, such issues as project monitoring and tracking, collaboration and communication, subject matter expertise, and lesson-learned repository should be documented. From the operational perspective, it is important to document the business processes and how they are mapped to the ERP software. From the IT perspective, hardware and software architecture, network configuration, and the like need to be documented. Structured and integrated visibility to the knowledge base (i.e., ERP Center of Excellence (COE)) is critical for easy accessibility and retrieval of information.

The team composition is likely to change in the Go-Live and Stabilization phases: Internal and external resources used in the Define and Build phases leave, especially third-party consultants, whereas new internal staff takes their place. As mentioned earlier, the boundary between the phases is a weak point. The first task in the knowledge management plan should therefore be monitoring the transition from one phase to the other, which enables a smooth transfer of knowledge. Other tasks include training guides, user guides, known problems, a troubleshooting guide, IT architecture and code repository, and third-party tools used to access the ERP system (e.g., reporting tools). The ERP COE is replaced with an Application COE at this stage.

In the ongoing support phase, the departments and users involved are likely to change again. This time, such supply chain partners as customers and vendors are added to the user base, along with analysts who use data warehouse tools for analysis of the ERP information. The knowledge base must therefore be revised to reflect the new communities involved.

There are knowledge management systems that can help streamline the process of knowledge and skill transfer. With such a system in place, one centralized data repository can then be used by the implementation team to store the documents. In addition, one data repository will eliminate confusion, duplication, and losing data. Moreover, there will be only one interface to be used by the entire team: The knowledge management system will store the data in one consistent format, thereby making it easier for new users to collect documentation input by different people.

---

[4] Brennan, M. (2004). *Knowledge Transfer Enables Enterprise Performance.* Working Paper, Carleton University's Sprott School of Business.

The project management office must be proactive and ensure that there is a good knowledge management plan as part of the ERP implementation process. A knowledge management plan will ensure knowledge is retained, reduce the cost of support due to lower number of support calls, facilitate faster learning, better maximize the capabilities of the system, cut time in troubleshooting problems, and ensure a correct use of the system.

IMPLICATIONS FOR MANAGEMENT

The closer an ERP implementation gets to its Go-live date, the more project management must focus on the issues, tasks, and activities to being ready. The readiness process will identify the issues and help project management focus its resources and efforts. The readiness process must be planned and organized well in advance of the Go-live date. The PMO must have plans for several readiness processes to understand the level of readiness of each project area fully. Each time the teams go through a readiness process, the level of risk should be reduced. If that is not the case, the Go-live date is very much at risk and should be reconsidered.

To ensure a successful and sustainable ERP implementation, one must have a well-thought-out and understood knowledge transfer process. Even though it is best to ensure as much continuity as possible during a project, the reality is that staff will change. This will happen with subject matter experts and technical staff. To lose this knowledge base and the history of decisions sometimes leads to revisiting problems and issues, and it can slow a project down. During the stabilization and postproduction phases most projects lose a number of staff. This will include consultants, implementation partner staff, full-time and part-time staff, and even end users. When this happens, a significant base of knowledge leaves and takes the project knowledge with them. New staff coming in will not have the history or knowledge base, and they will need to learn and acclimate themselves to the team and system. Without a well-understood knowledge transfer process the PMO is risking the long-term sustainability of the ERP system.

Summary

- Assessing readiness in an ERP implementation is critical to the overall implementation process. Without the readiness process in place it will be difficult to meet the Go-live date with any assurance. The readiness process should start well in advance of the Go-live date and be repeated about every month to six weeks until the system is ready to Go-live. The process in itself clarifies all the open issues, tasks, and activities required for the implementation for the project team.

- For the project management office, the readiness process works to focus project managers on the high-priority tasks and activities and identifies where workarounds are possible. Resources can be added or

- shifted to meet deadlines. In addition to focusing on the teams the readiness process also creates a greater awareness for the project team and organization that the implementation is not that far away from going live.

- Just-in-time and continual training is the mark of a good ERP implementation training plan. This will ensure that the ERP system will be supported for the lifetime of the system. The budget for training is often only for the Go-live process. Setting continual training expectations early on in the project will help the training process sustain itself.

- Stabilization is generally a 60–90-day period that takes place after Go-live. It is possible that the time frame will vary depending on the number of issues that arise during the stabilization process and the number of cycles the system needs to go through to ensure the operation is in place to address stabilization concerns. During the stabilization period, the project team needs to focus on fixing identified issues, working through the daily, weekly, and monthly operation cycles, and ensuring that users can effectively use the system as it was designed. There should be no development during this period.

- Postproduction support is all about operationalizing the ERP. The production staff, users, and information technology staff must know what to expect daily, weekly, monthly, and yearly from the system. Postproduction support includes both the expected inputs and outputs of the system and the detailed operations schedules of

data and system backups, archiving, reconciliation, and the system change process (i.e., upgrades or fixes tested and moved to production).

- Knowledge transfer must be a process set up early in any ERP implementation. A roll-on and roll-off process for consultants and staff is needed to ensure the long-term system sustainability. Losing expertise will occur throughout the life of the system. Developing the knowledge transfer process will help to keep the system moving forward. In the life of an ERP system, a knowledgeable user or technical person leaves and much of the system knowledge leaves with them and inefficient or new processes are started where the knowledge vacuum was created. An effective knowledge transfer process will help to sustain the system over time.

Exercises

1. ERP implementation readiness is a key success factor to going live. Research two businesses that have implemented an ERP system that have used a readiness process, and describe the process to determine the level of success they had with that process.

2. Good ERP implementation training plans usually include just-in-time training and ongoing training after the system is implemented. Compare and contrast the two ERP implementation training plans, and identify why they were successful or not.

Review Questions

1. Why is the readiness process so important to an ERP implementation?
2. What project areas need to be assessed in a readiness process?
3. What is included (and not included) during the stabilization time frame?

4. Why is the knowledge transfer important to the long-term stability of the ERP system?
5. What are the five areas addressed in postproduction support?

Discussion Questions

1. ERP systems need ongoing support to ensure that the system does what it is supposed to do. Identify and describe the support structures needed for stabilization and postproduction support.

2. The knowledge transfer process is something that is needed throughout a project. Discuss why it is vital to the sustainability of the system.

CASE 7-2
Real-World Case
Hewlett-Packard SAP Implementation

Hewlett-Packard was founded in 1939 by Bill Hewlett and Dave Packard, both students at Stanford University. They built an audio oscillator—an electronic test instrument used by sound engineers. One of their first sales was to Walt Disney Studios, who used the device to develop and test a new sound system for the movie *Fantasia*. From 1939 to the present, HP has grown and changed as technology has grown and changed, often inventing new and useful technology products for businesses and consumers. They are now a worldwide information technology company headquartered in Palo Alto, California, with $85 billion in revenues. The company is currently organized into three divisions or groups:

- Personal systems—business and consumer PCs, mobile computing devices, and workstations
- Imaging and printing—inkjet, LaserJet and commercial printing, printing supplies, digital photography, and entertainment
- Technology solutions—business products including storage and servers, managed services, and software.[5]

For several years, Hewlett-Packard had been working to centralize its ERP systems. They had migrated five product groups into two SAP systems and had been very successful. A couple of years earlier HP had purchased Compaq and, as a result, needed to incorporate the two operations into a single model. In May 2004, however, Hewlett-Packard was implementing the SAP ERP system in its largest North American division. Prior to that the ERP implementations in previous divisions were successful, and there was no reason to think that this next one would be problematic. The company had a number of successful implementations under its belt and believed that even though this was a much larger division, there was a good, experienced team that could address most any implementation issues. The Go-live plan allowed for about three weeks of problems and issues related to interfacing between the legacy order-entry system and the new ERP, SAP. The project manager had identified one of the biggest risks and had a plan in place to address the issue.

When the system went live, however, there were some technical glitches between the legacy and the SAP system. Although the problems on the technical side were not a big issue and were mostly resolved in four or five weeks, about 20 percent of orders were stopped dead in the water until the problems were fixed. This created a backlog of orders, and the manual workarounds were not sufficient to keep the flow of orders to meet customer demand. Customers called HP to complain, but, even worse, they called their competitors to deliver the products not supplied by HP. HP had estimated the financial impact at about $160 million, $120 million in order backlogs and $40 million in lost revenue.

The implementation was considered a disaster. It was in fact the result of some very minor technical problems that created a snowball effect on the business. The implementation team did many things right. They tested the system and the interface between the legacy and SAP. The team also trained the end users two weeks prior to Go-live and made them pass a

---

[5] Extracted from HP Web site:www.hp.com (accessed July 15, 2006)

test to certify they knew how to use the system. A number of the issues could have been addressed prior to Go-live with some added investigation and more timely training.

CONCLUSION

Hindsight being what it is, the obvious conclusion to be drawn from this implementation is that care needs to be taken when assessing readiness. The contingency plan was lacking and needed to be expanded to include both technical issues and workarounds that also addressed the business issues.

Two specific key components for the end users were problematic:

- The training did not coincide with going live. The two-week period between the training and going live allowed the users to forget some of the details on how to use the system. This may have been alleviated by providing a practice instance for end users from the time they were trained until beyond Go-live.
- The second issue involved more complete testing. In a supply chain ERP implementation, the development of a robust test plan and test data, along with testing using "real" data and "real" customer information, is essential for a successful Go-live. This will ensure that orders can be filled on a timely basis and end users will develop a high level of confidence in the system and its processes.

CASE QUESTIONS

- What are the common threads between the Hugger-Mugger and HP ERP implementations?
- What were the key project management strategies that may have been used to minimize Go-live problems with the HP SAP Go-live process?
- When implementing an ERP system, especially supply chain systems, identifying risks and minimizing them requires planning. Discuss how IT needs to work with the business to address Go-live planning and issue resolution.

APPENDIX A

READINESS STATUS TABLE SAMPLE

Seq	Category	Criterion	Criticality	Site 1	Site 2	Group 1	Group 2	Key Measures	Contingent Workaround(s)	Decision Owner	Task Contact	Minimum "Pass Status"	Current Actual Status	Assessment	Assessment Date
1								**Tech Infrastructure Readiness**							
1.01	Tech Infrastructure Readiness	Database servers.	M	X	X			Production servers installed, tested, stable. All required software installed, tested (system, database, network, application) Production servers available during scheduled hours. Utilization assessments.	Go-live on production server. Go-live on reporting server. Go-live on development server. Implement disaster recovery process.			95% HR available for 1 month prior to Go-live; 80% fin; 80% rep.			
1.02	Tech Infrastructure Readiness	Application servers.	M	X				Application Servers installed, tested, stable. All required software installed, tested (system, network, application). Application server available during scheduled hours.	Go-live on Production Server using logical three-tier approach.			95% available for 1 month prior to Go-live.			

(Continued)

Seq	Category	Criterion	Criticality	Site 1	Site 2	Group 1	Group 2	Key Measures	Contingent Workaround(s)	Decision Owner	Task Contact	Minimum "Pass Status"	Current Actual Status	Assessment	Assessment Date
1.04	Tech Infrastructure Readiness	Web servers.	M	X				Web server installed, tested, stable. All required software installed, tested. Server available during scheduled hours.	Go-live on production Web server.			95% available for 1 month prior to Go-live.			
1.05	Tech Infrastructure Readiness	Report distribution (online view and remote distribution).	M	X				Product installed, configured, tested. Ability to view reports online. Ability to print to remote printers.	Print centrally and distribute manually through internal mail.			Product/operations test results indicate Go-live readiness.			
1.06	Tech Infrastructure Readiness	Patches and fixes applied to database environments.	H	X				Patches and fixes applied.	None			Patches and fixes issued 1 month prior to freeze date have been applied.			
1.07	Tech Infrastructure Readiness	Network availability.	H	X				Network availability during scheduled hours. Performance test complete.	None			95% availability for 1 month prior to Go-live for all campuses.			

No.	Category	Item	Priority				Readiness Criteria	Contingency	Metric
1.08	Tech Infrastructure Readiness	Connectivity between sites and Internet (if needed).	M	X	X	X	Connectivity from each site LAN to the production server established through connectivity test.	Move user(s) to alternate site(s)—dependent upon site Go-live with subset of user population.	Minimum latency of 100 milliseconds from point to point.
1.09	Tech Infrastructure Readiness	Local site network.	M	X	X		Planned upgrades complete, if any. Site network performance test complete.	Move user(s) to alternate site(s)—dependent upon campus—need to assess validity.	Minimum latency of 100 miliseconds from point to point.
1.11	Tech Infrastructure Readiness	Workstation	H		X		Workstations in place connectivity test complete all required software installed, tested (system, network, application, OA).	Move user(s) to alternate site.	Percentage of campus key users: A (80%), B (80%), L (80%), and W (75%).
1.12	Tech Infrastructure Readiness	Application availability during business hours—production.	H	X	X	X	Application available during scheduled hours.		95% available for 1 month prior to Go-live
1.13	Tech Infrastructure Readiness	Application availability during business hours—reporting database.	M	X	X	X	Application available during scheduled hours.		95% available for 1 month prior to Go-live
1.14	Tech Infrastructure Readiness	Application availability during business hours—development database.	M	X	X	X	Application available during scheduled hours.		95% available for 1 month prior to Go-live

(Continued)

Seq	Category	Criterion	Criticality	Site 1	Site 2	Group 1	Group 2	Key Measures	Contingent Workaround(s)	Decision Owner	Task Contact	Minimum "Pass Status"	Current Actual Status	Assessment	Assessment Date
1.15	Tech Infrastructure Readiness6	Batch window.	H	X				Batch performance test passed. Heaviest batch schedule can complete within allocated batch window.	Extend batch process into normal online hours. Quantify the number of hours that the schedule would extend if necessary. Move or eliminate some processes if possible.			During performance test, batch processes can be completed in the designated window.			
1.16	Tech Infrastructure Readiness	Key transaction throughput.	H	X	X	X	X	Online performance test passed.	Implement "shifts" for online users to minimize concurrency workload balancing. Deploy additional staff on temporary basis. Work overtime.			Performance test results indicate Go-live readiness. Performance test scripts test the minimum requirements.			

No.	Category	Item	Pri.		Detail	Note	Status
1.17	Tech Infrastructure Readiness	Production user classes and user IDs loaded.	M	X X X X	Production classes configured and tested. Production User IDs loaded. Production user authorization received. Production User IDs linked to classes.	Manual creation of operator IDs and passwords.	95% of classes and IDs loaded.
1.18	Tech Infrastructure Readiness	Production environment is stable.	H	X X X X	Production environment tested during conversion dress rehearsal (after data are moved over).		Test results indicate Go-live readiness.
2	**Operational Readiness**						
2.01	Operational Readiness	Backup/restore ability.	H	X	Production instances backed up on regular schedule. Restore works successfully. Production instances available for restore on demand. Both proven through ad hoc testing.	None	Operations test cycle 2 passed.
2.02	Operational Readiness	Disaster recovery plan (includes both technical and business aspects) — HIGH AVAILABILITY.	L	X X X	High-availability plan defined, documented (including manual steps). Recovery plan incorporated into operations test plan.	Utilize backup offsite server.	First draft complete.
2.03	Operational Readiness	Disaster recovery plan (includes both technical and business aspects) — CATASTROPHIC.	L	X X X	Procedures defined JOIs include manual steps.		First draft complete.

(Continued)

Seq	Category	Criterion	Criticality	Site 1	Site 2	Group 1	Group 2	Key Measures	Contingent Workaround(s)	Decision Owner Task Contact	Minimum "Pass Status"	Current Actual Status	Assessment	Assessment Date
2.04	Operational Readiness	Central high-speed printer and other central printing services.	M	X				Equipment in place (including backup). All required software installed, configured, tested.	Split print file for multiple printers. Employ temps for folding. Utilize backup printer. Utilize backup folder.		Operations test cycle *N* passed.			
2.05	Operational Readiness	Critical forms in place.	L		X	X	X	Available for use during functional training.	Utilize existing forms. Utilize "baseline" forms.		Approved forms distributed to campuses available to end users.			
2.06	Operational Readiness	Batch scheduler and production schedule.	H		X			Product installed, configured, tested. Batch performance test complete. Scheduled jobs entered and tested. Ad hoc jobs entered and tested.	Project team executes jobs until scheduler trained and available.		Operations test cycle 1 passed.			
2.07A	Operational Readiness	Table maintenance—key procedures in place for the high-impact data areas.	L		X			Procedures defined, documented.	Update tables centrally.		First draft complete. Operations test passed for critical tables.			

#	Category	Task	Priority					Completion Criteria	Assumption(s)/Constraint	Comment
2.07B	Operational Readiness	Additional key site procedures in place—system requests—release development—interface management—interface development—testing—training—migration—postimplementation.	M	X	X	X	X	Procedures defined, documented.		
2.08	Operational Readiness	Define production user IDs.	H	X	X	X	X	Map of users to classes complete.		Sign-off operator classes.
2.09	Operational Readiness	Method to handle reporting requests from the sites.	L	X	X	X				

3   **Testing**

#	Category	Task	Priority					Completion Criteria	Assumption(s)/Constraint	Comment
3.01	Testing	Critical function 1.	H	X	X	X	X	Ability to complete test of function 1.	None	Successful pass of key scripts with no outstanding critical issues.
3.02	Testing	Critical function 2.	H	X	X	X	X	Ability to complete test of function 1.	None	Successful pass of key scripts with no out-standing critical issues.
3.03	Testing	Parallel test complete.	H	X	X	X	X	100% reconciliation; discrepancies identified and understood; new processes defined; manual steps defined.		100% Reconciliation with discrepancies identified

(Continued)

213

Seq	Category	Criterion	Criticality	Site 1	Site 2	Group 1	Group 2	Key Measures	Contingent Workaround(s)	Decision Owner	Task Contact	Minimum "Pass Status"	Current Actual Status	Assessment	Assessment Date
3.04	Testing	Report security—ensure that security is set up appropriately.	H	X	X	X	X								
4								**Conversion Readiness**							
4.01	Conversion Readiness	Conversion criteria 1.	H	X				Data converted successfully.	Postconversion fixes of small volume (manual).			XX% of key data successfully converted.			
4.02	Conversion Readiness	Conversion criteria 2.	L	X				Data converted successfully.	Use legacy programs to view retirees. postconversion fix.			YY% of data converted successfully.			
4.10	Conversion Readiness	Network resources committed for conversion to production time frame.	H	X				No power or equipment outages scheduled. Primary and backup contacts established and staffed.	None			Documented and reviewed on-call and change control schedule.			
4.11	Conversion Readiness	Application support resources committed for conversion to production.	H	X	X	X	X	Primary and backup contacts established and staffed.	None			Documented and reviewed on-call and change control schedule.			

			H			None / Steps	Result
4.12	Conversion Readiness	LAN support resources committed for conversion to production weekend.	H X			None	Documented and reviewed on-call and change control schedule.
4.13	Conversion Readiness	Technical resources committed for conversion to production time frame.	H X			None	Documented and reviewed on-call and change control schedule.
4.14	Conversion Readiness	Facilities available for conversion to production weekend.	H X			None	Facilities confirmed.
4.15	Conversion Readiness	Manual conversion—updates complete during conversion window.	H	X	X X	Manually updated data.	ZZ% of data is accurate.
4.17	Conversion Readiness	The conversion window has been tested and is appropriate given the technical routines, reconciliation, manual entry, etc.	H	X	X X	Calculate the manual conversion effort and ensure that it fits within the conversion window.	
4.18	Conversion Readiness	Reconciliation process defined and tested.	H	X	X X	Convert to standard schedule.	

(Continued)

215

Seq	Category	Criterion	Criticality	Site 1	Site 2	Group 1	Group 2	Key Measures	Contingent Workaround(s)	Decision Owner	Task Contact	Minimum "Pass Status"	Current Actual Status	Assessment	Assessment Date
5								**Training**							
5.01	Training	Key training module 1.	H	X	X	X	X	All functional courses for module offered and conducted.	Superusers/department contacts (one-on-one coaching). Learning lab and practice environment. Make up training sessions.			Key users getting trained. No major readiness issues with key campus users.			
5.02	Training	Key training module 2.	H		X		X	All functional courses for module offered and conducted.	Superusers/department contacts (one-on-one coaching). Learning lab and practice environment. Make up training sessions.			Key users getting trained. No major readiness issues with key campus users.			

6 Communications

	Category	Criterion	Clinics	Site 1	Site 2	Group	Group	Key Messages	Production support messages	Notifications/Concerns
6.01	Communications	Executive communication.	L	X	X	X	X	Identified sponsors have received continued information on the progress of the project.	None	Continual meetings have occurred on each site; Go-live decision communications have occurred.
6.02	Communications	Employees notified about new functionality.	H			X	X	Employee communications complete.		Distribution of communication.
6.03	Communications	Campuses notified about freeze and Go-live dates.	M	X	X	X	X	Communication distributed.		Each site has distributed key project dates
		Additional communications regarding Go-live.	M	X	X					delivered to users.

(Continued)

Seq	Category	Criterion	Criticality	Site 1	Site 2	Group 1	Group 2	Key Measures	Contingent Workaround(s)	Decision Owner Task Contact	Minimum "Pass Status"	Current Actual Status	Assessment	Assessment Date
7								**Production Support Readiness**						
7.01		End-user assurance approach implemented and completed.	H	X	X	X	X	Approach defined. Staff assigned. Employees scheduled for appropriate training sessions: Training materials; job aids; coaches; Learning lab facilities; critical end users identified and have been through assurance test.	D: Implement coaching and buddy system. B: No workaround for training, critical users must attend; If practice environment not used, pursue via end-user readiness sessions; if end-user readiness sessions not used, rely on feedback from training, practice environment, and coaching.		Key at-risk employees identified and completing program.			

7.02	Production Support Readiness	End-user support for stabilization defined and implemented (Go-live stations).	H X X X X	End-user support options selected for your campus: training materials, job aids, coaches, learning lab facilities. Go-live kit distributed. Go-Live stations defined and ready for implementation; staff assigned; employees scheduled.	D: No work-around. Go-live kits will be available in the central location B: Distribute Go-live kit information electronically; designate workstations in departments for learning lab exercises; set up workstation with application, training materials, and job aids; use help desk office location temporarily to field all calls and triage issues.	Site draft plans complete. Go-live kit distributed.
7.03	Production Support Readiness	Functional second-level support staff.	H X X X X	Functional site staff identified and assigned. Contact list established.	Project team to provide user support on temporary basis.	Staff assigned.
7.04	Production Support Readiness	Technical second-level support staff.	H X X X	Technical site staff identified and assigned. Contact list established.	Project team to provide user support on temporary basis.	Staff assigned.

(Continued)

Seq	Category	Criterion	Criticality	Site 1	Site 2	Group 1	Group 2	Key Measures	Contingent Workaround(s)	Decision Owner Task Contact	Minimum "Pass Status"	Current Actual Status	Assessment	Assessment Date
7.05	Production Support Readiness	User help desk facilities.	M	X	X	X	X	All necessary equipment is acquired and in the help desk facility. File servers are installed and tested. Tracking databases in help desk application are created and ready to support ticket entry. ACD and telephone capabilities have been set up and tested.	Route calls to Project Team on temporary basis. Utilize site "super users."		Site physical spaces fitted and equipped. File servers installed, tested. Tracking databases created. ACD and telephone capabilities established.			
7.06	Production Support Readiness	User help desk staff.	M	X	X	X		Staff identified and assigned.	Project team to provide user support on temporary basis. Utilize campus "super users."		Help desk staff trained			
7.07	Production Support Readiness	User help desk procedures.	L	X	X	X		Procedures for tracking, response, and escalation defined, tested. Procedures documented. Frequently asked questions available. Approach defined.	Work without written procedures on temporary basis.		All procedures for escalation and communication.			

Between Tiers 1, 2, and 3 are defined and tested. All procedures have been documented and communicated with help desk staff, Tier 2 function SMEs, Tier 2 functional support, and Tier 3.

Successful pass of system testing with no outstanding critical issues. File loaded successfully.

8 **Third-Party Readiness**

| 8.01 | Third-Party Readiness | Inbound interface 1 ready. | H | X | None | Technical test complete. Functional test complete. Third-party confirmation received. Procedures in place to update system. |

(Continued)

(Continued)

Seq	Category	Criterion	Criticality	Site 1	Site 2	Group 1	Group 2	Key Measures	Contingent Workaround(s)	Decision Owner	Task Contact	Minimum "Pass Status"	Current Actual Status	Assessment	Assessment Date
8.01A	Third-Party Readiness	Outbound interface 1 ready.	H	X				Technical test complete. Functional test complete. Third-party confirmation received. Procedures in place to update system.	None			Successful pass of system testing with no outstanding critical issues. File loaded successfully.			
8.04	Third-Party Readiness	Outbound and inbound interfaces ready.	M	X	X			Technical test complete. Functional test complete. Third-party confirmation received.				Successful pass of functional and technical tests. Bank accepts interface files.			

9 Audit

9.01	Audit	Auditor agrees that project is ready to implement.	H	X	X	X	Critical issues (if any) addressed. Auditor has provided assessment letters. The governing agency(s) acknowledges that requirements have been met or deferred to post–Go-live and agrees that the project can implement on the selected date.	Need specific and measurable items from audit.
9.02	Audit	Audit objectives have been met.	M	X	X	X	If a negative assessment was received, company has formally acknowledged the risk and project mgt team or site(s), as appropriate, have established plans to address the risk.	

10 Risk

10.01	Risk	Project identified risk 1.	H	X	X	X	Risk 1 documented and managed appropriately.	Risk 1 manual procedure.	Risk 1 mitigation defined, documented, and completed.

(Continued)

Seq	Category	Criterion	Criticality	Site 1	Site 2	Group 1	Group 2	Key Measures	Contingent Workaround(s)	Decision Owner	Task Contact	Minimum "Pass Status"	Current Actual Status	Assessment	Assessment Date
10.02	Risk	Project identified risk 2.	H	X	X	X	X	Risk 2 signed off.	None			Risk 2 mitigation defined, documented, and completed.			
11	**Corporate Management**														
11.01	Corporate Management	Acclimation and understanding of new processes.	H				X	Documented schedule. Successful test application cycles end to end.	None.			Successful test cycle end to end.			
11.05	Corporate Management	Acclimation, understanding and capability to accomplish monthly, quarterly, annually, and ad hoc processes.	M					Inventory of needed reports and activities. Activity map for high-priority responsibilities.	Additional consultant support.			Successful test cycle end to end.			

224

8

Program and Project Management

LEARNING OBJECTIVES

After reading this chapter, you should be able to:

- Understand the difference between program management and project management.

- Describe the makeup of the project management office (PMO) and the areas it needs to address in an ERP implementation.

- Appreciate the skills needed to be a project manager.

- Identify critical success factors in an ERP implementation.

- Realize the value of a change control process for managing scope creep.

CASE 8-1
Opening Case
ABC Manufacturing: A Hypothetical Case in Unresolved Issues

The manufacturing company called ABC Manufacturing, which produces do-dads and thing-ama-bobs that fit on the dashboards of cars, decided to take a look at their competition. A team made up of senior management, area directors, and staff concluded that a new ERP system would help to integrate its processes and speed up order processing, thereby improving time to market. Several competitors had already completed an ERP implementation and claimed dramatic improvements in order processing and increased customer satisfaction. Even though the company believed that the ERP would improve the overall bottom line, many of the staff were skeptical. The company proceeded to purchase an ERP system, and the project teams were assembled. A project manager, Mr. Trevor Mackenzie, was assigned to the project from the internal IT department, but no one in that department had ever implemented an ERP before. The staff assigned to the project were chosen by the department heads to work on the project full time, and an implementation consulting firm was chosen to work with the manufacturing company to implement the system.

All of the teams were excited and eager at project start-up. The teams evaluated the software based on current practices and identified areas that did not fit the current environment. The team leads passed the recommendations along to the project manager for review and submission to the change control board. The board agreed to all but four changes. Those four changes were turned down because there were indications that there were workarounds and that the business practice needed to change. The subject matter experts on the teams believed that the four modifications should be made and that the workarounds would be very time consuming. Several months went by as the implementation proceeded and modifications were made to the system. Testing the system was now well under way. During the testing phase it was clear a number of changes needed to be made for the system to work in the manufacturing company's environment. The project slowed, more changes were made, and the testing time was extended. Training was delayed due to the changes in the system, and users continued to make requests for changes. After several delays the system testing was at a standstill. At this point the project executive, Kathleen Taylor, called a halt to the project to find out what was happening and what needed to be completed for the system to go live.

CONCLUSION

Management often does not realize that ERP projects are doomed for disaster. ABC Manufacturing seemed to have a number of components in place to be successful: enthusiasm and buy-in from both management and staff, along with a good rationale for change. Without realizing what was happening, initial project decisions, especially in the skill set and experience of the project manager and those assigned from the functional departments, set the project up for failure. After several delays caused the project to flounder, Kathleen Taylor made the right call to halt what was happening in order to evaluate what needed to be addressed for the implementation to move ahead.

PREVIEW

The project team, with a solid understanding of the concept of teamwork, will create a strong foundation for implementing an ERP that will meet the business objectives on time and budget. This was not the case with the ABC Manufacturing ERP implementation. The lack of project management skills and experience and the make-up of the teams were problematic from the project's start. Most project teams are made up of a variety of staff and consultants. Each team member should have expertise in an area (i.e., functional or technical) and understand the importance of teamwork. Even though the ABC Manufacturing teams were eager, they lacked the full understanding of the task in front of them and the teamwork needed to sustain the implementation. Teambuilding exercises, training, or both will make for a work climate in which progress and creativity will thrive.

The project management office (PMO) is responsible for ensuring that project teams are working well together and addressing the functionality issues in a timely, open, and efficient manner. The PMO needs to make certain that team activities stay synchronized and that progress is made. If teams become fragmented, it will often slow down an entire project, especially if teams are dependent on each other for decisions. The PMO must manage scope, resources, and time, as shown in Figure 8-1. If any one of the three sides of the triangle changes, then the other two sides will also need to change or the sides of the triangle will never meet. In other words, if the scope changes, then either resources or time will need to change (or both) for the sides of the triangle to remain connected.

The skill set of a project manager must be varied and robust. This was not the case for ABC Manufacturing. In fact, their project manager had never before implemented such a large ERP system. A project manager must be able to address issues related to how the system works, and have good negotiation skills, work well with the teams, and be politically savvy to navigate through the implementation. For these reasons and others, being part of the PMO can be both high risk and high reward. Even though a project manager is mostly focused on tactical areas within an ERP implementation, a program manager or project executive is strategically focused. The role of the program manager is to ensure that business goals are met. Both project and program managers must address areas that are critical to the success of the project.

Although the PMO must focus on the implementation, it must also address the critical success factors on a regular basis as they relate to the decisions process, project scope or changes to scope, teamwork, and communications with the team and executives. There was not enough time spent on the scope and developing user buy-in in the ABC Manufacturing example. In addition, the project manager was not skilled enough to manage "scope creep" to ensure that the project moved forward. The project manager may have avoided many of the issues around the modifications and scope through an

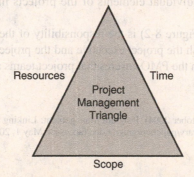

FIGURE 8-1 Project Management.

increased use of communications and discussions with the teams to understand the team issues better and how the scope and modifications would affect the implementation. As the project moved forward, the project executive needed to bring the project manager and teams together to review the status of the project. In doing this, management would begin to regain the trust lost early on regarding the project.

PROJECT TEAM

Program management and project management are often used interchangeably, yet there are significant differences between the two. Before discussing the topic of what role program management has, it is important to define what it is. "Program management is the coordinated management of interdependent projects over a finite period of time in order to achieve a set of business goals"[1] and "focuses on achieving business results to create a competitive advantage while project management focuses on planning and executing the work required to deliver the end product."[2] Project management is tactically focused, whereas program management is strategically focused. Companies sometimes choose to use only a project management approach to projects (e.g., an ERP implementation). This approach is often problematic in that projects may meet their goals with regard to cost, quality, and time, yet fall short of meeting the business objectives originally outlined in their business case. ERP implementations often consist of several projects simultaneously. Each project manager is concerned with his or her own piece of the overall puzzle; but it's the program manager who must link many different individual projects, that are often missing, together and make sure that the overall business goals are managed and addressed. The program manager might also be managing projects that have nothing to do with the ERP implementation, but which do contribute to the overall business goals. "In the program management model, the program manager manages across the multiple functional projects, while the project manager manages within a single functional project."[3]

When a company decides to implement an ERP, a business case must be created that outlines the business goals to be achieved. The primary goal should never be simply to upgrade existing legacy systems to a more robust ERP. There should be true business goals that the company must meet as a result of the implementation (e.g., improved customer service, increased market share, and cost savings or cost avoidance). The actual ERP implementation will require several different project teams over the course of several months or years. It is the role of the program manager to keep all of these projects moving in the same direction to achieve the business goals outlined in the business case. Each individual project manager has his or her own goals to manage in a project. The sum of the successful individual projects equates to the achievement of the overall business goals. "Program management integrates the individual elements of the projects in order to achieve a common objective."[4]

Program management (Figure 8-2) is the responsibility of the project executive (sometimes called the project director). Both the project executive and the project manager(s) make up the majority of the PMO. Even though the PMO ensures that project teams are moving forward, they must

---

[1] Martenelli, R., and Waddell, J. (October 2004). Program Management: Linking Business Strategy to Product and IT Development. www.pmforum.org/library/papers/prgmgmt.doc (accessed May 1, 2005).
[2] Ibid.
[3] Ibid.
[4] Ibid.

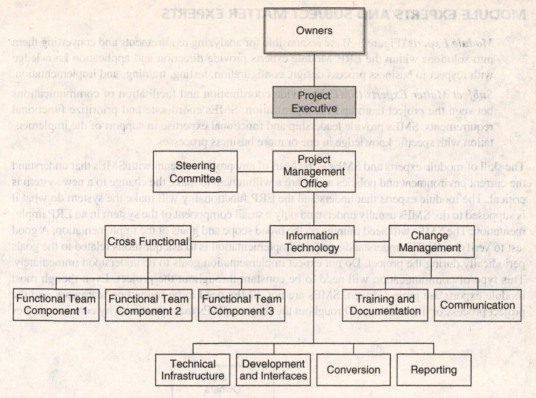

FIGURE 8-2 Sample Organization Project Executive.

also continue to evaluate risks, manage the resources (i.e., human and financial), and be sensitive to new issues arising that may cause delays. This work can be both exciting and exhausting; in addition, it is complex and time sensitive. The PMO's ability to work well together often determines how well the implementation meets its goals.

In Chapter 4, the roles, responsibilities, and skills needed for each area within the project organization will be discussed. The PMO will need to address the skills of each team in evaluating risks and success factors. Even though the technical and functional skills are important, the skills related to teamwork and productivity are just as important. As with any organization, projects must address the team and cross-team dynamics. The issues of ensuring that team players are in key positions and identifying the team players from the individual contributors are one of the many factors the PMO will need to address. It is critical not to put individual contributors in a lead role. This will increase risk and create problems within the team. Projects require a lot of communication and face-to-face meetings. Training in conducting efficient and effective meetings, along with how to participate in meetings, will increase the concepts of teamwork and productivity.

MODULE EXPERTS AND SUBJECT MATTER EXPERTS

Module Experts (Figure 8-3) are responsible for analyzing requirements and converting them into solutions within the ERP. Module experts provide direction and application knowledge with respect to business process design, configuration, testing, training, and implementation.

Subject Matter Experts (SMEs) provide coordination and facilitation of communications between the project team and the organization. SMEs coordinate and prioritize functional requirements. SMEs provide leadership and functional expertise in support of the implementation with specific knowledge in one or more business processes.

The skill of module experts and SMEs is the heart of any project. A team with SMEs that understand the current environment and policies and share a willingness to make the change to a new system is critical. The module experts that understand the ERP functionality will make the system do what it is supposed to do. SMEs usually understand only a small component of the system in an ERP implementation. The SMEs will need training on the broad scope and goals of the implementation. A good test to verify an SME's understanding of the implementation is to ask questions related to the goals periodically during the project. Do not expect implementation goals to be understood immediately. This type of communication will need to be constant throughout the project. Even though most module experts are project driven, SMEs are not. SMEs need to be trained on teamwork and the project process or methodology. Throughout the project, SMEs may question why certain activities

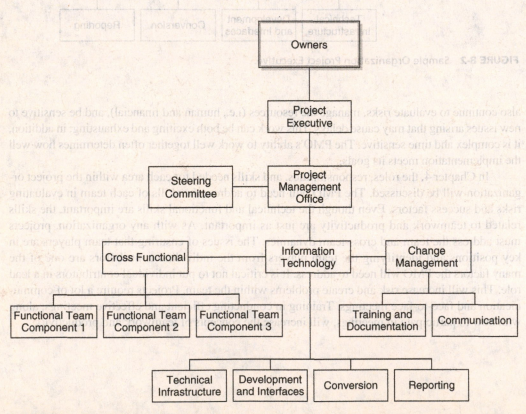

FIGURE 8-3 Sample Organization Teams.

are taking place and why some activities have not begun. SMEs will get frustrated with activities related to testing, reporting, and data conversion. It will be difficult for them to understand fully how the system is going to work until they can see their own data flow through it. The SMEs' understanding and trust of the project methodology will reduce anxiety and increase productivity.

PROJECT LEADERSHIP

In an ERP implementation, project leadership (Figure 8-4) is not for the "faint of heart." It is considered high risk and high reward. That being said, "perhaps the single most decisive element of ERP success or failure is the knowledge, skills, abilities, and experience of the project manager."[5] Trepper added, "A successful ERP project manager is flexible, disciplined, a quick learner, a good decision maker, has ERP and business experience, has political clout with a formal education, is well liked, and finally has the ability to motivate his staff."[6]

The PMO must manage the risks involved in a project implementation to be successful. Below are some examples of issues the PMO will likely need to monitor or address during an ERP implementation:

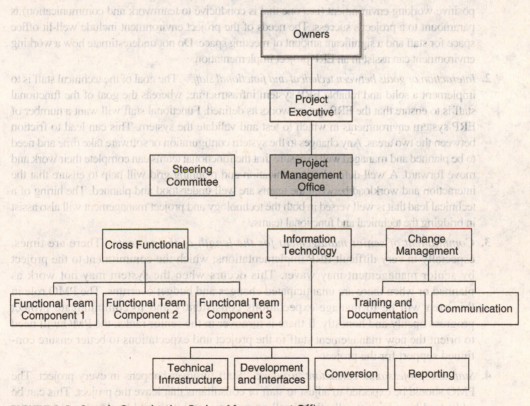

FIGURE 8-4 Sample Organization Project Management Office.

[5] Trepper, C. (August 1, 1999). ERP Project Management is Key to a Successful Implementation. www.peoplesoft-planet.com/Projectmanagement.html (accessed May 1, 2005).
[6] Ibid.

1. *Project start-up.*   As is often the case, ERP projects can take longer to start than anticipated. This can be the result of many issues including the following:

   - Hiring skilled staff can take longer than planned.
   - Bringing in professional consultants is time consuming.
   - Looking for and building out a single work location are important for the success of the project.

   Even though you may want to move through this step quickly you will need to resist the temptation. Hiring the right skilled staff and finding the right skills in professional consultants is one of the most important activities a PMO can address. The abilities of technical and functional project staff, whether they are hired full-time staff or as consultants, will take a coordinated effort. Professional consultants will often need to complete an existing engagement before they can join the project. The organizing and planning for a realistic project start date will depend a lot on when the key staff are in place.

   Another issue that sometimes arises with projects is finding the right space or location for the project to do its work. A single location is best. In fact, if a single location is not part of how an ERP project is implemented, it should be identified as a risk and managed closely. If the location is not set up for projects, then the build-out takes a significant amount of time. A positive working environment (i.e., one that is conducive to teamwork and communication) is paramount to a project's success. The needs of the project environment include well-lit office space for staff and a significant amount of meeting space. Do not underestimate how a working environment can assist in an ERP project implementation.

2. *Interaction or goals between technical and functional staff.*   The goal of the technical staff is to implement a solid and reliable ERP system infrastructure; whereas the goal of the functional staff is to ensure that the ERP system works as defined. Functional staff will want a number of ERP system environments in which to test and validate the system. This can lead to friction between the two areas. Any changes to the system configuration or software take time and need to be planned and managed well to ensure that the functional teams can complete their work and move forward. A well-defined communication and planning grid will help to ensure that the interaction and workload between the teams are well understood and planned. The hiring of a technical lead that is well versed in both the technology and project management will also assist in bridging the technical and functional teams.

3. *Commitment of senior management for the length of the project.*   There are times, especially in very difficult ERP implementations, which the commitment to the project by senior management may waver. This occurs when the system may not work as planned or when there are unanticipated changes and budget overruns. The PMO role in this area will be to manage expectations consistently and to communicate project progress openly and honestly. If there is turnover in the senior ranks, the PMO will need to orient the new management staff to the project and expectations to better ensure continued support for the project.

4. *Staff and professional consultant turnover.*   Staff turnover happens in every project. The PMO should be expected to adjust to staff or consultants that leave the project. This can be addressed by a project roll-off and roll-on process, and it should be developed from the beginning. For a roll off, the knowledge transfer must take place to ensure that activities and tasks are turned over to the appropriate staff. In addition, even though the PMO is hiring replacement staff or finding another professional consultant, the workload will need to be reprioritized until the new staff begins on the project. As new staff is hired, a roll-on process

will need to occur. This roll-on process includes orienting the new staff to the teams, implementation methodology, project assumptions, and current project status, as well as their role within the project organization.

5. *Second guessing project decisions.* As with most projects, there will be second guessing of decisions made, by both team members on the project and even those outside the project. The one that can be the most damaging is the second guessing from outside the project. This can lead to more implementation issues as the project nears completion and is ready for production. Staff that are not on the project do not understand the project methodology and may not even want the new system, so they may try to undermine the implementation. The role of the PMO will be to ensure the change management (i.e., managing change) process continues to communicate and to meet with staff to ensure they are up to date on the implementation progress and major functionality decisions. While you will not be able to convince all staff, they will appreciate the effort to communicate, especially when it comes to listening to the issues.

6. *Passive–aggressive staff and users.* Any ERP implementation project should encourage open communication and build a sense of trust so that staff and users feel free to express opinions and raise issues related to the functionality of the system. For a variety of reasons, however, this is not always the case. Passive–aggressive staff or users can undermine a project's motivation and morale. The best approach to ensure that this behavior is minimized is through accountability. The PMO must be sure that there is open and honest communication within the project and that the project team is accountable for decisions and direction. All team members must understand that project decisions and direction are made for the best of the organization, and they must abide by those decisions. Without accountability the project will become chaotic and team morale will drop.

CRITICAL SUCCESS FACTORS

Decision-Making Process

A well-defined decision-making process will minimize a number of issues related to scope, efficiency, and productivity throughout the project implementation cycle. The team must understand how and when decisions are made. If this process is not in place, decisions related to the project will increase scope (see next section) and may therefore not meet the overall goals agreed to during project start-up. In most projects there may be disagreement on how to use the system, what if any modifications should be made, the reports needed for Day one, and how to convert data. This is all very normal, but the project will soon break down if the decision process is not similar or the same with each issue or activity. If decisions are not communicated properly, the input and options will not be vetted with the proper groups or users and buy-in will not be achieved.

Project Scope

The project manager has many responsibilities. One of the most critical is the management of project scope. "Scope defines what needs to be delivered by the project, and a changing scope means the project will have difficulty in achieving project goals."[7] The PMO works through the business

---

[7] Aniceto, J. (March 2003). Project Management—Managing Scope Creep. www.suite101.com/article.cfm/17106/99319 (accessed May 1, 2005).

processes that will be included in the implementation based on the projects goals. These goals have a direct effect on which software modules will be implemented and the number of business units that will participate in this implementation. Scope creep is defined as constant changes to the parameters outlined in the original project goals. It was stated earlier that one of the roles of project management is to make sure the project meets its goals in relation to cost, quality, and time. Scope creep has a detrimental effect on meeting this objective. To prevent scope creep, the project manager must ensure that the parameters of the project are outlined in the business case, a project charter, or a mission statement. There is always some change in scope as a project progresses, but the project manager must make sure to have a formal process in place in order to manage that change effort. It is not unusual for organizations to implement a change control board, which includes users and senior management to address these instances.

Teamwork

The teamwork concept cannot be emphasized enough (Table 8-1). In most ERP implementations, project teams are assembled by bringing together staff from the existing organization, new hires, and possible external consultants. Teamwork does not just happen without some effort in training and team building. Each team will have its own set of dynamics based on the knowledge and personalities of the people involved. It takes savvy project managers and project leads to develop and build teams to address the many issues that will confront the teams as the project moves forward. If teamwork is not incorporated into a project, it will be much more difficult to keep on track, and it will likely cost more in resources.

Table 8-1 presents the result of a survey response from IS professionals in Australia and New Zealand. Respondents were asked to rate the importance of differing business skills by selecting a value from 1 to 5, with one representing very low and a five representing very high. They were also asked to indicate their level of expertise in relation to these skills. Table 8-1 shows the means and standard deviations for the importance of business skill of the cohort.

Teamwork scored the highest, with an approval with a very tight standard deviation. Solutions, deadlines, and projects scored equally, placing in second, followed by change management. The least-favored business skill was the need to have sales and marketing skills. This skill also showed a high standard deviation. A knowledge of business politics was not favored and was ranked 9 out of 10.

TABLE 8-1   Business Skills Importance to E-Business/E-Commerce ($n = 27$)

Skills	Mean Rating	Standard Deviation	Respondent Level
Teamwork	4.6	0.9	4.5
Deliver Business Solutions	4.3	0.7	3.1
Meet Deadlines	4.3	0.8	4.0
Project Management	4.3	1.1	3.2
Change Management	4.2	1.0	3.9
Client Consulting	4.1	0.9	3.6
Personal Communications	4.1	1.0	3.4
Client Negotiating	3.9	1.1	3.3
Internal Business Politics	3.4	1.2	3.3
Sales and Marketing Skills	2.8	1.5	2.4

The respondents rated their current skill level in the areas of personal communications and project management considerably below the level that they believed to be important to industry.[8]

Change Management

Change management is another critical factor that must be addressed by the project manager (i.e., managing change). Communication and training are the keys to a successful change management effort. It is normal for people to resist change and have a fear of the unknown. The project manager must have the skills to empathize with the affected employees, realizing many of them might have been doing their job in the same fashion for many years. It is up to the project manager to communicate the importance and significance of the project to the entire organization, top to bottom. There is no better way to calm a user's fears than to implement an aggressive training program. "Nothing eases a team's apprehension when starting a new project better than knowing they will be trained in what they have to do."[9] It pays to get these same users in the fold early. The project manager should make sure that their issues and needs are taken into consideration along with those of the organization. Let the team share in the ownership of the system, and it will provide for a smoother changeover.

Implementation Team and Executive Team

The program manager and the project manager are critical to a successful ERP implementation, but there are other groups that are also critical to that success. One of those groups is the implementation team. There are typically three options in choosing an implementation team: the internal IT organization, consulting organizations, and the package software vendors' client professional service group.[10] A critical element in choosing what combination of the three will be used largely depends on what type of resources the organization has within its own walls and how quickly the implementation must take place. It is a common edict in today's fast-paced environment that the sooner a solution is rolled out to a business, the faster a company will begin to see a return on investment.[11] It is unusual to find internal IT personnel who are up to speed on all the intricacies of the ERP, so relying solely on internal IT personnel will slow down the implementation process. Outside consultants have the experience of doing prior implementations at other organizations working in their favor, so they understand what has and has not worked in those other implementations. They are unbiased because they neither work for the software package vendor nor for the organization implementing the ERP solution. Finally, the vendor's client professionals bridge the gap between the internal IT personnel and the outside consultants. They have all the up-to-date information on the software package and can help explain the software's latest enhancements. It is essential that consultants are well integrated with the internal IT personnel in order to realize the benefits of knowledge transfer. This ensures that once the project is over and the consultants are gone, the internal IT personnel have absorbed all the necessary information to operate independently.

What role does the executive management branch of the organization play in a successful ERP implementation? Executive management support and commitment throughout the project is essential. Executive management can also assist with the change management process, especially

---

[8] Hawking, P., and Stein, A. E-skills: Proceedings of the Thirty-Sixth Hawaii International Conference on System Sciences (HICSS'03). *The Next hurdle for ERP implementations, School of Information Systems.* Melbourne, VIC: Victoria University of Technology.

[9] Strub, J. A. (February 2003). Top 10 Reasons for Having a Project Kickoff. www.technology-evaluation.com/Research/ResearchHighlights/ERP/2003/02/research_notes/prn_MI_ER_PJ_02_24_03_1.asp (accessed May 1, 2005).

[10] Bhuta, V. (April 30, 2001). Eight Mantras to a Successful Software Implementation. www.gantthead.com/article.cfm?ID=18833 (accessed May 1, 2005).

[11] Ibid.

TABLE 8-2   Executive Sponsor Speaks to the Organization

---

1. Impact of the product on the business   All departments were represented

        Cost savings   Vendors considered

        Cost avoidance   Preparation of the RFP

        Efficiencies to be gained   Site visitations and demos

        Competitive advantage   **3. Long-Term Impact of a Successful Project**

2. Description of Selection Process   Sustainability

    Who was on the selection committee   Growth

---

communications that will be needed with the new system. Change management helps employees feel secure about the changes that will come as a result of the implementation. It is very important to have the chief executive of the organization speak at the project kickoff meeting to explain in his or her own words why this project is so important, what the project means to the organization, and how their business goals will be met because of this implementation. Items that might be covered by the executive are outlined in Table 8-2.[12]

Managing Scope Creep

A well-thought-out process to manage changes to scope is critical to a project's success. The team can do everything in its power to understand the functionality of an ERP system; however, seeing it work in the company's environment is vital. Project plans and deadlines are made early on in the project planning without fully realizing the detail of how the ERP functions will meet the company goals and needs. For example, the functional teams begin evaluating the ERP functionality in the test environment after the project scope is approved. If a key element of the functionality does not work well during this process, there may be a need to make changes to the original scope. These new changes must then be built into the implementation. "Change Control" is managing these changes through a change process and governance. There must be a clear understanding around the decision-making process. When changes are made in the scope of the project, the options, costs, and time frame must be documented for the project to evaluate and decide a direction. Changes in project scope or new functionality are often addressed through the research and development of a white paper. A "white paper" consists of a description of the issue or new functionality, including the options available with advantages and disadvantages. A white paper should also list the implications to the project, including a time frame and budget considerations and a recommendation. If change control is not enforced, "scope creep" can quickly get out of control, leading to missed deadlines and project budget overruns.

IMPLICATIONS FOR MANAGEMENT

The success or failure of a project often rests with the skills and abilities of the PMO, project staff continuity, and a well-defined communications process. Well-managed projects are those where the scope is well understood and the project team is motivated to see the project through to Go-live. On the other hand, many projects fail due to a lack of open and honest communications and staff continuity throughout the project.

---

[12] Strub. Top 10 Reasons for Having a Project Kickoff.

BOX 8-1   Sample Change Control Document

Date:
    Issue Number: xxxx
    Description of issue or new functionality:

Option 1:

- Description of option
- Technical implications
- User implications
- Advantages
- Disadvantages
- Amount of additional functional and technical staff time
- Cost
- Additional project time frame

Option n:

- Description of option
- Technical implications
- User implications
- Advantages
- Disadvantages
- Amount of additional function and technical staff time
- Cost
- Additional project time frame

Recommendation

The PMO must monitor a number of activities and issues throughout the length of the implementation. Hiring and selecting skilled and competent staff from the beginning will ensure that the Go-live is smooth and the system is sustainable. An experienced and skilled PMO will know how to address implementation issues and activities. ERP implementations require teamwork and a high level of trust. This is accomplished by open and honest communication within and across teams. To accomplish this, meetings and discussions must be well organized and facilitated to ensure that everyone gets a chance to express ideas, thoughts, and opinions. Team members must be very aware that not all their issues will be accepted, but that they will be heard and considered.

The PMO needs to be sure that management is informed and up to date on the project status. This will ensure that the project stays on schedule and within budget (i.e., that teams are working together and moving through the implementation methodology). Managing senior management's expectations is an important activity for the PMO. Senior management must remain committed to the project through every phase, and they must show their commitment. In addition to regular meetings with management on the implementation status, management must also be informed as to how the system will function. This should be presented at a high level, but not a detailed level. ERP projects often take a few years to implement, and even though management is informed as to the benefits of a new ERP, they often forget some of the key benefits as the project team moves through the implementation phases. The PMO will know if they have communicated the benefits and expectations well enough when management starts to talk, on a regular basis, about how the system will work for the organization.

Summary

- Project management and the PMO must identify and monitor the critical success factors of an ERP implementation. Several factors were identified in this chapter as it relates to scope, teamwork, processes, and

communication. Each project will have these as it moves forward.

- The PMO must address a number of project priorities daily, but it will need to continue to focus on the business goals and to communicate them continually to the teams. This is the role of the program manager (executive) and project managers. It becomes especially difficult when the system is finally in-house and used with data from the business.

- The term "scope creep" is often used during a project when changes are requested that are not in the initially defined project scope. Some amount of change in scope needs to be planned for and must be addressed in a systemic fashion because change will happen during a project implementation.
- Project leadership is an important ingredient to the success of an ERP implementation.

The skills, knowledge, and abilities of a project manager and a program manager are perhaps the main factors of a successful implementation. An implementation is considered successful if it meets the identified business goals and is on time and on budget.

- Project manager and program manager should work together closely during an implementation. The difference between the two is that the program manager addresses the strategic points of a project, whereas a project manager is more tactically focused on the issues of the project.

Exercises

1. Project scope is difficult to manage. Research two businesses that have implemented an ERP system that have used change control, and describe the process to determine the level of success they had with that process.

2. Find job descriptions for program managers and project managers. Compare and contrast the descriptions and how they may focus on different project areas.

Review Questions

1. What is the role of a project manager and a program manager?
2. What are the skills, knowledge, and abilities required to be a project manager?
3. Name five critical success factors and why they are important to the success of a project.

4. What role can the company executives play in an implementation?
5. What is "scope creep," and why is it important to manage during an ERP implementation?

Discussion Questions

1. ERP implementations usually bring together staff from a variety of places, both internal and external to the business. Discuss the value that training and teamwork will bring to the success of the project.

2. The PMO is perhaps the single most important group related to the success of an ERP implementation. Describe the role and components of the PMO and why it is critical to the success of the project.

CASE 8-2
Real-World Case
Human Resource Implementation at the Institute

Source: Based on the Smithsonian Web site: www.si.edu/ocio/PDFs/SITP2006-2011.pdf.

BACKGROUND

The institute employs several thousand employees. It is the home of museums, research centers, and offices. Millions of people each year, ranging from visitors to scientists, visit the sites. Like most institutes, it has grown over the years and has outgrown its information technology infrastructure. The aging application systems were based on technology that had become very difficult to change and adapt to the increasing needs of the institute. To address the need for change, the institute developed a vision and plan to update the IT environment. The vision included all areas of the institute. This case study will focus on the governance structure and the implementation of a human resources management system.

Governance

At the institute, an IT governance structure was put in place to address the modernization. This included the following:

- The Information Technology Advisory Committee (ITAC) advises and assists the CIO in establishing and implementing IT management policies, procedures, and practices.
- The Change Control Board (CCB) for hardware and software changes to the IT infrastructure. The CCB addresses the impact of changes to the infrastructure and ensures minimal disruption in services and operations.
- The primary objectives of IT Management Review Board (IMRB) are to address project success factors and ensure that risk is managed by completing assessments at key project milestones.

This structure ensures consistency throughout the institution by standardizing hardware, software, and data. The following four governing strategies represent fundamental principles for managing IT resources and meeting the information needs of the institute:

1. Project management, including a proven implementation methodology and support process, baselined project plans in order to evaluate project progress and ensure the proper mix of functional and technical resources are available and working together on the project.
2. Application software and business process reengineering, thereby minimizing modifications.
3. Data management standards to ensure the interoperability across systems.
4. IT infrastructure: hardware, network, and system software that is current, secure, scalable and consistent across applications.

HUMAN RESOURCES MANAGEMENT

Human resources provide recruiting, compensation and recognition, planning and consulting, employee and labor relations, and training services. The legacy system did not have the ability to capture data at the source and use it for multiple purposes, resulting in errors and delays. The integrated HR management system (HRMS) that replaced the legacy system provided information, immediately delivering the services required, and it replaced current labor-intensive paperbound processes.

The project to implement the PeopleSoft HRMS took three years and was delivered in phases. The system was in full production and stable in a relatively short time frame.

Benefits

The HRMS ERP investment supports and modernized the institute's HR management systems. In addition, the IT infrastructure was state of the art. The approach had three critical success factors:

- Implementation team was involved in all aspects of the implementation from the hardware configuration to the "fit-gap" analysis.
- All changes were evaluated based on the original set of requirements.
- This involved the functional users from the beginning all the way through testing and stabilization.

CONCLUSION

This is a good example of setting up an ERP system implementation effectively from the beginning: It had the support of senior management, the reason for change was developed and conveyed to the organization, and an overall vision for the institution was incorporated into the IT strategic plan. The organization developed measurable goals for the HRMS project (see Appendix A) with actual results documented as each component was implemented to determine the level of success.

CASE QUESTIONS

1. What were the key strategies or success factors for HRMS ERP implementation?
2. Why was the governance so important to the project?
3. In setting up goals for each system component, what did the institute do that many businesses or institutions do not with an ERP implementation?

APPENDIX A

Sample Goals and Measures

Human Resource System Performance Goals and Measures

Office	What is Measured	Goal	Current	Improvement	Actual Results
Customer Results	Timeliness	Reduce the time it takes to process various types of actions	Awards 15 days	90 percent of actions processed within customer service standards	Awards reduced by 40 percent
			Data change 20 days		Data change reduced by 50 percent
			Extensions 10 days		Extension reduced by 25
			Pay change 10 days		Pay change reduced by 30 percent
			Position change 20 days		Position change reduced by 25 percent
			Promotion 15 days		Promotion reduced by 20 percent
Technology	Reliability and availability	Hours each day that users can access HRMS	Available to some users from 7:30 AM to 5:00 PM, 5 days a week	Increase HRMS hours of availability to an expanded user base 20 hours a day, 7 days a week	The HRMS hours of availability have been expanded to 18 hours a day, 7 days a week
Customer Results	Timeliness and responsiveness	Work days to complete hiring action	70 work days to complete hiring action on strategic positions	Reduce work days to complete hiring action to 50.	Reduced time to hire to 50 work days

9

Organizational Change and Business Process Reengineering

LEARNING OBJECTIVES

After reading this chapter, you should be able to:

- Comprehend why ERP systems are implemented to include business process reengineering (BPR) and "best practices."

- Realize that senior management must be committed to the implementation to assist in overcoming resistance to the change in business processes that meet the company vision and goals.

- Develop an awareness of Organizational Project Management Maturity Model (OPM3) and how it is used to assess an organization's ability to implement an ERP system successfully.

- Introduce business process management (BPM) and discuss its relationship with BPR.

CASE 9-1
Opening Case
FoxMeyer Drugs

Source: "The FoxMeyer Drugs' Bankruptcy: Was it a Failure of ERP?" in *Proceedings of the Association for Information Systems Fifth Americas Conference on Information Systems*, Milwaukee, WI, August 1999. Pages 223–225. Reprinted by permission of Dr. Judy Scott, University of Colorado–Denver.

FoxMeyer Drugs was one of the largest distributors of pharmaceuticals in the world, with a value of more than $5 billion. In 1993, they began an implementation of an ERP software package by SAP, and within four years they were bankrupt. The company officials have taken the stance that their failure was the responsibility of SAP and that the technology failed them; however, in-depth analysis leads one to conclude that the management of FoxMeyer Drugs is to blame because they did not understand the role organizational change was going to play in this implementation.

The failure at FoxMeyer was "not a failure of automation. It was not a failure of commercial software. It was a management failure,"[1] according to Judy B. Scott. FoxMeyer had senior management's support, but it did not have the proper communication channels in place for dealing with the organizational change. As a result, the morale of the workers was hurt and the quality of the products they produced diminished drastically because many felt they would soon be out of their jobs. To make matters worse, many of the workers decided to not wait until the implementation was complete, and there was a mass exodus out of the company to avoid what was seen as inevitable layoffs. If the situation had been communicated more effectively, the workers may not have fled, and the quality would have stayed at the prior standards, such that the business could sustain itself through the implementation; unfortunately, that was not the case.

Things went from bad to worse when the senior management "buy-in" became too powerful. Looking from the outside, it appears as though the belief of senior management was that the technology was the answer to everything. Instead of addressing the changes affecting the organization, and holding off or scaling back some of the technological enhancements, the company redoubled their efforts to implement the software package. They were essentially throwing good money after bad because the failure within the organization had doomed the system to failure regardless of the best-practice processes the system may have been able to deliver. Misunderstanding the role of organizational change in an ERP implementation may have bankrupted one of the world's largest pharmaceutical distributors.

In conclusion, a successful ERP implementation requires organizational change, and business processes are often reengineered to complement the benefits of the new software package. As we see in the case of FoxMeyer, failure to understand this connection can lead to severe financial woes or even bankruptcy. Because an enterprise-wide implementation is such an expensive undertaking, the role of organizational change cannot be overlooked. The success and failure of many ERP implementations do not lie with the technology, they lie within the organization. A stagnant organization that does not adapt its structure, people, and processes to its ERP system is doomed to fail. The role of organizational change in an ERP implementation is a decisive one that can have dire results if overlooked and spectacular results if embraced.

---

[1] http://www.ndsu.nodak.edu/ndsu/bklamm/BPandTCreferences/BPTCScott1999Foxmeyerdrugs-bankruptcy%20was%20itafailure.pdf

PREVIEW

Many ERP implementations do not get off to the right start, as shown by the FoxMeyer opening case. An implementation can be plagued from the beginning by a lack of a vision, a set of unrealistic goals that will be achieved by the ERP system, or both. The development of a rationale for change and communicating it to the company will set in motion a number of activities that will help with a clear direction and process for moving forward. This was not the case with FoxMeyer's ERP implementation. The rationale for changing from legacy systems to an ERP system is often a result of using business process reengineering (BPR) to streamline processes and procedures, thereby creating a competitive advantage. FoxMeyer's would have been served better by taking more time in the beginning to set the stage for change with their ERP implementation. ERPs and BPR have become linked over the years. ERP vendors have worked to include "best practices" in their system within a given industry, whereas BPR identifies current processes and the change requirement to implement "best practices."

Although BPR is used to assess the organizational process change needed, the Organizational Project Management Maturity Model (OPM3) will assess the company's level of skills and ability to implement an ERP system successfully. OPM3 is relatively new and has the support of the Project Management Institute (PMI). The OPM3 consists of three steps: knowledge, assessment, and improvement. These will be presented in more detail in this chapter.

Beyond BPR and OPM3, the project organization and roles and responsibilities will start to bring the project into clarity for the business. ERP implementations require their own organizations and reporting structure. Reporting lines, expectations, and even evaluations need to be included in the structure. Staffing the organization with existing staff, new hires, and consultants creates the need for the project management office to develop a sense of teamwork. Teamwork often takes a number of years to develop under normal circumstances. With ERP implementations, the sense of team needs to be something that is addressed early and quickly on a project and will need to be worked on throughout the implementation. The continuity of teams during the implementation helps to ensure that there is a basis for moving forward as decisions are made and business processes change. If an implementation does not have continuity, as found in the FoxMeyer example, it can lead to a lack of understanding of how business processes were changed and why.

REASON FOR CHANGE

What's "Organizational Change?"

Typically, the concept of organizational change is in regard to organizationwide change, as opposed to smaller changes, such as adding a new person, modifying a program, etc. Examples of organizationwide change might include a change in mission, restructuring operations (e.g., restructuring to self-managed teams, layoffs, etc.), new technologies, mergers, major collaborations, "rightsizing," new programs such as Total Quality Management, re-engineering, etc. Some experts refer to it as organizational transformation. Often this term designates a fundamental and radical reorientation in the way the organization operates.[2]

---

[2] Organizational Change and Development (includes the Field of Organization Development) Written by Carter McNamara, MBA, PhD, Authenticity Consulting, LLC. Copyright 1997–2007. Adapted from the Field Guide to Consulting and Organizational Development and Field Guide to Consulting and Organizational Development with Nonprofits.

ERP implementation projects usually mean radical changes to an organization. This includes fundamental changes in procedures and processes, job functions, and, initially, in the bottom line. According to Appleton, "Approximately one half of all ERP projects fail to achieve anticipated benefits due to managers underestimating the efforts involved in managing change."[3] The decision to implement an ERP must be addressed logically and communicated to key management and staff in order to achieve the desired company goals.

The reasons to move to an integrated ERP system are to improve the bottom line by streamlining business processes and to create a competitive advantage. It was believed for years that ERPs would almost immediately increase profits and provide a short-term return on investment. In most instances this is not the case. Expectations are now changing with the understanding that ERP implementations are much more of a long-term investment. For change management reasons, however, each company must develop a logical and strategic reason to implement an ERP system. Bypassing this step will, at best, result in an ERP system that does not meet management expectations and, at worst, be a complete failure even to get through the implementation.

The rationale to implement an ERP is often a result of an organization conducting a BPR study. These studies both identify process and procedural changes to streamline the business and they identify best business practices that can create industry advantages. In addition to identifying and documenting organizational changes, BPR sets the stage for the implementation. In almost all cases legacy systems will not be able to meet the needs identified in BPR, whereas ERP systems have been sold for a number of years on the fact that they are built around "best practices." In any case, BPR is one of the best methods for determining the need to move to an ERP system and set the high-level goals and project implementation scope.

The next step is to communicate the BPR results to the company so they can begin gaining an overall organizational commitment in replacing legacy systems with an integrated ERP.

ORGANIZATIONAL COMMITMENT

The commitment to implementing an ERP system is sometimes akin to jumping off a cliff with a parachute and hoping it opens. A prime component of a successful implementation is the unwavering commitment and "will" of senior management and key staff to see the implementation through to the end. There will be problems and issues to overcome and resistance to change, both open and passive, so senior management and key staff need to be steadfast in the quest to succeed.

There are two key areas to consider to ensure organizational commitment to the project: components of change management and the OPM3. The first, a component of change management, is a well-defined communication plan. The communication plan should reflect the organizational experience and build upon the ERP benefits and expectations. The second, OPM3, is a process that will help in understanding the existing organizational experience in implementing systems. Using OPM3 will assess an organization's ERP system implementation experience. It will also assist in understanding the implementation skill level and therefore the level of risk involved in the implementation.

---

[3] Appleton, E. L. (March 1997). How to Survive ERP. *Datamation, 43* (3), 50–53.

Change Management

Change management was discussed in Chapter 4. There are also a number of books and research papers on change management that will offer you much more detail on the change management process.[4] The following is a standard definition:

> **Change Management** is the process of developing a planned approach to change in an organization. The objective is typically to maximize the collective benefits for all people involved in the change and to minimize the risk of failure of implementing the change. The discipline of change management deals primarily with the human aspect of change, and is therefore related to pure and industrial psychology.[5]

The mention of change management at this point is to clue you in to the fact that change management must be an integral part of the overall implementation planning strategy to implement an ERP system successfully. The focus of this section will be more on the OPM3 area.

ORGANIZATION PROJECT MANAGEMENT MATURITY MODEL Project Management Institute describes OPM3 as "seeking to create a framework within which organizations can re-examine their pursuit of strategic objectives via Best Practices in organizational project management."[6] In other words it will help companies to understand the level of competency and ability to implement an ERP system successfully. In this case *successfully* means meeting the overall needs of the organization as described in the project scope and delivered on time and on budget. The more skilled companies have a greater chance of implementing ERP systems than those with lesser skills. The lesser-skilled companies can raise those skills through the use of other resources. This can be accomplished through external resources (i.e., consultants) or a combination of hiring new staff with the proper skills and training existing staff to meet the project skill requirements.

The OPM3 model is a three-step continuous improvement process. The steps include knowledge, assessment, and improvement which are shown in Figure 9-1.

For the purposes of an ERP implementation, the steps that need to be addressed to ensure a successful ERP implementation will be clear after the knowledge and assessment steps. The timing of when to start an implementation must be based on the current state of the organization and the plan to improve, if needed. Without the OPM3 methodology or a methodology similar to it, an ERP system implementation runs the risk of not meeting expectations, as well as of being late and over budget. The benefits of an OPM3 analysis are as follows:

- OPM3 helps organizations identify and deliver the right projects to advance their strategy. With OPM3, you will use organizational inputs to align projects across operations and select only the projects that will deliver business results.
- Improved project performance and return on investment with OPM3—experience a shift in thinking that will position your organization for immediate gains and long-term success. OPM3 isolates process improvements while forcing organizations to consider external pressures increasing operational and organizational efficiency.
- OPM3 helps your organization align its strategy with the projects that sustain business success. Through a comprehensive collection of best practices, OPM3 guides your organization on when to stay the course and when to change direction.

---

[4] Esther Cameron, *2004, Making Sense of Change Management.* Publisher: Kogan Page.
[5] www.findwhitepapers.com/enterprise-applications/change-management/ (accessed March 5, 2007)
[6] Project Management Institute. (2003). Organizational Project Management Maturity Model. *Knowledge Foundation,* xi.

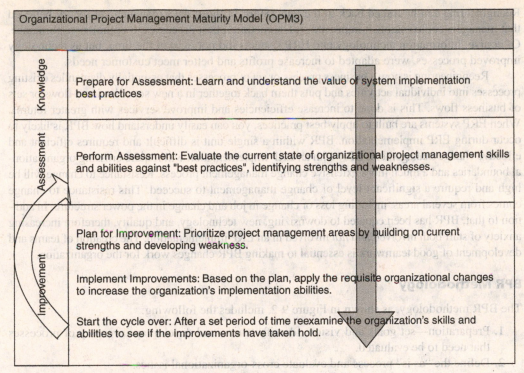

FIGURE 9-1 Organizational Project Management Maturity Model.

- OPM3 mitigates operating costs by keeping projects aligned to business strategy. Scalable by size and maturity, OPM3's diagnostic capabilities can guide any organization to improved performance.

BUSINESS PROCESS CHANGE

As mentioned earlier, BPR is often used as the reason to move from legacy systems to an integrated ERP. To fully utilize the ERP, the BPR results need to be incorporated into the ERP implementation scope and plan and continually measured to understand the effectiveness of the new processes.

Business Process Reengineering

Business process is defined as "a set of logically related tasks performed to achieve a defined business outcome."[7]

A *process* is "a structured, measured set of activities designed to produce a specified output for a particular customer or market. It implies a strong emphasis on how work is done within an organization."[8]

---

[7] Davenport, T. H., and Short, J. E. (Summer, 1990). The New Industrial Engineering: Information Technology and Business Process Redesign. *Sloan Management Review*, 11–27.
[8] Davenport, T. H. (1993). *Process Innovation: Reengineering Work Through Information Technology*. Boston, MA: Harvard Business School Press.

Reengineering can be traced back to the late 1800s. In those days management theory believed that managers could establish improved and, sometimes, best processes to optimize performance. Of course, information technology and ERP systems did not exist at the time, but as technology improved processes, were adapted to increase profits and better meet customer needs.

Reengineering is now a business process or set of processes that essentially dismantles existing processes into individual activities and puts them back together in a new set of business flows or sets of business flows. This is done to increase efficiencies and improve services with greater returns. When ERP systems are built to apply best practices, you can easily understand how BPR is likely to occur during ERP implementation. BPR within a single unit is difficult and requires efficient and effective change management. BPR with an ERP implementation will require crossing organizational boundaries and a much more extensive change management process. Resistance to change will be high and require a significant level of change management to succeed. This resistance to change comes from several areas, including loss or change in job and change in the power structure. In addition to that, BPR has been equated to downsizing, new technology, and quality, therefore increasing anxiety of staff both involved and *not* involved in an ERP implementation. The creation of teams and development of good teamwork is essential to making BPR changes work for the organization.

BPR Methodology

The BPR methodology, as shown in Figure 9-2, includes the following:

1. Preparation—set goals and vision, identify teams, and develop an inventory of processes that need to be evaluated.
2. Define the "as is" process and evaluate cross-organizational issues.
3. Map out "to be" processes based on best practices (i.e., related to ERP).
4. Test and measure new processes based on meeting goals and vision.
5. Reevaluation—revise, adjust to improve processes.

BPR steps are relatively straightforward and seem on the surface to be benign. The complexity of BPR is in its implementation. The setting up of the measurements to achieve the desired results and the monitoring of new or modified processes are the more difficult sides of BPR. Setting up measurements is the key to improvement. You cannot improve what you do not measure. The following is a brief description of each phase of BPR.

Preparation   The very first step in BPR is to develop and articulate what is to be accomplished by reengineering, including goals and scope as it relates to BPR. These goals should be measurable

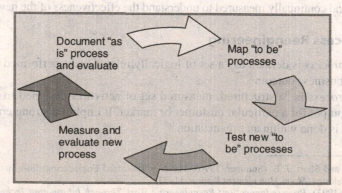

FIGURE 9-2   BPR Framework.

and fully understood by the organization. In the case of an ERP implementation, the functions included in the scope must also be identified. In addition to the goals, during the preparation phase the implementation teams should address goals that need to be created along with an elaborate and extensive communication plan. The teams will be made up of functional users and managers, initially along with facilitators, to walk the teams through the BPR phases. The ERP system is sometimes not purchased until after the "to be" processes are defined and communicated. In that case the BPR process can then be used to define functionality needs and requirements within the system.

Here are some of the drivers behind the need for BPR:

- Implementing a current purchased ERP system
- Automating current manual or error-prone processes
- Improving service to customers
- Streamlining current processes to decrease time to market
- Participating in or conducting e-marketplaces
- Reducing costs
- Addressing accountability
- Conducting e-Procurement

"As Is"   Working with the vision and goals, the functional teams must define the existing processes. The processes will need both a written description and graphical depiction of each and every process. Each process will likely have predecessors and successors linking processes together for future analysis in the "to be" phase. Expect a lot of discussion during this phase, especially around processes that cross functional boundaries. This usually results from one functional area not knowing what occurs in another functional area. Ensuring that a process is well understood by the team during this phase will be important for the "to be" phase. There needs to be clarity around decision points for who is responsible and why. Last, the teams will need to develop a sense of timing for each process. This will assist in the measurement process later in the methodology. In working through the "as is" phase it is often tedious and stressful. This can often be countered with team-building exercises and events. Part of the goal of this phase will be to develop good interaction between and among the teams and to prepare them for the much more difficult "to be" phase.

"To Be"   This is the phase where facilitators earn their stripes. This phase must address timing of processes and the changes needed to meet the original set of goals. This phase requires much thought and analysis. The questioning of current processes is a must. A team member will often say things similar to, "we've always done it like that." The understanding of *why* a process does what it does needs to be uncovered, irrespective of who does it. Some team members, although not all, will be threatened by the idea of changing a process. It is critical to work through this phase and all the processes objectively and thoroughly. It will assist in developing trust and minimizing some of the anxiety created by the "to be" phase. As stated earlier, this phase dismantles processes and puts them back together with a new sense of purpose. Some processes will even be eliminated, and all new processes must have estimates of timing and who is responsible. This sets the stage for the measurement phase.

If the ERP system is already purchased, then this phase must address the existing ERP system functionality and how the changed processes will work with the system. If the system is not purchased, then the defined processes should be used to compare systems on the market for an organizational match.

Testing and Measurement   Even though the "to be" processes are clearly documented and the timing for each process estimated, the testing and validation of each process is necessary to ensure that a step was not missed or that a process not achievable. If the system is already purchased, then this can be accomplished with a test system configuration. If the ERP is not purchased, then the teams must develop a methodology that will either walk them through the processes or have the vendors set up a test system that will help to validate the new business processes. It will not be perfect, but it helps the teams get a sense of what is doable and what is not. This process often identifies further improvements that can be made. It is essential to set up measurement processes that are meaningful and measure the goals set out in the preparation phase. It may take a couple of iterations of BPR to realize the goals fully, but continuing to examine processes and to make adjustments creates a sustainable ERP system environment.

As noted earlier, ERP systems are based on "best practices." BPR processes are designed to meet company goals and vision. Even though it must be done, care should be taken to address combining ERP and BPR into a single process. This gets back to the overall implementation methodology and how the "to be" processes fit into an ERP system. Almost all purchased ERP systems are very flexible and most of the time can be adjusted to meet organizational vision and goals; however, it is likely it will not "fit" all "to be" processes. This does bring you back to the discussion of modifying the system or adjusting the business process, communicating expectations, and overall governance.

Current BPR Tools

There are a number of BPR tools on the market today to assist in mapping out existing and new business processes. These software packages can help the team analyze the dynamics of existing processes and can provide greater insight to redesigned processes that meet project goals.

Some packages are comprehensive and take teams through the entire BPR process, whereas others address certain market niches. The appendix at end of chapter shows some of the BPR tools currently available on the market.

BUSINESS PROCESS MANAGEMENT

Over the last decade, business process reengineering has become very complex and difficult to implement manually or even with business process reengineering tools mentioned in the appendix, without a structured and consistent approach based on best practices. This has increased the need for business process management (BPM) and similar other approaches that have emerged to help organization with implementing BPR.

According to Gartner, BPM is defined as

> a management discipline that treats processes as assets that directly contribute to enterprise performance by driving operational excellence and business process agility. BPM employs methods, policies, metrics, management practices and software tools to continuously optimize the organization processes to improve business performance against goals and objectives.[9]

The goal of BPM helps achieve "business process improvement (BPI)." BPM improves the performance of business processes of the firm and also the processes involving external parties like suppliers and others in the supply chain. BPM helps to keep the business process model in line the with process execution. BPM tries to increase the agility. The modeling of business processes improves the transparency and makes it easier to change.[10]

---

[9] Gartner Research. (July 27, 2010). Hype Cycle for Business Process Management, 2010.
[10] Ibid.

BPM processes have been derived from the study on workflow technologies that aimed at eliminating the manual intervention in the process implementation.[11] BPM became popular in the 1990s for improving the performance of organizations. Business process improvement involved the usage of process benchmarking and BPR along with the implementation of ERP systems. The key for improving processes is for management to understand of the differences between firm's processes and the best practice processes.[12] Management that sees these differences will succeed in improving their business processes. Process improvements occur by knowing the customers better, devising processes to meet the needs of the customer, and continuously reevaluating to keep the focus on high-level performance in this time of rapidly changing environment.[13] BPM institutionalizes this continuous process change in organization. One of the Gartner surveys for top-level executives held in December 2009 showed that more than two-thirds realized the value in using a BPM approach to be successful in achieving their business goals. According to this study, the top-level executives are proactive and think about the high volatility in the marketplace before making the changes in their business models. As per the Gartner 2010 survey, organizations that have BPM system in place spend around 55 percent of IT budget to run the business, while the industry's average spending is 64 percent.[14] IDC research reported that the BPM market increased almost 80 percent in 2006, reaching $890 million, and that this market will expand to $5.5 billion by the end of 2011.[15]

Difference between BPR and BPM

BPR and BPM are not the same, and the differences between them are discussed in this section. BPR suggests that businesses will become competitive by redesigning core business processes. It aims at eliminating the human intervention and automating the process, wherever possible. BPM is not about radical automation; instead, it follows an iterative approach of making incremental improvements in the processes. For any industry, this approach enables to make frequent adjustments to the business processes according to the rapidly changing operational conditions in the global markets. BPM put processes in place to make continual incremental changes rather than aiming at one perfect solution, as the cycle time between changes is really short in current business situation. BPR is all about automation and downsizing of the organization. The aim of BPM is not to eliminate the human efforts, but to understand the dependencies and interactions among the people, system and the information needed to do the tasks better. BPM starts with process modeling to understand the workflows and figure out the manual and automated tasks and to improve the efficiency of the business processes. The business model improves the transparency of the work steps and resources in the business process and also clearly shows the information flows and business rules. The developed business model is then interpreted by the BPM software (BPMS) and becomes executable. This makes the process to be visible to the managers responsible for making decisions. Managers can modify the model by knowing where the bottlenecks are present. The modifications are reflected in the execution right away. Business managers can easily manage the processes, with IT deciding the implementation of some specific tasks.[16]

---

[11] O'Connell, J. (September 12, 2003). Measuring IT's Effectiveness to the Business. *Computer Weekly*, 00104787.

[12] Juan, Y.-C., and Ou-Yang, C. (April 1, 2004). Systematic Approach for the Gap Analysis of Business Processes. *International Journal of Production Research*, 42 (7), 1325–1364.

[13] Baker, B. (August 1997). Process Redesign: The Implementation Guide for Managers. *Quality Progress*, 30 (8), 174, 2 pgs, http://proquest.umi.com/pqdlink?did=13457720&Fmt=7&clientId=1531&RQT=309&VName=PQD

[14] Gartner Research. Hype Cycle for Business Process Management, 2010.

[15] IDC Predicts Rapid Growth for Business Process Management Software Market Reaching $55 Billion by 2011. http://www.askwebhosting.com/story/8347/IDC_Predicts_Rapid_Growth_for_Business_Process_Management_Software_Market_Reaching_$55_Billion_by_2011.html

[16] BPM is Not the Same as BPR, By: Janelle B. Hill, Vice President, Gartner, Friday February 9, 2007. http://www.bpminstitute.org/articles/article/article/bpm-is-not-the-same-as-bpr.html

Best Practices of BPM

BPM systems help managers in understanding the working of the business processes better so as to manage them more efficiently. The successful implementation of BPM requires separation of the following two broad categories of processes from one another.

HUMAN-INTENSIVE PROCESSES   These processes are also known as "knowledge work." They depend on people to do the work. The interaction of people with one another and with the business applications and databases are important. Human intervention is required to make effective decisions. Examples: loan approvals, customer service.

SYSTEM-INTENSIVE PROCESSES   These processes involve a large number of automated transactions each day that do not require human judgments and can be easily automated, for example, bank transactions processing.

TABLE 9-1   BPM Process Categories

People-intensive processes	Involve a high level of interaction between individuals for routing, approving, and fulfilling requests such as customer service requests, travel, and purchase requests and usually high rates of exception handling. Although this type of open-ended process translates into a need for flexibility on the part of the end user, it doesn't mean that the processes can't be automated in some way, shape, or form.
Decision-intensive processes	They are fairly complex processes that involve gathering and deciphering information and often include mission-critical decision making as well. A rules engine that sets "if then" rules (e.g., at a manufacturing company, a rule could be implemented that said: "notify sales when inventory is lower than 10 and we have more than five pending orders on a Monday") is absolutely necessary for this type of process. Ease-of-information access (i.e., no wasted time in repetitive searches and minimizing multiple database screens) is just as critical for employees performing this type of task.
Document-intensive processes	Require users to review documents for approval, enter data from those documents into a back-office system, and make decisions based on the documents in hand. User activity is driven by information found in scanned images or electronic forms, or often electronic documents created in Microsoft Word or other office automation software tools. Other examples of document-intensive processes include new account opening and invoice processing.
Integration-intensive processes	They are not only descriptive of a certain type of business activity but, according to the Forrester report, also a goal to aspire to for a company looking to cut down on wasted operator time in exception handling, for instance. This means that a best practice in BPM implementations is always to examine the other three types of processes and look for ways to improve on or significantly modify the process to get it to an integration-intensive level.

Source: Adopted from Best Practices in BPM.

BPM Software Vendors

The major BPM software vendors are listed in this section. These vendors have great opportunities, because of the increasing growth rate of BPM market. According to Gartner study, the global market for BPM software was $1.97 billion in 2008 and is estimated to reach $3.17 billion by 2013, at 10 percent annual growth rate.[17]

   Forrester Research classifies the BPM software vendors by their functionality, and some players are found in many categories. The categories include integration-centric, human-centric and document-centric providers.[18]

Vendor[19]	Category
Adobe	Document-centric provider. Adobe achieves its BPM market strength from document integration that then automates process.[20]
Appian	Human-centric provider
Cordys	Human-centric provider. Targets mainly services-oriented architecture (SOA) market.[21]
EMC	Document-centric provider[22]
Global 360	Human-centric and document-centric providers
IBM	Integration-centric and document-centric providers. IBM is able to leverage its SOA market dominance to support innovation, providing BPM software that supports flexible response to changing market conditions.[23]
Lombardi	Human-centric provider
MetaStorm	Human-centric provider
Oracle	Integration-centric provider
PegaSystems	Human-centric provider
Progress-Savvion	Human-centric provider
Software AG-IDS Scheer	Integration-centric provider
Tibco Software	Integration-centric provider

Core Business Processes

BPM improves the efficiency of all the core business processes[24] in an organization due to the interactions among the business processes; for example, the order-to-sales process (M/S) and revenue collection (RC) processes interacts with the revenue collection part of the order-to-cash

[17] http://www.crmbuyer.com/story/67813.html (accessed November 5, 2010)

[18] Ibid.

[19]http://www.gartner.com/DisplayDocument?id=1395425&ref=g_sitelink&ref=g_SiteLink

[20]http://www.researchandmarkets.com/research/912168/worldwide_business

[21]http://www.it-director.com/business/content.php?cid=10295

[22]http://www.crmbuyer.com/story/67813.html

[23]http://www.electronics-ca.com/products/Worldwide-Business-Process-Management-(BPM)-Market-Opportunities-Strategies,-and-Forecasts.html

[24]Gelinas, Ulric J., Sutton, Steve G., and Fedorowicz, Jane. (c2004). *Business Processes and Information Technology.* Mason, Ohio: Thomson/South-Western.

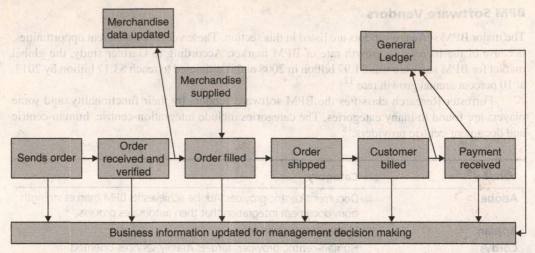

FIGURE 9-3   Example of the Order-to-Sales Process (M/S) and Revenue Collection (RC) Processes.

process, which also interacts with the purchasing and manufacturing processes by sharing information, as shown in Figure 9-3.

The M/S process includes interaction between employees, system, methods, and controls designed to reach the goals. This process has to support the following:

- Repetitive work procedures of the credit department, sales order department, the warehouse and shipping department.
- Requirements of the decision makers of the different marketing and sales functions.
- Information flows and data stored to support the operations and management processes.

The process supports the sales order department in capturing important customer and order information, facilitating the credit granting to the customers, and ensuring the timely delivery of goods to customers. The information flows are automated by the ERP systems.

M/S process involves:

1. Processing of the orders placed by the customers
2. Delivering goods to the customers

R/C process involves:

1. Charging the customers
2. Management of the customer accounts
3. Obtaining payment for the products or services provided

Order-to-Cash BPM Solution from Dell Services

Dell Services' automated, rules-based order-to-cash processing optimizes workflow to reduce costly errors, decrease receivables and DSOs (day's sales outstanding), increase collections, and enhance the customer experience. The Dell/Perot Systems suite[25] includes five modules as shown in Figure 9-4.

---

[25] http://www.perotsystems.com/MediaRoom/Library/ServiceOverviews/ServiceBrochure_OrdertoCashProcessing.pdf

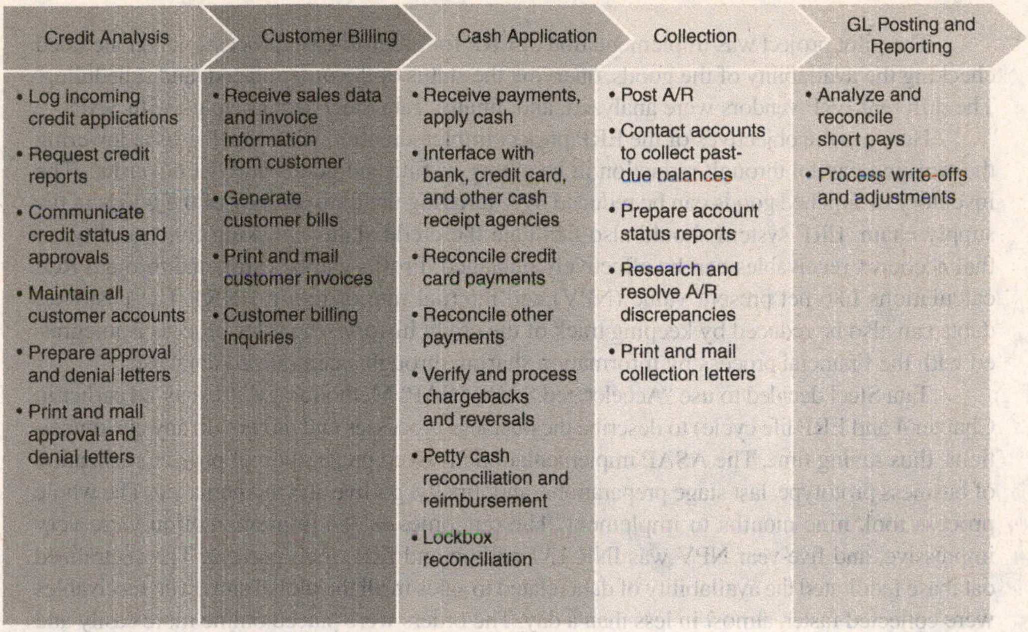

Credit Analysis	Customer Billing	Cash Application	Collection	GL Posting and Reporting
• Log incoming credit applications • Request credit reports • Communicate credit status and approvals • Maintain all customer accounts • Prepare approval and denial letters • Print and mail approval and denial letters	• Receive sales data and invoice information from customer • Generate customer bills • Print and mail customer invoices • Customer billing inquiries	• Receive payments, apply cash • Interface with bank, credit card, and other cash receipt agencies • Reconcile credit card payments • Reconcile other payments • Verify and process chargebacks and reversals • Petty cash reconciliation and reimbursement • Lockbox reconciliation	• Post A/R • Contact accounts to collect past-due balances • Prepare account status reports • Research and resolve A/R discrepancies • Print and mail collection letters	• Analyze and reconcile short pays • Process write-offs and adjustments

FIGURE 9-4 Example of Dell's BPM System.

SAP ERP Implementation at Tata Steel[26]

The Tata Steel Company implemented ERP in three stages to support their order fulfillment process:

- Generation and fulfillment of the orders
- Financial and accounting processes
- Auditing and assessing the advantages of ERP system

Tata Steel, a major conglomerate founded in 1907 by Jamsethji Tata in India, has been a low-cost provider of steel in the global market. Internationally, the steel prices started to decline and became closer to their costs. The company had to maintain its low-cost image, serve customers with quality products, and also remain profitable by improving efficiency of the core business processes. Tata Steel is spread across different geographic locations and involves many independent applications and hence leading to increase in the number of databases. It was hard to track the finished goods inventory in the different plants and other financial data, as there was no integration of the systems and consistency of information. Management of the processes and decision making became difficult. This led to the need for a central business application to support the core processes.

(continued)

[26] Kumar, S., and Keshan, A. (2009). ERP Implementation in Tata Steel: Focus on Benefits and ROI. *Journal of Information Technology Case and Application Research, 11*.

The pilot project was implementation of ERP for order-to-cash process, which included checking the availability of the goods, querying the status of the order placed, and scheduling. The different ERP vendors were analyzed, and, finally, Tata Steel decided to go with SAP.

Here are the objectives of the ERP project implementation: Tata Steel aims at lowering the working capital through reduction in inventory of finished goods and debt overdue. The inventory of finished goods can be reduced by improving the transparency of the goods in the supply chain. ERP system should also facilitate the credit status checking functionality, so that accounts receivables can be effectively managed. Profits can be estimated through ROI calculations like net present value (NPV) and internal rate of return (IRR). The customer debts can also be reduced by keeping track of the credit history. The sales process is integrated with the financial process by information sharing through a centralized database.

Tata Steel decided to use "Accelerated SAP (ASAP) Methodology" (discussed earlier in Chapter 4 and ERP life cycle) to describe the business processes and did not do any customizations, thus saving time. The ASAP implementation involved preparation of project, realization of business prototype, last stage preparations, and, finally, go-live and maintenance. The whole process took nine months to implement. The outcomes of the implementation were very impressive, and five-year NPV was INR 139 million and IRR of 23 percent. The centralized database facilitated the availability of data related to sales in all the global sites. The receivables were collected faster, almost in less than a day. The orders were placed online more easily and at a quicker pace. Finished goods inventory was reduced by improving the transparency, thereby cutting the inventory costs like holding costs and other costs. Thus the pilot project was successful, and Tata Steel proceeded with the other stages and was successful.

Optimizing Business Processes

BPM software helps to optimize the business processes of an organization and improve the performance. This section describes how BPM software functions and helps to improve the business processes. BPM is very important for the process-intensive industries like insurance. Gartner's research says that BPM helps firms to model, analyze, and test business processes without the interference of the core systems and then to figure out process problems more easily. BPM involves proper utilization of people and resources to do the work and also automate the processes that do not require human expertise and judgment.[27] BPM combines a range of features—process design and modeling, integration, and postdeployment monitoring and analytics—but the most important function is to help companies increase process efficiency and, therefore, reduce costs.[28] The visible process models can be fine-tuned or optimized by the managers to serve the customers better. Business process management (BPM) and services-oriented architecture engine markets were at $1.8 billion for licenses, maintenance, and services in 2008 and are forecasted to increase to $6.2 billion by 2015.[29]

---

[27] LexisNexis Academic. (July 5, 2010). What can BPM do? *ITWeb Brainstorm.*
[28] Voelker, Michael. (December 1, 2003). BPM Targets the Bottom Line—Enabling Change, Easing Compliance and Maximizing Efficiency, Business Process Management Technology Proves its Value in Cutting Costs. *Transform Magazine.*
[29] http://www.electronics-ca.com/products/Worldwide-Business-Process-Management-(BPM)-Market-Opportunities-Strategies,-and-Forecasts.html

BPM has functionalities obtained from application integration, process modeling and monitoring, and rapid application development tools. BPM software helps to model processes graphically and execute these processes within the business. The software also serves as a tool to measure the process performance, identify the bottlenecks, and then make adjustments more easily at a quicker pace. BPM software improves the method in which people and the applications work. The firms get more agility by developing more new processes as required by dynamic business environments. In short, BPM software is a set of tools that helps a company in extraction and management of the business processes efficiently.[30]

Smaller companies will have simpler workflow that can be easily managed, but as they grow, the workflow gets really complex and hard to keep under control and hence BPM comes into picture. BPM software helps to overcome workflow bottlenecks and improve productivity.

Benefits of Implementing BPM[31]

- Smooth business operations in an organization require communication and synchronization. BPM software aids in facilitating those efforts, resulting in high productivity.
- The employees become more efficient, because the workflow bottlenecks are removed using BPM software and thereby reducing the idle time of the employees. This increases productivity.
- High efficiency means reduced costs, and hence BPM software helps companies to cut costs.
- Employees feel better to work in an organized business processes architecture that was created using BPMS.
- Improved workflow results in better-quality products and services and thus BPMS makes customers happy and improves customer loyalty.

Three governments have implemented BPM projects:

- Kent County, Michigan—BPM software was used to streamline processes like accounts payable and invoice management.
- The City of Norfolk, Virginia—BPMS was used to lower construction permit turnaround time from 19 days to a few days.
- The Supreme Court of Louisiana—BPMS was used to lower the time staff requires to issue Certificates of Good Standing to attorneys from three to five hours a day to one hour a day.[32]

Following are some of the major features of BPM software to manage business processes:

- Process modeling and simulation—Users can directly use the software to design the processes that need to be automated, graphically. BPM software has drag-and-drop features to develop processes.
- Systems integration—BPM software lets other information systems like ERP to be connected to the processes, and hence information can flow between the systems.
- User interaction and collaboration—BPMS has Web forms and other user interfaces to help the user to enter inputs and make other changes to the process.
- Process execution and monitoring—BPMS lets job to be routed through the process steps and sends notifications electronically and also tracks performance indicators of processes.

---

[30] O'Connell. Measuring IT's Effectiveness to the Business.

[31] http://office-software.suite101.com/article.cfm/bpm_software_improves_corporate_workflow

[32] Boyle, B. (April 2008). Business Process Management: A New Way to Conduct Operations. *Government Finance Review*, 24 (2).

The benefits of BPM are driven by the *"Four Rs of Process"*:[33]

- Roles—establishing a set of defined user roles that will not change with employee absences or departures
- Relationships—identifying the interactions necessary to complete a process
- Rules—developing a fixed set of process steps that will be followed in most situations
- Routing—electronically transferring forms and documents for review, approval, and so on.

BPM software does not want the user to write code and is very user friendly. It facilitates the entire process-implementation life cycle and also interactive tasks like development of business rules that are managed centrally, development of portals and flexible forms, and feedback provided for process improvements. After the process models are developed, BPM software then works on automating, controlling, and recording new processes and also managing the allocation of resources to the different steps. Automation has many benefits like staff time reduction and high-quality services. BPM software also assists in tactical management by giving right information to the right people. It tracks process performance by measuring the time taken for each stage in the process, the number of unprocessed items, and the total time taken to finish the process. The BPM software sends e-mail alert messages, points out bottlenecks at a step, and gives information for effective decision making.

Other Examples of Success Stories[34]

Here are a few other examples of using BPM suite in different organizations like Facebook Inc, AT&T Inc., and McDonald's. The benefits of using the BPM suite by these organizations are also specified.

- **Facebook Inc.,** the famous social networking Web site, uses Oracle E-Business Suite Release to support the order-to-cash process. The suite helps in managing orders, sales process, and also the financials. The suite is integrated with the other applications, thus facilitating the information sharing throughout the organization. It also helps to improve the efficiency and increase the visibility of the business processes. Revenue collection process cycle is automated and also the SOX compliance is taken care of. The suite enhanced the business reporting and forecasting functionalities in order to provide the management with right information to make effective decisions.
- **AT&T Inc.**—The recent acquisitions have forced AT&T to upgrade to Oracle E-Business Suite Release 12 in order to centralize the worldwide accounting operations and also enable SOX compliance of all the global financial data.
- **McDonald's**—It decided to upgrade to Oracle E-Business Suite Release 12.1 to improve the business processes and productivity and also to reduce the downtime.

Role of ERP

ERP and BPM systems are not mutually exclusive. Implementation of BPM software does not need revamping of the existing ERP components. Actually, they both interact with and complement each other. The different hierarchical levels in the organization include corporate, functional, and informational levels (lowest level). The corporate level is "big picture" of the entire enterprise; functional level includes marketing, human resources, and other departments in the organization;

---

[33] Four Rs of Processes (Adapted from *"Business Process Management: A New Way to Conduct Operations." by, Brenda Boyle.* Government Finance Review).
[34] Customer Success Stories. (April 2010). Information for Success, Oracle E-Business Suite Release 12 and 12.1.

and the informational level includes day-to-day operational activities in a firm. ERP is at the functional and informational levels, and BPM system is at the corporate level. ERP does not satisfy all the process management requirements, but the BPM software aids and enhances ERP. BPMS not only supports workflow methods in ERP systems but also connects processes in other applications. BPM software records process performance metrics and also helps in automation and integration of processes throughout the organization, but ERP doesn't perform these functions.

EXAMPLE 1

At the City of Fresno, California, the link between ERP system and BPM software permits workers to create requests for leave electronically. Workers then use BPMS for checking the requests' status and receive notification e-mails. ERP alone cannot carry out this function.[35]

EXAMPLE 2

In 2009, SAP started working on integrating BPM and ERP, that is, including Net Weaver BPM as a component in ERP suite, to serve the SAP customers better and also provide greater agility to the ERP business processes. SAP is also working on merging BPM and BI to improve the monitoring functionalities.[36]

ERP system implementations aid in thorough redesigning of the business processes and the deployment of new software to support the newly developed business processes (Robey et al. 2002; Ross and Vitale 2000). Estimates suggest that the adoption of ERP is about 75 percent among medium to large manufacturing firms, 60 percent among service organizations, and about 80 percent among Fortune 500 firms (META Group 2004). The ERP system implementation caused greater change with huge impacts on employees, basically changing the nature of workflows and tasks. The importance of understanding change management procedures for implementing ERP is very critical because data indicated that the rate of ERP failures is greater than 60 percent.[37]

ERP software is a great asset in interconnecting the business processes and people and enabling access to latest information among the different divisions and locations. ERP system enables planning, scheduling, and monitoring of the entire manufacturing process. It also helps the organization to centralize the information fed into the system so that it can be shared across different departments like marketing and sales, material management, production planning, and finance and accounting. Thus ERP system provides the firm a chance to reduce costs, turn much more efficient, and reduce the manual intervention and automate the business processes to suit the dynamic business conditions. The ERP included modules like production planning, material management, quality assurance, sales and distribution and financial accounting. The ERP systems bring in great business benefits like increasingly visible operations, integrated business operations, and increased revenues.[38]

---

[35] Ibid.

[36] Kemsley, S. (October 26, 2009). SAP NetWeaver BPM: A 1.0 Product With Promise. *Intelligent Enterprise*—Online; Manhasset (1524–3621).

[37] Morris, M. G., and Viswanath, V. (March 2010). Job Characteristics and Job Satisfaction: Understanding the Role of Enterprise Resource Planning System Implementation. *MIS Quarterly (0276–7783)*, 34 (1).

[38] Rajendra Chaudhary The ERP Effect. (May 3, 2010). *Express Intelligent Enterprise.* http://www.expresscomputeronline.com/20100503/expressintelligententerprise02.shtml (accessed Mar 28, 2011).

IMPLICATIONS FOR MANAGEMENT

Senior management buy-in and support are needed, but these must coincide with a strong rationale for change. A prime component of a successful implementation is the unwavering commitment and "will" of senior management and key staff to see the implementation through to the end. There will be problems and issues to overcome and resistance to change, both open and passive, so senior management and key staff need to be steadfast in the quest to succeed. In addition, for change management reasons, each company must develop a logical and strategic reason to implement an ERP system. Bypassing this step will, at best, result in an ERP system not meeting management expectations and, at worst, in a complete failure even to get through the implementation.

OPM3 can help to assess the organizational skill set to implement an ERP system successfully, meeting the goals set out at the beginning of the project. It will help companies to understand the level of competency and ability to implement an ERP system successfully. The more skilled companies have a greater chance of implementing ERP systems than do ones with lesser skills. Following the OPM3 methodology will at a minimum identify skill gaps within the organization that must be filled before an ERP implementation starts.

As with most ERP implementations, *using BPR can create a lot of anxiety in the workforce.* Management involvement, especially in the communications to staff on the business process changes, will help to reduce staff anxiety. BPR with an ERP implementation will require crossing organizational boundaries and a more extensive change management process. Resistance to change will often be high and can be reduced with a significant level of change management early in the process and often. This resistance to change may be due to a fear of loss or change in a job and an overall change in the control structure. Over the years BPR has been equated to downsizing because of the new technology, therefore increasing the anxiety of staff involved and *not* involved in an ERP implementation.

BPM can improve success of ERP implementation and institutionalize continuous change of business process in organization. BPR can be scary to the employees as it involves radical changes and job loss; also, in today's competitive business marketplace discrete process change can make the organization ineffective and inefficient. BPM overcomes these problems as management, employees, and partners are all aware and used to the small incremental changes in business processes on an ongoing basis. This can increase the success rate of ERP implementation and bring down the costs of implementation.

Summary

- There are many tools and a significant amount of research in the industry to assist a company in putting together a successful project. Business process reengineering and organizational project management maturity model are two such tools.
  - BPR will help develop rationale for moving from a legacy system to an ERP system.

- OPM3 will assess the company's skills and abilities to implement an ERP successfully.
- BPM will institutionalize small incremental changes to improve the success of ERP system.
- In addition to using the tools to understand and communicate the rationale for moving to an ERP system, the project organization must be well understood. This chapter discussed the issues with business process change.

Exercises

1. Research two recent ERP implementations and compare and contrast the organizational structure with the level of implementation success (i.e., meeting vision and goals).

2. Research two ERP implementations (i.e., one that used BPR as a part of the implementation and one that did not), and then determine how well each company met the vision and goals of the implementation.

Review Questions

1. What are the steps in business process reengineering?
2. Why is BPR important in an ERP implementation?
3. What does the organizational project management maturity model do for a company's ERP implementation?
4. What are the steps involved in OPM3?
5. What is the role of the project management office in an ERP implementation?

6. Why is change management critical to the success of a project from the beginning?
7. What is usually the critical path of an ERP implementation?
8. What is the role of the cross-functional lead in an ERP implementation?

Discussion Questions

1. Discuss the need to have a strong rationale for moving from a legacy system to an integrated ERP system.
2. Describe the steps involved in business process reengineering and how they are closely linked to ERP implementation.

3. Discuss how project accountability is created within the project and within the company.

CASE 9-2
Real-World Case
Nike ERP Implementation

BACKGROUND[39]

Nike was founded in 1964 by Bill Bowerman and Phil Knight in Beaverton, Oregon. It began as Blue Ribbon Sports (BRS). In 1972, BRS introduced a new brand of athletic footwear called Nike, named for the Greek winged goddess of victory.

The company employs 26,000 staff around the world with revenues in fiscal year 2005 of $13.7 billion. It has facilities in Oregon, Tennessee, North Carolina, and the Netherlands with more than 200 factory stores, a dozen Nike women stores, and more than 100 sales and administrative offices.

Its subsidiaries include Cole Haan Holdings, Inc., Bauer Nike Hockey, Hurley International LLC, Nike IHM, Inc., Converse Inc., and Execter Brands Group LLC. As of

(continued)

---

[39] www.nike.com (accessed May 2005).

May 31, 2004, manufacturing plants included Nike brand, with 137 factories in the Americas (including the United States), 104 in EMEA, 252 in North Asia, and 238 in South Asia, providing more than 650,000 jobs to local communities.

OBJECTIVE

Nike grew from a sneaker manufacturer in the early 1970s to a global company selling a large number of products throughout the world. Nike's sneaker supply chain was historically highly centralized. The product designs, factory contracts, and delivery are managed through the headquarters in Beaverton, Oregon. By 1998, there were 27 different and highly customized order management systems that did not talk well to the home office in Beaverton, Oregon. At that time Nike decided to purchase and implement a single-instance ERP system along with supply chain and customer relationship management systems to control the nine-month manufacturing cycle better, with the goal being to cut it down to six months.

PLAN

The company developed a business plan to implement the systems over a six-year period, with multiple ERP rollouts over that time. The plan called for the implementation of the demand planning system first while working through the ERP system and supply chain implementation.

IMPLEMENTATION

The demand planning system was implemented first for reasons that made a lot of sense. The total number of users was small in comparison to the ERP system and was thought to be relatively easy to implement; however, this turned out not to be the case. When the system went live, there were a number of problems related to the software, response time, and data. In addition, training was not adequately addressed, causing the relatively small number of end users to use the system ineffectively. The single-instance ERP system and supply chain implementation plan differed from the demand planning system and called instead for a phased rollout over a number of years.

The ERP system implementation went much more smoothly. Nike started in 2000 with the implementation of the Canadian region, a relatively small one, and ended with the Asia-Pacific and Latin America regions in 2006, with the United States and Europe, Middle East, and Africa in 2002. This included implementing a single instance of the system, with the exception of Asia-Pacific, and training more than 6,300 users.

The total cost of the project as of 2006 was at $500 million—about $100 million more than the original project budget.

CONCLUSION: WHAT WAS LEARNED?

- The demand planning system interfacing to legacy data from a large number of systems that already did not talk well with each other was a root cause for misinformation and resulted in inadequate supply planning.
- The demand planning system was complex, and end users were not trained well enough to use the system effectively.
- System testing was not well planned and "real" enough to find issues with legacy system interfaces.
- The overall business plan for all the systems and reasons for taking on such a highly complex implementation were well understood throughout the company. Thus, Nike had exceptional "buy-in" for the project and was able to make adjustment in its demand planning system and continue with the implementation. The goal was to ensure business goals were achieved through the implementation, and not so much to get the systems up and running.
- Nike exhibited patience in the implementation and learned from mistakes made early in the process.
- Training was substantially increased for the ERP implementation. Customer service representatives received 140–180 hours of training from Nike, and users were locked out of the system until they completed the full training course.
- Business process reengineering was used effectively to clarify performance-based goals for the implementation.

CASE QUESTIONS

- How could OPM3 have helped to identify the problems with implementing the demand planning system?
- What were the three primary reasons Nike was successful with the ongoing ERP implementation?
- Why was a phased rollout the correct decision for Nike?

Sources: Koch, C. (December 7, 2004). Nike Rebounds. *CIO Australia's* magazine for executives.

APPENDIX A

BPR Software Tools

BPR Tool	Company	Description
ActionWorks®	Action Technologies, Alameda, CA	The product suite consists of a business process builder, process engine, and front-end executive dashboard.
AllFusion® Process Modeler	CA, Islandia, NY	Modeling tool that helps analyze, document, and improve complex business processes. Provides an integrated view of workflows to complete tasks and activities.
BizFlow	HandySoft, Vienna, VA	Delivers process management solutions in the areas of collaboration, administration, application, and integration.
BPSimulator	Technology Economics Inc, Rockville, MD	The activity-based analysis software enables teams to track cycle times and costs of multiple business processes.
Composer	Texas Instruments, Texas	Enables organizations to use model-driven development to design rapidly, build, test, install, and maintain reengineering applications.
Corporate Modeler	CASEwise Systems, Waltham, MA	The software comprises six diagramming modules that enable organizations to depict organizations, locations, processes, technologies, applications, and data from different perspectives.
Extend+BPR	Imagine That!, San Jose, CA	Includes 90 prebuilt blocks to assist teams in creating reengineering models. Includes drag-and-drop modeling, animation, spreadsheet connectivity, and customized reporting.
FirstSTEP	Interfacing Technologies Corp, Quebec, Canada	The software provides reporting and analysis on static and dynamic states of BPR models. Export and import capabilities are also included, along with workflow connectivity.
Framework	Ptech, Cambridge, MA	Integrated set of object-oriented tools that enable teams to create interactive blueprints of business processes. Software code can be generated from the hierarchical layout, providing rapid and consistent application development.
Icetools	CSP Group, Inc., Lee's Summit, MO	Combines documented enterprise processes and requirements with business modeling.
iGrafx	iGrafx, Tualatin, OR	Features process modeling, simulation, and reporting capabilities. Designed for the front end of reengineering projects. Teams can quickly create and edit presentation-quality process maps.

BPR Tool	Company	Description
iThink	isee systems (formerly, High Performance Systems), Lebanon, NH	Powerful tool for communicating interdependencies between processes and problems. The entire business team will understand the variables that impact business processes. A shared insight enables teams to work together, further ensuring that decisions are fully implemented and mitigating risk.
KBSI Tools	Knowledge Based Systems, College Station, TX	The tools in this suite enable teams to tailor the framework program to individual reengineering needs. Integrated modeling helps identify redundancies and non–value-added activities and creates a better understanding of relationships.
Looking Glass	Avatar, Jacksonville, FL	Provides workflow management and automated value chain management capabilities specifically designed to address the challenges that are posed by service sector business requirements and processes.
Mercutio	ProcessSoft, Lausanne, Switzerland	A solution for the reengineering of administrative processes that automatically generates and implements the necessary workflow components directly from the graphical design.
ProModel	ProModel, Orem, UT	Enables users to test the behavior and prove the benefits of redesigned processes before committing to change.
ProVision Workbench	Proforma Corp, Southfield, MI	Provides a process modeling and simulation tool set.
ReThink	Gensym Corp., Burlington, MA	Combined object-oriented technology with interactive graphics that provides modeling and simulation. The software helps teams monitor process performance and manage real-time operations.
SIMPROCESS	CACI International, Arlington, VA	Hierarchical simulation tool that is designed for business process modeling and analysis. Helps to reduce the time spent on mapping reengineering components.
Vision Manager	Cape Visions, Brookline, MA	Tool addresses the entire BPR life cycle, including data capture, process modeling, simulation, implementation, and continuous improvement. The software enables teams to test assumptions, analyze alternatives, and measure results.
Visual BPR	ProcessModel, Inc., Provo, UT	The product capture and design process allows for trying the process first on the computer, tracks process performance statistics, shows where things will bottleneck and why, and hunts for best solutions.
WorkPoint	Insession Technologies, Omaha NE	The product automates and models complex business processes across the enterprise.

Source: http://www.ndsu.nodak.edu/ndsu/bklamm/BPandTC%20references/BP%20TC%20Scott%201999%20Foxmeyer%20drugs%20bankruptey%20was%20it%20a%20failure.pdf
Quote by Christopher Cole, Chief Operating Officer, Pinnacle systems.

10

Global, Ethics, and Security Management

LEARNING OBJECTIVES

After reading this chapter, you should be able to:

- Learn generally about outsourcing and more specifically offshore outsourcing (offshoring) and their business and cultural implications, as well as the Software as a Service (SaaS) model.

- Know the ethical and legal issues related to ERP systems and implementations and how to protect the company assets.

- Understand the various components to system security and why security must be

planned, tested, and ready by the time the ERP implementation is at Go-live.

- Understand green computing phenomenon and ERP's role in green IT.

- Examine the impact of compliance and of laws such as the Sarbanes–Oxley Act on ERP implementations.

CASE 10-1
Opening Case
Outsourcing at FERC

Source: Based on McKenna, E. (March 5, 2001). Enterprise Computing Rings in a New Era, *Washington Technology.*

The Federal Energy Regulatory Commission (FERC), an independent regulatory agency within the Energy Department, was one of the first federal agencies to use an integrated enterprise resource planning application from start to finish, including human resources, base benefits, time and labor, and payroll. In October 2000, FERC implemented PeopleSoft Financial Management for Education and Government software, including the general ledger, payables, and purchasing modules. The two systems cost about $5 million for implementation and maintenance. According to Janet Dubbert, FERC's director of management administrative and payroll support, the agency's decision to acquire the systems was prompted by a couple of issues. First, the Department of Energy would no longer support FERC's human resource, time and attendance, and payroll functions. The department made the move as part of its efforts to streamline operations under the National Performance Review. Second, the ERP systems allow the agency to add functionality at its own pace. Because the systems are integrated, they provide real-time management information to help with workforce planning efforts.

In 2001, FERC decided to outsource the ERP system to the private sector. Dubbert said, "FERC will pay less than $2 million for the hosting and day-to-day management of its human resources and financial operations, including transition and production costs, under a five-year contract." The key reasons to outsource were to relieve FERC from maintaining, upgrading, and distributing software and services to its customers, who pay a periodic fee. FERC moved to this arrangement after it began re-engineering its operations using PeopleSoft Human Resources Management for the U.S. federal government. After contracting with PeopleSoft, Inc., the organization went live with the human resources application in less than six months. With outsourcing, FERC hopes to focus on its core functions of adding new human resources and financial features, such as training and budget and accounts receivable.

- Do you agree with FERC's decision?
- What other benefits can FERC achieve with this outsourcing agreement?

PREVIEW

The rationale for outsourcing is compelling. As seen in the FERC case, outsourcing an ERP environment is not new. The key benefits of outsourcing for FERC were a predictable monthly payment and the avoidance of the headache of running the application. From the FERC perspective this was therefore a good decision. In general, outsourcing helps organizations to lower the high software ownership and maintenance costs; simplify, or eliminate, or both, the traditional difficulties in implementation; and avoid the problems of hiring and retaining IT staff to run the applications. Today, more and more organizations find outsourcing to be a better strategy for lowering the maintenance costs of ERP systems. For example, three months after the implementation of a SAP R3 system, it was outsourced at Sebastian International, Inc., Woodland Hills, California. "Confronted by unacceptable system performance and the loss of key IT personnel, we made the decision to outsource," said Dianne King, director of IT. "We probably would have saved quite a bit if we had outsourced right at the beginning."[1] Companies thinking of outsourcing, however, need to have a strategy that is appropriate for their organizations. Management needs to evaluate whether it makes sense from both a cost and quality perspective and to make decisions on what should be outsourced and how. Outsourcing should not be used to abdicate responsibility. It requires proper oversight and a well-defined relationship with the outsourced partner.

In addition to outsourcing, this chapter will focus on the issues of ethics, legal environments, and security with ERP systems. ERP and other enterprise systems generally have a broad-based impact on organization structure, process, and people. They can also change the ethical and legal environment of the organization. Security is another major concern, both during and after the ERP implementation. ERP systems, with their power of integration and their ability to link with external systems, can create major havoc or disaster when a hacker or virus infiltrates the system's security perimeter.

OUTSOURCING

What Is Outsourcing?

Outsourcing occurs anytime a company decides to subcontract its business processes or functions to another company; therefore, instead of hiring employees to perform a task, the company (*outsourcer*) enters into an outsourcing arrangement with another firm (*outsourcee*) to provide these services under contract for a certain price and period. As mentioned earlier, outsourcing in the ERP area has been successfully used by organizations worldwide for some time. Peter Drucker,[2] the famous management guru, gave his blessing to outsourcing in 1995 when he predicted that "in 10 to 15 years organizations may be outsourcing all work that is 'support' rather than revenue producing, and all activities that do not offer career opportunities into senior management." Although he may be referring to outsourcing in general, Drucker's prediction has reached early fruition in the IT industry and ERP system.

Even as early as 2000, two respected IT research firms, Forrester Research, Inc., Cambridge, Massachusetts, and Syntacom IT-Services, Inc., Waltham, Massachusetts, had predicted ERP outsourcing to become a $6.4 billion market by 2001 with 50 percent of all ERP implementations outsourced by 2006, respectively.[3] High IT spending has been on the radar of top management in recent years, and the chief information officers (CIOs) are being asked to do more with less. Several key trends exist in ERP deployments that are helping implementation teams exploit technology in new ways to improve quality and reduce costs. Offshoring capabilities have strengthened over the years through the emergence of new global players, and they have allowed many organizations to take advantage of highly skilled labor at more cost-effective prices. Outsourcing (i.e., the delivery of IT and application software via service-oriented architecture (SOA) and Web services) is a new model that provides better value for customers than the traditional model of purchasing software licenses, installing the

---

[1] Teresko, J. (September 6, 1999). ERP Outsourcing: Can I Meet Market Demands? *Industry Week Magazine.*
[2] Drucker, P. (1995). Why Buy When You Can Rent? *Harvard Business Review.*
[3] Travis, L., and Stiffler, D. (2005). Offshoring Decisions for 2005 Time to Consider a New Model. www.amrresearch.com/Content/View/asp?pmillid=17890 (accessed January 14, 2005).

software, and managing application upgrades with internal resources.[4] In both cases, ERP teams face the challenge of integrating external partners with their global IT and business community.

Most IT outsourcing initially occurred in such back-office functions as technical support, software development, and maintenance areas. This was mainly triggered, in the mid- to late 1990s, by the Y2K (year 2000) software problems. The urgency in fixing these problems created a tremendous shortage for IT personnel and triggered an outsourcing boom in which U.S. and European companies hired a large number of software programmers and developers from all over the globe from such countries as India, Russia, and Ireland. The Y2K problem gave a major boost for IT outsourcing because it provided tremendous cost savings for these companies. This eventually progressed into other IT functions within the organization, where management of many companies figured that outsourcing was both cost-effective and provided tremendous flexibility. Many companies slowly started moving to front-office functions (e.g., customer support and help desk, call center functions, customer relationship management, and sales force automation). The front-office function generally includes IT solutions and support that have direct interaction with the customer. This area can be risky because many companies feel customers are too important to turn over to someone outside, particularly if the outsourcing company is from a different country (offshore) with a different cultural background. Therefore, it is very important for all parties to define their outsourcing relationship similar to one shown in Figure 10-1.

Organizations planning on ERP software are probably too wrapped up in implementation to worry about how they will maintain and update the system in the future. Most experts, however, say that in order to maximize your benefits, the sooner you start thinking of this the better. The benefits for ERP outsourcing depend on the organization. There are many other benefits beyond

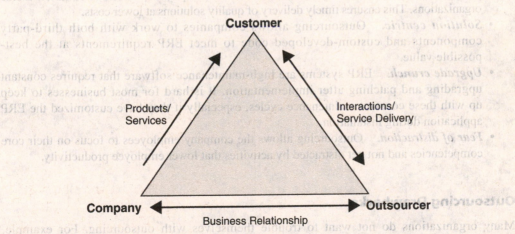

FIGURE 10-1 Outsourcing Relationship.

4 Howarth, F. (September 16, 2005). Software as a Service-Salesforce.com's New Application Shop. *Practice Leader.* Bloor Research, Publisher: IT Analysis Communications Ltd. www.it-director.com/services/content.php?cid=8075 (accessed June 2007).

cost savings when management considers outsourcing as a business strategy. Some of the key benefits of outsourcing are as follows:

- *Economics.* Outsourcing provides a predictable monthly payment. A company can solve all of the problems of running an application at a lower cost. Outsourcing enterprise applications can save a company anywhere from 30 to 50 percent, depending on the task, method, location, and how the relationships are structured.[5]
- *Market agility.* Outsourcing the ERP function offers a faster time to solution and removes a major distraction from a company's core competence.
- *Breadth of skills.* Many organizations do not have in-house personnel with ERP implementation and maintenance skills. Outsourcing provides an avenue to access these advanced expertise areas quickly.
- *Technical expertise.* Outsourcing arrangements cost-effectively enable a company to provide access to cutting-edge IT solutions to its employees and clients. Such service providers as Accenture and IBM typically have alliances with such key ERP vendors as SAP and Oracle, which puts them in the loop of the newest and latest changes in the applications.
- *Multiple feedback points.* Outsourcing provides an organization with an outside or external perspective during implementation and maintenance.
- *Best practices.* Outsourcing can provide companies with access to best practices in ERP planning, implementation, and maintenance.
- *Scalability.* One secondary benefit to outsourcing is flexibility for the company to grow or shrink quickly, depending on the market demand for its products and services. Outsourcing agreements allow companies to scale their service agreements with minimal disruption as opposed to doing them in-house.
- *Process-oriented.* Outsourcing, by default, forces process perspective (i.e., cross-functional teams, customer focus) rather than a functional perspective, which is common inside organizations. This ensures timely delivery of quality solutions at lower costs.
- *Solution centric.* Outsourcing allows companies to work with both third-party components and custom-developed code to meet ERP requirements at the best-possible value.
- *Upgrade crunch.* ERP systems are high-maintenance software that requires constant upgrading and patching after implementation. It is hard for most businesses to keep up with these constant maintenance cycles, especially if they have customized the ERP application during installation.
- *Fear of distraction.* Outsourcing allows the company employees to focus on their core competencies and not get distracted by activities that lower employee productivity.

Outsourcing Drawbacks

Many organizations do not want to trouble themselves with outsourcing. For example, Allegiance Healthcare Corp. of McGaw Park, Illinois, a 20,000-employee, $4.5 billion medical products company, decided to go in-house on its ERP implementation and maintenance. CIO Kathy White did give the outsourcing option serious consideration, but found it wanting for both reliability and cost-effectiveness. What is there not to like about outsourcing? ERP outsourcing is still a relatively new concept compared with IT outsourcing, which is simpler and involves

---

[5] Travis. Offshoring Decisions for 2005.

external companies operating your data centers (or IT support) either on-site or remotely. Some of the key drawbacks are as follows:

- *Lack of expertise.*   ERP outsourcing model targets an application that may need integration with other applications and systems in the organization. An external company may not know or have the expertise to understand the in-house-developed application or how to accommodate ERP extensions like barcode data collection, warehouse management, and e-commerce. For example, a company planning an internal e-commerce implementation while seeking to outsource ERP might discover little or no cost benefit in terms of IT staffing.
- *Misaligned expectations.*   Companies outsourcing often cannot anticipate changes in their business circumstances or in technology, resulting in surprise charges, delayed delivery, or delivery of wrong products and services. Misunderstandings can often occur between the outsourcer and the organizations.
- *Culture clash.*   The business processes and mannerisms followed by the outsourcing organization could be very different from the organization's culture. The work habits, communication processes, and reporting habits can be very different, causing enormous tensions in the outsourcing relationships.
- *Hidden costs.*   Surprise or unanticipated charges like travel costs, monitoring costs, lower productivity, and long-term loss of relationships with clients are hard to determine. The cost savings can often turn out to be a myth.
- *Loss of vision.*   Outsourcing arrangements often result in a loss of institutional knowledge (e.g., feedback from clients, problem-solving capability, and new idea generation).
- *Security and control.*   Outsourcing requires companies to share their trade secrets, which can be risky in a competitive environment. Companies have little control over employees of outsourcees, especially in global or high-turnover markets. Protection and control of intellectual property can be a critical issue when companies outsource. Companies therefore need to sign comprehensive service-level agreements to protect themselves and their partners.

Offshore Outsourcing

In recent years, outsourcing has become a global industry. When a company selects an outsourcing partner (outsourcee) from another country, it is called *offshoring,* as shown in Figure 10-2. Offshore partners are often selected from developing countries to lower the labor costs. The latest trends in IT implementations call for offshoring critical developmental tasks to improve quality, reduce costs, and speed delivery. According to AMR research, "The effective use of offshore resources means being able to do more with less. Users of offshore services for ERP implementation and support can expect savings between 15 and 20 percent the first year of the relationship, growing to 40–50 percent in ensuing years."[6]

Countries like India have a big IT industry that provides services in design, development, implementation, support, and help desk, while other developing nations are slowly emerging (e.g., Brazil, Argentina, China, Eastern Europe, Russia, and the Philippines). Three Indian IT companies (i.e., Infosys, Tata Consulting Services (TCS), and Wipro) each reported respective revenue growth of 51 percent, 44 percent, and 47 percent in Q404 more than Q304 in a $12.5 billion market in 2004 and over $16 billion in 2005. Because the worldwide spending on IT and offshoring services is estimated to be $600 billion, India accounts for only 2 percent of the total amount.[7] These global contenders are proving to be as innovative and expertly run as

---

[6] www.amrresearch.com/Content/View.asp?pmillid=17633 (accessed February 2001).
[7] www.amrresearch.com/Content/View.asp?pmillid=17723 (accessed February 2001).

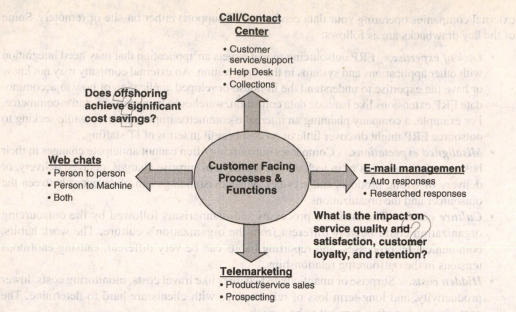

FIGURE 10-2   Offshore Outsourcing.

any in the business, intelligently absorbing consumer trends and technologies. "Their key advantages are access to some of the world's most dynamic growth markets and immense pools of low-cost resources, be they production workers, engineers, land, petroleum, or iron ore."[8]

With global ERP implementation teams, however, it is usually not cost-effective to colocate all team members. A successful ERP implementation team will recognize the potential risks associated with global offshoring due to differences in language and culture. The team will also recognize the importance of adhering to the highest of ethical standards (i.e., delivering a final product that secures and protects the organization, promotes financial growth, and provides significant return on investment to executives, board members, and public shareholders).

For a significant systems implementation like ERP, organizational change management plays a very important role. Offshore implementers can face barriers of language, culture, and values, making the ERP implementation more challenging. One example of language barrier is accent difference: Getting key messages to team members and frontline end users can be a delicate and complex issue. Savvy project managers will acknowledge the communication challenges and take the time to translate and distribute key messages through multiple channels to reach its intended audience effectively. Furthermore, not all people around the world are motivated by the same things that motivate Western society. Many Western countries value history, tradition, and work–life balance, whereas many countries in Eastern Europe and Asia value hard work, entrepreneurship, and teamwork.[9]

Offshoring requires consideration of the organization's local requirements, understanding of best practices, and an overall willingness to change. Each country is going to have its own set

---

[8] www.businessweek.com/magazine/content/06_31/b3995001.htm (accessed February 2001).
[9] http://blogs.ittoolbox.com/erp/roi/archives/its-not-a-small-world-after-all-managing-change-on-international-erp-projects-8437 (accessed February 2001).

of local requirements—whether they are currency related, regulatory, resource, or employee constraints (e.g., the high number of bank holidays and shorter workweeks in some European nations). Global ERP systems are equipped with handling foreign currency exchanges and value-added tax (VAT),[10] two critical areas that enable financial consolidation in complex organizations with multiple company codes. Employees in different countries also have different views on "best practices," and their belief in its effectiveness can impact the amount of justification required to support the change in business process.

Finally, different countries have varying desires to change. More-developed countries have business operations that have worked for decades, whereas many developing nations have less-mature operational models. Local culture and available resources will dictate how willing the organizational unit will be able to embrace the change required by the new ERP system. Completely localizing an ERP system increases complexity and customization, while defeating the purpose of a global solution. Corporate and local office management needs to be clear in the message for global change.

GLOBAL ERP VENDOR SELECTION   In order to create a successful outsourcing or offshoring project, companies need to perform due diligence in vendor selection. When evaluating an outsourcing partner, ERP selection teams should consider financial status, technical certifications, licenses, qualifications, and related work experience (e.g., familiarity with the industry). The employees of the offshore provider are also critical: What are the working conditions like, and what kind of retention policies are in place? This is a very critical issue for security where personnel could suddenly leave the offshore service provider and go to work for your top competitor without your knowing or approval. "In the U.S. [there are] strict controls on intellectual property rights and noncompete clauses, but if you're hiring overseas much of that goes out the window. Your competitor can outsource with a firm that works down the street from your outsourcer and advise them to hire the 10-person team that works on your projects."[11] Companies also need to be prepared if the offshore experiment is a disaster: What do you do about it? Can you bring the project in-house? For this reason, a careful risk assessment needs to take place before any offshore services contract is signed.

One of the biggest challenges facing companies that offshore their ERP initiatives is culture. Making sure that your company culture meshes with that of your offshore partner ensures a successful implementation. Cultural differences include such tangible discrepancies as time zone and language or such intangible differences as nationalism or corporate pride. Dion DeLoof, CEO of Anteo Group, a project-based IT staffing and consulting firm in Atlanta, said "many of his clients have sent IT projects to India only to find out that hard-to-quantify attributes like innovation and creativity are lacking and that people there do not have the freedom to speak up or the entrepreneurial culture that rewards them if they tell their boss what they're really thinking."[12] Companies that decide to offshore their ERP projects should be prudent about the total cost of outsourcing. Securing cheaper rates for SAP or Oracle developers in India might look good on paper, but when savvy managers factor in time required for contract setup and management, time differences, travel and communication costs, and reduced productivity due to language and cultural differences, the total cost of outsourcing may not be as attractive as it was initially.

---

[10] http://en.wikipedia.org/wiki/Value_added_tax (accessed February 2001).
[11] www.projectsatwork.com/article.cfm?ID=223467 (accessed February 2001).
[12] Ibid.

Software as a Service (SaaS)

Software as a Service (SaaS) is a model of software that can be rented or leased from a software vendor that provides maintenance, daily technical operation, and support for the software. SaaS is a model of software delivery rather than a market segment; it assumes the software is delivered over a secure Internet connection. Software can be accessed from a browser by any market segment, including home consumers and small, medium, and large businesses. The SaaS model brings lower risk in the implementation cycle and better knowledge transfer from integrators to users of systems. "When the implementation partner leaves, the implementing hosting vendor is still there managing the solution. So the knowledge transfer happens seamlessly, automatically, for no additional cost, no impact on schedule, and, of course, lowering risk. With conventional implementations the opportunity exists for disconnects that could hamper the knowledge-transfer process to the customer's support staff."[13]

BENEFITS OF THE SAAS MODEL   The traditional rationale for outsourcing of IT systems is that by applying economies of scale to the operation of applications, a service provider can offer better, cheaper, more reliable applications than companies can themselves. The use of SaaS-based applications has grown dramatically, as reported by many of the analyst firms that cover the sector. But, it's only in recent years that SaaS has truly flourished. The advent of PCs and high-speed Internet has provided an opportunity to the way we work and made this rapid acceptance possible. Some benefits of the SaaS model are as follows:

- *Universal access.*   Most information workers have access to a computer and are familiar with conventions from mouse usage to Web interfaces. As a result, the learning curve for new Web applications is lower, requiring less hand-holding by internal IT staff.

- *Ubiquitous computing.*   In the past, corporate mainframes were jealously guarded as strategic advantages. The applications were later viewed as strategic. Today, people know it's the business processes and the data themselves (i.e., customer records, workflows, and pricing information) that matter. Computing and application licenses are cost centers. As such, they're suitable for cost reduction and outsourcing. The adoption of SaaS could also drive applications to become a commodity.[14]

- *Standardized applications.*   With some notable, industry-specific exceptions, most people spend most of their time using standardized applications. An expense reporting page, an applicant screening tool, a spreadsheet, or an e-mail system are all sufficiently ubiquitous and well understood that most users can switch from one system to another easily. This is evident from the number of Web-based calendar, spreadsheet, and e-mail systems that have emerged in recent years.

- *Parameterized applications.*   In older applications, the only way to change a workflow was to modify the code. In more recent applications, however, and particularly Web-based applications, significantly new applications can be created from parameters and macros. These allow organizations to create many different kinds of business logic atop a common application platform. Many SaaS providers allow a wide range of customization within a basic set of functions.

---

[13] Traudt, E., and Konary, A. (June 2005). *2005 Software as a Service Taxonomy and Research Guide* 7. IDC.
[14] www.saasblogs.com/2006/09/26/scale-as-a-commodity-2/ SaaSBlogs: Scale as a Commodity (accessed February 2001).

- *Global market.*   A company that made software for human resource management at boutique hotels might once have had a hard time finding enough of a market to sell its applications. A hosted application, however, can instantly reach the entire market, making specialization within a vertical both possible and preferable. This in turn means that SaaS providers can often deliver products that meet their markets' needs more closely than traditional "shrink-wrap" vendors.
- *Reliability of Web.*   Despite sporadic outages and slowdowns, most people are willing to use the public Internet, the hypertext transfer protocol, and the TCP/IP stack to deliver business functions to end users.
- *Transparent security and trust.*   With the broad adoption of SSL and HTTPS protocols, organizations have a way of reaching their applications without the complexity and burden of end-user configurations or VPNs.

LIMITATIONS WITH THE SAAS MODEL   SaaS is conceptually similar to the original mainframe computing model that had a centralized control, minimal user privacy, and limited flexibility allowed to the individual user. Much of the explosive success of the PC after its introduction in the late 1970s and early 1980s was due to the power it gave to individual users. This empowerment will erode once users feel that with SaaS they lose their privacy and control. Another mitigating factor is the need for disconnected use. Many users (e.g., traveling salespeople) with expensive wireless connections need access to data in offline mode. Although some vendors provide offline modes that synchronize data, solutions are not optimal and not all vendors provide such functionality.

Although there is no large investment for software license at the onset of the project, the ongoing costs of SaaS are categorized as monthly expenses and do not depreciate over time as would a capital investment of perpetual software licenses. Such vendors can easily mislead customers into thinking that with SaaS there is no cost to configure the software or customize integrations because it's all delivered "out of the box." Smart ERP teams will see through this myth and realize that in order for any ERP solution to be successful, there needs to be significant investment in resources (and possibly third-party technology) to configure and support the solution, perform change management, and facilitate business process redesign so that ERP efficiencies can be realized. This cannot take place without thorough understanding of the requirements of the business, the SaaS configuration capabilities, and the difference between the two. It is quite possible that over a three-or five-year period, traditional ERP architecture might even be cheaper than a SaaS solution.

TYPES OF SAAS PROVIDERS   There are two types of SaaS providers. The first has often been referred to as an application service provider (ASP) where a customer purchases and brings to a hosting company a copy of software, or the hosting company offers widely available software for use by customers (e.g., hosting Microsoft Office and making that available across the Web to customers who pay a fee per month for access to the software). The second type of SaaS provider offers what is often called software on demand (SOD), where a company offers to customers' software specifically built for one-to-many hosting. This means that one copy of the software is installed for use by many companies who access the software from the Internet.

In the first type of provider, a licensing fee and a monthly fee are separate and are paid to the maker of the software and to the software host like an ISP. With the second type of hosting there is no division between licensing and hosting fees, and there is traditionally little or no customization of software for customers. With mature SaaS providers (e.g., Salesforce.com) on-demand solutions can be highly customized.

Outsourcing Best Practices

Balancing outsourcing and in-sourcing approaches can be a complex process, but the relationship can yield very successful results when done correctly. To maintain a higher success rate with outsourcing and offshoring ERP implementations, two best practices have emerged. First, a better way to manage the offshore relationship through a practice called "in-sourcing," where good ERP managers invite a representative or entire team to work on-site.[15] This allows the project manager to supervise the work personally to ensure that agreed-upon metrics are met, as well as to facilitate the collaboration that is only possible when the entire team is colocated in the same office. The second emerging best practice is for the creation of a formal governance process to manage the offshore relationship. A report by Meta Group in Stamford, Connecticut, said, "Vendor governance is becoming a critical success factor and must include global relationships and business-process outsourcing with formal methodologies followed to refine quality and improve consistency."[16]

Companies considering outsourcing must first understand what they want to accomplish, benchmark their current costs and level of quality, and then build an infrastructure to ensure the expected value is realized. A good example of this relationship is shown in the McCormick and Patni Systems vignette.

McCormick and Patni Systems Offshoring Partnership

McCormick and Patni Systems partnered together on McCormick's global SAP implementation. McCormick, a Fortune 500 company, is a global leader in the manufacture, marketing, and distribution of spices, seasonings, and flavors to the food industry worldwide. Patni, based in Mumbai, India, is one of the leading global IT and business solutions providers with more than 12,000 clients supported from 23 offices across the Americas, Europe, Asia, and eight offshore development centers in India. In order to enhance its competitiveness, McCormick wanted to improve the time to availability for its products and enhance the overall efficiency of its business channels.[17] They searched and found a global partner that provided a cost-effective solution by scaling resources up and down as they rolled out SAP to more than six worldwide manufacturing locations. Patni provided the collaborative approach they were looking for— leveraging local engagement teams to ensure a strong customer focus. Patni's cross-functional team aligned with McCormick's business model to conduct on-site activities, such as functional/technical specifications and integration testing, while delivering offshore tasks, such as effort estimation, technical analysis, and development. The in-house ("in-sourcing") team focused on the quick resolution of project issues so that the offshore team could continue to provide quality deliverables—on time and on budget. This relationship was successful because of the flexibility of Patni's technical resources and the creativity of McCormick's management team. Jeff Malat, director of process solutions and ERP implementations at McCormick, describes the engagement as follows: "Patni has demonstrated a high degree of flexibility, scalability, and service orientation to enable us to meet the strategic goals for some of our largest IT initiatives. Their sheer commitment, execution excellence, and ability to work with us to envision our overall program had made a tremendous difference."[18]

---

15 www.projectsatwork.com/article.cfm?ID=223467 (accessed February 2001).
16 Ibid.
17 www.patni.com/resource-center/collateral/manufacturing/McCormick_SAP_ERP.html# (accessed February 2001).
18 Ibid.

ERP experts say it's never too soon to plan for installing upgrades, maintaining modules, troubleshooting problems, and policing platforms once the software enters the longest phase of its life cycle—ongoing operations. When and for whom does an outsourcing ERP operation make sense? Furthermore, once that decision has been made, what are the major contract-negotiation and management issues IT executives should consider as ERP implementation begins to wind down? In 1999, *CIO Magazine* put those questions before a number of companies that were exercising their outsourcing options on ERP operations—and one that considered that path but rejected it in favor of taking care of the work itself. Small and midsize IT organizations will be most inclined to outsource ERP operations because they lack the resources to handle them internally, but larger companies can also derive advantages. The reasons for ERP outsourcing are ultimately as varied as the participants.

ERP implementation teams should not consider outsourcing and offshoring when they want someone else to take accountability or to deflect blame in the event something unfortunate transpires. Another reason for bringing on an offshore partner is for expediency. In the event resources are not available due to competing priorities or the resources lack a general set of knowledge or maturity, send the work to a qualified partner and reap the benefits of watching and learning for the first time. This approach may, in fact, reduce risk and give the staff a chance to improve their skills for the next project.

No matter whose logo is on the paychecks, the challenge of managing the folks in the ERP trenches doesn't go away. "It takes more work on our side of this than I originally thought," says Coup. "You can't just turn (any part of SAP) over to someone and then sit back while they go and do the job. We've found that we have to have very active involvement from good technical people working with the vendor."

ETHICS

Ethics is a general term for what is often described as the *science of morality*. In philosophy, ethical behavior is that which is good or right in a certain value system. Ethics is different from law. Whereas laws are enacted by the government or developed through a process of jurisprudence and enforced by the legal system, ethics are developed through culture, value, and belief system of an individual with influence from family or society. Ethical violations cannot be curbed unless they are made part of the law. For example, some of the disclosure rules enforced by the Sarbanes–Oxley (SOX) Act were enacted into law for enforcement across all U.S. corporations; however, they were considered unethical and implemented in many companies even before SOX.

ERP implementations can have a wide variety of impacts on the ethical principles of the organization. Consider the following scenario:

> The ERP system integrates information from various departments of the organization. What if the one department finds out the expenses of another department and reports to everyone in the company? Should this sort of information sharing be allowed? Should the company have developed a policy on accessing information from the system?

Abuses like the preceding one are eventually observed, converted into authorization policy, and enforced by the security system of the company. Two forces endanger privacy in the information age: one is the growth of information technology and other is increased value of information in decision making. Misinformation has a way of "fouling up" people's lives, particularly when the party with the inaccurate information has an advantage in power and authority. There are substantial economic and ethical concerns surrounding property rights, which revolve around the special attributes of information itself and the means by which it is transmitted. There are also very few institutions that can protect intellectual property rights globally. Thus, ethics play a crucial role in governing the use of information. ERP system facilitates easier access to vast amounts of corporate data from a single source, thereby making them vulnerable. Very little corporate governance exists on how to use or share this information. As such, the principles of ethics should influence the development and operations of ERP systems.

Ethical Principles

As shown in Figure 10-3, information technology can impact ethics in four ways, which can be summarized by means of an acronym, PAPA, which stands for privacy, accuracy, property, and accessibility.[19] Privacy is concerned with how personal information is safeguarded in the system. Accuracy requires systems to validate the correctness of the data in the system and who is responsible for this accuracy. Property governs who has ownership rights to the information. Accessibility is concerned with who has access to what information. The PAPA principles of ethics have been tested in a variety of systems in the last 20-plus years and are an important influence on the development of information systems.[20]

What does PAPA have to do with ERP? "If an ERP team leader says 'I've never faced an ethical issue,' they're not living in the real world," said Larry Ponemon, chairman and founder of the Ponemon Institute, a security and privacy research think-tank based in Tucson, Arizona.[21] ERPs have the capability to access and provide detailed information on various aspects of business and customers from the databases. PAPA can provide some guidelines for implementation and operation of ERP in organizations. The TJX example that follows highlights how a small security breach can create havoc with the privacy of millions of users in today's digital economy. Unless ERP users are knowledgeable with privacy regulations and take active measures to protect their privacy, frauds like identity theft will keep rising.

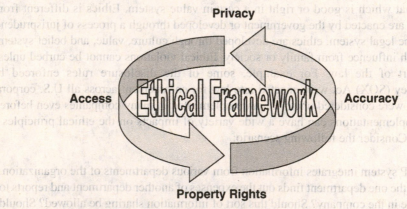

FIGURE 10-3 Ethical Framework.

[19] Mason, R. (1986). Four Ethical Issues of the Information Age. *MIS Quarterly,* 10 (1), 5–12.
[20] Peslak, A. R. (Spring 2006). PAPA Revisited: A Current Empirical Study Of The Mason Framework. *The Journal of Computer Information Systems,* 46 (3), 117.
[21] Levinson, M. (March 1, 2005). Ask the Ethicist, *CIO Magazine.* www.cio.com/archive/030105/ethics.html (accessed January 15, 2007).

TJX Cos., parent of T.J. Maxx, Marshalls, and HomeGoods retail stores had a major security breach in 2006 when hackers entered their network and stole the data on millions of consumers from the United States, Ireland, the United Kingdom, and Canada. The hackers were able to access a wide range of financial information, including credit cards, debit cards linked to checking accounts, and transactions for returned merchandise, and make fraudulent purchases with the stolen customer data. For example, one TJX customer reported that $6,700 in unauthorized transactions—including purchases from Wal-Mart Stores Inc., Flowers.com, and iTunes.com—were made with his card account number.[22] This breach could impact more than 40 million credit card users. Although U.S. retailers are required to follow stringent card industry rules (e.g., the establishment of firewalls to protect databases and prohibited from storing unprotected cardholder information), many merchants don't comply with them. Of its 330 largest merchants, 31 percent comply with the requirements, according to Visa.

PRIVACY   Privacy means providing individuals with the right to be left alone. In most societies, adult human beings have the right to control what information about themselves needs to be safeguarded and what can be made available to the public. This right, however, must be balanced with the public's right to know or societal needs (e.g., Patriot Act of 2001). Any organization that collects personal information must follow a process on how this information is collected, used, and shared. This process is influenced by laws of the land and ethics. Information systems in general provide easy mechanisms to collect, use, and share these data without any knowledge of the information owner. Temptations exist in a competitive market for organizations to use such information systems as ERP to violate individual privacy rights for marketing or accidentally releasing this information to third parties that do not have the right to it. Other problems are hacking, snooping, and virus attacks on the system, which also violate the privacy rights of individuals.

Until recently there have been very few privacy legislations around the world. Examples of privacy laws passed in the United States are the Privacy Act of 1974, which mostly applied to governmental agencies, the Children's Online Privacy Protection Act of 1998, and the e-Privacy Act of 2002. The latter two laws take into account for system-related or online violations. The European Union, ASEAN, and other countries have similarly passed regulations to protect individual privacy. The key tenets of these regulations are getting prior consent of the individuals before collecting the data, getting approval for sharing, informing individuals when their information is requested or shared with a third party, and setting regulations on collecting information on individuals from Internet browsing, junk-mail, fraud prevention, and others.

The biggest threat to privacy from ERP systems is from data mining activities. ERP systems simplify the process of collecting, sorting, filing, and sharing information on customers with external organizations. It was very complex, cumbersome, and expensive before to collect and look for consumer patterns on buying or predicting purchasing behaviors. With easy access to large amounts of data, new data mining software can reveal hidden consumer spending habits for business or identify patients with high risk for health care and insurance companies or reveal terrorists for security agencies or reveal fraudulent transactions for financial and credit card companies. Although these are beneficial to companies and society, they can be dangerous if they end up in the wrong hands. Identity theft (i.e., crooks using another individual's profile for fraudulent transactions) is now the number one crime in many parts of the world. ERP systems

---

[22] Pereira, P. (January 25, 2007). Wide Credit-Card Fraud Surfaces in TJX Hacking. *Wall Street Journal,* D3.

must therefore be proactive in embedding the best practices on privacy principles to increase the confidence of management and users in organizations.

ACCURACY The accuracy principle of ethics requires organizations that collect and store data on consumers to have a responsibility in ensuring the accuracy of this data. Its major concern is to protect an individual or consumer from negligent errors and to prevent intentional manipulation of data by organizations for their advantage. With the amount of data that is being collected today and integration of data from multiple sources there is a great possibility of these data being corrupted. There needs to be policy and mechanisms to prevent and correct these errors. ERP systems must embed these best practices on data accuracy and make them available to organizations. Through an ERP system companies can enforce traceability and manage data quality across the supply chain. Data tracing enables you to comply with such regulations as the EU General Food Law Regulation, the U.S. Public Health Security and Bioterrorism Preparedness and Response Act of 2002, and other import–export regulations. In addition, ERP systems can help in synchronizing data with the trading partners.

For example, most consumers who use credit cards have their profiles maintained by companies like Visa and MasterCard, but they are also reported to credit reporting agencies (CRA) that collect and disseminate information about consumers to be used for credit evaluation and certain other purposes. They hold the databases that are the origins of a consumer's credit report. Examples of CRA in the United States are companies like Experian (which purchased the files and other assets of TRW), Equifax, and TransUnion. These organizations are for-profit entities and possess no governmental affiliation. During this reporting what if errors occur by these credit card companies or during the storage process by credit reporting agencies? This can create problems for the individuals because it affects their credit rating, and they may not be able to get loans or approval for new credit cards. The accuracy principle was developed to prevent this problem. Such laws passed by the federal government as the Fair Credit Reporting Act (FCRA)[23] have focused on this issue of accuracy by regulating the collection, dissemination, and use of consumer credit information. Along with the Fair Debt Collection Practices Act (FDCPA),[24] it forms the base of consumer data rights with credit reporting agencies in the United States. These laws require information providers to report under the following guidelines:

- They must provide complete and accurate information to the credit rating agencies.
- The duty to investigate disputed information from consumers falls on them.
- They must inform consumers about negative information that has been or is about to be placed on a consumer's credit report within 30 days.

When organizations are caught violating these guidelines, a consumer may collect $1,000 for each willful or negligent act that results in the violation of the FCRA. Any person may file suit in local court to enforce the FCRA, which entitles individuals to repair their credit report. You have a legal right to dispute any information you find on your credit report. The FCRA, which was enacted in 1971, stipulates that the credit bureaus investigate all consumer disputes if they challenge credit information on their credit reports. As per this act, the credit bureaus must complete the investigations within a 30-day period. Any information that cannot be verified or is found to be inaccurate must be deleted immediately.

---

[23] www.ftc.gov/opa/2004/06/factaidt.htm (accessed February 10, 2007).
[24] FTC Statutes. www.ftc.gov/os/statutes/fdcpa/fdcpact.htm (accessed February 10, 2007).

PROPERTY   The property principle of ethics makes organizations realize that they are not the ultimate owners of the information collected on individuals. Consumers give organizations their information on a condition that they will be guardians of this property and will use it according to the permission granted to them. Organizations do not have a right to share information collected without getting explicit permission from the user. Sharing information in the digital economy is very easy with the advent of data warehouses, networks, and Internet. In addition to information sharing, property rights extend to issues of piracy that can involve copyrights, trademarks, and other intellectual rights issues.

Although a comprehensive look at property rights is beyond the scope of this book, ERP systems can be a *double-edged sword* when it comes to information property rights. On the bad side, ERP systems facilitate the process of sharing information easily by integrating information within the organization and across organizations. If implemented without proper controls, ERP can make it hard to safeguard information. On the good side, ERP systems can enforce corporate policy on data sharing consistently and embed best practices that can highlight the property rights issue in an organization.

With the vast ability to store data in corporate databases, and with the growth of online transactions, organizations are tested on data property rights by various stakeholders. For example, in 2006, the U.S. Department of Justice wanted to compel Internet search giant Google to share records that detail millions of Internet searches.[25] Google denied requests for the data under the Child Online Protection Act (COPA), which protects children from online pornography. Given revelations about illegal wiretaps and state spying on American citizens, Google refused to share this data because the government was planning to use the data to conduct an experiment to show that Internet porn filters were ineffective. Access to data held by Google and the other main search engines was not going to target named individuals, but a data mining operation to detect pornographic activity against children. With the passage of the Patriot Act the U.S. government has gained access to vast databases of telephone records and e-mails provided to it by airlines and telecommunications companies, and the government was not doing the same with Internet search engine companies. The user data collected by Google is among its greatest assets due to the revenue it raises from targeted advertising and other services.

ACCESSIBILITY   The accessibility principle of ethics forces organization to have proper controls for authorization and authentication. ERP implementation teams must ensure that information stored in the databases about employees, customers, and other partners is accessible only to those who have the right to see and use this information. Adequate security and controls must be in place within the ERP system to prevent unauthorized access. More details on authorization controls will be covered later in the security section, but an organization needs to develop a wide policy on accessibility before implementing ERP.

In the information society, organizations need to balance the needs of the workers who need access to vast amounts of data to make good decisions with the needs of society, which is increasingly hostile when data privacy rules are violated. In addition, hacking, snooping, and other fraudulent access to data are a big concern to organizations. There has been a recent surge in identity theft crimes to $55.7 billion in the United States,[26] where hackers steal individual profile data to open bank accounts and credit cards, apply for loans and driving licenses, and conduct

---

[25] Hafner, K., and Richtel, M. (January 20, 2006). *San Jose Mercury News.*
[26] Identity Theft Resource Center. www.idtheftcenter.org/ (accessed February 10, 2007).

fraudulent activity using a victim's name. All of these have made it difficult for organizations to balance the needs of various stakeholders. The good news is that identity theft in the United States is declining. According to the third annual survey by Javelin Strategy & Research, a research firm in Pleasanton, California, the estimated number of victims dropped for the fourth consecutive year in 2006, by about 500,000, to 8.4 million persons. Researchers attributed the decline to better consumer education and awareness as well as to the increased use of online banking and financial sites that allow individuals to monitor their accounts more frequently.[27]

Code of Ethics for ERP

With advances in new technology becoming a routine, organizations constantly face ethical challenges in dealing with information. ERP systems have become key tools for improving operational efficiency and building strategic alliances and partnerships. In the urge to gain competitive advantage, these systems also become tools for violating the code of ethics. Due to the newness of this technology, this area lacks the norms of ethical behavior one would find in established disciplines. Nonetheless, managers implementing ERP systems in organizations must assess the implementation in light of such ethical principles as PAPA, discussed earlier. There is a distinct possibility of an ERP development team in which most members or team leaders with training in computer sciences and engineering fields may not possess the background in ethics and social norms to incorporate the code of ethics in ERP system.

There are three normative theories of ethical behavior[28] that can be used by organizations to influence the ERP implementation. They are as follows:

- *Stockholder theory.*   Protects the interest of the investors or owners of the company at all costs. This is the ultimate implementation of the free market concept, where the responsibility of management is to maximize profits with legal and nonfraudulent methods.
- *Stakeholder theory.*   Protects the interests of everyone having a stake in the company success, namely, owners and stockholders, employees, customers, vendors, and other partners. Management using this theory has to balance the interest of these various groups while making organizational decisions.
- *Social contract theory.*   Includes the right of society and social well-being before the interest of the stakeholders or company owners. Management using this theory must think of the well-being of society first (e.g., protecting the environment or helping the socially challenged individuals before thinking about profits of the organization).

In context of ERP implementation, the stockholder theory would implement very few restrictions on using the information from this system to monitor employee performance or to collect and share consumer information from the system. On the other hand, the stakeholder theory would put restrictions on using the preceding information because the organization is committed to protecting employee and consumer rights. Both these theories, however, would implement the ERP only if the savings are greater than the costs, and they must improve the organization's efficiency and effectiveness. In context of the social contract theory, the ERP system would not be allowed to share or collect consumer information unless the consumers were notified of this plan and only if this activity would result in a net benefit to the society. These theories, even though not perfect, provide management with guidelines on developing the code of ethics for their ERP implementation based on their organization's culture and moral principles.

---

[27] Mincer, J. (February 7, 2007). Identity-Theft Incidents Declined 12% Last Year. *Wall Street Journal.*
[28] Hasnas, J. (1998). The Normative Theories of Business Ethics for the Perplexed. *Business Ethics Quarterly*, 8 (1),19–42.

Thus, it is practical for all organizations to develop a code of ethics for ERP systems implementation. In order to formalize the implementation of ethics consistently, the code of ethics policy of the organization must be explicitly communicated to all the stakeholders, including external partners and community. Without this, it will be very difficult to enforce the desired ethical behavior and deal with violators. This code should generally address the four principles of privacy, accuracy, property, and access in context of the organization's position on the normative theory, discussed earlier. It should provide guidelines on such issues as dealing with offensive content, copyright information, employee education on who has right of access to certain information before sharing, and how to protect consumer data (e.g., not downloading consumer data files in nonprotected areas of their computers or destroying such data after usage).

The following is an example of code of ethics for ERP implementation policy:

- Protect the interest of its customers.
- Privacy decisions are made free of owner's influence.
- We insist on fair, unbiased access of all information.
- No advertising that simulates editorial content will be published.
- Monitoring fellow employees is grounds for dismissal.
- Company makes prompt, complete corrections of errors.
- Implementation team members do not own or trade stocks of ERP vendors.
- No secondary employment in the ERP industry is permitted.
- Our commitment to fairness is our defense against consumer rights.
- All comments inserted by the employees will be clearly labeled as such.
- CIO will monitor legal and liabilities issues with the ERP system.
- Company attorneys regularly review our ERP system policy to make sure that there is nothing unethical or illegal in the implementation process.

GLOBALIZATION AND ETHICS   The legal and technical costs of complying with an expanding patchwork of state, federal, and foreign privacy laws are mounting for global companies. Jay Cline,[29] an expert on privacy, has outlined seven global privacy principles that can improve the global privacy climate. These principles include (1) giving notice to consumers before collecting data, (2) collecting only relevant consumer data and retaining these data only until needed, (3) providing access for consumers to correct data for accuracy, (4) protecting data with firewalls to prevent unauthorized access, (5) giving consumers choice of sharing their data with third parties, (6) giving consumers a choice on whether marketers could contact them, and, finally, (7) ensuring every organization has an officer enforcing the compliance of privacy principles.

Globalization and offshoring have raised the level of ethical concerns. For instance, the International Association of Outsourcing Professionals (IAOP) has released a code of ethics and a set of business practice standards that are designed to help companies improve their processes for awarding and managing outsourcing contracts. The standards apply to IT deals as well as other forms of outsourcing, and they provide guidelines to the parties in an outsourcing agreement based on a common business framework. The standards are general, but they weigh heavily in favor of disclosure, candor, and the use of objective metrics that are agreed on by both sides. The benefits are that everyone is up front with the governance, so there is therefore less confusion and fewer misunderstandings in dealing with third parties.

---

[29]Cline, J. (January 29, 2007). *Computer World Magazine*. http://www.computerworld.com/s/article/280320/ It_s_Time_to_Forge_Global_Privacy_Rules (accessed February 2001).

GREEN COMPUTING

Green computing or green IT is extremely popular with organizations. With business always growing and more and more cars and people on this planet, we are beginning to come to the harsh realization that our natural resources are not infinite. Countries around the world are trying to take the initiative and reduce the amount of wasted resources and pollution of our planet. This is especially true for businesses that are faced with increasing energy costs and an expanding need for power consumption. Governments and companies are working hard to portray themselves as being "green."

Green is not only good for the environment but also for business. Today, a green company is viewed as a responsible and caring company. Poland Spring, for example, has reduced the amount of plastic it uses in its water bottles. Automakers are making their vehicles much more fuel efficient. People, especially in America, are seeing how their waste and overuse of utilities like electricity or using plastic bags every time they go grocery shopping is affecting our environment. A company going green can also cut costs by eliminating waste and being more efficient. Anheuser-Busch has saved lots of money by trimming an eighth of an inch off of the diameter of their beer cans and saving 21 million pounds of metal every year.

These are some common examples of companies being green. Companies can go green simply by successfully implementing an enterprise resource program. ERPs are systems that facilitate all of the real-time data flow inside of an organization and manage connections to outside stakeholders. ERPs focus on efficiency within organizations to allow data to only be processed once. They have eliminated much waste by incorporating best practices into their software.

Companies are able to have some tangible and intangible results in regard to the greenness of their ERP. Primarily the tangible results are immediate and measurable. They can cut back on resources like paper by being able to do much more reporting electronically without the need for a hard copy on paper. Customers are also able to view order statuses and obtain much product information online, eliminating the need for printed product catalogs or printed receipts. This can save much on paper and ink costs.

Computer hardware has also come a long way toward being more energy efficient in today's business world. The Energy Star Program created in 1992 by the U.S. Environmental Protection Agency has helped to ensure the energy efficiency of the hardware components that go into an ERP. These include, but are not limited to, the desktop computers, laptops, and servers with one to four processor sockets. Computers marked with the Energy Star logo may only consume 15 percent of their maximum power use while inactive. This has set a benchmark for hardware manufacturers to strive for and continually improve. Consumers are also aware of this rating, allowing them to make a smarter decision in purchasing a machine that will reduce electricity costs for the home or business.

The NetApp's data center at Research Triangle Park in North Carolina was the first data center ever to receive an Energy Star for superior energy efficiency. NetApp scored 99 out of 100 and has reduced CO_2 emissions by 95,000 tons annually. This is a big step in maximizing the efficiency of a data center. By using overhead air distribution and a pressure-controlled room, NetApp's data center has really set a precedent for the industry that will become a model for data storage in the future. ERP relies on data storage 24/7. This requires running servers at all hours of the day that use up electricity. Data can be efficiently stored on servers in a room like NetApp's data center and be more effective in reducing a company's carbon footprint.

Another important hardware development has been made by General Dynamics Itronix in Cupertino, California. They have developed the Tadpole ultra thin client, which replaces and consumes 50 percent less power than a laptop. They have labeled it a "green computing alternative." This is possible because of the following reasons. It is free of hard drives, memory, and operating system or application software. The Tadpole's core computing is done at a secure centralized server. As this will replace many laptops that have spinning hard drives and where computing uses up precious resources, this will cut costs for the company. These Tadpoles are already being used in enterprise systems by Derby College in the United Kingdom and Cascade's IT departments.

Not only is ERP's hardware green, but the software is where ERPs really have green potential. The newer ERP software allows organizations to track their carbon emissions. Virtualization allows multiple applications to run on a single server. It can significantly reduce the amount of hardware necessary for an ERP implementation. Less hardware means less energy needed to run that hardware. This is one of the leading green practices for IT. People in F5 Networks and Pace Harmon say that virtualization allows an organization to eliminate about 5–10 pieces of hardware equipment and improves the utilization of a server by up to 85 percent.

A nonvirtualized data center can have all of those servers running at about 5–15 percent of their capacity. This means about 10 servers are being used to do the job that virtualization allows 1 server to do. Undoubtedly this allows an organization to drastically reduce power consumption and its carbon footprint, not to mention the equipment needed for cooling all of those servers. Virtualization allows for maximum power management, permitting an organization to only use what it needs. If a company can regularly and effectively monitor the metrics on applications and servers, they can get the most out of new virtualization tools, including moving virtual machines to lower energy costs.

Virtual data centers can be moved to different areas depending on electricity costs. If costs are cheaper, let's say in Montana than in New England, a company could move its virtual data to Montana to decrease its costs further. This would not do much for its carbon footprint, however.

Virtualized computer resources will also allow workers to work from home. This will allow an organization to save on heating a facility. This is useful especially in climates like that of New England, where the winters are very cold and will require much heat to get through a day. An employee would be taking that heat cost from the organization to heat his or her home while he or she works in comfort, reducing the need for a facility to be heated.

Another big step for green ERP is that ERP vendors are now including carbon-monitoring applications in their software suites. These allow organizations to track the amount of carbon they are producing by powering and heating their businesses as well as using fuel to deliver goods and move equipment. These factors are becoming increasingly important to companies, especially package delivery companies like UPS and FedEx. They have been able to alter delivery routes to minimize greenhouse gas emissions by using ERP software.

The government has taken a great initiative in setting an example for green business. In addition to the Energy Star Program, the government will offer tax cuts to organizations that can reduce their carbon emissions, which is a very positive incentive. It is not always easy or cheap for a company to implement green ERP. However, over time, an organization can save a lot of money by becoming green and this will also contribute to the health of the planet. There is a common saying by hardware vendors that "green desktop and server hardware is good for the planet, and what's good for the planet is good for business." This is the view that needs to be shared by all businesses in today's global economy.

The future of ERP is definitely green. Companies benefit greatly by becoming green, whether it be by reducing heating and electricity costs and materials costs, being more efficient in their data processing, or using their greenness in their marketing. Monitoring CO_2 will become a more and more common module for ERP in the coming years. Companies will be able to receive tax benefits by having greener practices and measureable results. This will not only benefit the organization but also the planet. Throughout the growth of business, history shows that we have done much damage by polluting the planet. Ideally ERP will help organizations to become wholly green and be able to recycle all of their energy and hardware. The green market is growing and is expected to go from $47 billion in 2009 to 223.7 billion in 2013. This will prove to be a very profitable venture for ERP vendors and organizations that use ERP.

COMPLIANCE ISSUES

The pressure in today's competitive environment requires the use of enterprise systems such as ERP to be effective and efficient in the management of the business operations. No commercial enterprise, government, or institution is an exception to this requirement. The validation of these systems to attest that they are fit for the specified purpose and meet user and compliance requirements is critical. Although no organization is subject to pressure to validate the system, other forces have pushed them toward embracing the concept. Thus, complying with specific regulations such as FDA, HIPAA, and SOX is becoming critical for the system to be valuable. It has been proven that only performing system validation or software validation does not mean that the system has been designed to meet these requirements. The validation concept and the compliance requirements of computerized systems are often misunderstood and thus need clarification. Business managers, who have the primary responsibility for ensuring that the ERP objectives in terms of compliance requirements are met, must know the principles surrounding ERP system validation and regulatory compliance. Ultimately, the validation would ensure that the system meets its requirements. According to Tim Flanigan and Robert Mackey, the fear of validation can be replaced with its embracement once it's understood that validation could be and should be beneficial to the overall ERP investment project.

SOX Compliance and EU Regulations

SARBANES–OXLEY ACT The Sarbanes–Oxley Act of 2002, sponsored by U.S. Senator Paul Sarbanes and U.S. Representative Michael Oxley, represents the biggest change to federal securities laws in a long time. It came as a result of the large corporate financial scandals involving Enron, WorldCom, Global Crossing, and Arthur Andersen. Sections 404 and 409 relate to IT controls. Section 404 illustrates rules set up on internal controls. It discusses the necessity for clear responsibility in IT systems, as well as for maintaining an adequate internal control structure and procedures for financial reporting. Section 409 illustrates real-time information concerning material changes in the operational or financial condition of a company.[30] In order to comply with these sections, companies must have adequate controls on the business processes and information systems that feed their financial reports.

In an article, Rob Smith describes seven different control considerations for information technology (see Appendix D). It is clear after reading these that SOX must be kept in mind when implementing an ERP system. You want to make sure that internal controls such as separation of duties, safeguarding of information, and the like are in place. With internal controls in an ERP system you will be able manage risks and monitor the reliability and integrity of financial reporting. Because most ERP systems contain data that feed the financial reports, compliance of SOX is definitely a topic to cover when choosing and implementing an ERP system.

---

[30] Smith, R. Seven Things You Need to Know About IT Controls. Sarbanes-Oxley 404/409. http://www.techrepublic.com/whitepapers/sarbanes-oxley-404409-seven-things-you-need-to-know-about-it-controls/113303 (accessed October 2004).

BOX 10-1   SAP and SOX

Systems Applications and Products (SAP) provides software for businesses in every type of industry. SAP is a major ERP provider, so when Sarbanes–Oxley sections 404 and 409 were introduced, they had to think about their market force and their own company. SAP is a worldwide company that was started in Germany. In a recent article, it was noted that as of July 15, 2006, overseas companies listed in the United States had to be SOX 404 compliant.[31] SAP is a "software giant" that has a lot of activity in the United States. Dirk Matzger, head of risk management at SAP Asia-Pacific, said in an interview that SAP has been actively researching and working on becoming SOX 404 complaint since the regulations first came about in 2002. They have involved process owners and have also chosen current employees to champion the project and are in charge of SOX 404–related tasks. They are working on their company's internal controls and incorporating them with SAP's risk management function. SAP currently has biannual audits by their auditor, KPMG, on SOX 404 compliance. They expect these audits to benchmark their progress in becoming compliant and hope to obtain first certification of compliance.

SAP is currently marketing their mySAP ERP Financials. They claim that "mySAP ERP Financials software provides extensive capabilities to ensure continuous compliance with regulatory mandates—enabling high governance standards and reducing IT and audit costs. Using mySAP ERP Financials, you can manage the complex documenting, testing, mitigation, and sign-off procedures associated with Sarbanes–Oxley sections 302, 404, and 409, as well as fast close and section 301 whistle-blower requirements."[32] Their software enables companies to manage their systems and financial information while supporting the regulations of the SOX Act.

SOX IMPACT ON PRIVACY AND SECURITY   Two key concerns for SOX are privacy and security violations. Audits are done to a company's ERP systems to test the privacy and security levels of the system (e.g., who has access to what information and what internal controls are involved in the ERP system?). The major areas of privacy include access to the system, user ID and verification, evaluating configurations relating to business processes, change management, and interfaces.[33] As discussed earlier, ERP systems integrate almost all business functions into one system. It uses one database, one operating system, and so on. People who have access to this system should have user IDs, passwords, and access controls. All users should not be able to change financial information, personnel information, vendor information, and the like. Most auditors get a list of users and what permission they have in the system. They also check to see what process is used for user IDs and passwords: How often are passwords changed? How complex are the user IDs? They also check on how easily changes or modifications can be made to the system. Change management is something that should be controlled by a limited number of experienced people in ERP software. Privacy and security are extremely important with ERP systems.

Along with SOX requirements related to privacy and security violations, other government entities also require companies to maintain certain standards of data integrity. The FDA requires that computerized data be as "accurate, authentic, attributable, current, and legible" as paper

---

[31] http://news.zdnet.com/2102-1009_22-6098931.html (accessed February 2001).
[32] www.sap.com/solutions/business-suite/erp/financials/sox.epx (accessed February 2001).
[33] www.isaca.org/Content/NavigationMenu/Students_and_Educators/IT_Audit_Basics/IT_Audit_Basics_Auditing_Security_and_Privacy_in_ERP_Applications.htm (accessed February 2001).

BOX 10-2   UC Berkeley—Privacy and Security Violations

Over the past few years, colleges and universities have been implementing ERP systems to integrate all student information into one main database. Students enroll in classes, drop classes, pay bills, receive grades, and update personal information all in one central location. This is a great idea because in the past, if a student moved, they would have to change their address at the registrar's office, financial aid office, and admissions office; it was just a very redundant and frustrating process. With the implementation of these systems, however, came violations of security. Most of the systems that are integrated are secure, but individuals with certain accesses are able to download information on their laptops or PCs, and that is when the information becomes very insecure and out of control of the CIO that oversees the centrally located systems. There was a major incident at Berkley in 2005: "As chancellor of the Berkeley campus, I was stunned to learn of the theft of a laptop computer in the graduate division, which contained personal information for approximately 98,000 current and former graduate students as well as persons who applied to our graduate programs. Our students, staff, and alumni expect us to protect the information they have given us confidentially, and we have not maintained that trust. This incident revealed serious gaps in our management of this kind of data. The campus has been instituting new policies to address these issues for several months, and we will do much more. Accountability for this effort ultimately lies with me."[34]

records (Colorado Analytical Research & Development).[35] Exhibits 1-1 and 1-2 present a more comprehensive list of requirements, but the main ones are that all data must be accurate and a record is available of when the data were entered or changed and by whom. SOX has more requirements regarding auditing data and access to the data. Digital data are now more common than data recorded on paper. Signatures on paper are being replaced with digital signatures backed by some sort of biometrics or as is more common an ID and password. But the most telling issue is that managers must now understand how their computer systems process data.

"If you can't explain how things going into the sausage machine come out the other end, then you will be in trouble," said a compliance officer with a London investment bank. For example, upcoming international capital adequacy rules, known as Basel II, will require firms to consider operational risk, such as the risk of a trade not being settled, when calculating capital levels. Without a clear view of how a firm's systems process trades, it will be very difficult to calculate operation risk, he noted. SOX, meanwhile, requires that firms audit and understand their own software. "Before it was like getting a drivers license, as long as you could drive the software you were fine," said Kusionowicz. "But now they are saying you have to show you know what IT systems are doing, so to get your driver's license you have to be able to strip down and rebuild an engine" (Compliance Reporter).

ERP systems are time-savers and money savers, but the very complexity of the system that makes them so advantageous also means that they have many potential areas of weaknesses. Security of the data is of utmost importance if a company wishes to satisfy an auditor that it is in compliance with all the regulations mentioned in SOX. In 2005, a study showed that a large company can expect to spend 70,000 man-hours and $7.8 million reporting and correcting material weaknesses in its financial controls (Dave McClure).

---

[34] www.educause.edu/apps/er/erm05/erm05613.asp?bhcp=1 (accessed February 2001).
[35] Keatley, K. L. (April–June 1999). A review of US EPA and FDA requirements for electronic records, electronic signatures, and electronic submissions. *Quality Assurance,* 7 (2), 77–89. Colorado Analytical Research & Development, an Operating Unit of Pyxant Labs, Inc., Colorado Springs 80907, USA.

However, there can be a significant point of material weakness in a company's financial controls. ERP systems have access to all data, thus incorrect data being used in a variety of a company's financial reports could render the entire financial report fraudulent under the law. Many companies have stepped up to market software that can be used to flag suspicious activity that would be in violation of the SOX. Some examples are DC2, OpenPages, Certus, MetricStream, and MKInsight. All these software packages are searching for multiple levels of access for a single user. For instance, setting up a new vendor in the company's account system, creating a purchase order against the approved vendor list, approving an invoice from that same vendor, and finally paying the invoice all four of these tasks should be handled by different people. If the same person has access to all four functions, then that person could single-handedly commit fraud (Jon Brodkin). Software packages would be examining the millions of transactions made by a company and searching for anywhere the same person was involved in all four steps.

SECURITY

Today's ERP systems are largely Web browser based, meaning they can be accessed anytime and anywhere. In addition, supply chain or e-commerce environments within the ERP are exposed to the intricacies of the Internet world. As ERP systems are implemented, they become exposed to the good and bad of the Internet. Hackers are becoming more and more sophisticated at gaining access to systems. Worms, viruses, and Trojan horses are common, and hackers are now using a variety of other methods to capture information to gain access to systems. An ERP system's security, as shown in Figure 10-4, is only as good as company employees are aware of the importance of

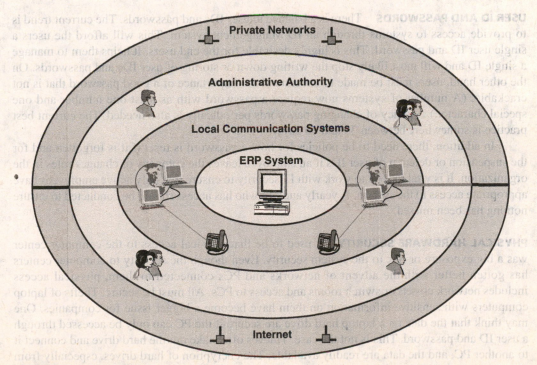

FIGURE 10-4 Security.

maintaining a secure environment. It is still the case that systems that are inappropriately accessed come from the stealing of user IDs and passwords because they are written down and posted on an employees' monitor or in an employee's desk. Securing an ERP system is complex and requires both good technical skills and communication and awareness. It is often said that a system's security is only as good as its weakest link. In the case of systems connected to the Internet, the weakest link may not even be the company's employee—it could be someone else that has been given access to the system for e-commerce purposes.

System security cannot be underestimated or overlooked in an ERP implementation. Like any system, a security plan must be developed to address all the issues related to access with an implementation methodology employed to ensure proper installation and testing. Organizations many times hire security consultants to attempt to access the ERP to see how secure the system really is, and even to continue to try to break in once the system is in production. This will include not only breaking in through electronic means but also accessing computers, stealing user IDs and passwords from employees, and even taking laptops or PDA devices that may contain sensitive information. It certainly seems to be the case, as in the nonelectronic world, that it is difficult if not impossible to keep up with the creative ways thieves or hackers can gain access to systems. ERPs are prime targets because they have so much information that can be harvested and used. A currently published statistic estimates that there are 100 million published data leaks.

Security needs to be in place, tested, and enforced from Day one. The Internet makes access from anywhere anytime possible, but it also opens up a company ERP to many more people than just the company employees.

A good security plan will consist of the software products needed to ensure proper and secure access but will also consider physical access and user security awareness.

USER ID AND PASSWORDS   There is a balance to user IDs and passwords. The current trend is to provide access to systems through an ID Management system. This will afford the users a single user ID and password. This is highly desirable for the end users. It helps them to manage a single ID and will most likely stop the writing down or storing of user IDs and passwords. On the other hand, users must be made to understand the importance of a good password that is not crackable. (A number of systems now require a password with as least one number and one special character.) A policy of changing passwords periodically is also needed. The current best practice is somewhere between 30 and 60 days.

In addition, there need to be policies for how a password is reset if it is forgotten and for the suspension or deletion of user IDs if an employee leaves the company or changes roles in the organization. It is vital for HR to work with IT security to ensure that only active employees have appropriate access to the system. A yearly audit of who has access should be conducted to ensure nothing has been missed.

PHYSICAL HARDWARE SECURITY   It used to be that physical access to the computer center was a big exposure or risk to the system security. Even though the security to computer centers has gotten better with the advent of networks and PCs connected to them, physical access includes network closets or switch rooms and access to PCs. All must be secure. Thefts of laptop computers with sensitive information on them have become a bigger issue for companies. One may think that the data on a laptop hard drive are secure if the PC can only be accessed through a user ID and password. This is not the case. Thieves often take out the hard drive and connect it to another PC, and the data are readily available. The encryption of hard drives, especially from laptops, is one solution that is becoming more and more available. PCs have been a weak link in

TABLE 10-1   List of Some Company Data Leaks

Institution	Type of Leak	Year	Records
UCLA	Hacked into database	2006	800,000
Aetna	Stolen backup tapes	2006	130,000
Boeing	Stolen laptop	2006	382,000
Bank of America	Lost data tapes	2005	1,200,000
Stanford University	Network breach	2005	10,000
University of Connecticut	Hacking program on server since 2003	2005	72,000
University of Southern California	Flaw in online application database	2005	270,000
Wilcox Memorial Hospital	Theft of hard drive	2005	130,000

overall system security. There are many published stories of hackers gaining access to a PC to gather information and to launch an attack on the rest of the company's systems of which the ERP is the prime target.

NETWORK SECURITY   The Internet has its share of less-than-ethical individuals accessing it. In fact, there are likely many people doing a wide variety of illegal activities on the Internet. The Internet and illicit activities seem to be in the news every day. This illustrates how big the Internet has become, and that network security is in its infancy. There are devices that will address significant amounts of network security, but it is complex and requires constant updating. Most companies implement some form of firewall(s), virus controls, and network or server, or both, intrusion detection to safeguard the networked environment. Operating systems need the latest patches, and virus software needs to be updated regularly with antispyware installed to prevent further access. All need to work together to ensure the network environment remains secure and stable. Network security is one of the more complex IT jobs around today. The staff needs to address its throughput and response time, and they must try to ensure the network is free from viruses, intrusions, and, in general terms, attacks to the environment.

INTRUSION DETECTION   Network and server intrusion detection comes in many forms of hardware and software. The notion is to catch and track intrusions in the best case as they are happening and worst after they have happened and been discovered.

BOX 10-3

An **intrusion detection system (IDS)** generally detects unwanted manipulations to computer systems, mainly through the Internet. The manipulations may take the form of attacks by skilled malicious hackers or script kiddies using automated tools.

An intrusion detection system is used to detect all types of malicious network traffic and computer usage that can't be detected by a conventional firewall. This includes network attacks against vulnerable services, data-driven attacks on applications, host-based attacks such as privilege escalation, unauthorized log-ins and access to sensitive files, and malware (viruses, Trojan horses, and worms).

An IDS is composed of several components: **sensors** that generate security events, a **console** to monitor events and alerts and control the sensors, and a central **engine** that records events logged by the sensors in a database and uses a system of rules to generate alerts from security events received. There are several ways to categorize IDS, depending on the type and location of the sensors and the methodology used by the engine to generate alerts. In many simple IDS implementations, all three components are combined in a single device or appliance.

From Wikipedia, the free encyclopedia.

All intrusions must be taken seriously and investigated. Hackers are very sophisticated and can sometimes access systems without it being noticed. Real-time monitoring and after-the-fact reporting of anomalies and misuse of network and server activities will assist in spotting intrusions and safeguarding systems from inappropriate access to information stored in the ERP. Infrastructure implementation planning should address intrusion detection during an ERP implementation. It may be that the IT organization has this capability and is trained adequately, but validation of their capabilities is needed along with a thorough test plan.

Sample List of Intrusion Detection Systems

VCC/TripwireTM

Computer Misuse and Detection System (CMDS) by SAIC

Kane Security Analyst by Intrusion Detection, Inc

NetRanger by Cisco Systems

Symantec Intruder Alert by Symantec

Real Secure by ISS now IBM

G-Server by Gilian Technologies

PORTABLE DEVICES   It may not be easy to steal desktop PCs, and thieves are finding that stealing laptops and PDAs is much easier. Society is demanding more and more portability. PDAs and even mobile phones can store large amounts of data. The theft of laptops and PDAs that have stored identity information is common. Safeguarding against stealing of portable devices is difficult. Society wants the convenience of portability, but it comes at a cost of less security. Laptops can be stolen from offices, cars, trains, airplanes, and homes. Once stolen, the storage media can be mined for information that can be used to gain access to confidential data. Use of passwords and data encryption is important in securing a portable device, but the key is for the users to be very aware of what is being stored and to ensure its safety from hackers and thieves.

AWARENESS   Users often do not understand the vulnerabilities of Web-based ERP systems to unauthorized access. Even though it may be difficult to convey these vulnerabilities to end users, making them aware of the possible issues is key to a successful security plan and program. There should be two facets to awareness. First, ensure that users are aware of security risks (e.g., writing down or choosing simple passwords). Second, enforce policies and procedures related to access. Security violations must be enforced or all system security plans will be compromised. It is often said that system security is only as good as the weakest link. Those seeking to gain access illegally will find it and expose that weakness.

SECURITY MONITORING AND ASSESSMENT   A good security plan will also detail how to provide for constant assessments of security. A periodic review of who has access, what they have access to, and how often they are accessing the system should be part of the review. Setting up and reviewing audit logs must be addressed with an ERP implementation. Logging transactions and reviewing them on a daily or, at worst, a weekly basis is a must for any financial transaction. Audit logs will reveal any unusual transactional activity and help to minimize revenue loss due to fraud or hacking. Intrusion detection must be in real time, and any anomalies or unusual happenings on the network or ERP servers uncovered through daily reporting should be investigated. Virus scanning and general malware must be addressed, along with an evaluation of physical security. Physical security includes those who have physical access to the servers and why. Some companies have hired consultants to provide this type of security assessment on a periodic basis. However it is accomplished, whether in-house or by outsourcing, this type of monitoring must be available to the production ERP system.

ENCRYPTION   The process of taking data and making it unreadable to those who should not see the data has been around for a long time. The complexity has been to encode the data in such a way that the data is reliable to those who should be able to read it. Encryption involves using a key, usually a very long prime number that is difficult to guess or program, to scramble at one end and unscramble at the other end. One way hackers gain access to systems is through monitoring data passing through a network. If the key is unscrambled, the process with the right tools and knowledge is relatively simple. In today's Web-based Internet applications, data encryption is highly desirable. Customers and users are sending and storing confidential data (e.g., credit card numbers and social security numbers) over the network. Encrypting that sensitive information will help to prevent theft of information. In today's ERP implementations, network data encryption and even storing encrypted data need to be addressed. Even the sensitive data on laptop hard drives or PDA storage should be encrypted for security purposes. If the laptop or PDA is then stolen, accessing the hard drive to retrieve data will be next to impossible without the proper key.

Disaster Recovery and Business Continuity Planning

Mission-critical systems must have a plan in place that will provide for the recovery of a number of disasters that can occur to a business. ERP systems play a key role in company business and profits. When a system is unavailable, significant revenues are often lost. It must be said that disaster recovery and business continuity planning are not just an IT responsibility. All departments that use an ERP system must play a part in providing business continuity while a system is unavailable. In planning for a disaster a company must address the level of risk versus the amount of money to ensure that systems are available as quickly as possible. Some of these costs include alternate sites or mirrored sites to ensure ongoing business availability, software and data backups stored off-site, alternative computer centers with the network connectivity, and workstations needed to run the business and the support to ensure that the sites remain in synchronization as the software and hardware configurations are changed. In any planning process (e.g., disaster recovery), evaluating risk or loss of revenues should compare the amount of funds necessary to recover any possible risks in a timely fashion. This planning process is very complex and time consuming and is well beyond the scope of this book. The key concept is to understand that planning for a disaster is part of ongoing business and must include all departments involved in a mission-critical system.

IMPLICATIONS FOR MANAGEMENT

Outsourcing

Outsourcing is certainly not a new idea; however, the face of facility service outsourcing is changing. You now have a wide range of companies with very assorted business models. There are companies that self-perform services, who subcontract services, and who contract manage services. Your next avenue of support lies somewhere in the middle of the crowd of service companies. When companies outsource, it raises ethical questions, especially in this post-Enron era. Casseres[36] said, "My favorite post-Enron cartoon, by Dan Wasserman, has two captains of industry discussing what to do about the fallout from corporate scandals. 'We are seen as ethical disasters,' says one of them. 'How are we going to rebuild public trust?' In a flash of brilliance, the other answers: 'We could outsource it!' " He further continues his article saying that when companies begin to outsource, you can't help but ask if they are shedding ethical responsibility for their company. The key to realizing the benefits of outsourcing or offshoring ERP implementation activities is to know when to use these services properly.

The first consideration is to determine the amount that companies should rely on outsourcing and the extent to which they do.[37] Even though IT budgets have been flat through much of this decade, government regulations (e.g., SOX) have required companies to innovate to remain competitive. Offshoring and outsourcing services include data center operations, help desk and application maintenance, and specialized project work (e.g., global ERP implementations). IT and business management need to determine where offshoring fits with their business goals and how much makes sense for the organization, both fiscally and culturally.

The second consideration is to reevaluate the level of support required for the ERP implementation. Companies need to decide if and when to replace traditional business and implementation services with comparable services from one of the major Indian offshore services providers mentioned earlier. ERP projects are one of the largest budget items of most IT organizations, enforcing the need for more affordable services in this area. ERP support is quickly becoming a buyer's market, and savvy IT organizations are exploiting this fact to their advantage, proving to be a more cost-effective option and improving the company's bottom line.

The third consideration is to evaluate business process outsourcing (BPO) and hosted applications for key business processes. BPO is the contracting of a specific business task (e.g., payroll) to a third-party service provider. Software as a Service (SaaS) is renting externally hosted enterprise applications on a fixed monthly, per seat cost from application service providers like Salesforce.com or NetSuite. The BPO and SaaS providers have matured to the point that they warrant consideration for key ERP-related business functions. IT and business leaders can be assured quality solutions through BPO providers or subscription-based hosted providers, and they can be cost-effective alternatives to traditional software purchase and installation. In fact, according to Dana Stiffler, a research director for AMR Research, "BPO can offer operational savings of up to 50 percent over purchased applications."[38]

Last, when considering outsourcing solutions (whether they be offshore development or SaaS providers), ERP management teams need to look beyond cost. Given the emotional

---

[36] Gomes-Casseres, B. (October 1, 2005). Outsource, Don't Abdicate. *CIO Magazine.* www.cio.com/archive/100105/keynote.html?page=1 (accessed January 15, 2007).
[37] www.amrresearch.com/Content/View.asp?pmillid=17890 (accessed February 2001).
[38] Ibid.

nature of the decision, managers need to focus on resource availability, staff experience, and motivation. In fact, there are six key assessment factors to consider when making the in-house versus outsource or offshoring decision: (1) ERP team's skills and experience; (2) resource availability; (3) project priority; (4) availability of funding; (5) severity of problem; and (6) development motivation.[39] Implementation teams should consider keeping the project internally if there is a high need for control (e.g., keeping company activities secret for competitive advantage). Furthermore, if the organization can afford the time and cost to educate the internal staff, then they may be better off in the long run to perform the implementation internally. The decision might be about national pride and ego (i.e., teams may not want to see these jobs go overseas).

ETHICS   Ethics should be a major concern of the ERP implementation team. An ethics guru should be appointed to the team to guide the team on privacy, accuracy, property rights, and access principles. The best ethical practices should be embedded into the ERP system with other business processes. The integration of ethics both in the system and in the change management strategy and training program would help create higher ethical standards with systems in the organization and improve the compliance with such government regulations as SOX and HIPPA. Another major concern for management should be with data mining activities with ERP systems. Setting high ethical standards during and after ERP implementation will prevent data mining from identifying individual consumer identities.

LEGAL   Management cannot assume all will go well with ERP implementations. Software products sometimes do not perform as advertised, software companies go bankrupt or are bought out by other companies, and consultants overextend themselves or do not have the skills necessary to be successful. It is important for management to address as many possible legal issues up front to protect the company's investing in the ERP and the successful implementation. Contracts must be scrutinized by both the legal department and the project director, project manager (PMO), or both.

AUDIT   The key issue for management with ERPs in general is the law around Sarbanes–Oxley. It has had a big impact on systems as it is related to the integrity and completeness of controls and processes that are oftentimes coded into the ERP. As the SOX law continues to be clarified in the courts and therefore in compliance, it will continue to have impacts on existing and new systems. Changes are often required to ensure that compliance is reached.

SECURITY   Securing an ERP system is complex and requires good technical skills as well as communication and awareness. As mentioned before, it is often said that a systems security is only as good as its weakest link. In the case of systems connected to the Internet, the weakest link may not even be the company's employee, but rather someone else that has been given access to the system for e-commerce purposes. System security cannot be underestimated or overlooked in an ERP implementation. Like any system a security plan must be developed to address all the issues related to access with an implementation methodology employed to ensure proper installation and testing.

---

[39] www.projectsatwork.com/article.cfm?ID=224597 (accessed February 2001).

Summary

- Global and ethical issues are major areas to assess when implementing or modifying an ERP system. These areas are also forever changing (i.e., the world is getting flatter; companies are competing and need to communicate with other companies worldwide).
- Outsourcing is gaining a lot of interest in ERP implementation because it is efficient, but unfortunately it is also steeped in controversy. The details concerning what to outsource, to whom, where, and at what cost can be a very challenging decision for even the most sophisticated companies; however, if handled strategically, outsourcing can provide tremendous benefits to the organization in terms of cost, flexibility, and diversity.
- Offshore outsourcing relationships must keep in mind language barriers, cultures, and international rules and regulations. As a result of this, our government continues to monitor and regulate the ethics of ERP systems.
- Software as a Service (SaaS) is emerging as a viable model of outsourcing. With SaaS, organizations do not have to worry about installation, maintenance, and upgrades. This allows them to focus on their core business processes and scalability options.
- Companies implementing ERP face several ethical challenges with such issues as data privacy, accuracy, property rights, and access rights of users to the system. With data mining on identity theft activities on the rise, organizations face considerable challenges in embedding best ethical practices in the system as well as educating ERP users toward higher ethical standards.
- With Sarbanes–Oxley coming to our world after the Enron crisis, companies have no choice but to ensure their systems are compliant. In our fast-changing world, it is more common to think on a global level, and it's very important also to think ethically.
- Protecting the asset, ERP system, is all a part of an ERP implementation. Legal issues can arise at any time before, during, and after the implementation. Addressing needs and performance in contracts provides a level of protection against a major loss of assets and expenses.
- An ERP system's security is good only as long as company employees are aware of the importance of maintaining a secure environment. Securing an ERP system is complex and requires good technical skills as well as good communication and an overall awareness. A system's security is only as good as its weakest link. In the case of systems connected to the Internet, the weakest link may not even be the company's employee; rather, it could be someone else that has been given access to the system for e-commerce purposes. System security cannot be underestimated or overlooked in an ERP implementation. Like any system, a security plan must be developed to address all the issues related to access with an implementation methodology employed to ensure proper installation and testing.

Exercises

1. Research offshore outsourcing companies that specialize in ERP implementation and maintenance. Prepare a report for management ranking the outsourcing companies with their strengths and weaknesses and provide recommendation on how management should proceed with signing the outsourcing contract.
2. Information technology security is essential to the general health of an ERP. Research a company that has discovered a breach in security; describe the breach and how it affected the business.
3. Find out how the major ERP vendors support SOX, HIPPA, EU regulations, and other compliance modules. Prepare a report for management of a large company with a matrix comparing the features supported by each vendor with your recommendation.

Review Questions

1. What is outsourcing and why would a company choose to outsource?
2. What are the advantages and disadvantages to outsourcing?
3. What are the key challenges in offshore outsourcing?
4. List five best practices in outsourcing.
5. What is SaaS and why is it considered as another outsourcing option?
6. Discuss the components of PAPA.
7. What are the components of a good information technology security plan?
8. With ERP implementations why would an auditor get involved?
9. Why is the Sarbanes–Oxley Act important to investors?
10. What should a disaster recovery and business continuity plan include and who should be involved?

Discussion Questions

1. Outsourcing is becoming more and more popular in companies today. Discuss why a company would want to outsource and how they should outsource ERP implementation.
2. Compare and contrast traditional outsourcing with the Software as a Service. Under what conditions should a company choose SaaS over traditional outsourcing?
3. Discuss how PAPA principles of ethics can be applied to ERP implementation.
4. The Sarbanes–Oxley (SOX) Act is important in a financial environment. Discuss how the operations of an ERP system are affected by SOX.
5. Discuss the major security concerns in ERP systems.

CASE 10-2
Real-World Case
TJX Security Breach

The TJX Companies, Inc., is the leading off-price apparel and home fashions retailer in the United States and worldwide, with $16 billion in revenues in 2005, 8 businesses, and more than 2,300 stores, with a rank of 138 in the most recent Fortune 500 rankings. TJX's off-price concepts include T.J. Maxx, Marshalls, HomeGoods, and A.J. Wright, in the United States, Winners and HomeSense in Canada, and T.K. Maxx in Europe. Bob's Stores is a value-oriented casual clothing and footwear superstore in the Northeastern United States. Our off-price mission is to deliver a rapidly changing assortment of quality brand name merchandise at prices that are 20–60 percent less than department and specialty store regular prices, every day. Our target customer is a middle to upper-middle income shopper, who is fashion and value conscious. This customer fits the same profile as a department store shopper, with the exception of A.J. Wright, which reaches a more moderate-income market, and Bob's Stores, which targets customers in the moderate to upper-middle income range.[40]

   In mid-December 2006, TJX discovered that a hacker had illegally accessed the network that handles credit card, debit card, check, and return transactions. The stores

(continued)

---

[40] www.TJIX.com (accessed February 2001).

affected were T.J. Maxx, Marshalls, Homegoods, and A. J. Wright stores in the United States and Puerto Rico. The stores affected in Canada were HomeSense and Winners. Current reports indicate the hacker had access from a time in July 2005 to mid-December 2006. Along with credit and debit card numbers that were stolen, some driver's license numbers with names and addresses were compromised. As the ongoing investigation continues there is concern that even stores in the United Kingdom are affected.

The announcement to the public occurred about one month after the breach was discovered. Once the breach was discovered, the areas that allowed for the network breach were closed. Law enforcement along with external security experts was called in to investigate and evaluate the breach and how to prevent it in the future. The cost for this breach and subsequent cleanup will be large. Affected TJX customers are being notified, banks are reissuing credit cards, and the security consulting and intrusion detection around the breach is going to be expensive in addition to the fraudulent activity related to the stolen numbers. A breach like this may last for years and affect consumers over the next five years or longer.

Breaches like TJX are more common with today's increased e-commerce and e-Business. Networks, servers, and services are constantly being stressed to look for weak links. Information technology security systems are in need of constant scrutiny by companies engaged in storing of personal information. In the TJX case, the costs involved in correcting the security hole and the ongoing investigation, along with notifying consumers, may also see a loss of sales revenue. Current analysis is not conclusive, but as time goes by consumers may lack trust in businesses that do not appropriately safeguard consumer identities from fraudulent activities.

CASE QUESTIONS

1. What are the costs involved in the TJX network breach?
2. As this investigation unfolds, research the additional costs or loss of revenue to TJX and the credit card companies involved.
3. What should TJX have done to prevent this breach from occurring? Could they have stopped it?

APPENDIX A

(½11.10) Controls for closed systems (environment in which access is controlled by persons responsible for the electronic records). Persons using closed systems to "create, modify, maintain, or transmit electronic records" need to employ the following procedures and controls, and need to ensure that the signer cannot repudiate the records as not genuine.

- Validate systems.
- Generate accurate and complete copies of records in a readable and electronic form subject to inspection, review, and copying.
- Protect records for retrieval during the records retention period.
- Ensure limited access to authorized individuals.
- Create a secure, computer generated, time stamped audit trail for date and time of operator entry or action. When creating, modifying, or deleting records; changes should not obscure the previous record.
- The audit trail must be retained and available for agency review and copying.
- Use operational system checks to permit sequencing of steps and events.
- Use authority checks to ensure that only authorized individuals use or access a system, alter records or electronically sign a record.
- Use device checks to determine the validity of data input source or operational instruction.
- Determine that those who develop, maintain, or use the system have the appropriate education, training, and experience for their assigned tasks.
- Have written procedures in place to hold individuals accountable and responsible for actions under the use of their electronic signature.
- Have controls of distribution, access, and use of documentation for system operation and maintenance.
- Have time-sequenced development and modification of systems documentation for revisions, and change control procedures for the audit trail.

EXHIBIT 1-1A   21 CFR Part 11 Subpart B—Electronic Records.

Subpart E—Purchasing Controls

Each manufacturer shall establish and maintain procedures to ensure that all purchased or otherwise received product and services conform to specified requirements.

- Evaluation of suppliers, contractors, and consultants. Each manufacturer shall establish and maintain the requirements, including quality requirements, that must be met by suppliers, contractors, and consultants.
- Evaluate and select potential suppliers, contractors, and consultants on the basis of their ability to meet specified requirements, including quality requirements. The evaluation shall be documented.
- Define the type and extent of control to be exercised over the product, services, suppliers, contractors, and consultants, based on the evaluation results.

(continued)

- Establish and maintain records of acceptable suppliers, contractors, and consultants.
- Purchasing data. Each manufacturer shall establish and maintain data that clearly describe or reference the specified requirements, including quality requirements, for purchased or otherwise received product and services. Purchasing documents shall include, where possible, an agreement that the suppliers, contractors, and consultants agree to notify the manufacturer of changes in the product or service so that manufacturers may determine whether the changes may affect the quality of a finished device. Purchasing data shall be approved in accordance with 820.40.

EXHIBIT 1-1B   21 CFR Part 820.50—Quality System Regulation.

Phase	Deliverable	Vendor Possible in Package	Comment
Planning	Change control form		
Planning	Business requirements		
Planning	Compliance assessment report		May have position papers
Planning	Validation plan	M	See below
Requirements	User requirements	T	See below
Requirements	User acceptance test plan/cases	T	Should be developed at this stage
Requirements	Product functional specification	E	See below
Configuration	Configuration specifications	T	See below
Install/Test	Installation plan and qualification	T	Installation qualification expected
Test	System/operational test protocol and report	E	If required
Test	System performance test protocol and report	T	See below
Test	Validation report	T	Possible, but not likely
Use	User manual	E	Manuals and SOP for system expected
Use	Support plan/contract	E	If required
Cross	Traceability matrix	M	

VENDOR DEVELOPMENT

Planning	Quality/project plan		These should be available for review as part of a vendor audit
Requirements	Product requirements		
Design	Design specification		
Develop	Program standards		

Develop	Source code
Develop	Source code review results and report
Test	Product test plan/cases
Test	Product test protocols/results and report
Test	Product validation report
Maintenance	Configuration management procedures
Maintenance	Change management procedures

E means expected; **M** means possibly available but requiring modification; **T** means probably only in template form, if at all.

EXHIBIT 1.2   Validation Package Contents

11

Supply Chain Management

LEARNING OBJECTIVES

After reading this chapter, you should be able to:

- Learn about the supply chain network and management drivers.

- Understand the complexity and importance of the integration of supply chain.

- Learn about supply chain components, processes, and flows.

- Know the different levels of supply chain integration.

- Examine the impact of the ERP on supply chain management.

CASE 11-1
Opening Case
Managing the e-Supply Chain at Cisco Systems

Source: Adapted from Managing the e-Supply Chain. Business Intelligence, 2001 and Shister, N. (March 2007). Cisco Builds a Supply Chain, *World Trade*, 20 (3), 34.

Headquartered in San Jose, California, Cisco Systems designs and sells the equipment needed to build Internet technology–based networks: remote dial-up access servers, routers, switches, and network management software. Cisco has the top market share in 16 of the 20 markets in which it competes and is number two in the remaining four. By the mid-1990s, Cisco's managers found that they simply could not increase production capacity fast enough to meet demand.

James Crowther, customer business solutions manager, enterprise, explained: "We realized that growth depended on our ability to scale manufacturing distribution and other supply chain processes quickly. Cisco also realized that we would require the services of far more people than we could reasonably expect to recruit in time. It was at that point that the idea of a new business model emerged. Cisco decided to turn itself into a Web-enabled company by outsourcing most of the manufacturing and logistics activities. In addition, it used networking technology to link supplier and distributors tightly to their in-house business processes. This left us free to concentrate on our real strengths: new product development, looking after customer needs, and brand management."

In Cisco's case, using the Internet to reengineer the organization did not mean pasting a thin dotcom veneer on to a bricks-and–mortar company; however, it was about fundamentally transforming the company from the inside out. Cisco used Internet-based technology to transform its entire supply chain into an extended enterprises system or what Cisco calls "an ecosystem."

Cisco's Internet ecosystem seamlessly links customers, prospects, partners, suppliers, and employees in a multiparty, multilocation electronic network. This e-network both acts as the glue that holds together all the internal operations of the supply chain and enables all the parties involved to present a unified face to the outside world, with the result that all the working parts look and act as if they are one company. At the heart of Cisco's ecosystem are two portals: Cisco Connection Online (CCO), which provides access to Cisco's customers or clients, and Manufacturing Connection Online (MCO), which provides access to Cisco's contract manufacturers, assemblers, distributors, and logistics partners.

CCO COMPONENTS

1. *Marketplace:* a dynamic online catalogue used by more than 10,000 authorized representatives of direct customers and partners to configure Cisco products online. It contains a suite of applications for order processing that enables customers to configure, price, route, and submit orders.
2. *Status agent:* gives Cisco's sales force, direct customers, and partners immediate access to critical information on the status of orders.

(continued)

3. *Customer service:* for after-sales nontechnical support and information.
4. *Technical assistance and software library:* to help IT staff and network administrators in installation and maintenance.

MCO COMPONENTS

1. *Access agent:* real-time manufacturing information, including data on demand forecasts, inventory, and purchase orders.
2. *Monitoring agent:* customer orders and ship product, without them actually touching an order.
3. *Payment agent:* collects payments for the parts used by Cisco.

When taken together, these initiatives have had an immense impact on value creation. Cisco estimates that its extended supply chain generated a total of $695 million in cost savings. Cisco's supply chain model has also provided scalability and agility that allow the company to grow with incredible speed. In the intensely competitive market spaces occupied by Cisco (i.e., where the timelines for new product introduction are counted in weeks rather than months or years) the company's ecosystem has become as great a core strategic capability as its strengths in product design and marketing. In 2005, Cisco announced the demand-driven supply chain (DDSC) solution, which links business applications throughout the supply chain over Internet protocol (IP). The second solution of the Cisco intelligent networked manufacturing strategy, the DDSC solution, enables customers better to integrate information and processes spanning the entire manufacturing workflow. By providing a highly secure visibility into the supply chain, customers can build in the flexibility needed in today's manufacturing world, meet expectations more efficiently, operate more profitably, and respond to market dynamics and mandates. Cisco is currently launching, in a staged approach, a manufacturing-focused product compliance review to be implemented throughout its supply chain. According to V. P. Darendinger, Cisco vice president, "SCM includes strategy development, business reviews, and scorecards, continuous improvement programs and ongoing supply base classification processes."

What do you think of Cisco's e-Business and supply chain management (e-SCM) strategy, and why has Cisco remained successful in its e-SCM strategy?

PREVIEW

As brick-and-mortar enterprises increase their Web-enabling processes, there is one area where more attention is necessary: the firm's supply chain. A good supply chain management (SCM) system can act as a digital nerve center for the entire business and save the company millions of dollars in costs in order fulfillment and other back-end support processes.

Cisco's implementation of their SCM was an optimal combination of technology and business processes that optimized the delivery of goods, services, and information from the supplier to the consumer in an organized and efficient way. SCM gives companies involved in developing, manufacturing, distributing, and retailing of products access to all of the critical information they need to plan their operations in an efficient way—whatever and wherever they need it. A complete supply chain management solution also includes customers, service providers, and partners. SCM is a large, dynamic network of complex but well-defined relationships with multiple channels in the business, which provides accurate information to everyone in the network. SCM provides companies like Cisco the flexibility and the agility to be in constant control of their businesses. It improves efficiencies and reduces costs substantially while also giving companies the adaptability to modify their business processes.

As the opening Cisco case showed, there are myriad parties and processes involved in the SCM. Availability of proper communication channels, good collaboration policies, continuous innovation, and seamless integration across the systems involved are necessary components for reaping benefits. Cisco's e-SCM strategy benefits include supplier base reduction, greater involvement of supplier management in new product introduction, and increased risk management strategies. In addition, it has also led to refinement of Cisco's outsourcing strategy so it could better leverage its business with electronics manufacturing services (EMS) providers and better use their capabilities.

SUPPLY CHAIN MANAGEMENT

Supply chain is the network of services, material, and information flow that link a firm's customer relations, order fulfillment, and supplier relations processes to those of its suppliers and customers. In practice, people tend to use the terms *value chain* and *supply chain* interchangeably. Supply chain management is the science of developing a strategy to organize, control, and motivate the resources involved in the flow of services and materials within the supply chain.[1] According to the *Council of Supply Chain Management Professionals (CSCMP)*, a professional association that developed a definition in 2004, supply chain management "encompasses the planning and management of all activities involved in sourcing and procurement, conversion, and all logistics management activities. Importantly, it also includes coordination and collaboration with channel partners, which can be suppliers, intermediaries, third-party service providers, and customers. In essence, supply chain management integrates supply and demand management within and across companies."

SCM is an outgrowth of the value chain concept developed by Michael Porter.[2] A business value chain, according to Porter, consists of a series of processes or activities conducted by the company to add value to the existing product or service and to provide a competitive advantage in the market. These business processes can be grouped into primary or secondary activities depending on the company's business strategy, product, or service and relationships with its business partners. Supply chain focus is on improving the efficiencies of the primary activities with a better flow of information across the activities and linking the with the company's external partners and customers.

Supply chain, therefore, improves the value chain of the firm. It has a direct impact on the company's bottom line. To achieve competitive advantage, companies today first need to understand their supply chain and build the strategy in such a fashion that its competitive strategy and supply chain strategy are properly aligned. The company can otherwise fail miserably in the market, even when its product or service is of good value. For example, Toys "R" Us, Inc., failed miserably when it first entered the e-commerce market in 1998. Their Web site got enormous attention from the end users during the Christmas season in 1998, and thousands of users placed online orders for toys to be delivered as gifts before December 25. At the time Toys "R" Us did not have a proper supply chain system in place to fulfill the number of orders it received; hence, it was not able to deliver the toys on time before Christmas Day. This became a major embarrassment

---

[1] Krajewski, L., Ritzman, L., and Malhotra, M. (2006). *Operation Management Processes and Value Chains*, 8th ed. Publisher: Prentice Hall, p. 371.

[2] Porter, M., and Millar, V. (1985). How Information Gives You Competitive Advantage. *Harvard Business Review*, 63 (4), 149 (12 pages).

for Toys "R" Us, because they made a lot of their customers angry and dissatisfied. Toys "R" Us eventually had to discontinue its business strategy of selling toys online on its own and created a partnership with Amazon.com, which never worked smoothly.[3] For any company to be successful, its supply chain strategy and competitive strategy must be aligned or work together toward a common goal. Strategic alignment means that both the competitive and supply chain strategies have the same objective. It refers to consistency between the customer priorities that the competitive strategy hopes to satisfy and the supply chain capabilities that the supply chain strategy aims to build.

A good SCM can assure the company agility and flexibility needed in today's Web-enabled competitive landscape. As corporations strive to focus on core competencies and become more flexible, they have reduced their ownership of raw materials sources and distribution channels. These functions are increasingly being outsourced to other corporations that can perform the activities better or more cost effectively. The consequence is that there is an increase in the number of companies involved in satisfying consumer demand, while there is a reduction in management control of daily logistical operations. Less control and more supply chain partners create the challenge for the SCM. The purpose of SCM is to improve trust and collaboration among supply chain partners and to integrate the processes to a wholesome system, thus improving supply chain responsiveness and efficiency, as shown in Figure 11-1.

Marketing, distribution, planning, manufacturing, and the purchasing departments traditionally operate independently in organizations. These departments have their own objectives,

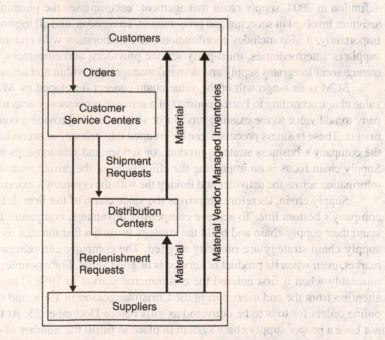

FIGURE 11-1 Collaboration in Supply Chain Information. *Source:* Sanjay Jain, Supply Chain Management Tradeoffs Analysis, in *Proceedings of the 2004 Winter Simulation Conference,* R. G. Ingalls, M. D. Rossetti, J. S. Smith, and B. A. Peters, eds. Reprinted by permission of Dr. Sanjay Jain. The George Washington University.

[3] Ouchi, M. S. (March 3, 2006). Toy Story Winds Up Leaving Amazon Grim. *Knight Ridder Tribune Business News.* Washington, 1.

and these are often conflicting to a certain degree. Purchasing contracts are often negotiated with very little information beyond historical buying patterns. The result of these factors is that there is not a single, integrated plan for the organization (i.e., there are as many plans as the number of departments). There is clearly a need for a mechanism through which these different back-office and front-office plans can be integrated together. Supply chain management is a strategy through which such integration can be achieved.

All functions that are part of a company's supply chain contribute to its success or failure. These functions do not operate in isolation: No one function can ensure the supply chain's success. Failure at any one function, however, may lead to failure of the overall chain. Thus, a company' success or failure is closely linked to the following key perspectives. The competitive strategy and all functional strategies must fit together to form a coordinated overall strategy. Each functional strategy must support other functional strategies and help a firm reach its competitive strategy goal. The different functions in a company must appropriately structure their processes and resources to be able to execute these strategies successfully.

To achieve strategic fit, a company must ensure that its supply chain capabilities support its ability to satisfy the targeted customer segments. They must understand the customer and supply chain uncertainty. A company must understand the customer needs for each targeted segment and the uncertainty the supply chain faces in satisfying these needs. This gap analysis will help the company define its desired cost and service requirements, and identify the impact of a disruption or delay, or both, in the supply chain. A company should also understand its supply chain system capabilities. There are many types of supply chains, each of which is designed to perform different tasks well. A company must understand what its supply chain is designed to do well. If there is a mismatch between the supply chain outcomes and the desired customer needs, the company will either need to restructure the firm's competitive strategy or alter its supply chain strategy as seen in the case of Wal-Mart (see Vignette) as it promotes the use of radio frequency identification (RFID) technology to its suppliers and partners.???

Wal-Mart's RFID Strategy

A typical U.S. Wal-Mart has 142,000 items, so multiplying those savings makes sense that Wal-Mart's efforts on enforcing new SCM technology on their suppliers make a big impact on the bottom line.[4] Wal-Mart has definitely started a ripple effect within its own supply chain.

Ever since 2002, when radio frequency identification technology proponents began insisting that it would dramatically change the way companies track goods in the supply chain, it has remained a niche technology because of the cost of RFID tags. The most generic RFID tags cost around 10 cents apiece, whereas latest generations of chips are getting better with standardization and improved functionality. Consumer goods companies always talk about 5-cent tags as a price that would open RFID up to broader uses and remove the difficulties pioneers like Wal-Mart have had in pulling in a critical mass of partners.

Just 600, or about 3 percent, of its suppliers have started using RFID since the retailer announced its famous supply chain "mandate" in 2003. The slow uptake is prompting Wal-Mart to change its strategy for the RFID technology drastically. It is moving away

(continued)

---

[4] Weier, M. H. (April 2, 2007). RFID: Hold the Revolution. *InformationWeek*, Manhasset, Issue 1132, 30–31.

from distribution centers, because so many cases and pallets still arrive stamped with bar codes, to stores. There, it can work with goods from the suppliers that place RFID tags to find ways to reduce out-of-stock situations and, more recently, to drive sales promotions.

On the store front, Wal-Mart has expanded its RFID use from 100 to 1,000 stores. Readers are typically located at loading dock entrances, at entrances leading from backrooms to sales floors, and at trash compactors where boxes are destroyed. Data are collected when product moves, including at the cash register, allowing Wal-Mart to generate printouts for employees to prioritize restocking duties. Suppliers can link into Wal-Mart's e-SCM system over the Web to check exactly where their products are. In addition, Wal-Mart is also starting to give employees handheld RFID readers that beep based on proximity to specified products, making them easier to find.[5]

One Wal-Mart supplier, consumer goods company Kimberly-Clark, is focusing on sales promotion through a pilot program that uses RFID to monitor promotions of its Depend adult diapers. The company created fully stocked promotional displays of Depend and put RFID tags on the displays before shipping them to Wal-Mart and Target, another RFID pioneer. Using software from OAT Systems, Kimberly-Clark could see on a color-coded dashboard how many stores received the product in the stockroom and how many put it on the store floor.

SCM Drivers

For companies, achieving strategic fit simply means achieving the balance between supply chain responsiveness and efficiency in its supply chain that best meets the needs of the company's competitive strategy. To understand how a company can improve supply chain performance in terms of responsiveness and efficiency, we must examine the four key drivers of supply chain: facilities, inventory, transportation, and information. These drivers determine the supply chain's performance in terms of responsiveness and efficiency, as well as whether strategic fit has been achieved across the supply chain.

FACILITIES Facilities are the places in the supply chain network where product is manufactured, stored, or transshipped. The two major types of facilities are production sites (plants) and storage sites (warehouses). Whatever the function of the facility, decisions regarding location, capacity, and flexibility of facilities have a significant impact on the supply chain's performance. For a certain company, it needs to decide how many suppliers, manufacturing facilities, distribution centers, and warehouses to have, and where these facilities should be located, along with where the market is for its products (i.e., where are its customers). The decision on facility directly affects the company's inbound and outbound transportation costs, responsiveness to the market, and inventory level. For example, increasing the number of warehouse locations decreases the average outbound distance to a customer and makes outbound transportation distance a smaller fraction of total distance traveled by the product. Thus, as long as inbound transportation economies of scale are maintained, increasing the number of facilities will decrease the overall transportation cost. The inbound lot sizes can become very small if the number of facilities is increased, which results in a significant loss of economies of scale for inbound transportation. In general, increasing the number of facilities increases total transportation cost.

---

[5] Wal-Mart. (July 12, 2010). *CIO Still "Bullish" on RFID*, http://www.rfidjournal.com/blog/entry/7315/

INVENTORY   Inventory is the raw materials, work in process, and finished goods that belong to the company. Inventory is an important supply chain driver because changing inventory policies can dramatically alter the supply chain's efficiency and responsiveness. For example, to deal with the high demand of the product during the holiday season, manufacturers can make it more responsive by stocking large amount of inventory. With large inventory, the likelihood of stock out for that product is low. It can better service its customer during the holiday season. A large inventory, however, will increase the manufacturer's inventory holding cost, thereby making it less efficient. Reducing inventory will make the company more efficient, but will hurt its responsiveness. To reduce the stockout probability, companies usually keep a certain amount of safety stock that provides the buffer for stock out. A successful inventory management policy is to achieve that right balance of responsiveness and efficiency. It is worth noting that there is no finished goods inventory for the service industry. For example, for an accounting firm their finished product is the accounting service, which is not stockable.

TRANSPORTATION   Transportation moves the product between different stages in a supply chain. Like the other supply chain drivers, transportation has a large impact on both responsiveness and efficiency. The type of transportation a company uses also affects the inventory and facility locations in the supply chain. Transportation can take the form of many combinations of modes and routes, each with its own performance characteristics. For example, a company can outsource the production to China and ship its entire finished product across the Pacific Ocean via an international container shipment. Such a practice clearly increases efficiency, but it decreases the responsiveness to the customer because shipment via sea takes long periods of time. On the other hand, Dell flies in several PC components from Asia because doing so allows the company to lower the levels of inventory it holds. This practice increases the responsiveness, but it decreases transportation efficiency because it is more costly than transporting parts by ship.

INFORMATION   Information consists of data and analysis concerning facilities, inventory, transportation, and customers throughout the supply chain. Information could be overlooked as a major supply chain driver because it does not have a physical presence; however, information is potentially the biggest driver of performance, or efficiency, in the supply chain because it directly affects each of the other drivers. Information presents management with the opportunity to make supply chains more responsive and efficient. Information serves as the connection between the supply chain's various stages, allowing them to coordinate and bring about many of the benefits of maximizing total supply chain profitability. Information is also crucial to the daily operation of each stage in a supply chain. For instance, a production scheduling system uses information on demand to create a schedule that allows a factory to produce the right products in an efficient manner. A warehouse management system uses information to create visibility of the warehouse's inventory. The company can then use this information to determine whether new orders can be filled. There are a lot of SCM solution vendors (e.g., i2, Inc.) currently on the market that provide sophisticated ways to store, analyze, and report the relevant information to the managers.

SCM Flows

Supply chains exist in both service and manufacturing organizations, although the complexity of the chain may vary greatly from industry to industry and firm to firm. One view of the supply chain is to see it as a network carrying different flows to satisfy the customer demand. Supply

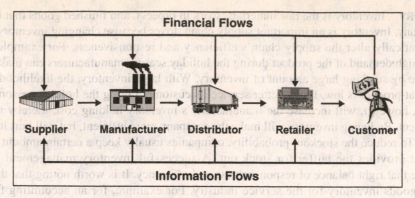

FIGURE 11-2 Flows in Typical Supply Chain.

chain management involves coordinating and integrating these flows both within and among companies. SCM is typically viewed to lie between vertically integrated firms, where the entire material flow is owned by a single firm, and those in which each channel member operates independently. Coordination between the various players in the chain is therefore the key in its effective management. It is said that the ultimate goal of any effective SCM system is to achieve the system's efficiency and respond to customer demand promptly.

SCM flows (Figure 11-2) can be divided into three main categories: product flow, information flow, and finance flow.

- The product flow includes the movement of goods from a supplier to a customer, as well as any customer returns or service needs.
- The information flow involves transmitting orders and updating the status of delivery.
- The financial flow consists of credit terms, payment schedules, and consignment and title ownership arrangements.

SOFTWARE AND TECHNOLOGY   Increasing numbers of companies are using the Internet and Web-based applications as part of their SCM solution. A number of major Web sites offer procurement marketplaces where manufacturers can trade and even make auction bids with suppliers.

There are two main types of SCM software: *planning applications* and *execution applications*. Planning applications use advanced algorithms to determine the best way to fill an order. Execution applications track the physical status of goods, the management of materials, and financial information involving all parties. Some SCM applications are based on open-data models that support the sharing of data both inside and outside the enterprise (this is called the extended enterprise and includes key suppliers, manufacturers, and end customers of a specific company). These shared data may reside in diverse database systems, or data warehouses, at several different sites and companies. By sharing these data "upstream" (i.e., with a company's suppliers) and "downstream" (i.e., with a company's clients), SCM applications have the potential to improve the time-to-market of products, reduce costs, and allow all parties in the supply chain better to manage current resources and plan for future needs. SCM applications are developed using a number of such scalable enterprise-level technologies as electronic data interchange (EDI) and extensible mark-up language (XML).

SCM Processes

Supply chain management involves many processes and procedures for efficient chain management. These will now be examined.

PROCUREMENT Procurement is the business-to-business purchase and sale of supplies and services. Companies usually develop strategic plans with suppliers to support the manufacturing flow management process and development of new products. The desired outcome is a win–win relationship, where both parties benefit, and reduction times in the design cycle and product development are achieved. It is more common to see this process being done over the Internet. An important part of many B2B initiatives, e-procurement Web sites allow qualified and registered users to look for buyers or sellers of goods and services. Depending on the approach, buyers or sellers may specify prices or invite bids. Transactions can be initiated and completed. Ongoing purchases may qualify customers for volume discounts or special offers.

OUTSOURCING AND PARTNERSHIPS Outsourcing is an arrangement in which one company provides services for another company that could also be done or have usually been provided in-house. Outsourcing is common in IT and other industries for services that have usually been regarded as intrinsic to managing a business. This is true both for outsourcing the procurement of materials and components and for the outsourcing of services that traditionally have been provided in-house. The benefit is that the company will increasingly focus on those activities in the value chain where it has a distinctive advantage, and let everything else be outsourced. This is particularly evident in logistics where the provision of transport, warehousing, and inventory control is increasingly subcontracted to specialists or logistics partners (3PL). In addition, managing and controlling this network of partners and suppliers requires a blend of both central and local involvement. Hence, strategic decisions need to be taken centrally with the monitoring and control of supplier performance and day-to-day liaison with logistics partners being best managed at a local level.

MANUFACTURING FLOW MANAGEMENT The manufacturing process is to produce and supply products to the distribution channels based on past forecasts or point of sales (POS) data. Manufacturing processes must be flexible to respond to market changes, and they must accommodate mass customization. Orders are processes on a just-in-time (JIT) basis in minimum lot sizes. Changes in the manufacturing flow process also lead to shorter cycle times, which means improved responsiveness and efficiency of demand to customers and activities related to planning, scheduling, and supporting manufacturing operations, such as work-in-process storage, handling, transportation, and time phasing of components.

ORDER FULFILLMENT This is the process that responds to customer demand by merging several important functions: order management, storage, and delivery of finished goods. It also involves the warehouse and inventory management and physical distribution. Warehouse execution may involve final assembly and packaging of products. In addition to better customer response, the benefits of this practice include more efficient inventory management, order entry, warehousing and transportation management, and an optimizing end-to-end order fulfillment process. Physical distribution concerns the movement of finished products, services, or both, to customers. In physical distribution, the customer is the final destination of a marketing channel, and the availability of the product or service is a vital part of each channel participant's marketing effort. It is also through the physical distribution process that the time and space of customer service become an integral part of marketing; therefore, it links a marketing channel with its customers (e.g., links manufacturers, wholesalers, retailers).

CUSTOMER SERVICE MANAGEMENT PROCESS   Customer service provides the source of customer information. It also provides the customer with real-time information on promising dates and product availability through interfaces with the company's production and distribution operations. In retail industry, product return is a big issue, and it contributes to the name "closed loop" supply chain because some of the products will return to the origin of the manufacturing facility due to imperfection or some other issues.

FORECASTING   Some literature includes forecasting into the demand management process. It is a crucial part for supply chain management. Forecasting seeks to predict levels of weekly or monthly product activity over a time horizon. The statistical methods proven to make such predictions have been used by manufacturers and distributors since the advent of MRP II systems. In addition to increased availability, the nature of forecasting is also changing. Forecast systems are used to increase agility. Companies are able to consolidate demands from multiple business units, reduce forecasting cycle times from weeks to days, and simultaneously increase forecasting accuracy, thereby eliminating excess inventory and ensuring that material is on hand for scheduled production. A failure to consolidate the forecasting information along the supply chain will result in bullwhip effect. The bullwhip effect is an observed phenomenon in forecast-driven distribution channels. Because forecast errors are a given, companies often carry an inventory buffer called "safety stock." Moving up the supply chain from end consumer to raw materials supplier, each supply chain participant has greater observed variation in demand and thus greater need for safety stock. In periods of rising demand, downstream participants will increase their orders. In periods of falling demand, orders will fall or stop in order to reduce inventory. The effect is that variations are amplified the farther you get from the end consumer.

E-BUSINESS AND SUPPLY CHAIN MANAGEMENT

Supply chain management is poised for a rapid evolution. Brick-and-mortar manufacturers are increasingly adding e-commerce capabilities and, as a result, facing new challenges (e.g., individual delivery of products). The biggest challenge ahead may be to overcome the notion that a single organization can achieve best-in-class SCM. The truth is that organizations must work together to help each other succeed. Everyone in the supply chain is a strategic link. Strong links make strong supply chains; weak links hurt everybody, from the raw material producer to the end customer, who evaluates how well a supply chain is performing every time he or she makes a purchase.

A Web-enabled supply chain management (e-SCM) solution is the digital nerve center of the entire business. An effective e-SCM solution can save companies millions of dollars in costs. e-SCM is the optimal combination of technology and business processes that optimizes delivery of goods, services, and information from the supplier to the consumer in an organized and efficient way. A complete supply chain management solution also includes customers, service providers, and partners. The creation of an integrated e-supply chain solution will be a major key or barrier to entry and would provide a critical edge over competitors as it speeds time to market, improves order fulfillment, improves customer service and satisfaction, improves order management, improves decision making, improves forecasting and demand planning, improves warehouse and distribution activities, reduces paperwork, reduces inventory buildup, shortens sales cycles, and strengthens partnerships.

The traditional concept of SCM is no longer valid in the digital economy. e-SCM focuses on globalization and information management tools, which integrate procurement, operations, and logistics from raw materials to customer satisfaction. With the widespread implementation and acceptance of e-Business, the traditional methods and rules have changed to improve profitability and fulfillment. e-SCM can use e-Business concepts and Web technologies to manage inventory and information beyond the organization, both upstream and downstream. It is the strategic approach that unites all steps in the business cycle, from initial product design and the procurement of raw materials, through production, shipping, distribution, and warehousing, until a finished product is delivered to a customer. Companies with a network of suppliers, vendors, and distributors need a fast, efficient way to disseminate information and enable two-way communications.

REPLENISHMENT SYSTEMS   Supply chain replenishment encompasses the integrated production and distribution process. CVS, a well-known drug store chain, almost completely relies on its e-SCM system to reduce inventory levels as well as to eliminate stocking points. CVS has 9 main warehouse facilities and 15 satellite facilities. These warehouses are placed in central locations around all of the CVS stores. As a purchase is made at CVS, the register captures the inventory replenishment needed via a bar code on the product. At the end of each day, the manager reviews the daily POS report and uses this report as a guide to place the order to replenish the stock that was purchased that day. All of the CVS stores report the amount of new stock needed for the next day to their designated warehouse. A delivery will be made the following morning to replace the exact number of products ordered. If the store needed five bottles of Extra Strength Tylenol Gel tabs, then the store would be delivered five bottles of Extra Strength Tylenol Gel tabs. The entire process will happen again at the end of each day. CVS does have the ability to automate this process.

The POS system can send the needed inventory order directly to the warehouse; hence, eliminating the store manager's involvement. CVS feels that by having a computer take over the responsibility of a human, however, customer service may be sacrificed if an issue arises and a product is not ordered. CVS wants the ownership to rest in the hands of the store manager. If a product is not ordered for a customer, the manager can then apologize and remedy the situation, as opposed to telling the customer that he or she doesn't know why the computer did not order the product. This is just simple depiction of how CVS makes its replenishments. The marketing, finance, and sales departments forecast each month's demands using Manugistics' Demand Planning System and Manugistics' Supply Chain Planning Suite. The system analyzes sales trend climates, market conditions, and seasonal promotions. Once the data are reviewed, the procurement group enters the demands into a Marcam Corp Prism capacity system that schedules the productions of, say, Tylenol needed and generates an electronic purchase order. As Tylenol fills the purchase orders, the boxes are sent to the various warehouses, where they are opened so that individual needs are filled based on each store's request.

E-Procurement

E-procurement[6] is the use of Web-based technology to support the key procurement processes, including requisitions, sourcing, contracting, ordering, and payment. The use of e-procurement has many benefits. With the use of e-procurement, companies can monitor and regulate buying

---

[6] Turban. (2005). *E-Business Book.* New York: John Wiley & Sons.

behavior, consolidate orders to reduce product costs, eliminate maverick purchases, improve payment process, and reduce cycle time and administrative processing fees. Ariba is a company that offers procurement solutions. Dell, a well-known online computer sales company, has written the book on front-end, made-to-order, on-time delivery of computers. According to a study by Ariba, however, Dell's back office was not quite as efficient. Dell has approximately 25,000 employees spread out across the United States. They spent around $5 billion a year on nonproduction supplies from consulting to office equipment. Dell followed the traditional procurement process that required a three-part form, needed between 8 and 10 signatures, and took weeks to complete. The entire process carried a cost of about $110 per transaction. Tracking was nonexistent, and maverick spending was out of control.

Dell researched three e-procurement systems with a five-part scorecard: ease of use, optimization on Dell servers and the Microsoft NT platform, e-commerce links to a broad base of suppliers, ease of integration with Dell's back-end systems, and cost-effectiveness. Dell took the big bang approach to implement the new system. Seven months were needed to create approximately 20 interfaces from the Ariba buyer to Dell's legacy systems. With the new systems in place, a Dell employee can make a purchase in less than one minute. Employees are able to search by product, by a service, or by a certain Dell-approved supplier. When a catalog item is selected, the necessary information is populated automatically, including Dell's preferred prices from that supplier and all accounting information. Once the requisition is submitted, an automated workflow approval process is followed. Once approved, the requisition moves out to the Ariba Commerce Services network, a shared infrastructure that enables connectivity between buyers and suppliers on the Ariba B2B commerce platform. Ariba takes responsibility for communicating orders via XML, e-mail, faxes, EDI, or whatever the supplier has required.

Dell benefited because there was no need to maintain a costly EDI infrastructure for purchasing indirect materials. Orders are submitted over the Internet via XML, and the supplier fills the orders. Once the orders have been received from the supplier, the receiving department can match the packing slip with the online order via Ariba and automatically send it to accounting for payment. With Dell implementing Ariba's e-procurement system, they were able to save 62 percent on the time it took to complete an order and ensure a 61 percent reduction in the cost of the order. Dell is also able to use the data collected by the e-procurement system to go back to suppliers and negotiate greater volume discount.

Collaborative Design and Product Development

Collaborative design and product development among parties in the supply chain are crucial when product design and shortening the time it takes to get the product to market are the goals. With online collaboration, all parties, engineering, suppliers, marketing, and even customers can get involved in a product development before the first dollar is spent. In the early 1990s, GM usually spent four years taking a car to market. When a GM vehicle would land on the showroom floor, it was already stale. Around 1990 GM had more than 9,000 outside suppliers and more than 7,000 legacy systems. Within GM, engineering and design departments had 23 computer-aided design (CAD) systems. No system integrated with another, and collaboration was a nightmare. In 1996, GM chose electronic data systems' (EDS) Unigraphics as its standard CAD program. This program allowed the three-dimensional design documents to be viewed, edited, and changed by more than 18,000 engineers and designers located in more than 14 different locations all over the world. GM also chose to give access to the EDS to more than 1,000 critical suppliers.

Today, with the use of Unigraphics, GM's collaborative design and product development, the time to market for a new vehicle is 18 months. With new systems in place, GM will be redesigning and turning out new cars once every three weeks for the next five years. In addition to reducing time to market, GM is enjoying quite a bit of savings. Before the collaborative design and product software was in place, GM would build around 70 cars per model to test crash. Since these models were prototypes, parts were ordered in small batches, thus carrying a heavy price tag. Each prototype car could cost around $1 million. Currently, GM builds only 10 cars per model for test crashing, and the rest is taken care of virtually. Once a virtual car is crashed, math-based models and real-time online reviews can be sent back to suppliers with new specifications for certain parts based on the virtual crash results.

SUPPLY WEBS   As stated before, supply Webs are also known as an exchange. A supply Web is a virtual location where buyers and sellers can meet and negotiate products, prices, and quantity. Back in early 2001, Forester Research recorded more than 2,500 exchanges worldwide. Within a few years more than 50 percent of the exchanges have gone out of business due to lack of customers, lack of cash, or lack of both. A few success stories exist. ChemConnect is an online chemical exchange that has been around since 1999. They are now part of Intercontinental Exchange and provide exchange services to several large companies worldwide.[7] So how does the exchange work for ChemConnect? One of ChemConnect's 9,000 members may hold a reverse auction. In a reverse auction Company X will post a request that it will purchase 10 tons of a certain acid for $1 million. Suppliers will bid against each other to sell Company X the acid requested. In the end of the reverse auction, Company X buys 10 tons of acid from Supplier Y for $900,000, $100,000 less than the original bid, as a result of the competitive bidding process via the reverse auction. The benefit? The entire reverse auction process only took 30 minutes! In the past Company X would have to call on suppliers around the world to see if they had the amount they needed and priced at what they wanted to pay and could take weeks or months to complete the transaction.

E-LOGISTICS   The Council of Logistics Management defines *logistics* as that part of the supply chain process that plans, implements, and controls the efficient and effective flow and storage of goods, services, and related information from the point of origin to the point of consumption in order to meet customers' requirements. Thus, e-logistics is applying the concepts of logistics electronically to those aspects of business conducted via the Internet. In today's world most companies outsource the handling of e-logistics. Amazon has partnered with almost all of the big delivery companies (e.g., FedEx and UPS). It is much easier and cost-effective to plug into FedEx's infrastructure than it is to hire a logistics department and purchase the expensive equipment that would be required to maintain e-logistics. The downside for Amazon is loss of control. If a customer of Amazon does not get their package as promised on a certain day, that customer will be calling Amazon, not FedEx. Online buyers today want to purchase a product online and then track that package until it arrives on their doorstep. The driving need for e-logistics is that today's buyer has much higher expectations. Online customers will not tolerate partial orders, back orders, or poor return policies. Traditional delivery of large bulk or stocking items to a single known location has changed; now many small parcels are being delivered to many unknown locations based on demand, price, and convenience.

---

[7] ICE Buys ChemConnect's Trading Business for Undisclosed Sum. (June 2007). *Gas Processors Report* [serial online], 25, www.proquest.com/ (accessed January 16, 2008). Available from: ProQuest Information and Learning, Ann Arbor, MI (accessed November 11, 2007), Document ID: 1295470561.

COLLABORATIVE PLANNING   Collaborative planning involves a shared forecast between business partners. These partners all have real-time access to POS information. The goal of collaborative planning is to match production plans and product flow, thereby optimizing resource utilization. Because collaborative planning involves input from multiple parties across different companies, unification is difficult. Rules and deadlines need to be put in place, and a manager must supervise the entire process for collaborative planning to be efficient. The Gem Group, Inc. is a manufacturing company based in Lawrence, Massachusetts. They have collaborated with their customer (i.e., Timberland) to produce T-shirts. Timberland has installed an instance of a retail application at Gem Group's site. That retail application is in turn closely integrated into Gem Group's ERP system. This way both companies have real-time information about their order status, advance shipping notices, invoices, UCC 128 carton labels, and so on.

A typical example of the collaborative portal is shown in Figure 11-3. This is an example of a commercial enterprise-level portal.

ERP System and Supply Chain

ERP and SCM today are commonly integrated in most companies. ERP focus is on providing an integrated transaction processing that enhances organizational performance by increasing information consistency and transaction efficiency. SCMs, on the other hand, are aimed at providing a higher level of business planning and decision support functionality for effective coordination and execution of interorganizational business processes. As these two systems have matured,

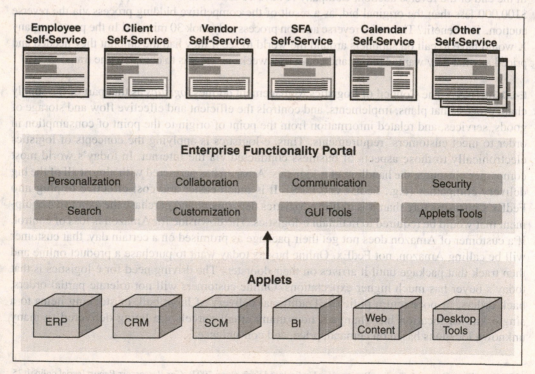

FIGURE 11-3   Example of Enterprise-Level Portal.   *Source:* Adapted from Oracle/PeopleSoft Enterprise One Collaboration Portal (www.oracle.com)

their capabilities are beginning to overlap based on normal product enhancements as well as due to business acquisitions and mergers. There is therefore a surge of integrated SCM–ERP solutions available in the market.

ERP was traditionally not considered for SCM; consequently, the information flow between various members of the supply chain was slow. This was because until the late 1990s the focus of organizations was on improving the internal efficiency alone. ERP systems therefore supported only internal organization functions instead of interorganizational supply chain functions.

The organizations soon realized, however, that although internal efficiency is important, its benefit would be limited unless they were complemented by increased efficiency across the supply chain. They also realized that seamless flow of real-time information across the supply chain was the key to success in the emerging market scenario, which was characterized by great advancements of technology, shorter product life cycles, and so forth. Organizations therefore started integrating ERP applications with SCM software. This ensured that the efficiency was achieved across the supply chain and there is a seamless flow of information. Thus, ERP becomes a vital link in the integrated supply chain as it serves as the integrated planning and control system.

In a simple, straightforward way ERP applications help in effective SCM in two ways. Data sharing is the first. They can create opportunities to share data across SCMs, which can help managers to make better decisions. They also provide managers with a wider scope of the supply chain by making much broader information available. Real-time information is the second way. ERP systems can provide real-time information, which can be a great help in supply chain decisions. For example, ordering raw materials can be based on the inventory details provided by the ERP systems.

In short, Web-based technologies have revolutionized the way business is carried on, and SCM and ERP are no exceptions. In order to leverage the benefits offered by this new technology enabler, ERP systems are being "Web-enabled." The Internet allows linking of the Web sites to such back-end systems as ERP and provides connections to a host of external parties. The benefits of such a system are that customers have direct access to the supplier's ERP system, and the vendors can in turn provide real-time information about inventory, pricing, orders, and shipping status. As stated in the section on e-supply chain, the Internet thus provides an interface between ERP system and the supply chain members, allowing real-time flow of reliable and consistent information. To illustrate, one of the benefits of Web-enabling ERP is that it would allow customers to go online and configure their own products, get price information, and know immediately whether or not the configured product is in stock. This is possible because the customer's request is directly accessible by the ERP system of the supplier.

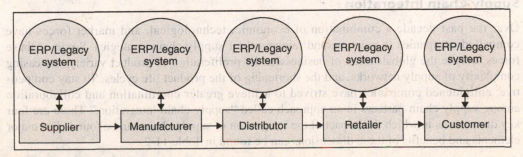

FIGURE 11-4 ERP/Legacy Systems Linkage Across the Supply Chain.

TABLE 11-1 ERP Versus SCM

Point of Comparison	ERP	SCM
Comprehensiveness	Covers a wide range of functionality	Limited to specific supply chain functionality
Complexity	Highly complex	Relatively less complex
Sourcing Tables	Relatively static	Relatively dynamic
Constraints Handling	All the demand, capacity, and material constraints are considered in isolation of each other	Simultaneous handling of the constraints
Functionality	Relatively less dynamic because they are mainly concerned with transaction processing speed and capacity	Relatively more dynamic because it performs simulations of transaction adjustments with regard to the constraints in real time
Processing Speed	Relatively slower	Faster

The differences between ERP systems (e.g., SAP, Infor, Oracle) and SCM systems (e.g., i2, Manugistics) has been subject to intense debate. One of reasons for the heated debate is that the ERP vendors are adding more SCM functionality to their products, whereas SCM vendors are also expanding their functionality, encroaching on the area handled by the ERP vendors. With the vendors of ERP systems and SCM systems adding more and more functionality, the differences between these two have been blurring. For example, major ERP vendors are introducing advanced planning and optimization as an integrated component (also a component in SCM) of their systems. Along with the current trend, it is legitimate to predict that the differences between the two solutions will be diminishing. Table 11-1 highlights the key differences between ERP and SCM systems presently available.

INTEGRATION

Integration is a broad concept that was discussed in Chapter 2. In this section, we will discuss the integration issues involved in supply chain, supply chain and ERP system, and integration of enterprise application. All of these are crucial to the success of the supply chain.

Supply Chain Integration

Over the past decade a combination of economic, technological, and market forces have compelled companies to examine and reinvent their supply chain strategies. Some of these forces include the globalization of businesses, the proliferation of product variety, increasing complexity of supply networks, and the shortening of the product life cycles. To stay competitive, enlightened companies have strived to achieve greater coordination and collaboration among supply chain partners in an approach called "supply chain integration." There are four key dimensions in which the impact of the integration of supply chain can be found. The major elements and benefits of these dimensions can be found in Table 11-2.

TABLE 11-2   Supply Chain Integration Dimensions

Dimension	Elements	Benefits
Information Integration	• Information sharing and transparency • Direct and real-time accessibility	• Reduced bullwhip effect • Early problem detection • Faster response • Trust building
Synchronized Planning	• Collaborative planning, forecasting, and replenishment • Joint design	• Reduced bullwhip effect • Lower cost • Optimized capacity utilization • Improved service
Workflow Coordination	• Coordinated production planning and operations, procurement, order processing, engineering change, and design • Integrated, automated business processes	• Efficiency and accuracy gains • Fast response • Improved service • Earlier time to market • Expanded network
New Business Models	• Virtual resources • Logistics restructuring • Mass customization • New services • Click-and-mortar models	• Better asset utilization • Higher efficiency • Penetrate new markets • Create new products

Information integration refers to the sharing of information among members of the supply chain. This includes any type of data that could influence the actions and performance of other members of the supply chain (e.g., demand data, inventory status, capacity plans, production schedules, promotion plans, and shipment schedules). Such information ideally can be accessible by the appropriate parties on a real-time, online basis without significant effort.

Planning synchronization refers to the joint design and execution of plans for product introduction, forecasting, and replenishment. In essence, planning synchronization defines *what* is to be done with the information that is shared; it is the mutual agreement among members as to specific actions based on that information. Hence, members in a supply chain may have their order fulfillment plans coordinated so that all replenishments are made to meet the same objective—the ultimate customer demands.

Workflow coordination refers to streamlined and automated workflow activities between supply chain partners. Here, *integration* means "what" we would do with shared information, as well as "how." For example, procurement activities from a manufacturer to a supplier can be tightly coupled so that efficiencies in terms of accuracy, time, and cost can be achieved. Product development activities involving multiple companies can also be integrated to achieve similar efficiencies. In the best-case situation, supply chain partners would rely on technology solutions actually to automate many or all of the internal and cross-company workflow steps.

Adopting e-Business approaches to supply chain integration promises more than just incremental improvements in efficiency. Many companies are discovering whole new approaches to conducting business, and even new business opportunities not previously possible. E-Business allows partners to redefine logistics flows so that the roles and responsibilities of members may change to improve overall supply chain efficiency. A supply chain network may jointly create new products, pursue mass customization, and penetrate new markets and customer segments. New rules of the supply chain game can emerge as a result of integration fueled by the Internet.

Integrating ERP and SCM Systems

ERP systems offer tremendous benefits by integrating functions across the organization. They help in automating the business processes and enabling reliable information capture and retrieval. SCM systems offer capabilities to integrate various entities that make up the supply chain and facilitate the seamless flow of information between all the supply chain partners. Given the intraorganizational and interorganizational advantages offered by ERP and SCM, respectively, integration of both systems can help in deriving substantial leverage and the potential of such integration is quite huge.

Integration of ERP and SCM is a very tough task because each member in the supply chain may have different hardware and software, and it is very difficult to insist that your company's supply chain partners maintain same systems. It would be ideal, however, if all the parties involved could agree up front to abide by open standards. This would help ease integration. Here are some of the approaches to integration. If the two companies want to integrate on the infrastructure level, and they happen to have the ERP system installed, then the process would be to have the ERP systems of the supply chain partners interlinked to each other directly to enable a seamless flow of real-time information. This might be possible when the ERP systems are sophisticated enough to include the necessary functionality to support SCM (interenterprise integration). If all systems use the same operating platform (or the same vendor's product), then the integration of the systems would be easy. If they are different, however, the necessary middleware software would have to be developed that could enable connectivity and integration of the disparate systems so that there would be a consistent and seamless information flow. If the integration of the supply chain is achieved by linking the ERP and SCM systems, then this integration could be viewed as a way to capitalize on the strengths of the two systems (i.e., ERP and SCM). For this purpose, sophisticated middleware interface software, which enables sharing of data and processes, are used to help in building up the linkage between ERP and SCM systems, specifically at the point where they have overlapping features. For example, i2 technology uses SAP's *ALE*™ (Application Link Enabling) to exchange data between SAP R3 and its SCM product, *Rhythm*™. There are also some specialized software called specialized integration software, which allow ERP and other systems to share processes and data. This software allows integration by simply choosing the sending application (e.g., SAP, Baan) and a receiving application (like Rhythm, Manugistics) and the process to be linked.

Enterprise Application Integration

Enterprise application integration (EAI) facilitates the flow of information and straps transactions among disparate and complex applications and business processes within and among the organizations. With the move toward market globalization, there have been mergers and acquisitions at a phenomenal pace. EAI has become an essential component for an organization to share data and business logic with its business partners within the supply chain. As IT aims to provide companies with a competitive edge, several factors can slow down its effectiveness. The move from the traditional brick-and-mortar operations to more sophisticated processes, along with the repercussions of mergers and acquisitions, makes it a necessity to respond to the ever-changing market demands. Application integration has become essential for a company's success in today's economy.

A standard EAI system provides a broad range of services that range from security management to protocol management to data mapping, among other related functions. These services define the functionality and flow of data in the application. EAI solutions can benefit an organization by providing end-to-end visibility and control of business operations. This control improves interactions with partners and customers, increases responsiveness to business changes, enables new market opportunities, and makes captured knowledge more widely available. Companies need integration that can be set up, taken down, and changed quickly, and that can work with a variety of partners, systems, and rapidly changing technologies. In case of application-integration, the focus lies largely on integrating one production application with the other, for EAI middleware is implemented in the form of connectors that handle data transformation and business logic with such outside systems as the ERP (i.e., SAP, PeopleSoft), Database (i.e., DB2, MS SQL Server, Oracle), Message Queuing (i.e., Mqseries, MSMQ), and the like.

As stated, integrating disparate systems is a very complex task. In the past application integration was a rare achievement and was restricted to a simple exchange of data. EAI requires a whole new approach to integration. The old approach involved building custom point-to-point integration one application at a time. This cannot meet the demands of the Internet economy, wherein companies need to integrate their business processes quickly with dozens, even hundreds, of other companies. Today, with the introduction of such component-based models as EJB, DCOM, and CORBA, it has become relatively easier to provide software applications as congregations of stand-alone and independent business components that communicate with the business processes through a standard set of APIs.

Many of the companies today are embracing the component-based applications. This is either by developing a new application or by componentizing their existing applications. The component approach involves splitting up the colossal applications into an assembly of numerous independent business components. DCOM and CORBA/IIOP are the two main protocols for object communication across networks, including the Internet. Both are platform independent programming models that support compatibility between applications in a complex system. DCOM is used for Windows-based applications, and CORBA is found on many platforms. Simple object access protocol (SOAP) is a communication protocol that defines a new way for processes on different systems to communicate, the heart of which is the extensible mark-up language. XML has emerged as the leading business-to-business integration and enterprise application candidate. XML is fast becoming the unifier among integrated systems.

Phases of Enterprise Application Integration Process

There are several phases of an EAI process, including the following:

- Solution outline phase
- Architecture phase
- Design phase
- Implementation phase

The end result of this process is a consolidated, consistent, and coherent view of the vital information that's accessible from multiple points across the enterprise.

Benefits of Enterprise Application Integration

EAI provides advantages through uniting disparate applications, reducing redundant data entry, merging diverse data sets, and reducing transaction costs. EAI proves beneficial to businesses for a number of reasons:

- *Increased efficiency:* The ability to automate business processes across the enterprise and across existing boundaries.
- *Value of information:* Redundant databases are aligned, eliminating duplicate data.
- *Lower costs:* The EAI strategy is to create one interface per application. This lowers the cost of upgrades or modifications/additions to applications.
- *Increased productivity:* Results from business process automation and access to real-time information.
- *Improved customer service:* Customer service employees have improved real-time access to give accurate information to customers.
- *Enhanced access:* EAI increases the ability to extend applications to more users from anywhere and anytime over the virtual private networks.

The integration of applications is compelled by the Internet and the need to connect interorganizational systems with customers, suppliers, collaborators, and partners of all sorts within the supply chain.

RFID

Radio **F**requency **ID**entification, or RFID, has been around since the 1950s. RFID is a small microchip (or tag as it is commonly referred to) that sends/receives data via radio waves sent on specific frequencies. Current RFID tags are less than half the size of a tictac. RFID has capabilities to speed updated information from a sales floor inventory to a CEO's reports in a matter of seconds. From detecting product shrinkage in real time to restocking shelves, the possibilities for this technology are almost endless. Many companies have already begun to implement RFID into their corporate structure; however, with the technology still being in its developmental infancy stage, the end result possibilities are yet to be imagined. Even though the technology is 50+ years old, it has never recognized its potential until recent years. We will discuss how RFID relates to ERP implementation, data accuracy, data timeliness, supply chain management, report structuring, and business process reengineering. One of the world's leading users of RFID technology is Wal-Mart. Wal-Mart's CIO Rollin Ford has been quoted as describing their stance on RFID as "bullish" ("Wal-Mart CIO Still 'Bullish' on RFID"). Wal-Mart is a primary reason why this technology is beginning to realize its real value.

RFID is Catching on

RFID is not the magical "do anything" technology many have made it out to be. RFID is an enabling technology that gives and ERP the means to communicate with itself. This allows for real-time automation of many data collection functions originally conducted by paid employees. The labor savings, which we will discuss first, is only a small portion of the savings realized via RFID.

Imagine you are a manager for a popular chain clothing store located in a mall. It is the last day of the month, and it is time to take an inventory. Inventory is taken only twice per month. The store closes and 10 employees begin working, counting every single article of clothing inside the store. It may take these 10 employees 5 hours or more to count every item in the store.

Assume 10 employees, for 5 hours, at $15.00/hr (overtime), that is, $18,000.00 per year in labor just to count inventory. Imagine this same scenario except that the store is using RFID combined with their ERP, that is $ 0.00 in labor, and the inventory is checked constantly with perfect accuracy. At the end of every night, every person in the chain of command has an exact count of inventories. This information will be automatically sent to marketing so they can consider what items they may want to put on sale. The information will be sent to the supply warehouses and a reorder will automatically be generated for the shelves. This streamlines the supply chain removing lag time and human error, all the while accounting for shrinkage. This information will be automatically generated into reports to be waiting in the inbox of regional managers first thing in the morning. Employees across the entire company, from the top of the pyramid to the bottom, can use this information.

RFID Technology

"RFID is a very complicated and costly technology"[8] and will thus increase the initial challenge and cost of a successful ERP implementation. If an organization decides RFID is a technology they wish to explore, this will help narrow the field of optional vendors in which they begin their ERP purchase search. Both hardware and software much be considered.

Hardware. Although the technology has been around for over 30 years, there are no "off the shelf" hardware packages. Each hardware implementation will need to be designed specifically to meet the needs of purchaser. Choosing a vendor with extensive RFID experience will be a critical choice to the success of the ERP. Tags range from passive to active, single unique identifier to writable, and come in sizes in shapes ranging from the tiny and round to the big and flat. Tag readers can be mounted just about anywhere: in a doorway, to a pallet jack, on a ceiling, in a shelf, or carried in a hand. Depending on the reader and tag they can read at distances of up to 300 feet.

Software. Unlike the hardware, software will be much easier to design. There are even cases where a near vanilla implementation would be sufficient. This would be great cost savings if possible. RFID, as far as the ERP is concerned, will be just another interface device.

Data Accuracy and Timeliness

As shown in the earlier example of Zara, Inc. a clothing store, data are only as accurate as the device collecting and entering the data. In most historical cases, a human is part of that device to collect and enter data. With a human doing the operational steps of collecting and entering data, you have a minimum of three places an error and/or retardation of the data can occur:

1. Physical counting of the data
2. Writing down of the data collected
3. Typing the data into ERP

Changing any process where these steps occur to automated RFID data collection will eliminate the possibility of human error. Data can be collected instantaneously and with 100 percent accuracy. RFID is so accurate and current; the clothing store would be able to view shrinkage as it is

---

[8] Chuang, M. L. and Shaw, W. H. (2008). An Empirical Study of Enterprise Resource Management Systems Implementation. *Business Process Management Journal,* 14 (5), 675, Print.

happening. In sum, RFID is a growing technology that has yet to see its full potential. With industries consistently driving to cut labor costs and increase speed and accuracy of data flow, not implementing an applicable ERP RFID solution is money being lost. The data generated from a RFID system are immense; ERP increases the speed and accuracy with which these data can be useful for business decisions.

IMPLICATIONS FOR MANAGEMENT

Managers should understand that SCM is an important component for the successful implementation of ERP systems. It does not matter whether SCM is an external or internal component of ERP as long as there is seamless integration between the two applications.

Balancing the supply chain efficiency and responsiveness is more an art than science. The competitiveness of products and services in the global economy is increasingly measured both by individual product or service characteristics and by the efficiency and responsiveness of the supply chain of products and services in catering to differentiated customer requirements. In the face of shrinking product life cycles, differentiation and diversification of customer requirements, and cost transparency and accountability, there is constant focus on supply chain efficiency and responsiveness. For supply chain managers, this translates to a need for managing and monitoring the partnerships in the supply chain with a strategic view to sense opportunities for improvement and growth. This also translates operationally to the need for balancing customer service requirements with the costs of operating the supply chain. SCM are complex systems whose success often depends on external environment. These systems need to be integrated or linked with the systems of a company's trading partners, suppliers, clients, and other external sources. The success of the system often depends more on standardization and agreed policy between trading partners rather than on sophisticated information technology. Management emphasis for IT departments should be on collaborative design rather than on a stand-alone design for SCM systems.

E-supply chain provides great competitive advantage in today's Web-enabled economy. High-speed, low-cost, communication and collaboration with customers and suppliers are critical success factors to managing the supply chain more effectively. The very essence of SCM is effective information and material flow throughout a network of customers and suppliers. The potential of e-supply chain for improved productivity, cost reduction, and customer service are enormous. Of course, the benefits are based on effectively employing the right processes and supporting IT. Providing the right amount of relevant information to those who need to know it, and when they need to know it, is in fact effective SCM from information point of view. Fast access to relevant supply chain information can pay off remarkably in lower costs, reduced inventory, higher-quality decision making, shorter cycle times, and better customer service. One of the biggest cost savings is in the overhead activity associated with a lot of paperwork and its inherent redundancies. The non–value-added time of manual transaction processing can instead be focused on higher revenue creation activities without proportional increases in expense. The result in cycle time compression, lower inventories, decision-making quality, and reduced overhead costs, among other benefits, makes e-SCM a highly desirable strategy. Supply chain processes are more streamlined and efficient today. For many companies, more effective e-SCM is where the profit and competitive advantages will emerge and be sustained. For e-commerce to be successful, efficient fulfillment of orders and good customer service are extremely important. E-SCM systems are critical components for serving better back-end business processes in e-Business. Companies similarly will not be able to develop good B2B operations with their business partners without a good SCM platform. Even companies that do not have online stores need an efficient e-SCM for their B2B operations, as well as for their intranet applications (e.g., warehouse management systems) that work hand-in-hand with the e-SCM system.

Integrating is the key issue to the successfulness of the supply chain. Integration must occur at multiple levels, and not just at the network or hardware platform level. An important aspect of integration is sharing and access. For integration to be successful, organizations must become comfortable with the idea of sharing critical information with their partners, and they must be willing to provide proper access to sensitive information. This can be a double-edged sword because sharing could potentially make the organization less competitive, and more access also means less security for the organization's information. Each organization will have its comfort level, depending on the industry, culture, and other environmental factors. Management will need to find a "sweet-spot" for their company. Finally, instead of just thinking about integrating ERP and SCM, management needs to think of enterprise application integration.

Summary

- Supply chain management (SCM) is a central piece of technology in today's enterprise system. They are interorganizational systems that provide an efficient and flexible operational environment between the company, its external partners, and suppliers, thereby saving millions of dollars in manufacturing and distribution costs.

- SCM provides a link for services, materials, and information across the value chain of the organization. It plays a major role in logistics management, procurement, and collaboration activities among others in the organization. The SCM strategy of the organization must be aligned with the corporate strategy of the organization; otherwise, the consequences will not be good for the company.

- ERP vendors have started including SCM as a component or module of the software. SCM was traditionally not part of ERP because the domain of SCM was to link the company with external partners, whereas the focus of ERP was mainly on the internal functions of the company.

- There are four main drivers for the SCM system performance: *facilities*, from which the product or service is delivered; *inventory* (i.e., the product or service that need to be distributed or procured with the external partners); *transportation*, which moves the product or service between two points of the supply chain; and *information*, which stores data and analysis of the other three drivers. Information is the most powerful driver for SCM performance.

- SCM involves the operation or management of many organizations' processes and procedures. They include procurement, outsourcing, manufacturing flow management, order fulfillment, customer service, and forecasting. The scope depends on the implementation of SCM in the organization.

- SCM plays a major role in the success of e-Business and e-commerce. Without a good SCM, an organization will not be able to build B2B partnerships with its trading partners, work on e-procurement from suppliers, and have proper e-fulfillment of client orders. A strong SCM implementation is necessary for e-Business.

- A good SCM is designed in collaboration with the organizations' partners rather than stand alone. SCM development should focus on standardized technology rather than sophisticated technology. Success is dependent more on agreed policy and standards with other trading partners.

- Integration with SCM system is of many types (e.g., supply chain, ERP system, and enterprise application). In addition, there are four levels of integration. Integration has to occur at the information-sharing level, at the design and planning level, at the workflow collaboration level, and at the new product development cycle.

- Enterprise application integration process is very complex and has a multiphase life cycle. If done correctly, it can produce a consolidated, consistent, and coherent view of critical information from anywhere and at anytime, with authorized access to different users in the organization. EAI has tremendous long-term benefits to the organization, including improved efficiency and increased productivity at cost reductions.

Exercises

1. Your boss is interested in purchasing SCM software and has requested that you find out about the major SCM systems and the vendors. Write a two-page report with a short summary and a table of SCM systems, vendor names, major functionality or features of the software, key clients, licensing cost, support and upgrade policy, and so on. Rank the SCM system or vendor in terms of size and popularity.

2. Locate a company that you know or work at and find out the details of the SCM system used in this company. Your survey could include questions on the SCM drivers for this company, the vendor used, components, benefits and drawbacks, and the level of integration between SCM and ERP or EAI at this company. Write a two-page report summarizing your findings as well as providing recommendations for improvement.

Review Questions

1. What are the motivations for an organization to have a good supply chain management (SCM) system?
2. Define SCM in your own words.
3. List the four drivers of SCM and how they impact the system's responsiveness.
4. What are the major types of SCM software?
5. Briefly describe the SCM processes.

6. Why is SCM implementation critical for the success of e-Business?
7. What are the major components of e-SCM?
8. What is e-procurement?
9. How should organizations design SCM systems? Stand alone or collaborative?
10. What are the elements and benefits of SCM integration?

Discussion Questions

1. Discuss the relationship between a company's supply chain strategy and competitive strategy.
2. Discuss the role and flow of SCM software.
3. Which SCM process according to you is most critical? Explain why.
4. Discuss the role of SCM in e-Business and e-commerce.

5. Discuss the differences between e-procurement and e-fulfillment.
6. Discuss the critical components in design of SCM systems.
7. How is EAI different from the integration of SCM and ERP systems? Explain.

CASE 11-2
Real-World Cases
Zara and the Limited Brands

CASE 1: ZARA

Source: Based on: Zara: Taking the Lead in Fast-Fashion, Rachel Tiplady, *BusinessweekOnline*, April 4, 2006.

Zara is the flagship brand of the Spanish retail group, Inditex, one of the superstars in the fashion retail industry in recent years. In 2005, Inditex reported 21 percent sales growth to $8.51 billion. That puts Inditex ahead of H&M, the world-leading purveyor of cheap-chic apparel, which posted $7.87 billion in sales. Zara has more than 1,000 stores in 31 countries. The fashion industry is a special industry. The products they deal with are highly perishable, and they are susceptible to seasons—gross margin is meaningless if the product does not sell as planned. For many retailers, 35–40 percent of the total merchandise being sold at hefty discount is quite the norm.

Zara contributes around 80 percent of group sales by concentrating on three winning formulas on which to base its fresh fashions: *short lead time, lower quantities,* and *more styles.* With an in-house design team based in La Coruna, Spain, and a tightly controlled factory and distribution network, the company says it can take a design from drawing board to store shelf in just two weeks. That lets Zara introduce new items every week, which keeps customers coming back again and again to check out the latest styles. With new styles being developed and introduced frequently, each style would provide only around $200,000–$300,000 of retail sales, a far lower figure than those other retailers or brands, and certainly not "cost-efficient" in terms of design and product development cost. Moreover, Zara's success is all the more surprising because at least half of its factories are in Europe, where wages are many times higher than those in Asia and Africa. To maintain its quick inventory turnover, however, the company must reduce shipping time to a minimum. The fast-fashion approach also helps Zara reduce its exposure to fashion faux pas. The company produces batches of clothing in such small quantities that even if it brings out a design that no one will buy, which happened during an unseasonably warm autumn in 2003, it can cut its losses quickly and move on to another trend. This higher cost of product development, however, is obviously more than adequately compensated by higher realized margins. The result is that Zara discounts only about 18 percent of its product, which is roughly half the level of competitors.

Information and communications technology is at the heart of Zara's business supply chain. Zara's quick response to the market and its high speed from design table to store shelf are enabled through four critical information-related areas.

The first is constant collection of information on customer needs. Trend information flows daily and is in turn fed into the database at the company's head office. Zara outfits its store clerks with handheld computers to record sales and customer comments and then integrates the collected data with design, manufacturing, and distribution functions. Designers check the database for these dispatches as well as daily sales numbers, using the information to create new lines and modify existing ones. Thus, designers have access to real-time information when deciding with the commercial team on the

(continued)

fabric, cut, and price points of a new garment. As a result, the company can spot trends early on—a rather critical quantity in fashion retailing—and adjust stock accordingly within days.

The second area is standardization of product information. Different or incomplete specifications and varying product information availability normally add several weeks to a typical retailer's product design and approval process. Zara, however, stored the product information with common definitions, allowing it to prepare designs quickly and accurately, with clear-cut manufacturing instructions.

The third area is product and inventory management. Its inventory management system is able to manage thousands of fabric and trim specifications, design specifications, and physical inventory, which gives Zara's team the capability to design a garment with available stocks, rather than having to order material and wait for it to arrive.

Zara's distribution management approach is its final advantage. Its state-of-the-art distribution facility functions with minimal human intervention. Approximately 200 kilometers of underground tracks move merchandise from Zara's manufacturing plants to the 400-plus chutes that ensure that each order reaches its right destination. Optical reading devices sort out and distribute more than 60,000 items of clothing in an hour. Zara's merchandise does not waste time waiting for human sorting.

CASE 2: THE LIMITED BRANDS

Source: Based on: The Limited Designs Supply Chain to Begin and End with the Customer, *Baseline Magazine*, April 3, 2006.

Founded in 1968, Limited Brands now is the holding company of Victoria's Secret, Express, Bath & Body Works, C.O. Bigelow, The Limited, White Barn Candle, and Henri Bendel. In 2005, the annual sales of Limited Brands reached $9.4 billion. Limited Brands achieved its expansion of brand and growth on the sales and market over the years through the active acquisitions of different retail companies. As the result of acquiring so many stores and brands, Limited inherited a complex hodgepodge of IT systems and software, including 60 major systems running hundreds of applications, many of them redundant, on numerous platforms. Many of these platforms (e.g., Hewlett-Packard HP-UX, Sun Microsystems Solaris, and IBM OS/390 and AS/400, as well as Intel-based servers and Tandem computers) are still in place today. Given the complexity of the company's IT operations, Limited's ability to stay on top of its supply and demand chains was going to be a challenge.

The situation became acute beginning in 2001. Discount retailers started encroaching on Limited's market space. In response, the company began shifting to a high-end product line that would generate better profit margins. To make this new strategy work, however, Limited needed new supply chain technologies and processes to drive the speed-to-market requirements of the new growth strategy—what Leonard A. Schlesinger, Limited's vice chairman and chief operating officer and a former Harvard Business School professor, has described as "integrated brand delivery" (i.e., integrating and leveraging the supply chain and logistics supporting a brand for maximum value).

Limited Brands buys merchandise from more than 1,000 suppliers worldwide and sells through multiple channels retail stores, the Internet, catalogs, and third parties. An enterprisewide view is critical in dealing with supply chain efforts. For an organization to make such a transition is difficult from a number of perspectives.

Indeed, when Limited Logistics Services (LLS), which supplies global logistics management and leadership in support of the supply chains used by Limited's brands, initially tried to integrate the far-flung supply chain logistics operations of Victoria's Secret, Bath & Body Works, and the like, it ran into strong pushback from brand executives. It was only after the brand managers saw retail sales increase and the time needed to get products to market reduced by as much as 10 days as the result of the effort—and COO Schlesinger began pushing the initiative—that brand executives got with the program.

Limited has worked with a lot of vendors on supply chain–related software projects, including Tibco Software, which develops business integration packages. Limited brought in Tibco to build a global application integration platform to track and manage the flow of information better as it moves through a supply chain that extended around the globe. As a first step, vendor and client went through an assessment phase beginning with business processes. Using Tibco's business integration software, Limited partnered with Tibco to establish real-time reporting and communications with delivery agents and to integrate Limited's outbound supply chain accountability and reporting (OSCAR) applications with its logistics applications. Limited stated in 2004 that as many as 45 delivery agents will be integrated into OSCAR, which aids with merchandise flow, data control, and data facilitation.

Limited has now managed to consolidate its technology operations into a single shared service for all of its brands. This is operated centrally by Limited Technology Services, a subsidiary company run by CIO Jon Ricker. It employs some 750 IT professionals and has an annual budget of approximately $150 million; however, there is still an enormous amount of work to be done before the overhaul is completed. What should Jon Ricker do?

CASE QUESTIONS

1. Discuss the role of SCM in retail industry. Give examples from the two cases.
2. Is Zara's competitive strategy aligned with supply chain strategy? Explain.
3. Discuss the role of Zara's SCM system. Suggest how it can be improved.
4. Discuss briefly the supply chain problems faced by The Limited.
5. Is "integrated brand delivery" a correct SCM strategy for The Limited? Explain.

APPENDIX A

This shows the benefits of RFID to the ERP at different levels of the pyramid.

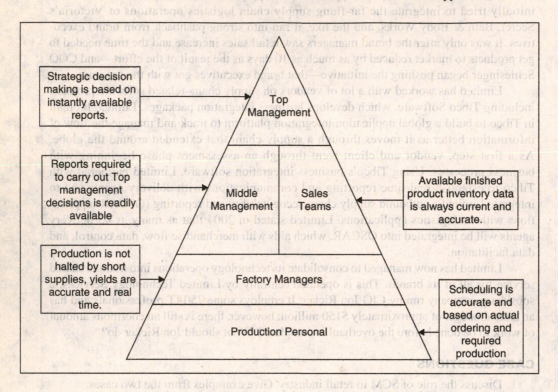

12

Customer Relationship Management

LEARNING OBJECTIVES

After reading this chapter, you should be able to:

- Understand the customer relationship process.
- Know the evolution, current status, and categories of the customer relationship management (CRM) system.
- Understand the components and architecture of CRM systems.
- Examine the CRM life cycle and its relationship with other enterprise software.
- Examine the impact of CRM on an organization.

CASE 12-1
Opening Case
Walt Disney's CRM Strategy

Source: Based on article by D'Agostino, D. (December 1, 2003). Case Study: Walt Disney World Resorts and CRM Strategy, *CIO Insight*. www.cioinsight.com/print_article2/0,1217,a=114960,00.asp

Disney was founded on October 16, 1923. The company presently has a wide portfolio of businesses, ranging from film to animation, theme parks, distribution, retail, television, music, and almost every aspect of the entertainment industry. Their commitment to entertainment has made them one of the leading and arguably the most popular entertainment companies in the world. Disney's total revenue for 2005 was $32 billion, and they currently employ 133,000 full-time employees worldwide, with significantly more part time. Disney currently has approximately 100 million people per year visit their stores and theme parks across the globe.

In order to improve the customer experience at Disney while simultaneously lowering the customer service cost, Disney is integrating such cutting-edge information technologies as the Internet, customer relationship management (CRM), and mobile connectivity. One example of this technology leveraging is Destination Disney. Disney experienced data issues that would make simple tasks such as tracking repeat customers while visiting their parks. Disney wants all the data accessible in real time to track the individual customer's buying behavior and personal preferences to be able to create easy-to-book Web sites for groups of people to plan their Disney activities.

Another example is the creation of a mobile CRM device called "Pal Mickey," a 10½-inch-tall stuffed doll with a central processing unit, an internal clock, small speakers, and a powerful infrared sensor in its nose. Disney park visitors are often frustrated with long lines and crowds at the amusement parks after paying a high entrance fees. Pal Mickey acts as a virtual tour guide, providing tips on which rides have the shortest lines and information on events. As the doll moves through the park, the sensor receives a wireless data upload from one of the 500 infrared beacons concealed in park lampposts, rooftops, and bushes that transmit location-centric information from a Disney data center. The signals let Pal Mickey know when to inform the owner of an event. For example, when it receives a new piece of information from a nearby beacon, it giggles and vibrates to indicate that it has something new to say. Squeeze its hand or stomach and Pal Mickey will tell you about an upcoming parade, a shorter line at another ride, or trivia on the current location of the park. With more than 700 prerecorded message variations, Pal Mickey always has something to say, whether it's telling a child a corny joke or keeping kids entertained with interactive games while they wait in line.

Pal Mickey is an example of bridging the gap between static customer support and dynamic customer support based on the customers' behavioral preferences, physical location, and movements at any given time. In other words, it's all about "dynamically matching data with context—a new concept and the next big development in the evolution of CRM," in the view of futurist Paul Saffo, research director of the Institute for the Future in Menlo Park, California, a technology think tank. Another futurist and business strategy guru, C.K. Prahalad, the Harvey C. Fruehauf Professor of Business Administration at the University of Michigan Business School and coauthor of *The Future of Competition* (Harvard Business School Press), agrees: "Disney is experimenting with a customer strategy

(continued)

that goes beyond today's CRM," he said, "using not just the data, but data in the context of individual customer behavior."

Due to technical and other problems, Disney has discontinued Pal Mickey since 2008 but supports customers who own a Pal Mickey and bring it to their theme parks. However, Disney has developed two new CRM applications recently, "Mobile Magic" with Verizon Wireless phones and several others with Apple's iPhone. These applications provide guests access to real-time park information similar to the Pal Mickey. Mobile Magic allows you access to real-time information on wait times for rides, return times for "fast pass" (which is another technology that prints a ride-specific card with a time on it when the guest can come back and wait in an express line), and information on character locations. This application also includes a GPS-enabled mobile map, which shows you your current location while you are wandering the theme parks. You can scroll through an extensive list of locations and easily route to any location you choose whether it be a character greeting or a short line for a ride that you found on the application or directions to a dinner you have reservations for in the park. The Apple iPhone applications include the following: (1) The "Walt Disney World Maps" application contains full-size maps for the Magic Kingdom, Epcot, and other Disney theme parks in Orlando. For each map, you can look for individual rides or attractions and make a schedule of the things you want to visit. You can also find your location on the map; (2) the "Disney World Dining," which includes full menus for all 160 restaurants and also locates the restaurants closest to you, with one-touch dialing for the Disney dining reservations number; and (3) several others such as the "Disney World Park Hours," "Disney World Notescast," "Disney World Wait Times Free," and "Mouse Memo." The appendix at the end of this chapter provides more details on these iPhone applications. Disney also relies on its guests to provide real-time updates to things like the wait times for rides, which really creates a network of people who are users and updaters of the applications.

What do you think about Disney's CRM strategy? Will Pal Mickey and newer mobile phone applications enhance the customer experience? Why?

PREVIEW

Disney's CRM strategy is methodical, logical, and organized. Business strategy plays a very important role in any CRM implementation. A good strategy coupled with a well-defined set of requirements, identification of key success factors, and good partnerships will usually lead to success in CRM technology. Disney's goal is to reduce the hassle for visitors to the park by creating a more personalized environment, with IT at the core. According to Disney CIO Russ Berry, "The role of IT is changing. It's not simply an organization that deploys technology, but one that now integrates technology from a lot of different angles to improve the customer experience." The complexity of implementing a CRM system in a company like Disney is to be able to adapt to the changing requirements of the customers during the implementation of a system. The implementation alone can take years for a project with as wide a scope and expectations of what this system will mean to Disney.

CRM focus should always be on customer experience. Because customer expectations often change, it is important for the company to understand that CRM implementation needs to be *customer driven* more than *technology driven*. That is, CRM implementation must involve people, process, and systems, rather than just a narrowly defined IT application. Investments in CRM technology that are technology driven have not been very profitable. In 2003, Gartner Group published a report stating that 75 percent of all CRM initiatives fail overall. Another report from Forrester Research also indicated that CRM spending was more than $13 billion in 2005, with less than half of all purchasers of CRM satisfied that their CRM systems achieved the business benefits they had expected. "Achieving positive ROI for CRM initiatives has often been a difficult task," said Bruce Culbert, cofounder and executive director of BPT Partners.[1]

This chapter will provide an overview of CRM systems, their evolution, and the types of CRM. In addition, it will discuss the customer relationship function and processes, the CRM technology, and the implementation life cycle of CRM. The chapter will conclude with the implications of CRM technology on management.

WHAT IS CRM?

When the term *customer relationship management* is mentioned, it automatically brings to mind such well-known software vendors as Siebel and Salesforce.com. In fact, CRM is much more than the software utilized to store, analyze, and manage customer relationships. A true CRM integrates corporate strategy, business methodology, and technology to accomplish a myriad of goals for companies that want to operate in a customer-driven environment. For example, Pal Mickey integrates with Disney's customer-driven strategy by providing real-time interaction with the customer and being responsive to their needs for quick information. It also solves the problem during peak loads when Disney employees cannot provide quick and accurate information. CRM as a concept is as old as business itself. No business can survive without understanding its customers and having a positive relationship with them. CRM provides support for the front-end customer facing functionality (e.g., marketing, sales, and customer service), which are usually not available in traditional ERP systems. Even though the ERP system focus is more on providing systems support for employees and business partners of an organization, the CRM system focus is on supporting the requirements of customers and clients of the organization. As seen in the Disney case, CRM's role is to improve the customer experience, thereby increasing revenues of the organization.

CRM Evolution

In the 1980s and through the mid-1990s, companies started using IT to automate customer processes with discrete customer-centric applications (e.g., sales force automation (SFA) for managing prospects and sales activities, customer center support systems for complaint management, and marketing automation for advertising campaigns and customer segmentation). In the late 1990s, companies began to take a full 360-degree view of a customer, as shown in Figure 12-1, and they started integrating these discrete systems into what is now known as CRM.

CRM began in response to a changing market environment as mass marketing gave way to focused segment marketing and finally to target marketing an individual. Mass marketing techniques presented one message to a wide and varied base and relied upon the notion that the more frequently you presented messages to the consumer, the greater odds you have of piquing the interest of a new or existing customer. As media proliferated and multiplied, mass marketing proved expensive, and measuring return on advertising dollars was ambiguous at best.

---

[1] RWD Technologies and BPT. (October 7, 2005). Partners Align Forces to Revolutionize Return on Investment in the CRM Industry. *CRM Today.* www.crm2day.com/news/printnews.php?id=115828 (accessed November 2005).

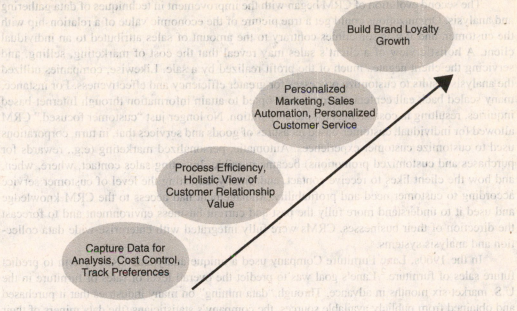

FIGURE 12-1   Evolution of CRM Programs

Enabled by new technologies that collected consumer data, companies progressed to focused segment marketing. Such tools as preference and satisfaction surveys, demographic collection, focus group data, and point-of-sales collection technology gave industry a better glimpse at why a customer purchased certain services and goods, along with the relative satisfaction level or impression he or she had with a company or brand. This turned the tide in marketing, manufacturing, operations, and customer service as all industries relied upon customers to dictate the product and not internal forces. By using technology to analyze consumer data, companies have found that incremental sales to loyal, repeat customers (i.e., existing customers) is much more profitable than acquiring new customers. This shifted the emphasis on maximizing the customer's experience with the brand and spawned the customer relationship discipline that gave way to CRM software.

The expectations of a CRM system have evolved over time. Organizations first implemented CRM to capture customer data for analysis to find out what aspects of their goods and services are important to their clients. A customer file is started from an initial point of marketing contact, whether it originated with a phone call inquiry to customer service before a sale, a purchased lead generation list service, a request for literature, an organized event, or a completed warranty or registration form. The software can track all aspects of sales from lead source tracking to meetings with a sales representative, thereby automating the sales process. After a sale, such customer service and support activity as complaint resolution or satisfaction feedback is captured. Each point of contact with an individual customer can be recorded as they conduct business with a company. This allows development of a business process across marketing, sales, and customer service. One limitation of this first-generation CRM was that this information did not filter to the management level. There was no corporate-wide sharing of customer experiences and adjustments of corporate strategy or tactic based on the CRM knowledge.

The second evolution of CRM began with the improvement in techniques of data gathering and analysis. Organizations could get a true picture of the economic value of a relationship with the customer, and it was sometimes contrary to the amount of sales attributed to an individual client. A holistic view of a client's sales may reveal that the cost of marketing, selling, and servicing the client negates much of the profit realized by a sale. Likewise, companies utilized the analysis results to customize processes for greater efficiency and effectiveness. For instance, many scaled back call centers, as consumers opted to attain information through Internet-based inquiries, resulting in cost savings for the corporation. No longer just "customer focused," CRM allowed for individual, customer-based measures of goods and services that, in turn, corporations used to customize customer experiences. Automatic, personalized marketing (e.g., rewards for purchases and customized promotions) became possible. Initiating sales contact, where, when, and how the client likes to receive contact, and, finally, adjusting the level of customer service according to customer need and profitability. Management had access to the CRM knowledge and used it to understand more fully the past and current business environment and to forecast the direction of their businesses. CRMs were fully integrated with enterprise-wide data collection and analysis systems.

In the 1960s, Lane Furniture Company used a unique analytical CRM system to predict future sales of furniture.[2] Lane's goal was to predict the overall level of sales of furniture in the U.S. market six months in advance. Through "data mining" on many industries that it purchased and obtained from publicly available sources, the company's statisticians (the data miners of their day) figured out that the strongest predictor of furniture sales six months in the future was the current month's national, regional, and local new car sales figures. The relationship was a negative one (i.e., the lower the car sales were for the current month, the higher furniture sales would be in six months). Armed with this analysis, Lane consistently made the right decisions on their furniture inventory and when to advertise to a receptive market. Lane used data from their CRM system, broadly defined as a predictive tool that gave it an "insight advantage" over their competitors.

CRMs have also triggered consumer advocates due to the fine line crossed by these systems on individual privacy. Profiling customers often involves data collection and close observation that create a feeling of "Big Brother is watching." Recent Internet technologies have become very intrusive in collecting data without consumer knowledge. CRMs indirectly encourage this behavior of collecting and tracking customers as they navigate through various software and Web sites. On one hand, tracking and profiling are the key tools for effective CRM; on the other, they create various negative feelings on the company image and brand in the mind of customers. A good CRM strategy should therefore incorporate the privacy and ethical principles discussed in Chapter 10.

CRM Today

CRM software is continuously evolving. Globalization and ubiquitous connectivity are forcing companies to reevaluate how to deliver value to customers. Globalization has leveled the playing field for large and small companies to deliver similar products at low cost with an abundance of options for customers. A Web-surfing customer today has much more bargaining power with the help of the Internet and can change a vendor any time with a click of a button. To be successful in this competitive environment, companies have to deliver both quality products and unique and

---

[2] Stanton, A., and Rubenstein, H. (2005). The Discipline of CRM. www.CRMGuru.com (accessed December 15, 2006).

dynamic experiences for the customer depending on his or her current "context" or the customer's precise physical location, time, and needs,[3] as shown earlier in the Disney case.

Companies that have realized the tactical value of CRM (i.e., reducing costs, improving process and communication, and managing customers) are discovering that CRM can also yield strategic value for a corporation. According to Montgomery Research, Inc.,[4] there is a shift in CRM focus from cost reduction to building brand loyalty and growth. The information collected and analyzed in a CRM program can be used to create a unique branded experience for each client. The theory is, if you can create a unique and meaningful experience for your customer, they will remain loyal to your brand, which will, in turn, increase sales. A study by Gartner Research[5] predicts double-digit increases, between 9 and 11 percent, in CRM software sales until the next decade.

Types of CRM

Various criteria can be used to categorize CRM systems. From a functionality perspective there are two types of CRMs: one related to customer service or support and the other to sales force automation. From a business strategy perspective, CRM systems can be categorized by three complementary perspectives, as shown in Table 12-1. Finally, from an implementation perspective, CRM systems can be operational, analytical, and collaborative.[6]

OPERATIONAL CRM   Operational CRM systems provide front- and back-end support for sales and marketing, administrative personnel, or customer service processes. They improve

---

TABLE 12-1 Business Strategy Perspective of CRM[7]

Business
- promotes customer-centric approach
- customer segmenting
- one-on-one marketing
- increase customer retention

Technology
- foster close customer relationship
- analyze customer information
- coherent view of customer

Customer
- increased interaction opportunity
- increase customer loyalty
- better "word-of-mouth" advertising

---

[3] Prahalad, C. K., and Ramaswamy, V. (2004). *The Future of Competition: Co-Creating Unique Value with Customers.* Cambridge, MA: Harvard Business School Press.

[4] The CRM Evolution Continues. (2006). From Relationship Management to Experience Management, Montgomery Research Inc., San Francisco, CA. www.crmproject.com/documents.asp?d_ID=3780

[5] Flinders, K. (September 18, 2006). Gartner Predicts Steady Rise in CRM Market. *MicroScope,* 6.

[6] Shahnam, E. The Customer Relationship Management Ecosystem. *Application Delivery Strategies Delta 724.* www.metagroup.com/communities/crm/ads724.htm (accessed November 17, 2003).

[7] Teo, T., Devadoss, P., and Pan, S. (2006). Towards a Holistic Perspective of CRM implementation: A Case Study of HDB, Singapore. *Decision Support Systems,* 42, 1613–1627.

the efficiency of CRM delivery and support processes. They are often embedded in campaign management and customer help desks. They are integrated with the corporate databases to provide a single and consistent view of the customer from anywhere in the organization.

ANALYTICAL CRM   Analytical CRM systems provide tools for collection and analysis of data gathered during the operational process to help create a better relationship and experience with clients or end users. They store and value add customer knowledge for better understanding of customer needs and behavior. Analytical CRMs utilize sophisticated data warehousing, OLAP, and data mining software for planning, monitoring, and analyzing business activities and to support business intelligence needs.

COLLABORATIVE CRM   Collaborative CRM systems deal with the interaction points between the organization and the customer. These outlets are referred to as channels. Common channels are the telephone, e-mail, Internet, and fax, among other forms of communication to facilitate open and effective communication with the variety of customers with a multitude of preferences. CRMs today integrate these channels via an integrated CRM portal that provides a gateway for customers to access information and to interact electronically with the company.

CUSTOMER RELATIONSHIP PROCESSES

CRM's role is to balance the corporate needs with successful fulfillment of customer needs. CRM needs a tight integration with business processes that involve customers. In addition, customer processes are hard to model because they rely on the underlying supply of knowledge on products, markets, and customers. Thus, a CRM cannot automate all the customer relationships, and it is often considered a knowledge-intensive process. Nonetheless, a good CRM should provide support for the following functions:[8]

- capture and maintain of customer needs, motivations, and behaviors over the lifetime of the relationship
- facilitate the use of customer experiences for continuous improvement of this relationship
- integrate marketing, sales, and customer support activities measuring and evaluating the process of knowledge acquisition and sharing

Research in the support of customer relationships processes has shown that these processes can be categorized into three areas: delivery processes, support processes, and analysis processes.

CRM Delivery Processes

The delivery processes focus on direct contact with the customer to support the sequence of activities to solve a specific problem (e.g., buying a car). Campaign management, sales management, service management, and complaint management are the key customer delivery processes that need CRM support.

---

[8] Geib, M., Reichold, A., Kolbe, L., and Brenner, W. (2005). Architecture for CRM Approaches in Financial Services. *Proceedings of the Thirty-Eighth Hawaii International Conference on System Sciences.* Track 8, 240b.

CAMPAIGN MANAGEMENT   The key goal of campaign management is to generate "leads" or potential clients for the organization. It involves planning, realization, control, and monitoring of relationships aimed at current and potential customers. Today's marketing campaigns require individualized or segmented contacts with the consumers with a feedback channel for consumers to interact.

SALES MANAGEMENT   The goal of sales management is to convert the lead generated by campaign management into a potential customer. It requires a thorough understanding of the customers' needs and provides alternatives to satisfy their requirements and to close the deal.

SERVICE MANAGEMENT   The goal of service management is to provide ongoing support for the client and to assist in the operation of the product or service purchased by the customer (e.g., through help desk support or contract or billing support). The underlying objective is to maintain an ongoing relationship with the customers, making sure they remain satisfied and will potentially buy more products or services in the future.

COMPLAINT MANAGEMENT   Sale of products or services often creates dissatisfaction with consumers that needs to be monitored and managed effectively. The goal is to improve customer satisfaction by directly addressing the complaint of the customer and supporting a continuous improvement process to increase customer retention in the long run.

CRM Support Processes

The customer support processes focus on supporting activities with customer contact rather than facilitating direct customer contact. These include market research, loyalty management, and others.

MARKET RESEARCH   Market research focuses on systematic design, collection, analysis, and reporting of data, and on findings relevant to specific sales activity in an organization.[9] This process involves integration of external and internal data from a wide variety of sources.

LOYALTY MANAGEMENT   In today's market, with increasing competition and decreasing customer loyalty, loyalty management provides the processes to optimize the duration and intensity of relationships with customers. It can increase the switching costs of the customers by providing incentives like the frequent-flyer programs or churn management tools, which provide early warning on customers planning to switch to competitors.

CRM Analysis Processes

These back-end processes collect, consolidate, and analyze customer knowledge collected from other CRM processes. The knowledge generated from these processes provides support to such customer contact processes as campaign management and loyalty management, thereby improving their effectiveness.

---

[9] Kotler, P. (2003). *Marketing Management*, 11 ed. Englewood Cliffs, NJ: Prentice-Hall.

LEAD MANAGEMENT   The focus of this process is on organizing and prioritizing contacts with the prospective customers. It involves integration with campaign management and service management, as well as customer profiling. A sub process of lead management is customer scoring, which uses quantitative and qualitative measures to rank the customer based on his or her interest in the product or service. This filtering process allows for more precise target marketing, and it lowers the contact costs.

CUSTOMER PROFILING   The focus of this process is to develop a marketing profile of every customer by observing his or her buying patterns, demographics, buying and communication preferences, and other information that allows categorization of the customer. The knowledge generated from this process feeds into campaign management, sales management, service management, and the other processes discussed earlier. In addition, this process allows more individualized contact with the customer.

FEEDBACK MANAGEMENT   A good CRM requires a closed-knowledge management loop that consolidates, analyzes, and shares the customer information collected by CRM delivery and support processes with the analysis process, and vice versa. The loop can provide a road map for continuous improvement process for the company's products and services. A good system will discard unnecessary data and focus mainly on the knowledge useful for making better decisions.

CRM TECHNOLOGY

The two key technologies applicable to customer service are CRM and call center technologies. Even though call center technology focuses on facilitating better communication between a customer and the telephone operator, CRM technology implements a companywide business strategy in an effort to reduce costs and enhance service by solidifying customer loyalty. There is a wide variety of CRM software in the marketplace.[10] With the rise of the Internet, data mining and analytics techniques have advanced to where they can be considered an integral component of CRM. True CRM brings together information from all data sources within an organization (and where appropriate, from outside the organization) to give one, holistic view of each customer in real time. This allows customer-facing employees in customer support to make quick, yet informed, decisions in resolving customer problems and issues. On one end you have call center technology being sold as CRM, and on the other extreme you have knowledge management systems also being sold as CRM software. How can you go about deciding what deserves your time and attention?

CRM Components

CRM is typically associated with so-called front-office functions (e.g., marketing, sales, customer service, and knowledge management, which includes data analysis, mining, and knowledge sharing) as shown in Figure 12-2.

---

[10] See http://en.wikipedia.org/wiki/Category:CRM_software (accessed January 15, 2007).

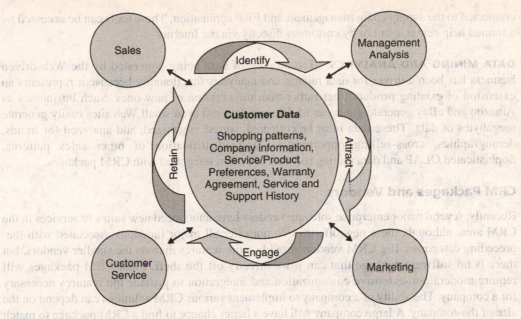

FIGURE 12-2 CRM Components.

MARKET RESEARCH　The two key functionalities here are campaign management and market analysis. Campaign management provides support for preparing such things as marketing budgets, ad placement, sales targeting, and response management. Marketing analysis tools provide statistical and demographic analysis, Web site traffic monitoring, and profiling tools. With the amount of data collected today, these tools provide sophisticated segmenting and targeting capabilities in real time.

SALES FORCE AUTOMATION (SFA)　Sales force automation software has been around since long before CRM became a buzzword. Some of the current CRM vendors were originally in the SFA market. SFA tools provide basic functionality for sales personnel to automate sales lead distribution and tracking, sales reporting, pipeline management, contacts centralization and management, and group collaboration. In addition, they include such software for sales managers and executives as opportunity management, forecasting, reporting, analytics, and customizable dashboard capabilities so that they can be confident that their teams are producing at their full capacity. The goal of SFA software is to give businesses the upper hand with their sales data and to empower sales reps to spend more time selling and less time on administration.

CUSTOMER SERVICE AND SUPPORT　The customer service function has gone through major changes since the advent of the Internet. Online help desks have become a common source for customers to find quick answers to complex technical questions. Customer service originally consisted of setting up a call center with access to a customer database and the frequently asked questions (FAQs) Web site page. Today, with sophisticated CRM back ends, companies have been able to consolidate the two areas into help desk support centers. Customer service functionality typically includes help desk ticket management software, e-mail, interactive chat, Web telephony, and other interaction tools connected to a fully integrated customer database, which is connected to the supply chain management and ERP application. These tools can be accessed by a trained help center agent or by customers directly via the Internet.

DATA MINING AND ANALYTICS   The amount of data being generated by the Web-driven business has been a driver for data mining and analytics functionality because it represents an extension of existing product lines rather than the creation of new ones. Such businesses as Amazon and eBay generate gigabytes of data per day, and even small Web sites easily generate megabytes of data. These data must be collected, sorted, organized, and analyzed for trends, demographics, cross-selling opportunities, and identification of other sales patterns. Sophisticated OLAP and data mining software are often integrated with CRM packages.

CRM Packages and Vendors

Recently, several major enterprise software vendors have announced new suites or services in the CRM area, although, these new offerings do not offer all major functions associated with the preceding categories. Big CRM vendors provide more features than do the smaller vendors, but there is no software package that can work directly off the shelf. Most CRM packages will require moderate-to-extensive customization and integration to provide the features necessary for a company. The ability of a company to implement various CRM solutions can depend on the size of the company. A large company will have a better chance to find a CRM package to match their needs. CRM vendors today provide software for big and small businesses (Table 12-2).

CRM Architecture

CRM systems architecture can utilize connections to multiple sources of data to provide support and service representatives detailed information that can aid a customer experience, increase sales revenue, and provide more efficient and faster real-time data.

The CRM hardware architecture (see Figure 12-3) depends on a number of factors and considerations. Typical CRM systems follow client–server architecture. The system environment would consist of the following components:

- Application server: runs either front-end processing or querying data and possibly a Web interface for the CRM system.
- Database server: houses the back-end database and possibly retrieves information from other database systems in the company to present through the application server.
- Web server: used if the CRM provides an extranet access point for such external users as vendors or customers and an intranet access point for employees.

Factors to consider when building the hardware architecture should be based on scalability for future growth, performance of the end-user and back-end processing, and security requirements

TABLE 12-2   CRM Vendors by Company Size

Target Market	Vendor
Large Enterprises	Siebel, Vantive, Clarify, and Oracle
Midsize Firms	Servicesoft, Onyx, Pivotal, Remedy, and Applix
Small Companies	Goldmine, Multiactive, and SalesLogix

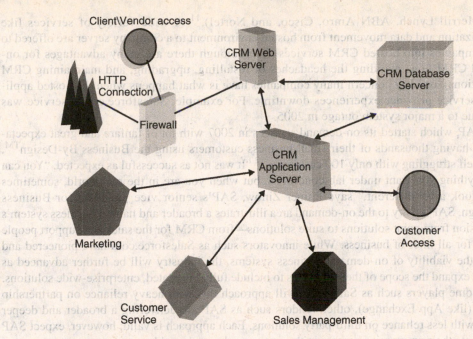

FIGURE 12-3   CRM Architecture.

of the CRM system. Hundreds of users could require multiple application and database servers, or hundreds of Internet users could require multiple Web servers.

The CRM software architecture is usually the standard client–server configuration. This can be best described as a company wants using a standard browser for a Web-based client. Choosing hosted architecture where the vendor hosts the CRM system or choosing an in-house CRM architecture is based on the requirements of the system. Customization is usually easier in-house, whereas scalability and performance are better in hosted models.

A good CRM system needs to be fully integrated with the enterprise resource planning and transaction systems, knowledge management system, and office automation and communication systems. CRM systems typically process such well-structured information as customer contact data and profiles. They are supported by knowledge management systems, which provide such unstructured information as documents and rule-based systems for guidance, and by ERP systems, which provide access to the transaction data. For example, customer support or help desk staff will need detailed information about the product and details on customer transactions from the ERP system and guidance on how to resolve the customer complaint from the knowledge management system.

On-Demand CRM

High-speed secure Internet connectivity has recently spurred a lot of interest and demand in hosted CRM systems. Using thin-client architecture, such vendors asNetSuite, Inc. and Salesforce.com have provided firms with the option of a scalable CRM application suite via a browser and pay a per-month, per-user set fee. Such vendors as Siebel, RightNow, Microsoft, and Oracle have all started offering hosted CRM solutions to small and large business (e.g., Merrill Lynch, ABN Amro, Cisco, and Nortel).[11] A wide variety of services like customization and data movement from hosted environment to a company server are offered to lure companies into hosted CRM services. Even though there are many advantages for on-demand CRM (e.g., avoiding the headaches of installing, upgrading, and maintaining CRM applications), one key concern many companies have is what happens when the hosted application service provider experiences downtime. For example, Salesforce.com's service was down due to a major system outage in 2005.

SAP, which started its on-demand services in 2007 with lot of fanfare and great expectations of having thousands of their small-business customers using the Business By-Design[TM], finds itself struggling with only 100 customers.[12] "It was not as successful as expected. "You can do everything you want under lab conditions, but when you are in the real world, sometimes things look a bit different," says Rainer Zinow, SAP's senior vice president for Business ByDesign. SAP's entry to the on-demand area illustrates a broader and natural business system's progression from point solutions to suite solutions—from CRM for the sales and support people to ERP for all lines of business. While innovators such as Salesforce.com have pioneered and proved the viability of on-demand business systems, the industry will be further advanced as vendors expand the scope of their offerings to include fully integrated, enterprise-wide solutions. While some players such as Salesforce will approach this with heavy reliance on partnership models (like App Exchange), other vendors such as SAP are delivering a broader and deeper system with less reliance on third-party solutions. Each approach is valid; however, expect SAP to replicate their on-premise success in the newer on-demand world.

Small businesses are slowly shifting to on-demand software due to high costs of installation, maintenance, and security. NetSuite, another company offering on-demand CRM, has added project management, billing, and other applications to its software suite. Microsoft Corp. has also introduced a Business Productivity Suite, which offers small- and medium-size businesses e-mail, Web site, file sharing, and other software services at low monthly leases, which they find are getting popular with small businesses as they are becoming aware of the benefits of on-demand software.

According to market researcher IDC, the software-as-a-service (SaaS) industry is slated to increase sales to $40.5 billion by 2014, up from just $13.2 billion last year. IDC predicts that in 2010 the shift to subscription software will result in nearly $7 billion less worldwide traditional software license revenue. Around the globe, including Europe, Middle East, and Africa, on-demand accounts for just a small piece of the software-as-a-service market, 13 percent last year, according to IDC, versus 74 percent in the Americas. By 2014, this region will increase its share of such sales to 35 percent.

Microsoft had also announced that Microsoft Dynamics CRM on-demand will be available in 40 markets and 41 languages by the end of 2010. Microsoft Dynamics CRM 2011 offers familiar, intelligent, and connection experiences for users both inside and outside an organization. It also enables MS partners, including independent software vendors, global system integrators, and value-added resellers, to quickly create, package, and distribute Microsoft Dynamics CRM extensions and custom solutions. In conjuction with this release, Microsoft has started new Microsoft Dynamics Marketplace Web site, integrated within Microsoft Dynamics CRM 2011, which offers an online catalog for partners to market and distribute solutions to

---

[11] Mohamed, A. (September 5, 2006). Web Services Lead the Way to CRM. *Computer Weekly*, 34.
[12] http://online.wsj.com/article/SB10001424052748703499604575512452496458586.html?KEYWORDS=SAP+AG#printMode#ixzz10vesNSRH

Microsoft Dynamics customers. The marketplace enables customers to quickly search, discover, and apply industry-specific applications and solution extensions from Microsoft and its partners to help them accelerate and extend their CRM and ERP implementations.

"We are excited to get the new release of Microsoft Dynamics CRM. The new features will give us even more power and flexibility to create and easily customize CRM solutions to meet the unique business needs of our customers and help them be more productive," said Jason Hunt, Avanade CRM and xRM evangelist. "We are also looking forward to the introduction of Microsoft Dynamics Marketplace, as it opens up new opportunities that will enable us to expand our reach and get our CRM solutions out to a broader, global audience."[13]

CRM LIFE CYCLE

As mentioned earlier, a customer relationship management system life cycle involves focus on people, procedures, company philosophy, and culture, rather than just information technology (see Figure 12-4). Up-front planning can minimize costly process and technology changes. The first step is to adequately outline the corporate CRM goals and the practical process changes that have to occur before focusing on possible technology solutions. It helps to identify a baseline and to understand how core processes are currently accomplished, the key people who are involved, and how the information is currently handled. Identify inefficiencies and areas of opportunity. A CRM program should ultimately be integrated into the company's philosophy and brand.

Functional requirements must be considered before making a decision on the architecture. These are extremely important pieces in implementing a CRM system. Functional requirements are the set of requirements defined by the key stakeholders of the CRM implementation. A functional requirements document should be created and reviewed by all key project stakeholders to determine if all the essential processing and functionalities are present during the implementation. Success or failure of the implementation is directly related to a thorough functional requirements

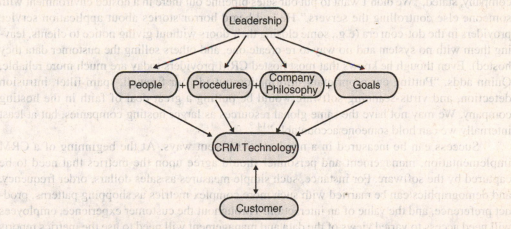

FIGURE 12-4 CRM Life Cycle.

[13] Microsoft Demonstrates Next-Generation CRM Release at Worldwide Partner Conference; Upcoming release delivers "The Power of Productivity" for businesses and introduces the Microsoft Dynamics Marketplace for on-demand and on-premises solutions. (July 12, 2010). *Anonymous*. PR Newswire. New York.

document. This document should be the outline for how the project progresses and be set as the measurable mark to the implementation to control scope of the project. A well-thought-out architecture can help the life cycle of a CRM system and minimize the implementation risks.

If a corporation is attempting to replace a myriad of legacy systems and software programs (e.g., ACT! Databases, Access Databases, or older call center software), sufficient time and resources are needed to implement CRM. Even when employees give input to the end product, there may be an adjustment period as they learn the new tools and adjust to CRM. Training is vital as well as visible support from the executive level. Deadlines should be flexible to account for the organization's ability to change, not a delivery schedule set by a vendor. It is crucial that management clearly defines and communicates how CRM fits into the corporate vision. Then they must demonstrate their commitment by allotting money, time, training, and personnel. Responsibility for the success of the CRM program should not lie solely with the IT department. A cross-functional team that includes IT, sales, marketing, customer service, and management among other users, should be assembled to ensure its implementation. IT must recommend technology that fits with the organization's goals, finances, and other resources.

There are many CRM products to choose from, depending upon the complexity of the information needed and the resources to manage the program. IT may recommend a hosted CRM from an application service provider such as Salesforce.com, which offers a relatively quick implementation for basic functions (e.g., sales force automation). Hosted CRM programs offer a less-expensive alternative to supporting licensed software. It has also become the choice for small to midsized companies that often lack enough internal IT professionals to manage other options.

On the other hand, purchasing a software license for a CRM package not only enables a company-wide integration but also requires significant technical support and implementation time. It is still regarded as the better choice for those corporations who require complexity and security. Gerry Quinn, chief operating officer at Qosina Inc., a medical components distributor company, stated, "We didn't want to put our sales pipeline out there in a hosted environment with someone else controlling the servers." He had heard horror stories about application service providers in the dot-com era (e.g., some closing their doors without giving notice to clients, leaving them with no system and no way to re-create one, and others selling the customer data they hosted). Even though he knows that most hosted CRM providers today are much more reliable, Quinn adds, "Putting our proprietary information outside our firewall, spam filter, intrusion detection, and virus-scanning software would be putting a great deal of faith in the hosting company. We may not have the same global resources as larger hosting companies, but at least internally we can hold someone accountable."[14]

Success can be measured in a number of different ways. At the beginning of a CRM implementation, management and personnel should agree upon the metrics that need to be captured by the software. For instance, such simple measures as sales dollars, order frequency, and demographics can be married with such more complex metrics as shopping patterns, product preference, and the value of an interaction. Throughout the customer experience, employees will need access to varied views of the data and management will need to use the metrics reports to attain a regular status check on the company. All should be considered before deciding upon a technology solution.

---

[14] Stephanie Overby, S. (2006). *The Truth About On-Demand CRM*, CXO Media Inc. www.cio.com/archive/011506/on_demand.html (accessed January 15, 2006).

IMPLICATIONS FOR MANAGEMENT

Managers introducing a CRM system in their company should remember that there are management implications for introducing a new system.

CRM is a strategic business solution and not a technical solution. Management therefore must not introduce CRM technology as an afterthought; rather, it must be part of the enterprise management solution. When organizations make a decision on a new ERP system, they also need to incorporate CRM in their vision because it is much easier and economical to implement CRM with the ERP system, rather than to do them separately. Even when a company does not have a budget to implement them together, it is still advisable to have a CRM solution in their vision and planning efforts and to roll out the two technologies at two different time periods. Another reason management should consider CRM as a business solution is that successful CRM implementation requires a proper mix of good people, business processes, and information technology. Management is in the best position to decide on this mix.

CRM should not be implemented as a single system or at one time. Companies should try to implement a system step by step (i.e., function by function). When considering a CRM implementation, there will be pieces of systems scattered all over (e.g., in sales (maybe a few), customer service). Start with the one where the need is most critical. Make sure there is buy-in from individual users and departments, as well as from management. Furthermore, the CRM implementation team needs the ongoing monitoring and involvement of top management; otherwise, their company may have a great CRM solution, but it will not be used effectively to improve the company's bottom line.

CRM systems come in a variety of shapes and sizes, but there is no real off-the-shelf solution. Every CRM implementation is unique and must be customized to the needs of the organization. CRM systems include a basket of technologies (i.e., market research, sales automation, and customer service) that can be implemented as a hosted solution or installed in-house on the company servers. There are benefits and drawbacks for each option that management needs to evaluate based on the organization's business, resources, in-house capabilities, and other factors. Another choice that management has to make is whether to go for a best-of-breed CRM solution or to select one vendor to support all the CRM requirements. In recent years, the CRM market is moving toward few vendors due to consolidation, mergers, and acquisitions, so selecting one vendor does have its advantages in vendor support and maintenance.

Even though CRM provides a great solution for one-on-one individualized marketing, it also provides good mechanisms for privacy and ethical violations. CRM and other technology-based processes that collect data on consumers have come under fire because there is great potential for the misuse of information. Organizations spend millions of dollars to keep databases secure from theft, loss, damage, or manipulation from hackers. Unscrupulous corporations have been accused of using customer data to coerce buyers by using high pressure or fear. There is also some debate whether the collection of consumer data encroaches upon one's right to privacy. Legislation has been passed that restricts collecting data from children, although they are a powerful buying segment. Many companies have pledged not to sell collected data to outside vendors or, if an Internet-based transaction is the source of data, consumers are often given the choice to opt out of such offers. Still, much of the CRM activity is self-regulated because the government cannot effectively regulate a constantly evolving technology.

Summary

- Customer relationship management (CRM) systems are an integral part of enterprise systems for today's global market where many organizations are competing for the same customers, who in turn have easy access to market information with ubiquitous connectivity. CRM provides one-on-one relationships with the consumers to improve their buying experience and to help organizations compete both efficiently and effectively.

- CRM as a concept is as old as business. No business can survive in a competitive environment without keeping a customer happy. The first generation of CRM was manual and focused on the narrow domain of sales management. With the advent of powerful computers and sophisticated data analysis techniques, the second generation of CRMs provided a holistic view of every customer interaction with the organization and increased the customer contact points with multiple media channels. Today, CRMs are integrated with enterprise systems, apply sophisticated data mining techniques to understand and predict customer purchasing patterns, and provide unique real-time experiences to consumers based on their "context" (i.e., physical location and current needs), as discussed in the Disney case.

- A wide variety of CRM systems are available today. They can be categorized by functionality, business strategy, and implementation perspectives. They are most popularly categorized into operational, analytical, and collaborative CRMs.

- The customer relationship process is complex and integrates several functional areas of the organization. The process can be divided into CRM delivery process, CRM support process, and CRM analytical process. It is not possible to automate the entire value chain of customer relationship due to its knowledge intensiveness. Good customer relationship management requires integration of people, business processes, and technology to deliver value to the customer.

- A CRM system combines a wide variety of computer and communication technology. They can be viewed on a continuum from call center technology at one end of the spectrum to knowledge management systems at the other. To be successful, CRM systems should be integrated with ERP and transaction systems, company database, data warehouse, data mining software, knowledge management, contact management, e-mail, Web, and telephony, among other systems.

- The major components of the CRM system are market research tools, sales force automation software, customer service and support tools, and data mining and analytics. Although several vendors offer comprehensive off-the-shelf CRM solutions, CRM software seldom works without customization. Each organization has unique customer relationship needs, and these must be integrated with the organization's culture and business philosophy.

- CRM solutions exist in hosted and installed environments. In recent years, the increasing costs of hosting and maintaining CRM has forced many companies to opt for a thin-client-hosted CRM solution. Such vendors as NetSuite and Salesforce.com have flourished with the recent surge for on-demand CRM solutions. Organizations must carefully evaluate their CRM needs before deciding on which option is best for them.

- CRM implementation must never focus on a technology solution. CRM solutions must be part of corporate strategy from the beginning, and they must be part of the enterprise system solution. CRMs cannot be an afterthought because they are a critical piece of software that touches the customer and allows the organization to build life-long relationships with the customer. CRMs today allow organizations to distinguish themselves from the competition and have a direct impact on the company performance.

Exercises

1. Your boss is interested in purchasing CRM software and has requested you to categorize the major CRM vendors by the customer relationship processes they support. Write a two-page report with a short summary and a table about CRM systems, vendor names, major features of the software, and how they match the customer relationship processes discussed in this chapter.

2. Locate a company that you know or work at and find out the details of the CRM system used at this company. Your survey could include questions on the CRM drivers for this company, vendor used, components, benefits and drawbacks, and the level of integration between CRM and ERP at this company. Write a two-page report summarizing your findings, and provide recommendations for improvement.

Review Questions

1. Why is it necessary for an organization to have a good customer relationship management (CRM) system?
2. Define the role of CRM in your own words.
3. What are the key differences between today's CRM and the early generation of CRMs?
4. How does CRM impact the company's bottom line or performance?
5. What are the major types of CRM?
6. Briefly describe the customer relationship processes.
7. What are the major components of CRM?
8. What is hosted CRM?
9. How should organizations design CRM systems?
10. List the major CRM vendors by their target market.

Discussion Questions

1. Discuss the relationship between a company's CRM strategy and business strategy.
2. Discuss the role of CRM software in improving the company's strategic advantage.
3. Which CRM process according to you is most critical? Explain why.
4. Discuss the role of CRM in e-Business and e-commerce.
5. Discuss the critical components and architecture of CRM systems.
6. Discuss the differences between hosted and installed CRM systems.
7. How is CRM life cycle different from ERP life cycle? Compare and contrast.

CASE 12-2
Real-World Case
Plexipave: A Failed CRM Implementation

Source: Based on Reed, T., and Desrosiers, A. (2006). Unpublished Case Study Report, College of Management, University of Massachusetts, 1 University Avenue, Lowell, MA 01854.

Plexipave is the world's largest manufacturer of acrylic sports surfacing systems and surface preparation products. Their acrylic sport surfaces are installed in residential, commercial, institutional, and tournament locations around the world, including Indian Wells, Tennis Asia, and the Davis Cup. Plexipave Sport Surfacing Systems is a division of California Products Corporation, a manufacturer of paints and coatings since 1926, headquartered in

(continued)

Andover, Massachusetts. California began manufacturing Plexipave in 1953 and is now the oldest and largest manufacturer of acrylic tennis court surfaces in the world. Plexipave sells its products to tennis court installation businesses.

After the loss of two long-term sales representatives, who collectively had more than 50 years in the business, the director of the Plexipave division was in search of a better way to capture customer data. Much of the customer and market information from the two territories was lost since the salesmen maintained prospecting information independently from the database in customer service.

Customer service maintained a Microsoft Access database of current customers. It was not integrated with any other systems (e.g., ordering, finance), but instead served as a stand-alone database to retain only the most basic information (e.g., addresses and employee names). In addition, Plexipave subscribed to a lead reporting service called the Dodge Reports, offered by construction publishing powerhouse McGraw-Hill. McGraw-Hill employed reporters from around the country to capture and report construction projects as they went to bid, detailing all aspects of the project. The Dodge Reports were e-mailed to customer service, read, sorted, divided by territory, and e-mailed to the sales representative who would then follow up on the lead. Any report updates were treated as a new report, and the information would be sent once again with the applicable updates.

McGraw-Hill and Seibel entered into an agreement in 2004 to offer a hosted CRM program as an upgraded option for the Dodge Reports. It would enable Plexipave employees to download the daily Dodge reports into the CRM database and to transfer information from legacy programs into the CRM as well. A small one-time fee of $5,000 plus $100 per seat annually provided a hosted database that could be accessed remotely through the Internet. The software was designed to eliminate redundant files: If updates were available for a customer or project, it would simply add the information to the existing file. If a user attempted to create a new file for an existing user, the software would likewise alert the user to the double entry.

The director of Plexipave purchased the CRM service and five seats to "test-pilot" the program with key salesmen and customer service personnel. A seat was used for a customer service representative so she could input the data from the Access database (about 175 customers), download the leads from Dodge into the CRM before pushing the data to the sales force, and enter new phone, mail, and fax inquiries into the CRM. Three seats were given to salesmen who volunteered to pilot the program. The last seat was utilized by the director to oversee the program. A Dodge representative trained the internal users by reviewing a "canned" capabilities presentation, and the salesmen were trained through computer-based training (CBT) software with an offer to meet face to face with a trainer if the CBT was not sufficient.

The service went live with no lag time for development. The salesmen spent hours sifting through the database of leads, but did very little in terms of information input. Many approached the automation by compiling notes offline (whether written or typed) and then waiting for downtime or office time to input the data into the CRM. The stockpile of information took hours to input, and, in a short time, the salesmen began to resent the time they had to put aside to use the program. The most frequent comment was, "We spend all this time recording what we are doing and should be out selling."

The customer service representative also felt as if the CRM created more work. Even though she was able to input information into the system directly while she was conducting business, other customer service representatives, who did not have access to the CRM, were funneling information transactions through her. She also became the de facto trainer because the salesmen found it easier to ask her how to manipulate the software when they ran into difficulties.

Another problem was that Plexipave's major business is outside the United States. McGraw-Hill did not extend its reporting services internationally, so the CRM service followed suit and did not account for fields to enter international postal codes, country codes, and the like. Plexipave salesmen also travel to remote areas, sometimes without wireless Internet connections or the proper technology to integrate the use of a remote CRM in their daily travels. Whereas training was given on how to operate the software, many lacked the knowledge to understand the strategic advantage that could be derived from CRM programs.

Last, the director's frequency of accessing the system decreased and his enthusiasm wavered after numerous complaints from the salesmen that the program created unnecessary work. In an attempt to save the program, the Dodge Reports representative showered the Plexipave division with offers of training and software upgrades. For these reasons, the director is unlikely to explore implementation during his tenure unless there is another decision maker who is willing to champion the program. What do you think?

CASE QUESTIONS

1. What was wrong with Plexipave's CRM strategy?
2. What was wrong with the McGraw-Hill/Siebel-hosted CRM application?
3. Do you think Plexipave should implement another CRM system? Provide detailed recommendations.

APPENDIX A

Disney's Mobile CRM Applications

iPhone Application Name	Main Features and Benefits
Walt Disney World Maps	• Full-size maps for Disney theme parks in Orlando • Look for individual rides or attractions • Customize your schedule • Integrated with GPS
Disney World Dining	• Full menus for all 160 restaurants • Locates the restaurants closest to you • One-touch dialing for the Disney dining reservations number
Walt Disney World Park Hours	• Frequently updated information on opening and closing times • Daily event schedules for shows and parades
Walt Disney World Notescast	• Everything you need to know about Disney • Three hundred pages of information and more than 500 photos • Details coming attractions, parade schedules, important phone numbers, Disney World tips, and the history of the park. • Can be used offline
Disney World Wait Times Free	• Up-to-date info on wait times for rides • Application is free • Many similar applications on market
Mouse Memo	• Organizes all of the travel information you'll need. • Enter and track hotel confirmation numbers, dining reservations, rental cars, flights, and more • Great for organization

INDEX

Note: The letters 'b', 'f', & 't' followed by the locators are referred to boxes, figures, and tables cited in the text